Finally, due to many requests -- we are republishing "Memories of Mackinaw". Corrections have been made but no new additions.

We are still gathering information for a second book of Memories and if we live long enough you just may see it in your lifetime!! Send us your stories and pictures to include in it.

"Memories of Mackinaw"

You asked for it -- here it is -- read and enjoy!

Judy & Nancy

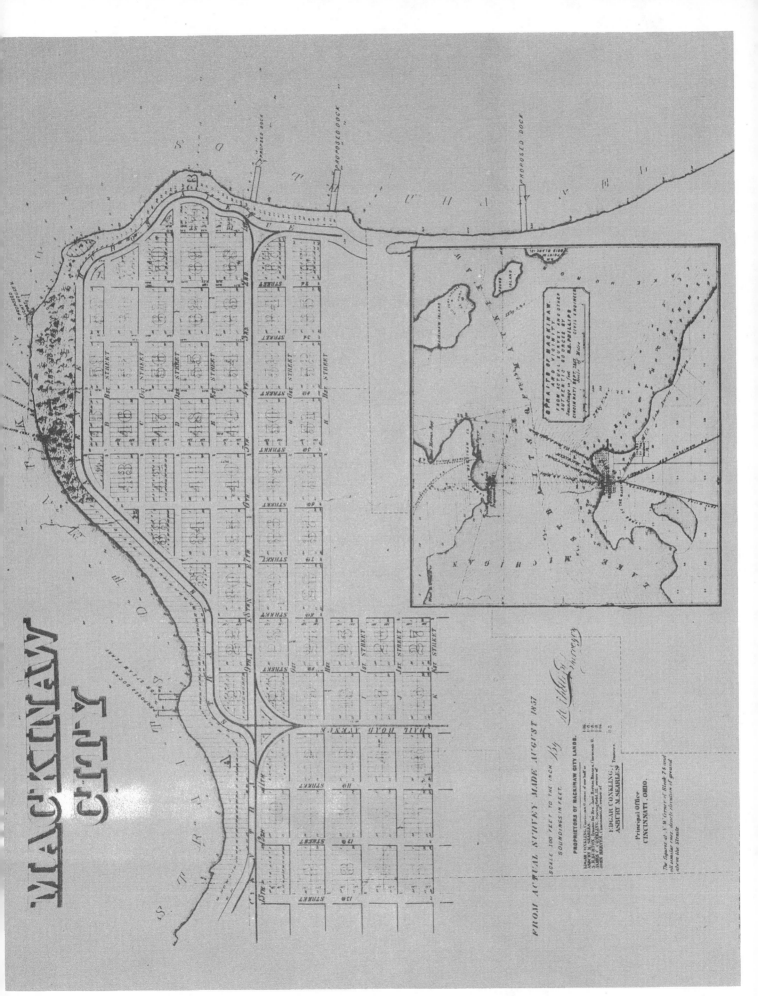

iii

MEMORIES OF MACKINAW

A
Bicentennial Project of
Mackinaw City Public Library &
Mackinaw City Woman's Club

Compiled By

Judy Ranville
Librarian
Mackinaw City Public Library

Nancy A. Campbell
Librarian
Mackinaw City Woman's Club

Printed in The United States of America by Little Traverse
Printing, E. Mitchell, Petoskey, Michigan. Copyright ©1976 by
Mackinaw City Public Library.

Second printing, 1993

PICTURE CREDITS:

Mrs. Bea Ackley, Mrs. Sara Anderson, Patricia Barnett, Leona Brown, Clifford Burroughs, Richard and Nancy Campbell, Mrs. Roy G. Cole, Martha Darrow, Mary Desy, Lloyd Desy, Elmer Dann, Harriet Evans, Celeste Jewell, Mary Poates Krueger, Mackinaw City Woman's Club, Mackinac Island State Park Commission, Marguerite Paquet, William Paquet, Jack Paquet, Carl Pierce, Jerry Pond, Robert Pintal, Ralph Preston, Edna Ranville, Judy Ranville, Marie Riggs, Fred Roueche, Thelma Shaw, Marne Smith, Capt. Wm. Schepler II, Christie Warner, Martha Wilkes, Keith Widder, Homer Walters, Gwen Wilson, Mickey McVey and Arnold Transit Company.

AUTHOR CREDITS:

Mrs. Bea Ackley, Virginia Alexander, Maribeth Barnett, Patricia Barnett, William Barrett, Leona Brown, Mrs. E. J. Bauers, Eric Campbell, Nancy Campbell, Steven Campbell, Edna Miller Coffman, Melinda Beyne, Mary Desy, Marie Fry, Mrs. Esther Gerdan, John E. Moore, Judy Oliver, Margaret Paquet, Ellis Olson, Robert Pintal - Wilderness State Park Naturalist, Judy Ranville, Marie Riggs, William Smith - Wilderness State Park Manager, Roseanna Smith, Marie Melms, Robert E. Strider, Thelma Shaw, Keith Widder - Mackinac Island State Park, Kenneth Teysen, Wawatam Beach Historical Committee, Michigan State Library, State Historical Society of Wisconsin, Mackinaw Woman's Club, Regional Chamber of Commerce of Petoskey, Clem Valot, David O. Voss, *Cheboygan Daily Tribune*, *Petoskey News Review*, *Detroit News*, Sault Ste. Marie *Evening News*.

Judy and Nancy wish to express a "sincere thank you" to all the above persons without whose help compilation of this book would have been impossible, and a special thanks to Mr. Joselyn for permission to publish the unpublished manuscripts of Frances M. Fox and to the many people of Mackinaw City who helped us identify pictures.

༒

We wish to dedicate this book
to the Citizens of Mackinaw City
Past, Present and Future

༒

TABLE OF CONTENTS

FOREWARD

The people who brought this book together worked like hell. The statement applies to the founding fathers and mothers of whom this is the story, and it applies to those who wrestled with the making of the actual book. Foremost, of course, Nancy Dagwell Campbell and Judy LaWay Ranville, who are descendents of Founders and librarians and researchers extraordinary. Theirs was the dream, and the gruelling work, and the most fun. Life is full of paradoxes and poetry!

For a long time these two have been giving birth to this book, and it may well be that it has become a permanent way of life for them. A second volume? It's a real possibility because this book, inevitably, suffers the sins of omission. And this is Judy's and Nancy's greatest regret. How could every son and daughter of early Mackinaw be given a full place in the sun? In an effort to do all the old timers and all the old stories justice, the work has truly been gruelling, demanding, parental-type labor--but with appropriate rewards, too.

Everyone who touched this effort felt the Mackinaw dimension of the early days when strong people chose it as their home place and sculptured the raw materials that became monuments....Those who worked on *Memories of Mackinaw* became a part of the old memories. Memories become distilled, and so they become poetry recreating the essence of past experience. The Ranville-Campbell team would not for anything have missed this exposure to new awareness, new appreciation of all that went before their time in Mackinaw.

Robert Frost has said, "Poetry is a way of taking life by the throat." In setting down the memories of old Mackinaw, the workers on this book have not intended a poetic effort, but if something of the valor and vigor of the early men and women who took life by the throat and, unafraid, bent life to serve and better mankind, then the poetic tribute is implicit and homage has been paid to those forefathers in this 200th birthday year.

Smell the sawn lumber of the old days, take deep breaths of the still-pure air of this northern world, know the Straits in silver calm and in fierce tempest, observe that people go their own way, yet person respects person; catch it all in the past, herein, and note its presence unto later generations--much of it still the homespun of an early people. Coleridge wrote,

"In every cell and every blooming bower
The sweetness of old days is hovering still."

Thelma Shaw

McGulpin Point
1976

viii

Chapter 1

The Traverse Region

CHAPTER XV.

VILLAGE OF MACKINAW CITY

Location—Original Proprietors—Early History of the Projected Village—Years of Waiting—The Beginning in 1870—Early Religious Worship—The School—Incorporated as a Village Under a Charter —General Progress.

The village of Mackinaw City stands upon historic ground, and the events which gave this point a conspicuous place in history have been narrated upon preceding pages.

The village as a reality is of recent growth, but as a projected enterprise dates back to the early years of progress in northern Michigan.

In the year 1857 Edgar Conkling and Asbury M. Searles, as trustees of the proprietors of Mackinaw lands, inaugurated a movement for building up a business center upon the south shore of the Straits. The principal office was at Cincinnati, Ohio, and the names of the owners and amount of their individual interests are as follows:

Edgar Conkling, Cincinnati, O., owner of 9-16
Asbury M. Searles, Cincinnati, O., owner of 1-8
S. H. Burton, Trustee for Mrs. Jane M. Messick,
   Cincinnati, O. 1-8
James C. Conkling, Springfield, Ill., owner of 1-8
John Reeves, Cincinnati, O., owner of 1-16
                                     ————
                                     8-8

Mr. Conkling was the largest owner and the leading spirit in the enterprise. His enthusiasm and confidence in the project were unbounded, and certainly no more captivating scheme was ever spread upon paper than that which contemplated the building of an important business center at this point. During the summer of 1857 ground was surveyed and platted for a village by R. C. Phillips, a civil engineer, and in October of that year a pamphlet of about fifty pages was issued by the trustees. This pamphlet contained a mass of information relative to this point, together with plats and maps, and a large edition was printed and circulated. An early writer had uttered the following prophetic opinion: "If one were to point out on the map of North America a site for a great central city in the lake region, it would be in the immediate vicinity of the Straits of Mackinaw. A city so located would have the control of the mineral trade, the fisheries, the furs and the lumber of the entire north. It might become the metropolis of a great commercial empire. It would be the Venice of the Lakes."

The projectors of Mackinaw City believed they were founding such a metropolis.

The pamphlet referred to contained an announcement of the trustees to the public, and also the report of the surveyor, Mr. Phillips. We give them herewith, as they define the enterprise as it was outlined at that time.

TO THE PUBLIC

The undersigned, trustees and proprietors of the lands of, and adjacent to "Mackinaw City", have the pleasure of presenting for the consideration of the capitalists, business men and others, what they will concede to be, upon investigation, the most reliable point for investment and settlement, now available in the west or north.

Mackinaw evidently occupies the most commanding natural position for a city of the first class; surrounded as it is, by a widely extended territory, abounding in elements of the greatest wealth, affording the utmost encouragement to the manufacturer and mechanic in their widest diversity of employment, and without the possibility of a competing city in any direction nearer than Detroit on the south.

They feel, from what has been so truly and ably said by E. D. Mansfield, Esq., a gentleman well and favorably known for his ability and habits of close investigation and comparison, that nothing more is left to be said, but to set forth the policy which they have adopted, and design to carry out, the more efficiently to promote the interests of this location, and at the same time to aid in the development of the vast resources of the surrounding region.

From the map it will be seen that the streets are laid out eighty feet in width, and the avenues one hundred, and one hundred and fifty feet, respectively. In the deed of dedication of these to the public, provision is made for sidewalks, fifteen feet width on each side, to be forever unobstructed by improvements of any kind, shade trees excepted, thus securing a spacious promenade, worthy of a place destined to become a principal resort for pleasure and health. Provision is also made for the proper use of the streets and avenues by railroad companies, adequate to the demands of the business of the city.

The lots, with the exception of those in fractional blocks, are fifty by one hundred and fifty feet, thus affording ample room for permanent, convenient, and ornamental improvements.

The park now laid off embraces the grounds of the old "Fort Michilimackinac", sacred in the history of the country. These grounds, now in their natural condition, are unequaled for beauty of surface, location, scenery, soil, trees, etc., by any park in any city in this country; and when the skillful hand of the horticulturist has marked its outline and threaded it with avenues and foot paths, pruned its trees and carpeted its surface with green, it will present the very perfection of all that constitutes a park delightful. The character of the soil (it being a sandy loam, with sand and gravel underlying it) renders it capable of the easiest and most economical improvement, securing walks always dry, hard and smooth.

This park, with suitable blocks and lots for county and city buildings, market houses, schools, etc., will be duly appropriated to these uses, whenever the proper authorities are prepared to select suitable sites; and lots for churches and institutions of learning and charity will be freely donated to parties contemplating early improvement. Thus the trustees propose to anticipate, by avoiding the errors of older cities, the wants of Mackinaw City in perpetuity, and free forever its citizens from taxation for any grounds required for the public good. They also design to place it in the power of the general government to secure, by like donation, at an early day, the grounds necessary for such fortifications as the wants of the country and commerce may require, on the simple condition of speedy improvement. This liberal policy, it is believed, will best promote the true interests of the city and country, and at the same time be productive of the greatest pecuniary profit, both to the original proprietors, and to all others who may make investments at this point.

It is also within the purposes of the trustees, to expend a large portion of their income from sales, in providing for the public wants, by the erection of docks at the most important places, and by the establishment of ferries, in view of which they have secured the land on the opposite side of the Straits. And they will also, as their means will justify, make loans to aid parties in the establishment of manufacturers, etc.

Building materials of great variety and in abundance are at hand. Lumber can be had for the mere cost of preparation, and the soil at no very distant point is suitable for making bricks; while for immediate use, Milwaukee can furnish the articles of the best kind in any quantities. The shores of Lake Superior abound with exhaustless quantities of granite, sand stone and marble; and limestone and sand are on the spot.

There are three harbors, the most eastern of which is well known to navigators, as affording perfectly safe anchorage at all times; and when suitable docks are built, they will offer unusual advantages to commerce.

The surface of the city itself is unrivaled, having a natural grade suited to city wants, and the soil being a sandy loam with sand and gravel underlying it, will form the cheapest and best foundation for streets and avenues.

Evergreen and other trees of full growth now cover the grounds, affording a healthful and delightful shade, and capable of varied embellishment, without the delay incident to artificial growth. The grounds adjacent to the city are of the same character, gradually ascending until an elevation of seventy-five or a hundred feet is attained, affording the finest views of the lakes and neighboring islands.

The following are the terms on which the trustees propose to sell the property which they have subdivided into lots, as represented in the subjoined plat of the city. Notwithstanding the superior facilities of this point over hundreds of others in the West, where lots have readily been disposed at ten, twenty, thirty, and even fifty dollars per foot, the trustees, in order to give impetus to the growth of Mackinaw City, and to afford a margin for others to profit by, propose to all settlers who will immediately improve the property by the erection of mills, hotels, dwellings, manufacturing and printing establishments, docks, etc., etc., to donate the lots necessary for such purposes, subject to the choice of the parties themselves; and to those who desire to profit by the inevitable advance of property contiguous to their own improvements, the trustees will sell lots on long time, if desired, at the unprecedentedly low price of five dollars per foot, front.

Capitalists and non-residents, desiring to avail themselves of the advantages of such a developing policy, and to invest upon a *real estate* basis, promising a rapid appreciation in value, can possess themselves for a very limited time, of lots, at the same low price of five dollars per foot.

The title to this property is unquestionable, having, within five years, been derived directly from the United States Government, as will be seen by reference to a title pamphlet issued by the undersigned for the information of parties interested.

Applications by letter will receive prompt attention. Asking a careful perusal of the annexed report on the subject, from the pen of E. D. Mansfield, Esq., we submit the matter to public investigation.

Edgar Conkling,) Trustees
A. M. Searles,   )

CINCINNATI, Oct., 1857.

MESSRS. E. CONKLING, AND A. M. SEARLES,

Trustees of Mackinaw City Company,

GENTS:—Having completed my surveys of "Mackinaw City" and the surrounding lands belonging to your company, at your request I herein embody briefly the result of my observations. "Mackinaw City", situated on the south side of the Straits, and upon the northern extremity of the southern peninsula of Michigan, occupies a position at once admirably adapted to the conveniences and necessities of a great city, and susceptible of easy and commensurate improvement. The land rises gradually from the water's edge, until it attains an elevation of about forty-four feet, just sufficient to secure certain drainage from every point, with very little expense in the grading of streets, while there is no portion of it subject to overflow of water.

By reference to the accompanying map of the city, its topographical features will be indicated by the figures at the corner of blocks, which figures denote their elevation in feet, respectively, above the level of the lake. The lands west of the city plat continue to rise until a height of seventy-five (75) feet above the lake is attained. From almost all parts of these lands commanding views are obtained of the surrounding lakes, the Straits and the numerous adjacent islands. That portion set apart as a park is covered with a beautiful growth of various evergreen and other trees, which only require the skillful hand of the horticulturist to render the place beautiful beyond description. The prospect from this site is particularly fine, and hardly to be equaled by that of any public park in the country, not excepting the far-famed Battery in New York, which is similarly situated. Looking westward, Lake Michigan is spread out in the distance, with the island of St. Helena in the northwest. Immediately north appear the Straits, and beyond, their northern shore, while Mackinaw, Round and Bois Blanc Islands dot the waters to the northeast and east, and the south channel of Lake Huron stretches away as far as the eye can reach, forming together a scene of unsurpassed natural and varied beauty.

The soil of the city is a sandy loam, sand and gravel, mixed with fragmentary limestone, underlying it, forming a perfectly dry and clean surface, admirably adapted for streets of a compact and reliable foundation, without the expense of paying.

The health of this locality, like that of the surrounding islands, is proverbial. The invigorating and pleasant breezes which prevail here have been the theme of the inhabitants, and of the thousands of visitors who annually flock here for health and pleasure. This testimony is confirmed by the fact that doctors find no encouragement in this whole region and are regarded as mere myths.

Ample and safe harbors are found adjoining your lands on the east, north and west. A reference to the city plat, and the United States charts of the Straits, will show you the depth of water at a great number of points -- a depth sufficient for any vessels that navigate the lakes. The eastern bay is well known to navigators as affording excellent anchorage and a safe retreat in time of storms. I have seen more than twenty vessels at anchor here at one time while a storm was prevailing. The northern and western bays are scarcely inferior, and, althogether, cannot fail to render "Mackinaw City" a place of favorite resort and secure retreat by the hundreds of steamers and sail vessels which are constantly traversing the Straits of Mackinaw.

Limestone for building purposes is abundant in your high lands, which, with the timber covering the same, furnish ample facilities for ready and substantial improvements.

I have also made surveys south of Mackinaw and in the vicinity of Little Traverse Bay, on the eastern shore of Lake Michigan, and have, therefore, had a good opportunity to see the country and to judge of its capabilities to promote the growth and prosperity of a city. I find the surface to be slightly rolling, or undulating, having an elevation above the lake of from seventy to one hundred and fifty feet. At a distance of half a mile to one and a half miles from the coast, the land is of an excellent quality generally, and improves uniformly as you go inland, as far as I have explored it. The timber consists mainly of sugar maple, wild cherry (red), beech, poplar, ash, oak, white cedar, Norway and other pines. The soil is a deep sandy loam, very warm, and producing luxuriantly.

Upon the whole, I can not but congratulate your company on the site you have been so fortunate as to possess for a prospective city, affording, as it does, almost unexampled facilities for settlement and improvements, while at the same time its commercial advantages, being at the center of an immense agricultural and mineral district, with many other minor pursuits inviting to human industry, give ample promise that in the onward development of the mighty northwest, it must become a great central metropolis.

The lakes being near one and a half feet higher than usual, will, of course, on receding, increase the depth of your water lots, my survey showing the present water line. Your lands on the opposite point of the Straits, and embracing the whole shore, I also surveyed and find similar in character to the south side, and well suited for the termini of railroads and ferry, the main channel of the Straits being near the south shore.

Yours truly,

R. C. Phillips, *Civil Engineer.*

CINCINNATI, Sept. 30, 1857.

After vigorous but unsuccessful efforts to found a city, Mr. Conkling became convinced that the project was matured at too early a time. The time had not arrived for extending railway lines to this point, and without railway connection a business center of any importance is impossible. Mr. Conkling, however, never lost faith in the ultimate success of his enterprise, and after waiting and watching nearly a quarter of a century died in December, 1881, a few days before the first railroad to this point was opened.

From 1857 to 1870 the village plat was undisturbed. In 1869 Mr. Conkling made arrangements to build a dock, and the contract was let to Mr. F. M. Sammons, of Cheboygan. In January, 1870, George W. Stimpson moved here from Cheboygan, having a contract to get out dock timber and 20,000 cedar posts. A small log house built for use of men working on the dock was the sole and solitary tenant of the site. Mr. Stimpson built a log house where the Stimpson House now stands, and became the first settler of the village.

George W. Stimpson was born in Somerset County, Me., in the year 1829. He was married April 5, 1849, to Miss Elvira A. Pillsbury, at Palmyra, in that state. Mr. Stimpson was a farmer, and in 1868, having several sons, decided it would be best to move into a new country where land was cheap. He accordingly removed with his family to Cheboygan, and kept the Cheboygan House about a year. While there he watched opportunities for securing desirable tracts of land and made several purchases. In January, 1870, he came to Mackinaw City, as heretofore stated, and engaged in getting out timber and posts. He also handled a lot of cord-wood for Mr. Conkling, and engaged in the wood trade on his own account. His house being the only one at this point, it became the stopping place for people who came here. The first religious services in the place were held in that house, and the first Sunday-school organized there. Mr. Stimpson was constantly on the alert for desirable land, and whenever there was an opportunity to secure a valuable water front or good farming land he purchased. The consequence is that he has become possessed of a large amount of valuable land in the vicinity. For several years he has carried on fishing quite extensively, and for this business his water frontage is invaluable. Mr. and Mrs. Stimpson have six children, four sons and two daughters. Charles and Forest J. have farms near Mackinaw City; George Stimpson is a veterinary surgeon at Quincy, Ill., and although a young man, has become distinguished for skill and remarkable success in his profession. He graduated with honors from the Ontario Veterinary College, at Toronto, Canada, in 1882, and located at Quincy, Ill., where he has already acquired an extensive practice. He is strongly endorsed by *Wilke's Spirit of the Times*, and is already in the front rank of his profession. John and Ida are at home, and Lydia is the wife of B. C. Milliken, of Cheboygan. Mr. Stimpson has engaged in various business enterprises, and has continued to keep hotel to the present time. In 1880 he built the present Stimpson House, a large and conveniently arranged frame building. He has accumulated some valuable and interesting relics from the old fort, among which is a set of charms consisting of a key and two charms, made of silver. Upon the ring is the date 1563 and the letter "M", upon the charms are engraved emblems, such as the heart and horn of plenty. He has also a silver cross, broad-axe, tomahawk, and a great quantity of beads. These were all found within a few years by parties digging in the soil in the vicinity of the old fort.

While the dock was being built the men engaged upon that work helped to relieve the place of its solitude, but that was soon finished.

L. I. Willets was the next person to become a permanent resident of the place. He came here in April, 1870, and purchased a lot. During the summer he had a store building put up, and in September removed here and brought his stock of goods. Mr. Willets was born in Orleans County, N. Y., but removed to Branch County, Mich., with his parents when quite young. In 1863 he was married at Coldwater, Mich., to Miss Elizabeth Fetterly. They have no children. Mr. Willets lived two years in Illinois, and then removed to Greenville, Mich., where he followed the business of painting until his removal to Mackinaw City in 1870.

July 1, 1871, the post office of Mackinaw City was established with Mr. Willets as postmaster, and he has continued to hold the office to the present time. He has carried on his mercantile business, and has taken an active interest in promoting the welfare of the place. He is a man of good education, and has been a leading spirit in educational matters, and taught the school in 1873 and 1874. He is superintendent of schools at the present time.

With the building of the dock and the business interests of Messrs. Stimpson and Willets, a beginning was made, but beyond that nothing was done for several years, and it still continued to look as though the greatest fame of this point would come from the past.

RELIGIOUS WORK.

Religious worship was introduced into the village of Mackinaw City as soon as the first home was established. In February, 1870, Elder Riley, of the M. E. Church at Cheboygan, came to the place and preached in the log house of George W. Stimpson that had been recently finished. There were a number of men at work upon the dock, and every person in the vicinity attended the services, filling the house to its utmost capacity. Shortly afterward Rev. Van Fleet came over from Mackinac Island, and preached in the old dock-house. In March Rev. Father De Cennick came up from Cheboygan and held services in the old boarding-house. After the work on the dock was finished, and the laborers went away, there were but few persons left at this point, and there was no preaching service held again until the summer of 1881, when the Presbyterians sent Rev. Cook from Harbor Springs once a month. He held services at the Stimpson House, and a Sunday school was organized with Dr. Henry Conkling, superintendent. Soon after a church society was organized. The first local pastor was Rev. Peoples, and the present one is Rev. Marsh.

Dr. Henry Conkling and his wife took an active interest in the welfare of the church, and in 1883 the society succeeded in building a house of worship. It was dedicated free from debt Sept. 26, 1883. This is the only religious orginanization in the village.

DISTRICT SCHOOL.

In the summer of 1871 application was made to the board of school inspectors of the town of Inverness for the organization of a school district. The application was signed by the following named persons: G. W. Stimpson, Charles Stimpson, James Nickelson, William Wright, G. W. Conrad, L. I. Willets, Octave Terrain, Lewis St. Andrew, Francis Dufney, John Kadott. July 8, 1871, School District No. 1 was organized, and the first meeting of the voters of the district was held at the house of George W. Stimpson, July 29, of the same year. William Wright was elected moderator; George W. Stimpson director, and George W. Conrad assessor. A school was kept during the following autumn in a log building that had been built by Mr. Conkling. The school was taught by Lydia J., daughter of George W. Stimpson, and there were seven pupils. George W. Conrad taught in 1872, and L. I. Willets in 1873 and 1874; Luella Smith taught in 1875 and 1876; Millie Wilson, 1877; Fred Bunker, 1878; and Mary Miner part of a term in 1878; Ella Eastman, 1879; Luella Smith, 1880. There was no school kept during the year 1881, and in 1882 the school was taught by Jessie Lomax; Miss Clark in 1883 and 1884. The school was kept in temporary buildings until the fall of 1883, when a school-house was completed.

In December, 1881, the Mackinaw division of the Michigan Central Railroad was completed to Mackinaw City, and railway communication with the outside world was established. In July, 1882, the Grand Rapids & Indiana Railroad had completed its line from Petoskey to this point, and the future prospects of the place assumed a more hopeful line. In 1882 it was thought advisable to organize under a village charter and push forward local improvements.

VILLAGE CHARTER.

At a meeting of the board of supervisors held in December, 1882, application was made for an order incorporating the hereinafter described territory into a village, to be known as Mackinaw City, to wit: Lots one (1) and two (2) of fractional Section seven (7) and Lots one (1) and two (2) of Section eighteen (18), all in Town thirty-nine (39) north, Range three (3) west, Cheboygan County, Michigan.

The petition was signed by the following named persons: E. C. Campbell, James Shepherd, E. M. Sutherland, S. B. Chamberlain, A. Laquea, M. H. Dunham, Chas. Goodell, L. I. Willets, James Converse, W. A. Johnston, F. S. Badge, Charles Bart, James Fox, W. M. Carpenter, R. G. Taylor, Benjamin F. LaRue, John H. Kintcel, Ed. Cuberson, George Gane, G. W. Stimpson, M. D. Ferry, F. J. Stimpson, H. L. Loomis, Charles Stimpson, F. L. Pierce, J. S. Apt, Henry Conkling, G. W. Kelker, A. D. McKay, James Bell, James K. Sizeland, George H. Todd, W. T. Waite, A. Torrey, John Paden.

This petition was granted by the supervisors.

In the winter of 1883 the village was reincorporated by act of legislature, approved April 10, 1883, under the general law relating to villages passed in 1875.

The first charter election was held in the spring of 1883, and the following officers elected: President, John Padden; clerk, E. M. Sutherland; treasurer, Samuel Chamberlain. Trustees: James Shepherd, James Fox, William Carpenter, John Andrews, James Ball,—Mercier.

1884: President, John Padden; clerk, E. M. Sutherland; treasurer, Samuel Chamberlain. Trustees: James Ball, James Shepherd,—Mercier, James Fox, D. B. Notson, J. Richards.

Considerable activity was exhibited during 1882 and 1883. A number of buildings were erected, and streets were graded. August, 1882, a signal station was established, with F. R. Day as observer. In March, 1883, he was succeeded by Dudley B. Notson, who is still in that position. This station ranks as first-class and a central office of sub-station.

The growth of the place is hindered by legal complications affecting the title to a portion of the village lots. When this hindrance is removed it is thought the village will continue to prosper. The village plat lies in both Cheboygan and Emmet Counties, but the village is built in Cheboygan County.

This place is the central point of early history, and for years was the center of trade for this great northwest region. Nature has made it a geographical and ocmmercial center, and what it may yet become is for the future to answer. The once famous metropolis of the Ottawas and Ojibwas, where the feet of thousands of warriors shook Pe-quod-e-nong (Mackinaw) while dancing their war dances, and going forth painted and plumed to war, may yet see the time when it will be to the whites what it then was to them.

Chapter 2

Emmet County
And Its Origin

Regional Chamber of Commerce of Petoskey

Emmet had its origin in the counties of Tonedagana and Kishknnoko, which were among the original divisions of Northern Michigan made in 1840. In 1843, these names were changed to Emmet and Charlevoix, which remained unorganized and attached to the old county of Michilimackinac until 1853.

In 1847, the township of Peaine was organized, embracing the territory of the Beaver Islands. In 1851, the Mormons elected all the officers and had full control of affairs.

In the winter of 1853, James J. Strang, the Mormon leader, was a member of the State Legislature. He succeeded in securing the passage of a bill uniting the counties of Emmet and Charlevoix, and organizing them under the name of Emmet.

In 1855, it was determined to secure better protection of the interests on the mainland; a bill at Lansing was passed reorganizing Emmet County. This same year the towns of Little Traverse, La Croix (Cross Village), Bear Creek (Petoskey), and Old Fort Mackinaw were organized.

The county seat was established at Mackinaw City, but the county business was transacted at Little Traverse (Harbor Springs) until 1867. In that year the county seat was moved to Charlevoix.

In 1869, the territory of Emmet County was divided, and Charlevoix County was organized. No new towns were created in Emmet County until 1876. In 1875, the name of La Croix had been changed to Cross River Township, and in the following year Friendship, Maple River, Bliss and Pleasant View Townships were organized; followed by Readmond and Littlefield in 1877, Center in 1878, and Carp Lake in 1879. Eggelston was added to the list in 1884--the name later changed to McKinley. Since that time the townships of Resort, Springvale, Wawatam and West Traverse have completed the sixteen townships in this County. The County seat was moved from Harbor Springs to Petoskey in 1902.

Emmet County is situated on the Eastern shore of Lake Michigan and immediately south of the Straits of Mackinaw. This county is noted for its great extent of coast. Including Little Traverse Bay, it has nearly 60 miles. It is bounded on the North by the Straits of Mackinac, on the East by Cheboygan County, on the South by Charlevoix County and Little Traverse Bay, and on the West by Lake Michigan.

Emmet County is characterized by North and South ridges. There are four of these ridges or ranges of hills starting on the north side of Little Traverse Bay. The first range rises to 350 feet from the shore of the lake, and gradually descends to a valley varying from one mile to two miles in width. Then commences another range which reaches an altitude of some 600 feet above Lake Michigan. Many parts of the ridges are table lands. Here some of the best farming of the county is found. The hills are equally fertile, but better adapted to fruit raising. The valleys are adapted to many varied purposes of agriculture.

Maple River is the principal stream in the county. It heads in the north and bears south through the eastern portion of the county, emptying into Burt Lake. The next stream of any importance is Bear Creek, entering Little Traverse Bay at Petoskey. It has its source in Walloon Lake.

The Cheboygan and Emmet County lake and river navigation improvements is one of the most important enterprises ever carried out in northern Michigan. The inland water route was opened to navigation in 1876. Starting from Lake Huron at Cheboygan, and continuing through Cheboygan River, Mullet Lake, Indian River, Burt Lake, Crooked River, and Crooked Lake, it traverses a distance of about 45 miles.

The early history of Emmet County centers around the Ottawa Indians. The Ottawas were originally established in the vicinity of the Straits. They then extended their settlements along the shore of Lake Michigan, from Seven Mile Point to Cross Village. (The French fur traders called this area L'Arbre Croche.) The Ottawas' principal and most permanent settlements were at Cross Village, Middle Village, Seven Mile Point and Little Traverse (Harbor Springs). A few of the Indian families had their homes at Bear Creek (Petoskey) on the south side of Little Traverse Bay.

From the massacre at Mackinaw until the war of 1812, their region was not the theater of any important event. The only inhabitants, so far as

14

known, were the Ottawas and such missionaries as may have labored among them. How long the Jesuits continued active work at L'Arbre Croche is not known. A great cedar cross remained standing on the brow of the bluff at Cross Village when the Catholics sent a missionary to reoccupy the long abandoned field in 1825.

The first occupation along our shores was that of fishing. As early as 1824, there were fish markets in Mackinac. By 1843, the whole shore was peopled with fishermen and with them, the traders. The first white settled in Harbor Springs in 1827. A French Canadian settled at Cross Village in 1840 and built a copper shop. The second white settler at Cross Village came in 1847 and operated a saw mill.

The Indian Treaty of 1836 was important to this area. This central government treaty with the Chippewas and Ottawas held the lands of this portion of the state as a reservation for the Indians for 20 years. At the expiration of the treaty, they were to move west of the Mississippi. In 1851, the Indians were given permission to stay, and in 1855, the Indians were allowed to select 40 acres of land for each unmarried person twenty years of age, and 80 acres for each man with a family. In 1872, by act of Congress, those Indians who had become of age since the last treaty, were allowed to select 40 acres each for patent, while the lands also were opened to them for homestead entry.

In 1852, an important Presbyterian Mission in the form of an Indian school was established at Bear Creek (Petoskey) by Andrew Porter, For the first two or three years the expense of the mission was born wholly by the Presbyterian Board. After the establishment of Indian schools by the government, the one at the mission was adopted by the agent as a government school, and the usual salary was paid to Mr. Porter as teacher. About 1871, the mission was discontinued. This was due to exhausted funds on the part of both the Indian treaty organization and the local board.

In 1853, a trading post was established at Harbor Springs (Little Traverse) and business began.

In 1855, the Benevolent, Charitable Religious Society of St. Francis was established by Rev. Father John B. Weicamp at Cross Village. He first purchased Harbor Point, but decided upon a location at Cross Village. He fitted up the saw mill, got out logs and sawed lumber with this mill. Subsequently, he erected a steam mill. The buildings were completed in 1857, and work began on the construction of a school, two convents, and a church. The religious community dissolved in 1896.

In 1874 and 1875, under the Homestead law, the Indian reservations were opened to all. The general settlement of the county and the development of its agricultural resources were delayed by the fact that the lands of the county were being held subject to the Indian Treaty. In August of 1874, the eastern tier of townships came into market and in April of 1875, the remainder of the county was thrown open to actual settlers. At that time, the white population of the county was about 150 people. The Grand Rapids and Indiana Railroad had just opened a highway of travel through the county as far as Petoskey in 1874. The village of Petoskey had just entered upon its career. So great was the rush for land that over 800 claims were entered during the first three days. Under an act of Congress, soldiers in the Civil War could homestead 160 acres of land, while a citizen could homestead only 80 acres. During the summer and fall of 1875, a steady stream of immigration poured into the wilderness of Emmet County; and wilderness it was indeed. There was not a road in any direction in the woods except one state road to Cheboygan. The settlers who came scattered over the county so that settlement was general. Cabins were set in the numerous openings in the wilderness.

This was during the hard times that prevailed throughout the United States, and many people were driven to seek homes in a new country where little capital was required to obtain a start. The rush of settlers continued through the summer of 1876, and most of them had no idea of the trials and hardships incident to pioneer life. The winter of 1876 was the worst, and an appeal was made to the outside for help. By 1877 and 1878, the worst was over; farmers began to raise enough food, and clearings were started. These early people were not practical farmers and became discouraged. Many deserted their homestead for the village while others took over the farms. Fruit farms became popular; vegetables and grain were grown also.

In 1875, the first talk of locating the campground of the Methodists of Michigan Association at Bay View began. Bay View is located outside the corporate limits of Petoskey, and is a complete village by itself. The land was then owned by a number of individuals, but the Petoskey residents, realizing the advantages of a permanent state campground on that location, donated liberally to raise a subscription to purchase the site. The amount paid was $3,300. The Grand Rapids and Indiana Railroad Company agreed to furnish money to buy the land, providing payment for it would be guaranteed. The railroad from Petoskey was continued to Bay View in 1876, and the first meeting was held August 1, 1876.

Bay View stands today as the outgrowth of splendid planning of the pioneers of the Seventies and is noted for its healthful climate, its programs for religious training, its conservatory of music programs, its department of theater arts, and arts and craft fellowship.

A year after Bay View was established, the Presbyterians began looking for a place to hold similar meetings. The people of Harbor Springs presented the Presbyterians with land where Wequetonsing now stands. In the spring of 1878, work began on these grounds. Numerous lots were sold and a large boarding house erected. Streets were laid out and a number of cottages erected.

In 1878, a group of people from Lansing bought

Harbor Point from Father Weicamp of Cross Village. They established a permanent resort. A stock company was organized under the statute from park association, and the grounds were laid out and a number of cottages erected. A hotel, dock, boat and bath houses were built, and the improvements added each year.

As early as 1882, the Western Hay Fever Association had its headquarters at Petoskey; they designated Petoskey as the most favorable resort for hay fever sufferers. Members of the association stayed at various points on Little Traverse Bay.

By 1880, the branch of the Grand Rapids and Indiana Railroad had extended to Harbor Springs and from Bay View to Mackinaw City by 1882. Many lumbering companies followed the extension of the railroad through Emmet County. Milling and lumbering were important industries on the Maple and Carp Rivers. Ties, posts, tan-bark and telegraph poles were taken out in large quantities. Other rivers that played an important part in lumbering were the Bear River, Crooked River, Wycamp Creek at Cross Village and Minnehaha Creek in Springvale Township. From lumbering came wood product industries. The fishing industry was still important. A number of men and boats were employed in this business at Petoskey and Harbor Springs.

Many lumbering towns sprang up that now cease to exist. Either the mills were destroyed by fires and never rebuilt, or when the timber was exhausted, the towns abandoned. Forest fires were quite common. The largest one was at Cecil Bay Village in 1918.

The Chicago and West Michigan Railway extended its main line from Grand Rapids to Bay View in 1892. It was later changed to the Chesapeake and Ohio. Several lumbering companys had their own private railroad track. As many as 1500 people lived in Pellston from 1903 to 1914. Lumbering went on there as late as 1930.

Many foreign people had come into Emmet County to work at the lumber camps, and at their closing, the French settled in Wawatam and Carp Lake Townships. Germans added to the population of the county. They bought farms and went into other businesses to help develop the county. Irish who had worked around Cecil Bay, settled in Bliss Township. The Poles coming later, helped to lumber around Larks Lake in Center Township. After the timber was cut, they bought farms in the township.

After taking the timber off their holdings, most of the big lumber companies in Emmet County sold what desirable land they could for farms. Having no further use for the land, they would not pay taxes, so in a few years it reverted to the State. Emmet County has thousands of acres of state land acquired that way. Wilderness State Park in the northern part of Emmet County comprises 6,409 acres of tax reverted lands.

Public opinion turned quickly against the lumbermen, who were accused of leaving nothing but stumps in their wake. This was only partly true. They did leave stumps, but they also left farms and cities.

City of Petoskey

PETOSKEY, county seat of Emmet County, is located on the south shore of Little Traverse Bay in the northwestern section of the Lower Peninsula, in the heart of Michigan's Water Wonderland. PETOSKEY is 70 miles northeast of Traverse City, 265 miles northwest of Detroit and 38 miles south of the Straits of Mackinac.

PETOSKEY was incorporated as a village in 1878 and as a city in 1896. First white settlers arrived here in 1852 to live in a town located at the mouth of Bear River and Lake Michigan on Little Traverse Bay.

The city was named for an Indian chief - Chief Pe-To-Se-Ga, an Ottawa who once owned all the land where the city is now located. His name means "rising sun," although Petoskey is famous for its "Million Dollar Sunsets" on Little Traverse Bay. Petoskey, once part of the Ottawa trail to Grand Rapids, is on US-31 and US-131, and is the gateway city to the $100 million Mackinac Bridge.

Petoskey has a 1974 population of 6,359 and has an area of four square miles. It is the retail trade center for approximately 50,000. This area includes Emmet County and parts of Cheboygan, Charlevoix and Otsego Counties. During the summer months of July and August, population grows to approximately 30,000 or more.

The altitude of Petoskey is 620 feet above sea level and the mean annual temperature is 45.2 degrees F.

Petoskey is served by US-31 which runs from Mobile Bay, Alabama to the Straits of Mackinac and by US-131 which traverses the length of Michigan. Interstate 75 passes a few miles east of Petoskey. This highway connects Sault Ste. Marie through Detroit south to the Tampa - St. Petersburg area in Florida. The opening of this highway and Michigan's general highway program have opened up the Petoskey area as never before and will continue to enhance its economy.

TRANSPORTATION

Pennsylvania RR and the Chesapeake & Ohio RR adequately serve Petoskey with freight service although there is no longer a passenger service. Petoskey is served by the North Star Bus Lines, Greyhound Bus Lines and Smith Bus Lines. Motor freight service is provided by Parker Motor Freight Company, REA and United Parcel Service.

North Central Airlines comes into Emmet County Airport at Pellston - 18 miles north of Petoskey. There is charter service from both Emmet County Airport and Harbor Springs Airport. Also, private aircraft can land at the Harbor Springs Airport, 4 miles north of Petoskey. Private landing strips are also at Boyne Mountain and at Boyne Highlands.

EDUCATION

Petoskey is the home of North Central Michigan College, a coeducational junior college with approximately 800 students. It was first established in 1958 and it is accredited by the Michigan Commission on College Accreditation.

Petoskey Public School District covers an area of over 170 square miles. The school system is accredited by the North Central Association, the University of Michigan and the State Department of Education. The Public School system consists of a recently constructed four-year high school, middle school, and six elementary schools. The school system also provides an area vocational center and special education for children with learning disabilities.

RETAIL TRADE CENTER

Petoskey is the retail trade center of a large area including all of Emmet County and sections of several others. This is evidenced by the many fine stores in the downtown area which are open all year.

HOTELS AND MOTELS

As far as Petoskey itself is concerned, there is really just one hotel, the Perry-Davis Hotel. The Perry-Davis Hotel was built in 1889 with a new wing added in 1926. The hotel has a total of 97 rooms. It also has a cocktail lounge and a dining room which doubles as a banquet room and overlooks the Little Traverse Bay.

Motels form an important part of the rooming facilities in Petoskey. Petoskey has a total of six motels with deluxe accommodations, three of which were constructed within the last six years, and many other motels with first-class accommodations. Motels and hotels in Petoskey offer accommodations for approximately 2,000 people, both summer and winter. There are many hotels, motels, inns and lodges in nearby Harbor Springs, Walloon Lake, Charlevoix and Indian River offering accommodations both summer and winter and bringing the total number of accommodations available in the area to over 3,000.

LOCATION

Petoskey is a "traffic hub" of Northern Michigan overlooking the beautiful Little Traverse Bay. US-131 and US-31 meet in Petoskey and traffic from I-75 diverts into Petoskey by way of M-31 and US-131 from Gaylord and M-68 from Indian River to US-31.

At the junction of US-31 and M-131, known as "Chimney Corners," 9,000 cars per day pass this spot according to Michigan Department of State Highways. This is the highest concentrated traffic spot north of the Midland - Muskegon line.

WINTER ACTIVITIES

Petoskey is the housing center for five major ski areas. Mr. Everett Kircher is the biggest corporate ski business owner in the United States with the Boyne Highlands, Boyne Mountain, Thunder Mountain and Walloon Hills ski areas. The Petoskey area, formerly publicized as the "Big 6 Ski Area," is now popularly known as "Boyne Country."

With constant upgrading of facilities and new equipment, "Boyne Country" which includes Boyne Highlands, Boyne Mountain, Nub's Nob, Thunder Mountain, and Walloon Hills, offers Midwest's finest skiing fourteen weekends during the winter. December through March finds 8 to 12 thousand skiers wending their way to Michigan's Winter Wonderland.

The Chamber of Commerce welcomes additional housing to provide modern accommodations for the people who visit the area during the four seasons.

Snowmobiling and cross-country skiing are fast becoming popular sports in the north, and the Petoskey area offers hundreds of miles of trails over scenic lakes and through virgin forests. Snowmobiling has opened areas heretofore unaccessible during the winter season. The most popular and well-marked trail in our area is the Moose Jaw Safari Trail just north of Harbor Springs on M-131.

MARINA

Petoskey is proud of its marina which marked its opening in 1970. The marina was built in cooperation with the Michigan Waterways Commission and the City of Petoskey.

The marina is capable of handling crafts up to 60 feet in length. The rowboat to the luxury yacht will be able to berth at the new marina with its 80 slips. Shoreside installations include toilets, showers and a recreation room. Each berth is equipped with electricity, water and telephone. Holding tank pump-out facilities are another service which is available. Gas, oil and marine supplies are available.

Marina facilities are also available in nearby Harbor Springs.

INDUSTRY

Another aspect of importance to the economy of Petoskey is its industries. The Chamber of Commerce lists twelve highly diversified industries. The largest is the Penn Dixie Cement Corp. Other important industries are Barnum Bros., Fibre Co., automobile parts; I.T.T. Thompson Industries, Elec. Div., wire harnesses; Curtis Wire Products Co., wire shelving and wire products; Kellogg Studios, ceramic specialties; The McLaughlin Co., clinchnuts, weld nuts, washer assembly; Michigan Maple Block Co., butcher blocks, maple table tops, carving boards; Northern Concrete Products, cement blocks, etc.; Petoskey Manufacturing Co., zinc die casting; Petoskey

Plating Co., chrome and copper plating; Petoskey Plastics, Inc., plastic bags, low density polyethylene. All of Petoskey's industries play a vital role in the economy.

AGRICULTURE

Although not as important as tourism, agriculture does play an important part in the economy of Petoskey and the area. Hay, potatoes and winter wheat are prime crops, as well as some feed grains. Apple and cherry orchards are important as well as dairy products. From a retail trade point of view, it is interesting to note that in 1968 according to Sales Management magazine, the total population of the counties which make up the retail trade area of Petoskey was 51,400 with 31,000 people or approximately 60% classified as non-urban residents. 1974 indicated that these figures have greatly increased.

MEDICAL CENTER

Petoskey is in a very real sense the medical center for a much wider area than its trade territory. Petoskey has two hospitals - Lockwood-MacDonald and Little Traverse Hospitals and Burns Clinic. Lockwood-MacDonald has 75 beds. Little Traverse Hospital has 178 beds and is known far and wide for its hospital care. People in Petoskey like to think of it as "Little Mayo." Little Traverse Hospital and Burns Clinic have wealthy and well-known personages among their clientele.

From a practical point of view, Petoskey's hospitals are Petoskey's largest employers. Little Traverse has 625 "personnel", Burns Clinic has 187 "personnel" of which 49 are doctors. Lockwood-MacDonald has 125 employees.

OTHER FACTORS

From almost every point of view, Petoskey is a very fine city. Petoskey has 22 churches representing all major denominations. Petoskey has a mayor-city manager form of government and an aggressive Chamber of Commerce. Petoskey has a fine daily newspaper with a circulation of approximately 11,000 daily.

Active social groups include: The Masons, Eagles, VFW, American Legion, Disabled American Veterans, Odd Fellows, Knights of Columbus, Knights Templar, B.P.O.Elks, Kiwanis, Rotary, Lions, Jaycees, Rebekahs, OES, WRC, Blue Star Mothers, Beta Sigma Phi, American Association of University Women, Business and Professional Women and Zonta. Petoskey has Boy and Girl Scouts, 4-H and many other youth organizations. With church groups there are a total of 287 organizations in this area.

Petoskey is served by Michigan Bell Telephone Company, radio stations WJML and WMBN. Television provides NBC, CBS and ABC networks.

Petoskey is also served by WGTU/TV, Northern Michigan's first UHF one million watt station.

Petoskey fire department has seven full time men and thirteen volunteers. The police department has eight full-time men, one meter maid, and two office clerks. Michigan State Police Post is located here. Consumers Power Company furnishes the city's lights and power. Petoskey has an unlimited water supply for home and industrial uses as well as a highly favorable tax rate. Two fine banks serve Petoskey - First National Bank and State Bank and Trust Company, which also provide five drive-in banks.

There are excellent camping, swimming, boating, fishing, hiking, bike trails and loafing facilities in the great north woods of the "Water Wonderland" state. For the summer visitors, there are numerous marinas and yacht clubs in the area, 12 golf courses within easy reach, and four tennis courts. At nearby Bay View, there is a two-month program of continuous artist's recitals and cultural activities, also a fine summer stock theatre. Year around activities include Little Traverse Racquet Club being completed this year and Little Traverse Theatre Group. For the winter visitor, there is skiing, cross-country skiing, and skating within the city limits, as well as at the numerous "famous name" ski and snowmobiling areas located within a short distance.

Petoskey has ten parks with a total of 70 acres and a public library with over 40,358 volumes.

The Petoskey State Park offers camping and swimming facilities under constant supervision.

In short, Petoskey is a community which offers many advantages to native and visitor alike.

Why the Name Petoskey?

One hundred and fifty-one years ago, while Chief Nee-i-too-shing and several members of the Chippewa tribe were hunting and trapping near the mouth of the Manistee River (now known as the city of Manistee), there was born to the chief in the early dawn, a son named Neyas Pe-to-se-ga (translated meaning "The Rising Sun"). Early missionaries persuaded the "patron Saint," after whom the hub and leading resort city of northern Michigan was named — Petoskey, that Neyas was an abbreviation for Ignatius, and he accepted it.

Shortly after the early morning arrival of Ignatius Pe-to-se-ga in the rudely constructed wigwam near the Manistee River, Chief Nee-i-too-shing, with his family and followers, moved northward and took up their abode on Little Traverse Bay, near Harbor Springs. When twenty-two years old, Pe-to-se-ga took for his wife the daughter of a neighbor Keway-ka-ba-wi-kwa. Through this union were born fourteen children. In 1830 Ignatius Pe-to-se-ga, with his family, moved across Little Traverse Bay locating on the south shore where he at one time owned a large portion of the territory on which is now located the beautiful and historic city of Petoskey, named in his honor. Just why Pe-to-se-ga was changed to Petoskey is not definitely known, and many early residents maintain that this change is an unhappy corruption.

Petoskey Stones

Summertime finds gem stone enthusiasts busy along the shores of Little Traverse Bay, collecting the numerous specimens available. Many of these hobbyists also are "lapidaries" – persons who practice the art of cutting and polishing stones.

A Petoskey Stone is a petrified coral of which there are several species. These fossils are found in many localities of the world, through drilling to great depths, but are found as an outcropping on the top of the ground in and around Petoskey on the shores of the Little Traverse Bay.

Corals are sea invertebrates which live in warm salt water. Their general structure is that of a membranous bag divided into radially arranged folds. These little animals may live singly or in a colony so intimately united that the separation of one body from the other is difficult to see.

PETRIFIED REMAINS

The stratified rocks, forming the crust of our globe, are frequently found to contain petrified remains of living organisms. Petrification may come about when a dead organism is saved from fungi, bacteria, scavenging animals, the air, and all agents that bring about decay. The only chance for a dead organism to be preserved as a fossil is for it to be quickly covered with sediment or volcanic ashes, especially if the organism contained hard skeletal parts. Petoskey Stones were formed when the original material was replaced, bit by bit, by a substitute mineral preserving the microscopic structure of each cell of the organism. The substituting or replacing mineral in this case was calcium carbonate in the water. This is the same chemical compound of which limestone is composed.

PRE-HISTORIC HISTORY

Paleontologists, those who study the life of prehistoric times, tell us that geologic history, like human history, falls into major divisions called eras. The names of the eras are based on the state of the organic evolution present: Archeozoic (primitive life), Mesozoic (medieval life), Cenozoic (recent life), and Psychozoic (the age of reason). Each era is composed of a group of periods. A period embraces one or more

invasions of the land by oceans; and therefore contains one or more sedimentary cycles. The name of the period is generally taken from the region in which the strata was first studied. Paleontologists have agreed that in certain strata outcrops, one is apt to find the same, or nearly so, kind of fossils.

The fossil corals, known as Petoskey Stones, lived in salty warm sea water in the Paleozoic era during the Silurian and Denonian periods. According to geologists, this was 280 to 300 million years ago. The most abundant coral in our Petoskey region belongs to the order of Zoantharia.

The area was under warm salt water. The Petoskey area is rich in unusual fossil stone.

The Petoskey Stone is the State Stone of Michigan.

Chapter 3

Cheboygan County --
Early Settlement

by Ellis Olson

Remnants of recorded history pertaining to the area now known as Cheboygan County offer us only vague and scattered glimpses of the early activities in this region prior to the 1840's, but those time-worn and tattered documents, when applied to the recent archaeological discoveries along the Inland Route, suggest a great deal of activity by our pre-historic brothers of the wild and the French and British that followed.

Early government survey maps by John Mullett and William Burt show numerous Indian "old fields", trails and sugar bushes scattered along the Inland Route and surrounding the inland lakes.

John Askin, trader of Michilimackinac, once maintained a trading post here and his youngest daughter, Catherine, wife of captain Samuel Robertson, spent at least three winters near the mouth of the Cheboygan river in a tiny but substantial log cabin.

Missionary priests, Baraga and Piret, both frequented the Inland Route administering their religion to the inhabitants. For the most part, though, what happened in Cheboygan prior to the Revolutionary War remains a mystery, perhaps to be unveiled at some future time by inquisitive historians and arduous archaeologists. Such an investigation is presently being conducted by the Mackinac Island State Park Commission, at Mill Creek, on Private Claim 334. This was the site of the first water-powered gristmill in Michigan, and also the earliest water-powered sawmill in Michigan. Private Claim 334 was once within the boundary of the Military Reservation of Old Fort Michilimackinac, and was controlled by John Askin who intended to build a fine house there.

The property fell into the hands of Robert Campbell, trader at Michilimackinac, at about the time John Askin left the Straits of Mackinac and the fort was removed to Mackinac Island.

Information about the early activity on Private Claim 334, in the township of Mackinaw, represents one aspect of our history that has neither been thoroughly explored nor completely understood. This claim was surveyed by Aaron Greeley in 1810 and granted to the heirs of Robert Campbell in 1811 by the United States government, and is one of few such grants made in Michigan. In order to secure a patent for a private claim, the petitioner had to clear the land and reside on the property before the Americans took possession of the Michigan Territory on June 30, 1796.

Little is known about the Indian trader, Robert Campbell, who eventually acquired the property after Fort Michilimackinac was moved to the island. His heirs sold the property, including the gristmill and sawmill, to Michael Dousman in 1811. Dousman operated the gristmill until 1839 and then abandoned it.

The idle mill remained intact until 1860, when the millstones were removed by William Meyers to a new location on the tiny island between the Cheboygan locks and dam. Five years later, he moved the millstones to his mill on Meyers Creek, in Grant township, which was to be its last location.

Only these two isolated little specks of settlement, Askin's farm at Mill Creek and Askin's trading post at the mouth of the Cheboygan River, are known to exist in Cheboygan County prior to 1796.

Between 1834 and 1843, the American Fur Company empire in the great lakes began crumbling and giving way to the ensuing wave of settlement. About this time, the government was busy surveying Northern Michigan to enable homesteaders to secure land along the lakes and rivers. This was a fortunate circumstance for the hundreds of clerks and traders of the fur company, who, with the almost abrupt end of the company, were forced to seek a new livelihood. Some turned to fishing, coopering, farming and lumbering, while others simply moved further westward.

Most of Cheboygan's early settlers were previously involved with the American Fur Company.

In 1840, the present county of Cheboygan included two counties which were created by an act of the State Legislature. The southern half was designated as Wyandot County and included Towns 33, 34, 35 and 36 North; Ranges 1 East, 1, 2 and 3 West. The northern portion, known as Sheboygan (sic) County, included Towns, 37, 38 and 39 North; Ranges 1 East, 1, 2, 3 and 4 West.

The first conveyance of land within the present boundaries of the City of Cheboygan, the county seat, was issued to Jacob Sammons in 1848. It was platted in 1851 and contained 45 lots which were designated, "Original Plat of Cheboygan". Sammons, who had been employed by the American Fur Company, spelled Cheboygan with a "C" in spite of the fact that Cheboygan County was spelled with an "S" by the State Legislature when it was set off from Michilimackinac County in 1840. The name Sheboygan was retained until 1853 when the county was officially organized. When he first arrived, there were no Indians making this their permanent residence, but they frequently camped at several places along the Cheboygan River.

In 1849, Sheboygan Township was organized and included all of the county of Sheboygan. One year later, in 1850, the township name was changed to Inverness, but retained the same boundaries. (The names of both the township and the county, in the acts of 1849 and 1850, are spelled Sheboygan.)

In the year 1853, the counties of Cheboygan and Wyandot were consolidated and organized into one county, to be known and designated as Cheboygan County, and so much of Range 4 West as had been included in Cheboygan County was detached and annexed to Emmet County. This act, which established the county seat at the village of Duncan on the Cheboygan River, was later amended that year to read "Bay" instead of "river". The county seat remained at Duncan until 1856, at which time it was removed to the township of Inverness.

These two townships, Inverness and Duncan, continued to be the only organized townships in the county until 1860, when the Board of Supervisors organized the township of Burt.

The first meeting of the Board of Supervisors was held in the office of the County Clerk, October 8, 1855. The Supervisors elected Jeremiah Woolston as their chairman. The purpose of this meeting was to examine the tax rolls, equalize and assess the necessary taxes to operate the governmental functions of the county.

The United States Land Office at Duncan was transferred from Flint where it had been previously known as the Genesee District Land Office. The Duncan Land Office was housed in the Duncan Court House. The land office was transferred to Duncan in the fall of 1855 and remained there until March 1, 1858. Medard Metivier conveyed the books, papers and fireproof safe to Mackinac Island on a sleigh, thus removing the office to its new location.

In 1846, a post office had been established in the village of Cheboygan; Ronald McLeod served as the first postmaster. The post office was situated on the west bank of the Cheboygan River near its entrance into the Straits of Mackinaw. It was named the Duncan post office and was on the Saginaw and Sault

Ste. Marie mail route. The name was properly changed to Cheboygan in 1870.

The term, "Duncan Village", was vaguely used in reference to the area on the east side of the Cheboygan River. It was first mentioned in 1853, when the legislature fixed the county seat at the "Bay", thus distinguishing it from Jacob Sammon's settlement. The land office was located in the township of Duncan because no legally defined boundary had been established for "Duncan Village". The first post office was located in the village of Cheboygan (Sammon's settlement) but was known as the Duncan post office. Until the early 1860's, Duncan was listed as a postvillage on the west side of the Cheboygan River.

During the 1860's, the principle means of transportation was by water for to that time suitable roads connecting the struggling northern Michigan communities were yet to be constructed.

Those who settled the interior, away from the water routes, cut crude and sometimes impassable roads to gain access to their farms or camps. As the numbers of pioneers grew and the need to travel from one small settlement to others increased, state roads were constructed.

The mail was carried by boat from Cheboygan to the west end of Crooked Lake and then transferred to stagecoaches which followed the Cheboygan and Little Traverse Bay State Road. This road had been completed by 1874.

The Laws of 1846 gave county boards of supervisors authority to lay out, establish, alter, discontinue or open state roads. This law, lacking a provision to supply the necessary capital for work on a road, was relatively useless. Some counties in Michigan may have taken advantage of this authority, but Cheboygan County lacked the population and a system of organized government to utilize its provisions. Each state road that was subsequently built in the county was financed by an appropriation of the State Legislature.

The Saginaw to Cheboygan State Road was authorized by the Legislature in 1858. The act under which this state road originated was amended in 1859 and the completion of the Saginaw to Cheboygan State Road was delayed indefinitely. The path that this road would have followed served as a mail route for many years but was not suitable for conveying anything but a horse and rider or dog sleighs. The mail route which followed this marked trail was called the Saginaw to Sault Ste. Marie mail route, carrying mail to Cheboygan once a week en route to the "Soo".

The Duncan, Alpena and Sauble River State Road was authorized by the Legislature in 1861 and additional legislation was given for improvements on it in 1867. The survey was made by D. D. Oliver, an early resident of Alpena. Oliver also surveyed the Cheboygan River to Old Mackinaw State Road. The final link of the Duncan, Alpena and Sauble River State Road was approved in 1877 with the appropriation of swamp lands to finance that section north from Alpena to Cheboygan. Portions of this road are presently referred to as the Black Lake State Forest Road.

The Cheboygan River to Old Mackinaw State Road was authorized in 1869 and completed in 1876. Today, this road is appropriately named the Old Mackinaw Road.

The Cheboygan and Little Traverse Bay State Road was legislated in 1871 and construction was begun in 1872. It passed through the Riggs settlement (Riggsville), Pellston, Alanson, Conway, Oden and Bay View. The section of this road from Pellston to Cheboygan has been altered in places and is called the Riggsville Road. At one time, in the late 80's, a stagecoach made weekly runs with passengers and mail from Petoskey to Cheboygan on this route.

These previously mentioned internal improvements came quite some time after the first settlers arrived and began to bring their families. Foremost among the early pioneers was Alexander McLeod, who was the first white man to come permanently to Cheboygan. He arrived in the fall of 1844 and built a small log cabin close to the river bank on what is now Water Street, just north of State Street. During the winter of 1844-45, he lived in that shanty with his brother, Ronald, and others. They spent the winter selecting and cutting hardwoods to be taken that spring to Mackinaw Island for the manufacture of barrels.

Jacob Sammons moved his family to Cheboygan in the spring of 1845. He built the first permanent house, situated on Water Street, just south of State Street. He is considered the first settler, although he was not the first person to live within the county.

Other early pioneers who made Cheboygan their place of residence shortly after Sammons were: John Vincent, Moses Wiggins Horne, Lorenzo Backus, R. N. Stephenson, Peter McKinley, Anson Delmadge, Alonzo Cheesman, James Starkley, Peter Labelle, George Kitchen, Stephan Winchell and the Fisher family.

It is difficult today to visualize Cheboygan during its first few years of growth. Its scattered homes lying alongside the few dirt trails, lacking even the crudest type of sidewalk, would hardly be the picture of prosperity. Good paint was still a thing of the future, so buildings were either left bare or were whitewashed. Behind each home, in an out of the way place, could be seen the familiar site of the outhouse collecting its share of lively bees. Women doing their washing on the river bank and the men piling lumber on the docks were common scenes during those early days. Most stimulating were the odors of freshly baked bread and burning pitch mushrooming from the chimneys of the quaint well-kept dwellings.

When navigation of the lakes stopped in the late fall, nearly every northern Michigan town became an isolated community. It was a matter of survival for everyone to have a full root cellar and a good store of staples in their pantry. The only connection with the outside world from November to May was by a difficult journey over a hostile and unsettled land or over treacherous frozen lakes. The trials and hardships of life were shared and it was easy to find friends during times of distress. They worked together, sharing what little they could and sometimes more.

The Cheboygan retail and wholesale business took second place to Duncan City until the late 1890's. Due to the extensive shipping carried on in both towns, the place was known as the port of twin harbors by all the captains who sailed the Great Lakes. Many vessels made regular refueling stops at Duncan, taking on slabs to "fire up" their boilers.

The importance of Duncan City as a merchandising outlet can be exemplified by the presence of its foundry, blacksmith shop, harness shop, machine shop, carpenter shop, barber shop, drugstore, warehouse and retail store. The foundary manufactured and exported over 800 "Brazel" snowplows at the time considered superior to any other type of horse-drawn plow in use. The foundry was well known on the Great Lakes for repairing heavy marine machinery and sawmill equipment and custom work of all kinds. The Smith stables at Duncan were large enough to accommodate 80 horses.

Many public services found in Cheboygan were also present in Duncan City -- in some cases shared by both. The City of Cheboygan extended a 12-inch water main to Duncan. In 1883 the first telephone was run to Duncan. In 1893, a track for a horse-drawn streetcar was laid down the middle of the old corduroy road. The Cheboygan Street Railway Co., owned by D. J. Kennedy of Bay City, was in service until it ran into financial difficulty about 1896. It started again in the summer of 1898 but was forced to close after the big mill in Duncan burned that fall, and there were not enough passengers to make it profitable.

The five docks at Duncan totaled over a mile with double frontage. They ranged from 40 to 60 feet in width. As many as 15,000,000 board feet of lumber could be air dried on the docks at one time. A 40x200 foot warehouse was located on the steamboat dock, which was 50x500 feet. The water depth at the dock was over 20 feet, more than adequate to float lumber hookers and schooners. The steamboat dock was sometimes called the D&C dock because boats of the D&C line made regular stops there. It was also used for docking the two tugs owned by the Smiths. Two other docks, the *Breakwater* and *L*, were used for a refueling point for steam vessels and for storing lumber, lath and shingles. Today, only a few weather-beaten piles and submerged slabs remain of the once impressive Duncan City docks.

While Duncan City was edging toward extinction, Cheboygan was boisterously making its way toward a position of prominence among northern Michigan communities. Unlike Duncan City, Cheboygan's advance was not due entirely to the lumbering industry, but rather to wood manufacturing, fishing, tourism, shipping and other related industries. But the most significant single industry by far was that concerned with cutting the saw log.

Most of the town's early activity centered around and near the river or bay. The first lighthouse was constructed in 1851 at Lighthouse Point by Rhodes and Warner of Ohio, under the supervision of Captain Shook of the U.S. Engineers. William Drew was the first keeper. This light was discontinued in 1929.

With the exception of a few sawmills in Cheboygan during the 1840's and 50's, coopering was the most substantial business in the infant settlement. This trade required an associated industry -- the blacksmith and his forge for making the hoops for the barrels. First among the coopers was Jacob Sammons who hired M. W. Horne to make the first fish barrels in his shop in 1846. The hoops for these barrels were manufactured on Mackinac Island because there was no blacksmith in Cheboygan until Peter Labelle arrived in 1848.

The first pioneer physician and surgeon who administered his patent medicines and cared for the sick was Dr. Strong of Duncan City in 1854. After he left, Cheboygan and Duncan were without a medical man until Dr. Arthur M. Gerow hung out his shingle at the corner of Main and Third (State) Streets in 1868.

Although it may seem that early business efforts were futile, they paved the way for more substantial improvements in the future. Many of the small mills later increased their capacity, extending their operations, and invested heavily in the economy of Cheboygan. One of the most progressive early lumbering firms was the W & A McArthur watermill company.

The W & A McArthur Co. provided the first electric power for the city in 1884. The plant was first located in the watermill and derived its source of power from the river's current. Sometime later, the plant was moved to the second floor of the old flour mill. The electric plant was moved to the Black River Dam when the W & A McArthur Co. Ltd. sold their interests to the Cheboygan Paper Company.

The first newspaper in Cheboygan was the *Manitawauba Chronicle*. Its first edition was issued on Saturday, January 28, 1871, by William P. Maiden. He published 13 editions in all. Maiden believed that every town should have and support its own newspaper. His primary purpose for starting the paper was to create an interest in politics among the local citizens and to nurture the thought of incorporating the village. His newspaper was well composed and extremely interesting. He printed several bold editorials, but in each instance displayed the tact and technique of a well-seasoned politician. For him, this endeavor was rewarding, for when the village incorporated May 9, 1871, he was elected the first village president.

Thus ends the first three struggling decades of settlement in Cheboygan County.

Mackinaw Township Supervisors

William Taylor	1884-85
E. M. Sutherland	1886-87
D. Barrett	1888-1892
Ed Blackmur	1893-94
Sam Smith	1894-1913
E. Wheeler	1915-1919
Sam Smith	1921-1931
Clark Trumbull	1932-1942
Elton C. Dagwell	1943-1969
Mrs. Amelia Cole	1970-71
Fred Grebe	1971-72
Clem Valot	1972-

Mackinaw's First Motorcycle

Very early in the 1900's, Bill Smith bought himself a motorcycle. Few in Mackinaw had ever seen one, so many were on hand to see it delivered and unpacked.

The crowd gathered on the boardwalk in front of the Stimpson house and began suggesting how to start this beastly machine. The gas tank was filled, and Bill, being no coward and anxious to show off his new toy, boarded it and slipped it into gear. Away he went! Each time he ran over a stone his speed accelerated, and he was having problems he hadn't thought of. Around the block he went, the crowd cheering him on--faster and faster until he thought he'd better stop. But how? He had no idea how. Round the block again, yelling as he flew past the Stimpson House, "Come help me stop this thing!" The crowd roared in laughter, enjoying the show. Round and round he sped, pleading on each pass, "Stop me!", not daring to take his eyes from the stony path ahead.

How long did it last? Until the cycle finally ran out of gas!!

----by Judy Ranville

PRIVATE CLAIM # 334

MILL CREEK AREA -(Only Private Claim in Cheboygan County)

****
Statement by Clem Valot:I believe this to be true to the best
of my knowledge.

March 1,1976
****
John Askin staked out claim,designated as PRIVATE CLAIM # 334

sometime between 1771 & 1777. I believe his claim was filed

in England.He left the Straits area in 1780 because he was

being tried for Treason. Before he left he transferred his

property to Robert Campbell,a Fur Trader.By 1793 Campbell had

built a Grist Mill and a Saw Mill.On April 15,1808 he made a

will,leaving his land to his children;John & Mary Campbell.

Robert Campbell died in the fall of 1808.

****
On July 1,1796 the United States took possesion of the NORTH-

WEST Territory which included the lands of Michigan.

****
The Revolutionary War was between 1775 & 1783.

On March 12,1819,John & Mary Campbell sold the farm to Michael

Dousman for $1,000.
****
Michigan became a State on January 26,1837,the 26th. State.

(Edgar Conklin platted out Mackinaw City in August,1857.

T 39 N R 3 N

Claim 334

Reservation at old Onchilmackinac
Description No 334 confirmed to the legal
Representatives, of Robert Campbell, deceased
commencing at a post standing on the
border of Lake Huron, it being the South
East corner of the Reservation at old
Onchilmackinaw, thence South thirty
five degrees, West one hundred and
ten chains thirty three links to a post,
thence North fifty five degrees, West
Sixty three chains twenty links to a
Maple tree, thence North thirty five
degrees East ninety two chains nineteen
links to a post standing on the borders
of Lake Huron, thence along the border of
said Lake, South Seventy one degrees East
Sixty five chains Seventy five links, to the
place of beginning, containing Six hundred
and forty acres. Detroit 2nd Oct. 1810,

Aaron Greely,
Surveyor of
Private Claims

Chapter 4

Cecil Bay, Michigan

A Land of Shingles, Staves and Strong Men

Pictures of Cecil Bay from the collection of Mike Krueger have been printed by permission of Mary Potes Krueger in memory of Malcolm (Mike) Krueger.

"Mike" was born at Cecil Bay, October 19, 1911, and spent his childhood there. When he was 13 his parents, Mr. and Mrs. John Krueger, moved into Mackinaw City and he attended school, graduating from Mackinaw High School. He was employed as butcher at L. H. Liebeck's Grocery until World War II when he worked for NYC Railway as car clerk until 1959 when the railroads started phasing out. He returned to his former vocation as a butcher at LaTocha's IGA where he worked until his death in 1973.

He is remembered by many as the butcher with a smile.

by Ken Teysen

At the time of Michigan's birth as the twenty-sixth state in 1837, government surveys indicated standing pine reserves of some 150 billion board feet. Sixty years later in 1897 only 6 billion board feet remained uncut. After the choice white pine was lumbered off so rapidly during this period the lesser quality woods were sought after and harvested. The introduction into the lumbering industry of the railroad beginning in 1880 made year around operations possible, rather

than just winter cutting and also made economically feasible the taking of marginal timber resources.

In Northern Michigan, although steam and sail vessels kept their importance as low-cost transportation facilities from our lumber towns, two major railroads came into being by the late 1800's. In 1882 the Michigan Central Railroad on the east and the Grand Rapids and Indiana Railroad on the west extended their lines north to Mackinaw City from southern Michigan. Soon every station along these lines became thriving villages with sawmills, shingle mills, and small factories processing forest products.

Two small lumbering towns in northern Emmet County were born, raised, and enjoyed their heyday for some forty years of lusty activity before quietly passing away by 1920. They were able to harvest the hardwoods and variety of softwoods that are native to the area.

The A. B. Kliss Lumber Company established a community at Sturgeon Bay just north of Cross Village and cut primarily maple and other hardwood trees. Further north on the Straits the Callam Lumber Company of 1878, followed in succession by the Davis and Caldwell Company of Battle Creek in 1898 (also known as the Cecil Bay Lumber Company) and finally by the Emmet Lumber Company in 1903, conducted a lumbering and milling operation at Cecil Bay until December 1917.

The land value as indicated by the purchase prices rose from $20,000 in 1878 to $125,000 in 1903. By 1925 this land was no longer productive enough to be retained by the Emmet Lumber Company and was completely disposed of by sale or by outright gifts.

Cecil Bay village was located on the Straits six miles southwest of Mackinaw City and the economy of the settlement of some 200 persons was based entirely on lumber. Initially, in 1878 the cutting of standing pine and hemlock timber and the production of lumber was the principal endeavor. By 1907 the pine was finished. However, in 1898 this work was expanded to include the making of shingles, barrel staves, cutting of pulpwood and so-called excelsior "bolts", railroad ties, as well as lumber.

Because most articles of merchandise and commodities of the late 19th and early 20th century were shipped in either barrels or boxes the demand for staves was high. Nearly the entire production of staves from Cecil Bay were purchased by the Morton Salt Company in Grand Rapids. The excelsior bolts were also sent there to the Excelsior Wrapper Company to be made into packing material for boxes or padding in furniture. A few staves didn't reach their destination as the children delighted in using them as skiis--complete with quick release bindings, called toe straps.

The village itself was situated on the mouth of the Carp River which drains Carp Lake because the river served as a source of water for the steam engines, as a power source for the small direct current electricity generator, and as a vehicle to transport logs to the mill. This latter use was a limited one although four dams were built in the first five miles of the river. Of course, being on the Straits offered access to the venerable sail and steam lumber "hookers" that transported the various forest products to the markets. The principal wholesale markets of the time were Chicago and Albany.

To the east toward French Farm Lake grew tall, straight, yellow and Norway pines--not as choice as Michigan's famed white pine, but still free of knots and highly usable lumber. To the west and southwest, ridges of spruce, hemlock and tamarack were found from which staves were made. To the south between present day Wilderness Park and French Farm Lake ranged poplar and balsam ridges interspersed with thick white cedar swamps. Pulpwood, excelsior wood and ties came from here.

The community by today's standards was unimpressive and even had a rundown look with its unpainted, vertically-sided mills, horse barns, warehouses, shingled homes and dirt streets. Yet it did possess a native beauty in spite of its rather crude buildings. The shining dark blue waters of the Straits outlined the huge old mill to the north and piles or "booms" of logs and stacks of finished staves and lumber were everywhere to be seen. In the hot July sun the pungent odor from the freshly cut wood, the stables and the wood smoke combined with the sweet fragrance of the evergreen forests on all sides and the call of the graceful gulls and other forest birds surely must have been enticing.

The big shingle and lumber mill was near the lake west of Carp River with the small or stave mill further east near the mouth of the river. Like most sawmills it was a two-story building (33'x115'x25' high) dominated by its two tall stacks, one 60 feet the other 48 feet high, of the steam engine room. Nearby was a silo-shaped refuse burner. A large, flat, wheel-like device known as a "ten blocker" fed cedar blocks, securely clamped, into the shingle cutting saws. The blades, being slightly offset with the wheel, cut the wedge-shaped shingles. Knots and sometimes fingers were cut off by a man called a "knot sawyer". To the north extending 200 feet into the Straits was the wharf where the "dock wallopers" loaded the lumber

hookers.

South of the mill and across the street the two-story boarding house, referred to by all as "the hotel", capable of housing and seating some 70 men, was located. Nearby was the company store, post office and livery stable (110'x36') capable of holding 60 teams at once. Also nearby was an ice house and office. To the east across the river twenty-five homes were located along with a school. Church services were held in homes with traveling ministers and Franciscan missionaries from Petoskey bringing the word.

Wagon roads to Mackinaw City and Carp Lake were supplemented in the winter of 1910-1911 by a five mile long spur line of the Pennsylvania Railroad from Carp Lake to Cecil Bay. A three-wheeled vehicle called a velocipide was used by persons to obtain supplies in Carp Lake. The propulsion was by a hand-operated eccentric gear which had to be pumped constantly during the five mile trip.

The life of the village of course centered around the mills and the piecework in the woods. It was a hard, rough and often dangerous work, both near the whining saws, edgers and the falling trees. Yet, it was also healthy and often exciting. Indians still lived and worked here. Devastating fires were common and sailing schooners often foundered in poorly charted waters. The average work day was 10 hours at a high rate of pay of $2.00 per day. All necessities were provided at the company store and since pay day was monthly "tin" money was issued the men for purchases at the store and charged against their account. Truly, they sold their soul to the company store, as the song says. The "tin" money was actually aluminum. Pennys were round, nickels octagon, dimes clover shaped and quarters square.

Since liquor was not available, the lumberjacks craved sweets, and the best of candy was provided from a supplier in Traverse City--Straub Brothers & Ammiote Company. Bliss and Levering farms supplied fresh meat and vegetables, and during the winter months Lake trout "as long as a hand sleigh" were commonly caught in the Straits and a welcome delicacy to the diet. At the boarding house a strick and customary rule of no talking by the seventy-odd men was observed, although the food was stowed away with great gusto.

Mr. and Mrs. J. B. Cain, who still live a few miles from Cecil Bay where they met, fell in love and married some fifty years ago, recall well the happy dancing parties at the old boarding house. Mr. Cain worked in the mill at a variety of jobs while his charming and witty bride-to-be rose from storekeeper to Company bookkeeper and eventually in the closing years to head bookkeeper and office manager of the operation while the superintendent managed another mill in Boyne City.

Both of the Cains were musically inclined and with a brother, Ray, provided music for the Saturday night dances when the tables would be pushed back to make room for the square dancing, the waltzes and the fox trots. Farmers, lumbermen and just plain people came from Carp Lake, Levering and the surrounding area to enjoy these affairs. The hard-working, low-paid men appreciated these wholesome diversions from their labor and seldom were altercations or drunkeness in evidence. On the contrary, good humor and real concern for others was much in evidence.

In December 1917 the Emmet Lumber Company ceased operation. For another year John Krueger, whose sons still live in Mackinaw City, lumbered pulpwood with a small crew of men. This was in an outlying area known as the Indian Camps, about a mile to the southeast. However, in the spring of 1919, a forest fire swept the area and burned 5,000 cords of his stacked wood and drained his resources. The end had come to the lumber era on this side of the Straits. Some families remained in Cecil Bay as late as 1924, but eventually all traces of this small village were erased by time. It is now being subdivided and developed by a downstate promoter.

Mackinaw's Cecil Bay Descendants

One of the two Callam brothers who first came to lumber the white pine married a local girl. She was the niece of Oscar, Sam and Will Smith. Mr. Callam built the house that Merritt Cole now lives in, as well as the buildings that house the Mackinac Fudge store, Coffman's hardware and Creekmur's bakery.

The two Desy brothers, James and Eugene, known to us as Jim and Sunday Desy, worked in the shingle mill. They were the fathers of Raymond Desy and Lloyd Desy.

Oscar Smith was foreman of the mill at Cecil Bay, and his children, Otis, Howard, Earl, Doris, Marie and Hazel, grew up in the village. Sam's daughter was Mrs. Virginia Sattler.

John Krueger moved to Cecil Bay when his children were young and they too grew up there.

One of the teachers at the Cecil school was Ethel Piehl and is referred to by a resident there as "one of the best teachers Cecil Bay ever had". Now she is Mrs. Ethel Carlton.

John Howard, a former Mackinaw City street superintendent, was an excellent mason as testified to by several dry, well-made, present-day basements. He also was postmaster at Cecil Bay despite the allegation he could neither read nor write!!!!

Four dams were built on the Carp River to raise the water level and then in the spring the dams were opened to float the logs downstream. The dam nearest the mouth would prevent the large runs of suckers from running upstream to spawn in the spring. Farmers would come with wagons, catch huge quantities in pond nets, hoist them into the wagon and return home. The many bears in the area also were attracted by the fish. George Coffman recalls hearing of five black bears at one time, in the river, scooping up pawfulls of fish onto the bank and continuing the fun after they had

eaten their fill. He also trapped, with his father, some twenty-seven bears in two years. The hides were sold to teamsters and others for coats and hats. These heavy, warm hides would bring from $40 to $50 each. The main feature was the warmth--not the beauty.

We would like to dedicate these pictures of Cecil Bay in memory of our wonderful father, Roy G. Cole, who moved from Cadillac to this little lumbering settlement to work as a jointer. Here he met our dear mother Emily Burns and they were married by the Rev. Frank E. Peck, U.B. Clergyman from Mackinaw City on July 3, 1913, at the Bay. They later ran a lumbering camp on the railroad spur to Carp Lake until his boss, T.C. Post moved to the Elkins W. Va. Box Co. and took several families with him including our folks as dad was considered an expert jointer.

After dad served 18 months in France during WWI, our folks moved to Pa., and in 1933 they came back to their beautiful northern Michigan.

We lost dad on June 17, 1966 and he is very sadly missed but he was very happy to be back home.

Dr. Kenneth L. Cole
Virginia (Cole) Alexander
Merritt C. Cole
Richard G. Cole

Mr. John Kreuger, Sr.
Last man in charge at Cecil Bay Lumber Mill.

He wasn't always right--but he was always the boss!!!!

Mrs. John Kreuger

A tribute to a top decker's loading skill.

Installing the Railroad
Cecil Bay, Michigan

Interior Car
Cecil, Michigan
1911-12

A wagon load of finished lumber.

Cecil Bay, Michigan - 1911-12

Mill at Cecil Bay, Michigan
1911-1912

January 10, 1912

Hazel Cain and Mrs. Roy Cole at Cecil Bay Mill.

Cecil Bay school. Mrs. Churchill, teacher. 1911.

(Left to Right) ?, Rose Smith, ?, Sarah Edgerton Smith (David's wife), ?, ?, ?, Mrs. Sailler, Mrs. Charlie Callam, with horse. The Callams owned the Cecil Bay Mill at one time.

The Company Store....
Cecil Bay

Andy Moore, Jenkins,
Howell Gilbert, Carl Saunders

Teamster ("Gabe") Charles Lett
Cecil Bay - 1917

"As Many Friends As a String of Bananas"

Mike Krueger grew up in the Cecil Bay Lumber Camp where his father was "Boss". Wages in lumber camps weren't very good, and luxuries were few and far between. The "Boss", however, fared a little better, moneywise, and once a month Dad Krueger would go to town via "handcar" to get a supply of groceries. He always brought back a special treat for his children--a whole stalk of bananas just as they had been cut from the tree.

Mike recalled how all the neighbor camp children kept track of Dad Krueger's shopping day and would gather at the Krueger's home to await his return. "We had a lot of friends as long as the string of bananas lasted," Mike would laughingly say.

****Judy Ranville

Superintendent Sam Parker on Dock at Cecil Bay.

Chapter 5

Trailsend Bay

by Mrs. Esther Gerdan

Trailsend Bay is fifty years old. It was started in 1925 by John G. Emery of Grand Rapids. Originally christened Trailsend Bay Colony, it extended from the beach inland to include French Farm Lake.

The first year the road was started. Trucks hauled gravel as far as they could go, dumped, and were pulled over the ridge by teams of horses to the then wide, hard beach for the return trip.

Driving those first years was a real adventure. Cars were not so dependable and the road was one track with a turnout here and there. If you met a car, someone had to back up to a turnout, or you took your chances leaving the one track. A shovel was standard equipment and you learned fast what to do and what not to do when stuck in the sand.

The first year two cottages and the club house were built. That was the end of building for quite a few years. The timing was unfortunate. The project was barely "off the ground" when the 30's came along. Most people had more pressing problems than where to spend the summer.

In due time, building started again. Now Trailsend is built up -- a combination of permanent residents and summer people. The club house is gone, but the chimney stands incorporated in a home. The original two cottages have seen things go from kerosene lamp and stoves and hand-pumped water to electricity and telephones. One of these cottages is housing the fourth generation.

It has always been and still has the greatest beach, the best swimming and the most spectacular sunsets in the area.

Trailsend Bay Colony

by Roseanna H. Smith

The Trailsend Bay Colony was surveyed and platted by Williams and Works, Civil Engineers and Surveyors, in April, 1925. It was recorded on May 7, 1925.

The Shore Drive (now known as Wilderness Park Drive) was rebuilt at the same time the Colony was platted. Enough land was acquired by Colonel John G. Emery to plat the Colony and the Shore Drive.

The Emery Realty Corporation had a booth at a Sportsman Show in Grand Rapids with an aquarium with live trout (furnished by the Conservation Department) and pictures to show the plat location. The lots were sold on land contracts, and three of the first buyers were Dr. Barrett, Dr. Bachman and Spoolstra's Dry Goods Store in Grand Rapids. In 1927, the Emery Realty Corporation became the West Shore Realty Corporation.

Colonel Emery built a house that is owned and occupied by his daughter, Mrs. Gerdon. Another house built then by the Denners is owned by Miss Florence Dean. Two houses were built across the road from the Lake, for selling, but neither house was sold or occupied -- all according to memory. The windows and doors in one (or the two) were removed and installed in a restaurant in Mackinaw. All were summer cottages built on piers. A large log cabin lodge, 36 x 62 with a fireplace, was built in the mid 20's. This lodge was used as a dance hall and was known as the Pavilion. It was to be for the use of the plat owners. No one is sure if it burned, but it was taken down and the logs used elsewhere. A Mr. Fochtman bought the building at a tax sale. In 1941, Clinton Bennett bought the pipes, some wood and firebrick to build a home which stands on the southwest corner of the Pleasantview and Levering Roads. Mr. Bennett bought these building supplies from Mr. Fochtman. The Watters family have built their home around the original stone fireplace from the lodge and use the fireplace today.

The third house was built by Ellsworth and Louise Sheldon with the help of their five children in 1949 and 1950. They used lumber (bought from Bill Paquet) from the old depot in Mackinaw City. They had 3 x 12 floor joists, 15-18 feet long. Louise and the children pulled out all the square nails (one is on display at the Mackinaw Public Library). They took the lumber to the Charles Page Saw Mill in Cheboygan where Mr. Page cut three inches off the top to avoid the nails and said, "You could not buy that size lumber today." The Sheldons found newspapers dated fifty years previous in the walls. Louise Sheldon taught school in Pellston in 1919 and her landlady was Mrs. Ruth Stevenson, who later owned the drug store in Mackinaw. Louise remembers seeing the sides of the roads in Levering stacked with logs higher than the cars. The logs were shipped to Chicago to be used to rebuild after the Chicago Fire. The Sheldons came to Mackinaw in 1925 for hay fever relief. They live in the third of three houses Mr. Sheldon built between the Gerdon house and the Dean house.

Helen Rouche (sister of Fred) in front of the Trails End Bay Club House.

The Case Of The Missing Woodpile

Then, as now, there were ambitious and less than ambitious people in the world. One story that never ceases to amuse me was about my grandfather, John LaWay, and his woodpile. He and his sons cut their wood a winter ahead so it would be well seasoned--walking each day to the woods (McGulpin Point area) from their home on Mackinaw Point, cutting the trees by hand and pulling them home at night on a large hand sleigh. This was hard, cold work, but they kept the fence row piled high.

As the winter progressed, Grandpa began noticing a "hole" in the woodpile each morning and realized he was keeping the "home fires burning" in more than one place. So he took an armload of wood inside, bored holes in the end of each piece, filled them with black gun powder and put a wooden plug in each. After carefully marking them for his own protection, he placed them at various intervals in the woodpile and waited. Sure enough--the next morning more wood was missing.

Now, one business downtown received a newspaper each day on the morning train and all the men in town gathered around the heating stove to hear the news of the world read to them. Old John went downtown as usual that morning and the big news of the day was--"Did you hear about poor old man   's stove? It blew up last night; why the lids blew off, the stove pipe fell down and nearly scared them to death."

The mystery of the missing woodpile was solved and the case was closed.

****Judy Ranville

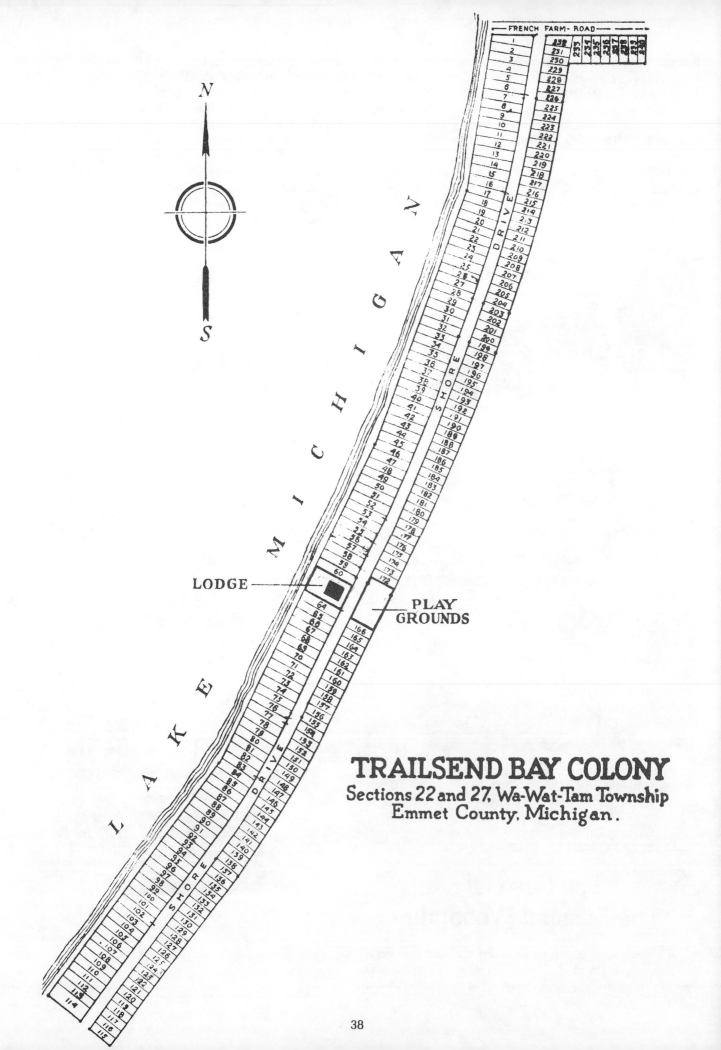

TRAILSEND BAY COLONY
Sections 22 and 27, Wa-Wat-Tam Township
Emmet County, Michigan.

Chapter 6

A History of
Wilderness State Park

By William Smith, Manager

The lands contained within Wilderness State Park and the waters bordering it are enveloped with history well known in the development of Michigan -- Fort Michilimackinac, and the presence of Chippewa Indians, the French voyageurs and soldiers, the English, and finally the Americans, and to the southwest, the Ottawa Indian village of Waganakisi, known by the white man as "L'Arbre Croche".

The interesting point seems to be that there were no Indian villages of any consequence within the lands of the park. One historian, Allen W. Eckert, in his book *Wilderness Empire*, places L'Arbre Croche at the mouth of Big Sucker Creek on Sturgeon Bay. However, the vast weight of historical evidence places the reaches of this once extensive Indian settlement as lying between Cross Village and Harbor Springs.

It is without doubt that the park area was used extensively by the Indians as a haven in times of trouble, for hunting, fishing, the gathering of fruits, overnight encampments, and even as a place to war. Waugoshance Point, a variation of the Indian word meaning "Fox Point", was specifically mentioned by Alexander Henry in a journal of his travels during the latter half of the 1700's. On June 6, 1763, two days after the fall of Fort Michilimackinac to the Chippewas, Henry and three other English prisoners were taken by canoe from the Fort. They were to be taken to Isles du Castor (Beaver Island). Because of a heavy fog that morning, the Chippewas followed the shoreline westward. The Indians would periodically sound four war whoops -- one for each prisoner aboard. As the party reached Waugoshance, the Chippewas again gave their war whoops and, surprisingly, received an answer from the foggy point of land. An Ottawa appeared and talked with the Chippewas, luring them close to land in the process. Then many Ottawas sprang from cover and charged the canoe and forcibly removed the four English prisoners, leaving the Chippewas unharmed to complete their journey. The four prisoners eventually were escorted to Montreal and freed.

No doubt many such conflicts took place in the course of time. According to Ottawa traditions, war was waged against the Mascoutens, a tribe then occupying the L'Arbre Croche area, when the Mascoutens insulted Ottawa warriors returning northward by canoe from a raiding venture to the south. The Ottawas returned in numbers and massacred most of the inhabitants of the Mascouten village. The Ottawas then took possession of the area and, in time, established L'Arbre Croche.

Indian artifacts have been found in the park and surrounding area -- such things as arrow and tomahawk heads. No doubt more will be found in the future.

The exploits and accomplishments of the early French explorers -- Jacques, Samuel de Champlain, Etienne Bruls, Jean Nicolet, and others -- are well known and need not be covered here. Also well documented in history is the coming of Christianity to the Great Lakes region through the efforts of the Jesuit priests and the establishment of their missions -- such men as Fathers Joques, Rambault, Hennepin and Marquette. The first mission near this area was established at St. Ignace in the 1640's.

By 1691 the Jesuit mission of Saint Ignace de Michilimackinac was established at L'Arbre Croche. In the years to follow, the very being of religious orders varied -- from suppression and disbandment to wide diversification. Then in 1855, Father John Bernard Weikamp came to Cross Village and established his Benevolent, Charitable and Religious Society of St. Francis. Father Weikamp had come to America from Prussia in 1850 and established a Franciscan Church in Chicago. He fell into disagreement with Bishop O'Regan there, disposed of the church property, and moved to Cross Village, Michigan. Father Weikamp's institution prospered well between 1855 and the time of his death in 1889. Eventually 2000 acres of land came under its domain, within which much of the land was farmed, cattle were raised, and a grist mill, saw mill, carpenter shop and a blacksmith shop were established. After his death, Father Weikamp's institution slowly deteriorated and was finally abandoned in 1896. Most of the buildings have been torn down or destroyed by fire through the years.

The 1840's saw the coming of more white settlers

to the area. As the years passed, various enterprises were developed -- coopers shops, mercantile stores, commercial fishing, real estate, schools and a post office.

In the late 1870's, the lumbering industry developed in the area and dominated the scene for the next 35-40 years. Numerous saw mills were in operation during this time -- three of which did business nationally and internationally.

The first of these was the saw mill at Cecil Bay. It was in operation from 1878 to about 1917. Wood products from this mill were shipped abroad -- first by schooners, later by railroad. At the peak of the mill's operation, the community developed around the mill contained about 300 permanent residents. There was a school, company store and post office.

The second mill was located in Cross Village. It was in operation from about 1880 to 1911. During the peak of the mill's operation, the population of Cross Village rose to about 500. As with the Cecil Bay mill, its wood products were shipped by sailing schooner. Mrs. Shurtleff states that "Schooners came in large numbers to take the lumber to market. Some of the finest oak timber was shipped to England." In addition to lumber, other natural produce, gathered by the Indian population, was shipped abroad -- untold bushels of blueberries and mokoks of maple sugar.

The third mill was owned and operated by A. B. Klise. It was located north of Cross Village on Sturgeon Bay. As with the other mills, it was in operation from the late 1800's into the early 1900's. Some foundations and pilings from this mill can still be seen. As with the other two mills, shipment from this mill was by schooner, later shifting to the railroad.

A story is told that one day Mr. Klise, wearing a long, heavy black coat, was helping a carpenter out on a dock in the bay. In order to reach some work beyond the dock, a plank was extended beyond the edge with Mr. Klise standing at the far end of the plank and the carpenter counterbalancing the plank dockside. In the course of their work, the carpenter found that he needed another tool and, not thinking, he stepped off the plank to get it. Mr. Klise went swimming and the carpenter did not return to work the next day.

According to local residents, the trees in the present park area were logged off in stages. First the prized white pine; then the Norway; and then continuing to the less prized species.

As the tree size and quality of lumber diminished, the mills, in order to survive, diversified their operations. Cedar shingles were made, barrel staves and tool handles produced, low grade materials were used for pulpwood and excelsior, and hemlock bark was processed for its tannic acid content.

Between locally severe fires and lumbering operations, the lands of Wilderness State Park were almost completely logged off. There remains a stand of virgin hemlock in the Mt. Nebo area and, here and there scattered amongst the wild interior, a stately pine tree of dimensions which brings to mind a time of long ago.

As the lands were denuded, they became useless to the landowners. What can one do with a bare sand ridge or a swamp? "One forty and surrounding land" was sold for as little as $1.00 in 1902. Much of this land reverted to the state for nonpayment of taxes.

In 1896, 1488 acres of land became the state's because of tax reversion. This was followed in 1909 by another 813 acres. In the late 1800's and early 1900's there were a few hardy settlers scattered within the present park boundaries: The LaWays at Big Stone Bay; Brewer's cabin, located westward on the Straits toward Station Point; O'Neal's camp on Big Sucker Creek; Parmerter's cabin inland along the Bliss Trail; and to the east, Hunt's camp and Nelson's camp. As the years went by, more private holdings came into state ownership through purchase and land exchange.

In 1921 and 1922, a house and outbuildings were constructed to house a resident manager. During this time of construction, a man by the name of Frank Lloyd was in charge.

In 1922, the state land became officially known as the "Emmet State Game Refuge", and a resident manager, Irish Saben, was placed in charge. Sometime during these early years, a steel fire tower was constructed atop Mt. Nebo. It was later dismantled when the Bliss Fire Tower came into being. While the Mt. Nebo Fire Tower was in operation, its towerman, a man named Jack Stewart, resided in a house near the present park entrance. It should be noted here that Mr. Stewart had but one leg -- the other was wooden! [His house stood in the clearing where the park entrance is, and that area was always known as "Old Jacks". In the gravel pit area south of the road there stood the haunted house -- a two-story place built by the Harvey's, who owned the acreage from there to Cecil Bay corner -- their descendants are in the Grand Rapids area.]*

In 1928, the lands were turned over to the Parks Division and the area officially became "Wilderness State Park". Its first manager was Thayer Denny, followed shortly by "Daddy" Bronson.

In or about 1930, primitive camping was allowed within the park, the area being along Big Stone Creek. From the end of the lumbering era to the early 1930's, the land was slowly healing from the effects of the axe and the saw and fire. Brush and young trees grew; seedlings were planted. Red and white pine, aspen, birch and other hardwoods flourished along the ridges and upland areas. Spruce, fir, tamarack and cedar abounded in the lowland pockets and swamps. Deer were becoming plentiful. Logging roads which crisscrossed the area slowly became obliterated with time. The land was blessed with a lack of large acreage fires, although one large fire in 1921 skirted the southern border, extending from Bliss eastward to

*supplied by Judy LaWay Ranville

Cecil Bay Road and then northerly toward Cecil Bay.

The Depression caused great strife in Michigan and in the United States. With the establishment of the Civilian Conservation Corps in the spring of 1933, the singlemost time of greatest development was about to occur within the park.

Officially, the program was called Emergency Conservation Work with Michigan tacked on for the state in which particular work was done, and several utility maps still on hand bear the name or initials "M.E.C.W." However, the C.C.C. label was far more popular and later became the official designation.

Beginning on October 1, 1933, a C.C.C. camp was built on the hill where the present outdoor center now stands. Structures ranged from "temporary" tarpaper dormitories 150 feet in length to "permanent" shingle-sided buildings used for administrative purposes. In all, there were about 16 structures eventually erected in the camp.

During their stay, which lasted until about 1937, the C.C.C.'s established an impressive building record. These building feats include the development of all interior roads including the bridge crossings -- these to be used as fire access roads; the construction of five trail cabins and one trailside shelter; the erection of a stone and log observation tower 60 feet in height, atop Mt. Nebo; the construction of several rest benches along the trail system and along the Straits shoreline; the establishment of hiking trails; seedlings were planted; a 15 acre area was cleared west of the camp in preparation for a campground; and the dredging and damming of Big Stone Creek to form Goose Pond.

When the camp was first established, trucks and heavy equipment had not yet been allotted to the camp, and as a result local residents with trucks and horses were hired to help in the work.

Mr. George J. LaWay, presently living in the privately owned community known as the "LaWay Settlement" located within the park boundaries, was one of the local people hired to help out with the pond project. He worked a team of horses used in the dredging phase.

Folkert Sikkens, presently living near the intersection of Cecil Bay and Gill Roads, was another of the local residents hired to help out. He was paid $1.00 per hour for man and truck -- furnishing his own gasoline. A glimpse of the conditions in which the C.C.C.'s worked may be shown by an incident told by Mr. Sikkens. One morning he was 1½ hours late for work. He had had great difficulties starting his truck and had had to drive several miles before he was able to shift gears. Upon reaching camp Mr. Sikkens was informed that the temperature was 52 degrees below zero.

The C.C.C. workers were unemployed men between the ages of 17 and 28, who were paid $30.00 per month -- $25.00 of which was allotted to the men's families. The camp was directed by a reserve Army officer, called back to active duty for a "limited time".

The method employed in bridging swamps was to lay corduroys of cedar logs, marl being placed between each corduroy layer. It is said that during the construction of the Sturgeon Bay Trail, a large caterpillar tractor sank in the muck near Big Sucker Creek and somewhere in that area, it remains yet today.

When the camp was discontinued in 1937, a pit was dug in the camp area and all of the hand tools were buried so that they would not be used by local residents and thus create hardships for local merchants.

1937 brought three changes to the park -- the burning down of a trail cabin at what is now appropriately called "Burnt Cabin Site"; a new park manager by the name of Bill Parker; and with the ending of the C.C.C. program within the park, the beginning of a new work program, the "W.P.A."

The Works Projects Administration had been established by the federal government in 1935 and was much broader in scope than the C.C.C. program. In addition to conservation projects and the employment of the young common laborer, the W.P.A. employed, in addition, craftsmen such as artists, writers, musicians, teachers, architects, etc., and constructed numerous public facilities such as police posts, firehouses, hospitals, town halls, etc.

While not residing within the park, W.P.A. workers completed several park projects between 1937 and 1942. They constructed the three log dormitories presently in use at the outdoor center. They developed the 15 acres cleared by the C.C.C.'s into a campground and, within this campground, constructed a stone and log toilet building. The entrance road to this campground passed through the C.C.C. camp. The W.P.A. program also produced a descriptive brochure entitled *Wilderness State Park*, written by Clifford Allen.

During these years (1937-1942) the buildings at the C.C.C. camp were used to store forest fire equipment. In the summertime, some of the buildings were used to house a University of Michigan summer school. Its director was Professor Kenneth McMurry of the University's Geography Department.

With the bombing of Pearl Harbor on December 7, 1941, and our entrance into World War II, little was done within the park other than maintaining the status quo. However, the old C.C.C. camp was taken over by the U.S. Navy and the western portion of the park, the Waugoshance Point area, was placed "off limits" to civilians.

Between 1942 and 1946, the C.C.C. camp was used as a base of operations and the Point was used for target and strafing practice as well as for experimentation with radio controlled aircraft. Planes were flown out of the Naval Air Station at Traverse City. Evidence of this military usage can still be found in the area. Shell holes can be seen in the boiler plating around Waugoshance Lighthouse. The fuselage of a target plane can still be seen from the

Point parking lot. Shell fragments and motor parts are scattered hither and yon, although most of the readily accessible items have long since been picked up for souvenirs.

With the conclusion of World War II, Dave Whithier became Park Manager for six weeks in 1946, followed directly by Grant H. Wykmuis who resided until 1956. During the war years and the years immediately following, camping continued on the hill where the present Pines Campground is located. The area by Big Stone Creek (formerly a primitive camping area) was used as a day use area -- swimming and picnicking. The usage conversion had been made when the W.P.A.'s had built the new campground and toilet building on the hill.

During these postwar years, the C.C.C. camp buildings decreased in number as they became decrepit and unsafe, or no longer served a useful purpose. Plans had been formulated since the late 1930's to convert this camp into an outdoor center, but none of the plans had come to pass.

On June 18, 1947, the Conservation Commission established a Game Refuge at Wilderness. Hunting and trapping was prohibited within its boundaries. Later, in 1964, these boundaries were modified.

Sometime around 1947, the observation tower at Mt. Nebo was dismantled as it had become unsafe. In October, 1949, the C.C.C. camp came under the direction of the Department of Corrections and was used as a minimum security work camp. Prison inmates came from the Southern Michigan Prison at Jackson. As the entrance road to the campground on the hill passed through the corrections camp and since the campground was so close to the camp, this campground was closed down and camping was again placed at Big Stone Creek -- a hand pump and pit toilets were offered.

In 1950, a saw mill was established in an area just south of the corrections camp. Logs cut from within the park were turned into rough building lumber and siding, cedar posts and shingles. The mill was discontinued in 1957.

In 1951, a new building was erected one mile to the west of the manager's residence by Big Stone Creek. This building served to house the manager and his family and was the headquarters for the park with office, garage and shop space being provided.

On April 19, 1951, the Conservation Commission dedicated four sites within Wilderness State Park as preserves. These sites are dedicated as follows:

Crane Island Natural Area Preserve.
Sturgeon Bay - Sucker Creeks Natural Area Preserve.
Waugoshance Point Nature Study Preserve.
Big Stone - Cecil Bay Nature Study Preserve.

WATERS SURROUNDING THE PARK

It should be emphasized that the waters surrounding the park have, do, and will continue to provide an excellent fishery. The Ottawa and Chippewa Indians fished, netted and speared these waters for their contents of "Mackinaw" trout and whitefish. The white man continued to do the same -- concentrating on the whitefish. Commercial fishing boats can still be observed setting their nets off the park beaches. Cabins and tarpaper shacks were erected on Crane Island and were used by commercial fishermen as a haven from the seas and by the ice fishermen as a base of operations. Waugoshance Point is still a renowned fishing spot for smallmouth bass.

As anyone who has plied its waters or stood along its beaches knows, the Great Lakes can be gentle and calm; a thing of mysterious beauty and peaceful awe. Or the Lakes can be a cruel mistress, wild beyond conception, crushing all that would be upon her waters. Many are the lakers who have surrendered their lives and bodies to her depths. Many are the vessels that lie at her bottom or whose bones are strewn along her shorelines.

Boating disasters have, through history, occurred in northern Lakes Michigan and Huron and in the Straits of Mackinac connecting them. No doubt such disasters will continue to occur.

Remnants of schooners can be found in the Station Point and Cecil Bay areas. In the late 1800's, the *California* faltered on the shoals surrounding St. Helena Island. Days later, seven bodies washed ashore at Cecil Bay. In 1894, the *Minneapolis* sank in the Straits. Two barges (converted schooners) that the vessel was towing were also lost. In the Great Storm of November, 1913, 19 ships were lost, 20 more were stranded. One of the stranded vessels went aground on Simmon's Reef in the Straits. In November of 1958, the *Carl D. Bradley* faltered and sank in rough seas near Gull Island at the west end of the Straits. Of the ship's company of 35 men, only two survived. On the night of May 6, 1965, a dense fog was present in the Straits area. The *Upson*, northbound from Chicago, rammed the lighthouse at Grey's Reef. Both the lighthouse and the ship were damaged. The fog persisted and the next morning the Norwegian motor vessel *Topdalsfjord* and the Great Lakes freighter *Cedarville* collided east of the Mackinac Bridge. Both ships were damaged -- the *Cedarville* mortally. An attempt to beach the ship at Mackinaw City failed. The *Cedarville* keeled over and sank with a loss of ten lives.

In speaking of maritime disasters, mention should be made of the lighthouses which guard the Straits and which are visible from the park. The oldest is Waugoshance Lighthouse, that lopsided, stoop-shouldered old relic located just north of Crane Island. Construction of the lighthouse began prior to the Civil War. Construction was suspended during the war and the lighthouse was completed shortly after the war ended. Upon the concrete foundation is a boiler room and a tower of brick with walls two feet thick. The lower part of the tower is encased by quarter inch boiler plating. The roof was solid copper. At the time, this lighthouse marked the shipping lane which ran close to Waugoshance Point. It used a geared mechanical means of rotating the reflector and had steam boilers to drive the fog horn. Waugoshance Lighthouse was abandoned in 1912, new and safer shipping lanes having been plotted further out in the Straits and which were marked by a new lighthouse at White Shoals. The equipment within was removed when Waugoshance was abandoned. The years have not treated this guardian of the Straits kindly. It has slowly deteriorated from weathering, from constant pummelling by the sea, from being used for target practice during World War II, and from vandalism and souvenir hunters.

The flashing light which can be seen from the Lakeshore Campgrounds in the evening off to the west-northwest marks the location of the "candy-striper" of the Straits, White Shoals Lighthouse. It was built between the years 1908 and 1910. It marks the current shipping channel at the west end of the Straits and is manned by Coast Guard personnel during the shipping season.

Visible to the west from Crane Island and the Sturgeon Bay area is Gray's Reef Lighthouse. It was built in 1937 and replaced a lightship which had been stationed at the reef to mark the danger point and guide vessels along the shipping lanes of Lake Michigan. It too is manned by Coast Guard personnel during the shipping season.

An attempt to determine the reasons behind the naming of some of the shoreline features has meet with mixed results. The reason for the naming of Station Point could not be conclusively determined. It is a point of location for the U.S. Geodetic Survey. Toward this end, there was a structure there in the past, and currently there is a monument located in this area.

Big Stone Bay, as the name implies, was apparently named after a huge limestone boulder that was located along the shoreline in the neighborhood of the present assistant manager's state residence. Edward "Cap" LaWay recollects as how the local residents used to build fires around the boulder and collect the lime which flaked off. This lime was mixed with sawdust from the mills and made into a plaster by adding water. This was then used in insulating the homes.

PARK MANAGERS
Frank Lloyd
Irish Saben
Thayer Denny
"Daddy" Bronson
William Parker
Dave Whithier
Grant H. Wykhuis
Dave Balbough
George Hughes

Clarence M. LaWay, Acting Manager
William Smith

Shipping History

By Robert Pintal, Park Naturalist

Wreckage of an old ship on the North Shore near Station Point Cabin makes an interesting piece of history. This ship is approximately 200 feet in length with a beam of about 30 feet. This ship has been in that area for 80 years or more. It is quite broken up at this writing but has evidence of being a sailing ship at one time.

According to Captain LaWay, two schooners went aground approximately 1887-1900 on the north shore of Waugoshance Point. One of these ships is still visible at this time just west of Station Point Cabin.

The ships were two masted but were not under sail when they went aground. They were being towed by a steam tug. The line broke and the ships went adrift. Before anchors could be dropped they ended up on a shallow rocky area. The ship which is still visible now did not break up. The partner ship broke in two. Salvage attempts were made on the still floating ship. A steam pump was being used to pump water from the holds. This pump was equipped with wheels for maneuverability. As one workman was passing the pump, he swung it to one side. Later as the ship listed the pump rolled to one side on the deck. The Captain was in direct line and it crushed him. It is not known if he died instantly, but operations for freeing the ship were stopped at that time. About seven years later it was burned to water level.

The partner ship broke up as it hit the beach. Captain LaWay states that a rowboat could be paddled through the openings in the ship. Both of these vessels were loaded with wooden ties in their holds and on their decks.

Approximate length of the ships was about 200 feet, and they had beams of about 30 feet. The cargo on deck was thrown overboard before the ships went aground to try to save the ships.

In later years salvage operations were undertaken to remove iron stock from the ship for use in making logging sleighs near Harbor Springs. Captain LaWay and his father did this work for the blacksmith and were paid approximately ½ cent a pound for the steel.

There is much other history in the area concerning shipping, sailing and fishing. Artifacts are being discovered along the shoreline and dunes. A pair of cast iron dock cleats have been found and are in park collection.

This area is rich in fishing history dating from the present day all the way back to the Indian days.

Chapter 7

E. J. LaWay

Captain LaWay's Unfinished Boat Purchased by State for an Exhibit in the Maritime Park at Mackinaw City

Colorful Skipper to Be Honored in Project

from the *Cheboygan Daily Tribune*
1972

EDITOR'S NOTE
The following story about Captain Edward J. LaWay was written by his daughter Judy. She is a former *Tribune* correspondent, and presently is librarian of the public library at Mackinaw City.

* * *

By Judy LaWay
now Mrs. Gordon Ranville

This is the story of a boat, and within it is the story of a man, and both are the last of a kind -- the last of the era of "wooden hulls and iron men". This boat, so seaworthy, will never sail the waterways or feel the tug of the wind in its sails, nor will its Master experience the thrill of guiding his craft through the swells of the lakes he knows so well. But this boat will be preserved as a memorial to those of its kind and the "iron" men who pioneered shipping on the Great Lakes.

The Mackinaw Island Park Commission has purchased the last vessel built by Captain Edward J. LaWay of Wilderness Park and a former Cheboygan resident. Captain LaWay, now 94 years of age, was nearly 80 when he began constructing this craft. The boat, a sailing schooner built entirely by his own labor, will be placed on display in the Michilimackinac

Marine Park.

The boat, built in the style of 19th century commercial schooners, is 47 feet long with a 13½ foot beam. She is double framed, one being oak and the other a natural bend of cedar, gathered for years by "Cap" in preparation to build this vessel. Her planking is oak, and she's lined with cedar. She has a drop centerboard weighing 1500 pounds, and there's a ballast shoe on her keel of cast iron weighing 2 tons.

Proposed plans for display of the schooner are that she will be placed in the beach area, with the hull parallel to the water, and that a wooden walkway will be constructed along the landward side of the vessel so that visitors may overlook the deck.

Until two years ago, when felled by a stroke, the Captain was active and continued to set his nets in Big Stone Bay and to fascinate those who came often to hear him tell tales of the past and the true experiences he lived. Fortunately many of his story times have been recorded.

Adjacent to the vessel, a shelter will be built containing a number of benches and two exhibit cases. One of the cases will contain pictures of the Captain and the other will contain the tools used by Cap in building the schooner. It is planned that the tapes of Cap's storytelling will be edited into a continuously playing tape, interspersed with folk music relating to the narration. Visitors will be able to sit for as long as they wish and listen to Cap's interesting tales.

The Captain came to this area at the age of four from Kingston, Ontario, and his first experience on the Lakes was at the age of 7, fishing gill nets with his father. He built his first boat when 10 years old from driftwood gathered on the shores near his home. He said it floated and he and his younger brother paddled it along the beach. It was their only toy.

Cap grew up working on the water, and when a young man bought a steam tug and went into the freight and salvage business. He became a hardhat diver and once said he had explored nearly every shipwreck from Bay City on Lake Huron to Manistee on Lake Michigan.

In the early 1900's he needed a larger boat, so he began to build the *E. J. LaWay, Jr.*, an 87 ft. steamboat. He was operating a planing mill and coal yard on his dock on the northeast side of the State Street Bridge, and it was there he laid the keel for the *E.J.*

Cap was a real sailor, knew how to navigate without the use of modern day navigational instruments, knew the water depths, all the shoals and natural harbours, so when weather was bad, he was always able to tuck away and wait it out. There was anxiety for his safety in the great 1913 storm, but when it was over and while assessment was being taken on the losses, Cap came sailing into the Cheboygan River, boat and crew safe. In other storms including the 1940 Armistice Day storm, Cap's ship was reported missing along with other freighters, only to turn up -- waiting out the storm in a sheltered area.

Late in April, 1929, Cap received a distress call from the residents of Drummond Island. They were fast running out of coal and would he bring a load to them. It was a late spring and there was still a lot of ice, but Cap fitted out his boat and set out for Detour. Early in the morning of the 29th they found themselves in a field of heavy ice, and it was too much for the *E.J.* and a hole was crushed in her side and water rushed in. Seeing it beyond the pumps ability to handle it, Cap headed his ship for shore hoping to be able to beach her, but progress was slow due to the ice and, realizing all was hopeless, he ordered the crew into the lifeboat. Cap stayed with his boat until he could swim from the upper deck and upon reaching the lifeboat, looked back to see the *E.J.* go bow up and slip beneath the icy water. His beloved ship was gone.

He and his crew reached home safely. Cheboygan men who were members of the crew who will be remembered by local senior citizens are: Fred Roberts, cook; Henry Houle, fireman; George Fisher, fireman; and Bill Redman, engineer. All are now deceased.

A few years later Cap bought the *M. H. Stuart*, a 120 ft. steamboat, and operated her from her Cheboygan River berth until the early forties when he retired and returned to his childhood home on Big Stone Bay, Wilderness Park.

During his retirement years he managed to keep busy building boats for various people -- aside from the 47 footer that will be displayed in the Marine Park, he built a 47 foot diesel powered boat for himself and his customers, three 28 foot sail, pleasure craft, three 18 foot pleasure craft and many small boats.

He spent several summers making charter runs to the bass fishing areas of Hog Island and had many notable names among his customers. One time when taking a client's own yacht through the rocky waters to the Island, the owner became more nervous as each huge boulder slid by and told Cap, "I have $25,000 in this boat and I don't plan to leave it here." Cap replied, "Well, I have my reputation in this boat and I don't plan to leave that here either." No more was said -- they had a successful day and in late afternoon sailed out past the boulders as easily as they had come in and headed for "Big Stone Bay" with their limit of game fish.

Cap, who will be 94 in March, is greatly disabled and nearly blind, but still maintains a sense of humor and laughs and jokes with his nurses. In his more serious moments he speaks of when he is able to walk again he'll go back to work, and John Masefield's poem "Sea-Fever" might well express Cap's thoughts.

"I must go down to the sea again,
to the lonely sea and the sky,
And all I ask is a tall ship
and a star to steer her by.
And the wheel's kick and the wind's song
and the white sails' shaking,
And a gray mist on the seas' face
and a gray dawn breaking."

Capt. Laway Has His 93rd Birthday

April 3, 1971

Sunday, March 28, was the 93rd birthday of one of this area's oldest citizens, Capt. Edward LaWay.

Captain LaWay is the oldest of eight children born to Sarah and John LaWay. When Captain was four years old he moved place in Canada to Cheboygan where they resided for three years. On April 20, 1885, the family came to Mackinaw City, traveling by horse and sled, on the ice from Cheboygan Captain states that the ice didn't move that year until the middle of May and there was still six inches then. (It must have been a year like this one.)

The LaWays drove ashore where the "Breakers" cabins are now and went across the way to the Mackinaw City House a hotel owned by Capt. Alexander Ranville and his wife, Margaret. This building is now the "Totem" Restaurant Captain says Mrs. Ranville took him upstairs to see her new grandson, Grover McVey, born the day before.

The next day the family again started out by horse and sled, destination, Cecil Bay. There at age 7, Captain worked with his father fishing to support the growing family.

Capt. LaWay has lived a long, interesting life. He has followed the Marine industry and since his retirement from sailing the Great Lakes in 1945, has kept busy fishing commercially and building boats. The latest a 47 ft. sailboat has been interesting to many people from all over the United States and Canada. Captain always enjoyed visiting with them and telling his many true experiences.

Times have changed for the Captain - he has been bedridden for the past fifteen months at the home of his daughter. His vision has dimmed and his speech comes slow but he still enjoys an occasional visitor and reliving amusing incidents from the past.

Sunday "Cap" spent a quiet day, his 93rd birthday. He says with a sly smile, that he feels it.

The E. J. LaWay, Jr., 86 foot steamboat built by Captain LaWay. Standing on the stem of the boat is Edward LaWay, Jr., who died in the big Cheboygan fire in 1922, aged 12. Frank LaWay is standing behind Edward, George in right, Ed, Sr. sitting on the rail below him. Others unknown. Picture about 1914.

Sarah LaWay, mother of Captain Edward J. LaWay, arrived in Mackinaw in 1884 and lived in this area until her death in 1940, aged 80. They built a home on the shore just east of Mackinaw Point Light.

DAY, APRIL 29, 1929.

SMALL FREIGHTER GOES DOWN IN LOWER ST. MARYS

CHEBOYGAN MEN FORCED TO SWIM ASHORE.

The small freighter "Leway" of Cheboygan sank in 60-feet of water with 125 tons of coal aboard last week off Cedar Island, near St. Joe Island in lower St. Marys river.

Captain Leway, also of Cheboygan, and his crew of six men were saved although having to swim to reach shore. The boat was carrying coal to Alex Purvis on Burnt Island when she struck an "iceberg" off Cedar Island. She filled rapidly and sank within a few hours.

Fed by 'Graveyard of the Lakes'

By Kendrick Kimball
Mackinaw City, Mich.

Wonder crept into the ruddy features of E. J. Laway, Cecil Bay fisherman, when his net brought up a glistening round object from 150 feet of water.

"What can it be?" asked his two sons, companions on a tug bobbing in a gentle swell off the White Shoals.

"Think I know," replied the fisherman with a faraway look in his eyes. "It's the second helping of a meal I had 46 years ago."

The object was a barrel, hoops of which had disintegrated from long immersion. When the barrel clattered upon the deck its staves parted like the frosted shuck of a hickory nut, and several slabs of a chalky substance rolled into the sunlight.

Laway cut a chip from one of the slabs, smelled it gingerly and applied a match. It burned with a sputtering flame. Then he placed the remainder in his mouth. Chewing slowly, he swallowed the morsel from the depths and pronounced the pork palatable.

"California," he muttered to his sons, who nodded understandingly, recalling the oft-told story of the wreck of that ship in 1887.

FED BY LAKE.

Laway's catch released a veritable Pandora's box of memories, dwelling upon the days when Lake Michigan filled larder, parlor and wardrobe with a generous hand.

Old residents, waiting for the ice to loosen its grip upon the Straits, are telling of a pork dinner that rolled ashore in a gale.

They are renewing tales of corn that "grew" on the water, of a floating island of flour off the White Shoals and occasions when the lake seemed a huge general store, offering anything from oranges to divans to families who went "marketing" on the beach.

They are describing the fabulous hauls of the "wreckers," a fearless breed of sailors who returned from sinking ships with salvage piled to the gunwales of their broad-beamed Mackinaw boats.

● ● ●

The village, once fed in a large measure by the waves, was ideally located for such enterprise. At its door lies that stretch of rock and reef extending from the Beaver Islands to McGulpin's point, and then known as the "Graveyard of the Lakes," because of hazards to navigation.

Apprehension spread along the coast whenever a gale came whooping out of the northwest. Fishermen on the Mani-

tou Islands listened for the dull, throbbing notes of the Indian drum, legendary portent of death and disaster, while Mackinaw City strained its eyes toward Waugoshance Point, Gray's Reef and the shoals, where many a brave vessel was pounded into kindling by the hammering of the seas.

WRECK OF THE CALIFORNIA

Of all the wrecks in the vicinity, and there were many, the light of public attention beat strongest upon that of the steamer *California*, which went down between St. Helen Island and McGulpin's Point, with the loss of nine lives, October 4, 1887.

Settlers and their

families, living a barren existence in cabins and shanties, ran pell-mell to the beach. Murky skies and the bending crests of the pines lent a grim tone to the scene. Horses struggled across the sands with clattering wagons, women and children milled about and men struggled shoulder deep in the combers to drag to shore articles of the *California* cargo cast to the waves by the breaking up of the ship.

Unattended babies among the stumps sucked on oranges cast up by the waves. Small boys tugged at firkins of lard and casks of machine oil. Souvenir hunters chopped off the keys of a melodeon that afterward provided the music for many a country dance. But the

Captain E. J. LaWay and E. C. Dagwell with pork from *California*.

prize most eagerly sought was pork, 600 barrels of which tossed and tumbled in the seas.

The day was the wildest in the village's history. A sailor drifted through the Straits on a pilot house, waving a red shirt to attract attention. Residents with spyglasses watched the crew of the *Faxton* rescue a woman clinging to a section of the *California's* hurricane deck. A rope lowered twice to the woman eluded her grasp. The third time, she fastened it about her body and was lifted aboard the ferry.

HER SON DROWNED.

In a dance hall which had been converted into a morgue the rescued woman, Mrs. Richard Connerton, of Detroit, knelt beside her 27-year-old son, Cornelius, swept away and drowned when a giant wave smashed the steamer's cabin. The Connertons lived at what was then 80 Sixth Street.

As a 6-year-old boy, Laway saw his father recover two barrels of pork from the *California* from a lagoon in Cecil Bay. Then, by a strange turn of fate, his net only the other day brought up a third, positively identified as a memento of the disaster of 1887 by the manner in which the meat was cut and packed.

• • •

The Canadian owned *California*, Capt. John Trowell, of Toronto, in command, put out from Chicago with her hold filled with pork, 20,000 bushels of corn and a general cargo. Her destination was Montreal. Among the five passengers were Mrs. Connerton and her son, a musician of high standing, and former organist at Our Redeemer Church in Detroit.

Tragedy had blighted the life of Mrs. Connerton, then in her sixties. She spent many years and a considerable portion of her fortune seeking a runaway son. The mother searched for him in New York, Washington and throughout the Atlantic seaboard, a forlorn figure with a shawl wrapped about her thin shoulders. She haunted the wharves, believing he had joined the Navy or merchant marine, and stopping officers and sailors with the words, "Have you seen my boy?"

The son, John, was never heard from. Time dulled the blow and the mother lavished her affection upon Cornelius, who had completed a course in a Chicago conservatory when he and his mother walked up the gangplank of the doomed steamer.

Halfway up the lake the *California* ran into bad weather. Passengers in the cabin glimpsed an inky sky as they prayed for safety and fitted on life preservers with trembling hands. Members of the crew knelt with them. Hymns played on the melodeon by the stewardess were sung in quavering voices.

"Be brave," whispered Connerton to his mother. "Everything will turn out all right."

But intuition told the mother otherwise. She had asked Capt. Trowell to put into the Beavers for shelter, but the bluff old skipper, confident of the staunchness of his ship, refused to do so.

"I'll take her through the straits or sink," the captain declared to an officer.

The *California* crept through the night like a crippled thing. Waves all but engulfed her and the gale's hum through the rigging increased to a shriek. In the pilot house the captain was confronted by an engineer whose face betrayed an ashen whiteness in the gleam of his lantern.

HOPE ABANDONED

Can't hold the fires," he shouted above the din of the storm. "The water has reached the grates and is climbing fast."

"We'll turn about and beach her," ordered Trowell, seizing the wheel with a mighty grip.

What then occurred was related by Mrs. Connerton to a reporter from *The Detroit News* on her return to Detroit with the body of Cornelius:

"The captain turned the boat and it struck a reef. Then there was a crash. If the city hall had fallen it could not have been more terrible than the noise of that fearful wave. The ship keeled over. I saw my son hanging to a door. Another wave carried everyone out of the cabin but a sailor and myself. The next wave took us. I grabbed him by the trouser leg and we went into the water together.

"Chairs and spars were all about me. I grasped at everything, but went under. The lifebelt brought me up. A big piece of cabin came near and I crawled partly on it. I called to my son, but there was no answer from the blackness."

The remainder of the story belongs to George V. Coffman, Mackinaw City druggist and antiquarian.

"We knew something had happened when we saw wreckage coming through the straits," he said. "Then the *Faxton* put about to rescue Mrs. Connerton and the sailor. News of the disaster spread like wildfire.

"The lake seemed to contain an endless array of barrels, dressers, lounges, mattresses and crates, all blowing onto the beach. Men risked their lives to get the pork. The would roll a barrel into the woods and go back for another. On their return they often discovered the original barrel had been stolen by someone hiding in the underbrush.

A SOUVENIR ORANGE

"One old fellow sat on his barrel until his 10 children appeared. Then he strung the pork on a pole, taking one end himself and giving the other to his oldest son. The remaining children were spaced along the pole according to their height. They walked off in lock step, the pole bending so far in the middle it touched the shoulders of the tots stationed there.

"I found the melodeon and tried to wrench off the lions' heads at its sides. A man with an axe knocked off a key. Then I ran into the water after an orange which I gave to a girl. Today it is preserved in alcohol in her home in Grand Ledge."

Nearly every family in Mackinaw City reaped its reward. A large portion of the steamer's linen was recovered, and the name board hung for years on a fence in the rear of a saloon. Someone took $900 in Canadian money from the body of the purser, washed ashore in Cecil Bay, but overlooked a similar sum in an inside pocket.

• • •

Other wrecks brought similar scenes. "Hundreds of sacks of flour, dumped by the crew of the *Cayuga* to lighten ship, formed an island upon which salvagers walked with safety," Coffman continued. "Tons of lard, peddled as far south as Petoskey, were taken off the *E. P. Wilbur* in 1895. "The *Briton, Bing-*

hamton and *Joseph Barnum* were corn wrecks. The salvagers ran their boats directly under the chutes through which the cargo was being discharged. 'Come and get,' yelled the crew. Tons of wheat were obtained the same way.

NOT ALWAYS A HARVEST

"Some wrecks yielded little if any salvage. A few axe handles were saved from the *Eber Ward*. The *Cicora* vanished with her cargo. The only survivor was a bedraggled Newfoundland dog which crawled onto the beach after swimming through the storm."

Troubles of the modern mariner are all but eliminated by adequate charts, buoys, lights, great power and sturdier vessels. Few of the steamers whistling sonorously as they parade through the straits come to grief in the troublesome stretch below. Should one run aground, its cargo would be transferred to barges and lighters furnished by insurance brokers.

No longer is Lake Michigan an open grab bag.

They moved two years later in April by horse and sleigh on ice in the Straits to Mackinaw City, where they stayed over night. Next day they crossed on the ice to Cecil Bay where the father got a job in the shingle mill.

Edward started a long sailing career when he was 7 years old. His father operated a fishing schooner, and young Edward helped in the work. He worked with his Dad in the fishing business until manhood.

His interest in boats led him into the tugging business. As a young man he operated tugs in salvage and hauling light freight. The tugs "Little Georgie" and the "Thomas Kane" were his first boats.

He built the steamboat E. J. Laway, Jr., for the freight and salvage business. The ship sank in Georgian Bay in 1929. Later he purchased the steamer M. H. Stuart, which he operated until his retirement in the early 1940's.

Along with sailing, he entered business in Cheboygan with a planning mill and coal dock, located on east bank of the Cheboygan river, north of State street.

Captain Laway was twice married. His first wife was Mary Tully of Manistique. To that union was born one son Edward J. Laway, Jr., who was killed in the Fost-Kessller Building fire in Cheboygan.

Mrs. Laway died, and he later married Flora Barclay of Whitefish Point, Michigan. Two daughters were born to them: Ann, who is Mrs. Wal-

ter Leist and Judy, (Mrs. Gordon Ranville). His wife died on August 9, 1967.

He is also survived by the following grandchildren, Mrs. Judy Anderson, Peggy Ranville, Gerald, James, Thomas and Kenneth Ranville and four great-grandchildren, also one brother, George Laway and one sister Mrs. Arthur Remer (Della), both of Wilderness Park.

One of Captain Laway's skills was shipbuilding. He built more than a dozen boats, in sizes ranging up to 100 feet long.

His last ship, is a 47 foot sailing schooner, which will be a permanent memorial. It is on display in the Maritime Park at Mackinaw City.

The Mackinac Island State Park Commission in recent years interviewed him and made tapes about many of his sailing experiences. The Commission purchased his ship-building tools. These and the tapes will be part of the permanent display in connection with his unnamed boat, known only as the Laway Schooner, in the Maritime Park, in which the closed former Mackinaw Point light house is located.

The body is at the N. J. Christian Funeral Home, where friends may call from 7 to 9 this evening, and from 2 to 9 p.m. Wednesday.

Funeral services will be held at St. Mary's Church in Cheboygan on Thursday, at 10 a.m., with Father Francis Partridge officiating. Burial will be in the family lot at Calvary Cemetery.

Captain E. J. Laway Dies Monday at the Age of 96

June 18, 1974

Captain Edward J. Laway of Wilderness Park, a colorful long time Great Lakes sailor, died Monday night in Lockwood-McDonald Hospital after a long illness.

He was 96 years old.

He was a sailor, businessman, and boat builder, and member of a pioneer Straits Area family.

Since becoming an invalid, he made his home with his daughter, Mrs. Gordon Ranville at Wilderness Park.

He was born at Havey's Locks, Kingston, Ontario, son of John and Sarah Laway. When he was 4 years old, the family moved by sailboat to Cheboygan. His father got a job in the Duncan City sawmill.

One of the many boats built by Captain LaWay.

49

The LaWay family in front of their humble dwelling in (Wilderness Park) Big Stone Bay.

Fishermen made a bare existence living, often picking berries to supplement their income. Captain said that when they had picked enough huckleberries to sell he would strap them to his back and walk to Cross Village, via the beach, to exchange them for needed groceries.

Left to Right: Mike, Jennie, Della, George, Ed, Mother holding Frank. Lady in back unknown. Picture taken about 1893.

The LaWays moved to (Wilderness Park) Big Stone Bay in the spring to fish. Their sailboat, fish shed and dock are shown in background.

Left to right: Ed, George, Mike, Jennie, Mother Sarah, Della.

Della, Mrs. Arthur Remer, lives in Wilderness Park; all others deceased.

Chapter 8

The Development of
Mackinaw City

by: Steven R. Campbell

PREFACE: The following article is an excerpt from a composition entitled "How and Why Mackinaw City Grew To Be What It Is Today", written for a composition class at Mackinaw City, Michigan, in 1971. Most of the material was obtained through interviews with my grandfather, Elton C. Dagwell, who lived all of his life in this city. Also, from old documents owned by him and my mother, Nancy Dagwell Campbell.

Mackinaw City should have become a large city because of its strategic location. There were many ways in which the city could have prospered but through unfortunate accidents and laws of the area, an increase in population was hindered by the limiting of industrial growth.

The Indians from far off came to the Straits of Mackinac for the vast fishing which this area provided. The area of Michilimackinac was also considered a sacred area and many tribes came to this area to make peace treaties, as no tribe was supposed to wage war here.

Although it wasn't until 1714 that a white man settled on the present site of Mackinaw City, it can be assumed that Father Marquette visited this site during his stay at St. Ignace. Also, Father Hennepin, who accompanied LaSalle on the *Griffin*, wrote the following account in his diary on August 27, 1679:

> "The 27th, in the morning, we continued our course northwest, with a southeast wind, which carried us the same day to Michilimackinac, where we anchored in a bay at six fathom water, upon a shiny white bottom. We went the next day to pay a visit to the Huron, who inhabit the land."[1]

In 1714 the French established a fort at the present site of Fort Michilimackinac. Little is known of the fort until 1761 when the English took over the fort

after the end of the French and Indian War. Its commander was Captain George Etherington.

The English were not on good terms with the Indians. They didn't trade in the same manner as the French and unlike the French, the English considered the Indians a lower class or savages. In 1762, the Ottawa chief, Pontiac, was conspiring against the English. His plan was simple but brilliant. All the tribes in the Great Lakes area were to attack the English forts at the same time. On June 4, 1763, a tribe of Ojibways, under Chief Minavavana, played a game of LaCross in front of the fort at Michilimackinac. The English were caught by surprise during the game when the ball went over the fort wall and the Indians rushed in to retrieve it. Instead, the Indians massacred most of the garrison and claimed the fort. A year later the English reestablished the fort.

The English moved the fort to Mackinac Island in 1781. In 1783, under the Treaty of Paris, the Northwest Territory, of which Michilimackinac was a part, became part of the United States of America, but it wasn't until 1796 that American troops occupied the Mackinac area.

Little is known of the history of Mackinaw City from 1781 until 1857. In 1857 Edgar Conkling and Asbury Searles, as trustees of the proprietors of Mackinaw lands, inaugurated a movement for building up a business center upon the south shore of the Straits.

Mr. Conkling was the largest owner and the leading spirit in the enterprise. He had the area surveyed and plotted for a village in 1857. That fall he issued a pamphlet of about fifty pages containing maps and information concerning this site. An early writer uttered the following prophetic opinion: "If one were to point out on the map of North America a site for a great central city in the lake region, it would be in the immediate vicinity of the Straits of Mackinac. A city so located would have the control of the mineral trade, the fisheries, the furs and lumber of the entire north. It would be the Venice of the Lakes."[2] The projectors of Mackinaw City believed that they were founding such a metropolis. The pamphlet and maps indicated the following provisions for the city: streets eighty feet in width and avenues one hundred feet in width; provision for sidewalks with fifteen feet width on each side, to be forever unobstructed by improvements except for shade trees; lots fifty by one hundred and fifty feet; the lands of Fort Michilimackinac to be a public park, and free lots to be given to religious and educational institutions.

From 1857 to 1870 the village plot was undisturbed. In 1869 Mr. Conkling had built a dock at Mackinaw City at the foot of what is now Central Avenue. In the same year the lighthouse at McGulpin Point was built. A year later the first permanent residents arrived. Mr. George Stimpson and family arrived here from Maine and developed a cordwood business. They later built the Stimpson House, which is today the Downtown Motor Inn. L. I. Willets was the next person to become a permanent resident. He built a dry goods store and a year later became the first postmaster of Mackinaw City. In December 1881, the Mackinaw division of the Michigan Central Railroad was completed to Mackinaw City. In 1883, the first school was built. In the same year Mackinaw City was incorporated as a village. At this time the growth of Mackinaw City was hindered by legal complications. The village plat lies in both Cheboygan and Emmet Counties but the village was built in Cheboygan County. Legal complications affecting the title to a portion of the village lots was in doubt. That portion, in Cheboygan County, was incorporated under a Village Charter and a few years later, that portion in Emmet County came under the same charter.

Lumbering was the major factor in the development of the Mackinaw City area. When Michigan became a state a survey was taken. The survey reported as much as 150 billion board feet of lumber was in the Northern Straits area. It was in 1878 when the first large lumber operation entered this area. They were the A.B. Klise Lumber Co. and Callam Lumber Co., located at Sturgeon Bay and Cecil Bay. The Callam Co. was taken over by the Davis and Caldwell Company of Battle Creek in 1898 and was known as the Cecil Bay Lumbering Company. Later, in 1903, the Emmet Lumbering Company conducted a lumbering operation at Cecil Bay until 1917.

The community of Cecil Bay was located at the mouth of the Carp River. It was very prosperous until 1917 when most of the lumbering trees were cut down. While the lumbering was here, many of the business establishments of Mackinaw City sold food, clothing, and other supplies to the people of Cecil Bay.

There were a few small lumber companies in Mackinaw City and the surrounding area. The only one of any size or importance was the Lewis Lumber Company. The Lewis Lumber Company was located in Mackinaw City and sawed white birch into slabs which were shipped to a toothpick factory in Saginaw, Michigan. This mill was located on the present site of the ValRue Motel. A clothespin factory was located near the present site of the State Dock.

Lumbering came to an end in the southern Straits area in 1919 when a large forest fire burnt out most of the forest land. The clothespin factory was also destroyed by a fire in the early 1900's.

The Citizens dock at the foot of Jamet Street was built by the city of Mackinaw. It wasn't a very good project as ice soon tore it down. The few years that it was used, it served as a docking place for ships picking up lumber and for steamships to pick up cordwood to burn in their large boilers.

In 1890 an ironworks company wanted to come to Mackinaw City. The city council refused to allow the company to establish itself in the city. The council was made up of business men who feared that the ironworks would bring other businesses to Mackinaw and take business away from their establishments. This company later became the Antrim Ironworks. It did send its pig iron to Mackinaw by rail which was then shipped away by boat. Thus the ironworks company did bring some business to this area.

When the railroads came to the Mackinaw area it brought many jobs. During the early 1920's there were twenty-two passenger trains running in and out of Mackinaw City and a countless number of freight trains a day. There were three major railroads that ran into this city: the Pennsylvania, the Michigan Central, and the Duluth, South Shore and Atlantic. In the late 1940's, due to the increase in automobile manufacturing, the passenger trains almost died out and in the early 1950's due to lack of freight, the freight trains and passenger service began to decrease. Today there are no passenger trains and few freight trains running into this city. The loss of rail service meant the loss of jobs, and several families moved from this city to other areas.

The ferry boats that transported the trains, autos and people across the Straits of Mackinac brought a great economic value to this area. There were a total of seven different ferry boats in Mackinaw City history. At the time the Mackinac Bridge was completed there were four State Ferries and two railroad ferries in service. Although the bridge brought a great deal of business to this area, the loss of the ferries meant a loss of jobs and several families again left the area.

Two little known businesses, which were private enterprises but brought economic value to this area, were farms and the Marine Reporting Service. The large farm of George Stimpson's raised grapes and potatoes which were shipped to southern Michigan. The Carl Pierce farm was a dairy which provided milk delivery to the city until the late 1930's. The Marine Reporting Service was conducted by the Dagwell family for sixty-two years. This service provided reports of vessel passages through the Straits to newspapers and various vessel owners throughout the United States and Canada. This station also acted as a weather observer for the U.S. Weather Bureau. The Marine Service, along with the railroads, was a major factor in the establishing of the Western Union business in Mackinaw City.

The businesses of Mackinaw City which were located on North Huron Avenue were destroyed by two disastrous fires, one in March 1900, when four business blocks were destroyed and another in 1916 when five stores were destroyed.

Mackinaw City has been a tourist town since the early 1900's. This area was a great relief to those suffering from hay fever and asthma because of the low pollen count. The area was also known for its natural beauty. In the late 1940's the tourist business began to grow, until today our natural beauty has been replaced by an over-abundance of motels, gas stations, gift shops and neon signs.

I have briefly told the history of Mackinaw City which concerned the progress and decline of the growth of the village. There have been several incidents which hindered the growth of this area beginning with the indiscriminate cutting of lumber which a conservation program would have prevented, to the lack of industry which would have provided freight for the declining railroads. The two most prominent incidents were the city government and nature. The lack of concern for the development of the city, other than for personal gain, prohibited industry from developing. The other incident was the physical factor of nature -- fire, which destroyed many of the established businesses, homes and factories. Should Mackinaw City have become a large city of many industries or should it remain as it is today, a tourist mecca?

BIBLIOGRAPHY

Footnote 1 *The Traverse Region.* (Chicago, Ill.: H.R. Page & Co., 1884), p. 16.

Footnote 2 *The Traverse Region.* p. 119.

Book: Andrews, Roger. *Old Fort Mackinac On The Hill of History.* Menominee, Michigan: Herald-Leader Press, 1938.

Stimpson House, Central Avenue, Mackinaw City. Now Downtown Motor Inn.

Railroad Ferry and lumber schooner at Railroad dock, Mackinaw City.

Citizens Dock - where water tower now stands (Ray Dorrance, Elton Dagwell, Unknown)

Central Avenue, Mackinaw City - 1920. Mr. and Mrs. Louis Liebeck in front of store. Marybeth Dagwell in car.

The interior of Leibeck's grocery. Elmer Dann behind counter, Mr. Leibeck and ? in center, Mrs. Liebeck is on the right.

Chapter 9

Historic Street Names

The village of Mackinaw City, Michigan, has a unique pattern of names for its streets. Few towns in the United States can compare with it. With the exception of a few streets on the fringe of the town, all are names of historical persons who had something to do with the region of Michilimackinac--the name given originally to the Straits area.

The main east-west street is Central Avenue, certainly not a distinctive name. Straits Avenue, Huron Avenue and Lake Side Drive are suitable names and descriptive of their location. Some new streets to the west have been given Indian names as Nokomis and Hiawatha. But all the rest of the streets in the main part of town have historic names. These were given many years ago by Miss Frances Margaret Fox, the author, who had a summer home here until her death.

The streets are listed as you go north from Central Avenue, toward the Straits. These are named for Englishmen.

ETHERINGTON - Captain George Etherington was the Commandant at Fort Michilimackinac in 1763, at the time of the famous massacre on June 2nd. The apparently peaceful Indians suddenly attacked the fort and its inhabitants, as part of Pontiac's Conspiracy, and killed a large number of them. Captain Etherington's life was spared and he, with a dozen others, was taken as prisoner to L'Arbre Croche. He was finally released and fled to Montreal, which he reached on August 13th of that year. We hear of him in April, 1765, with the First Battalion of the Royal American Regiment at Lancaster, Pennsylvania.

JAMET - Lieutenant John Jamet (or Jamette) was killed in that massacre on June 2, 1763. He had been located at Sault Ste. Marie the previous year, but his post there was accidentally destroyed by fire. He was then assigned to Fort Michilimackinac. In the massacre his fate was witnessed by Alexander Henry, a British trader, who later wrote an account of the whole affair.

SINCLAIR - Major Patrick Sinclair was the Lieutenant

Governor of Michilimackinac in 1779-1782. It was under his command that the Fort was removed from the mainland to Mackinaw Island and re-established there. This was done because he was afraid of the American Colonel George Rogers Clark, who in 1779 had captured the Fort at Vincennes, Indiana, and was threatening Detroit and Mackinac. In 1780, Major Sinclair sent Charles Langlade and 750 men from Fort Mackinac to attack the Spanish at St. Louis, but they were defeated.

DE PEYSTER - Major Arthur Schuyler de Peyster was the Commandant and Lieutenant Governor of Michilimackinac in 1774-1779, just preceding Sinclair. He was transferred to Detroit in 1779. He was of American birth and served in the British army in various places. He retired to Scotland, where he was a friend of the poet, Robert Burns. He died at the advanced age of 96.

For the streets which run north and south, we begin at the east end of the village, right after Huron Avenue, which runs along the water.

LANGLADE - Charles Langlade was born in Michilimackinac in 1724, the son of a Frenchman and an Ottawa woman. In 1752 he brought Indians from Michilimackinac to Piqua, Ohio, to fight the British, and captured three traders whom he took to Governor Duquesne. In 1755 he took an important part in the defeat of General Braddock and George Washington at Fort Duquesne in Pennsylvania. In 1756 Langlade was an officer of the French troops at Michilimackinac. He was in the battle of the Plains of Abraham at Quebec in 1761; it was Langlade who pulled down the French flag. At the time of the massacre of 1763, Alexander Henry, the British trader, sought refuge in his house for a time. Later Langlade was Indian Agent at Green Bay, Wisconsin.

HENRY - Alexander Henry was the brave British trader at Michilimackinac who survived the massacre of 1763 and wrote an account of it later.

He was born in New Jersey about 1739. When he was 22 years of age, he traveled from Montreal to Michilimackinac in two months' time, by way of the St. Lawrence River, the Ottawa and Mattawan Rivers, Lake Nipissing, the French River, Georgian Bay and Lake Huron. He was captured in the massacre but was befriended by a friendly Indian, Wawatam, and his life was spared. Later he was active around Lake Superior, engaging in some copper mining ventures which were unsuccessful. In 1809 he wrote an account of his travels and adventures. He died in 1811.

DU CHARME - M. Laurent de Charme was a friendly Canadian at Michilimackinac in 1763, who warned Captain Etherington of the possible danger of an Indian uprising. But Etherington was only annoyed at the suggestion and did nothing about it.

NICOLET - Jean Nicolet, for whom the street alongside the bridge approach is named, was born at the end of the 16th century. He was a protege of the early French explorer, Sameual de Champlain. He lived with the Indians and learned their language and ways. In 1634 Nicolet went through the Straits of Mackinac in a birch bark canoe, on a journey which he thought might be through the northwest passage to China. He was the first white man to pass this way, as far as is known. Three years later he married a young girl, a godchild of Champlain. In 1642 he drowned in the windswept waters of the St. Lawrence River.

LOUVIGNY - This name is misspelled on the street signs put up in 1958. Louis de la Ports, Sieur de Louvigny, was sent by the French Governor, Frontenac, in 1690, from Quebec to Michilimackinac. He had 150 men with him to strengthen the fort which at that time was on the north side of the Straits, and to replace its commander. He was a brother-in-law of the Frenchman Dulhut, for whom Duluth, Minnesota, is named. He was a vigorous commander and permitted an Iroquis prisoner to be tortured to death by the Indian allies of the French. In 1694 he was succeeded by Cadillac. When Detroit was founded in 1702, the fort on the north side of the Straits was ordered closed. But later it was deemed advisable to reopen it, and Louvigny was sent back about 1712. It is thought that he was the one who re-established the fort on the south side of the Straits, where Mackinaw City now is located.

MAREST - Father Marest, S. J., was a French missionary at St. Ignace when the French fort was on the northern side of the Straits. He was friendly with Louvigny but did not get along with Cadillac. He was opposed to military control and the sale of liquor to the Indians. With the withdrawal of the French to Detroit after 1701, his work became very difficult and he burned down his chapel and left. But he came back, and it was largely due to his persuasion that the French Governor sent M. Louvigny back about 1712 to re-establish the fort.

DU JAUNAY - This name is misspelled on the street signs put up in 1958. Father Pierre du Janunay (or Jonois as it is sometimes found in old journals) was in charge of a French mission at L'Arbre Croche (near Cross Village) in the middle of the 18th century. Just after the massacre at Fort Michilimackinac in 1763, his advice and help were sought by the British prisoners. He was instrumental in saving Etherington and Henry and others. He even carried a letter from Etherington to the garrison at Detroit asking for help which was not given.

ASKINS - John Askin was a Scotch-Irish soldier of a Highland regiment which came to America in the Seven Years War. After the fall of Quebec in 1759, he elected to stay in America and entered into a business partnership with the famous Major Robert Rogers, which however failed. He came to Michilimackinac after 1763 and began a successful business of trading with the Indians. He married an Ottawa woman of L'Arbre Croche. In 1768 he cleared a plot of ground at the Grand Portage on the north shore of Lake Superior. Later he had a fleet of ships on the Lakes, plying between Grand Portage and the Soo and Mackinac, and between Mackinac and Detroit, where he became a prominent merchant.

PERROT - This name is misspelled on street signs put up in 1958. Nicholas Perrot was a French voyageur in these parts as early as 1665. Some of his activity was among the Indians around Green Bay. In 1688 he persuaded the Indians of the Mississippi and Lake Michigan areas to go to Michilimackinac to join the French against the British. In 1690 he accompanied Louvigny to Michilimackinac and carried a letter from Frontenac to the Indians to hold them loyal to the French. He kept a journal of his experiences and wrote a book, *Memoirs of the Manners, Customs and Religion of the North American Savages*. He died in Montreal in 1718.

David O. Voss

Chapter 10

Mackinaw City Terminus

The East Michigan Pike, The West Michigan Pike
The Mackinaw Trail and The Dixie Highway

from the *Cheboygan Daily Tribune*
October 5, 1918

One can readily see that as terminal point for railroads Mackinaw City bears some importance; however, Mackinaw holds another important position, for it is also the terminus of the East and West Michigan Pikes, the Mackinaw Trail and the Dixie Highway, all of which are leading auto routes through Northern Michigan and traveled yearly by thousands of people.

Mackinaw is an enterprising city, one keenly alert to the possibilities it possesses, and nothing is being left undone that will further the advancement of industry or summer resorting in its locality.

To the south of the city and bordering on its limits lies, without a doubt, the finest summer resort location in Michigan. During the past year this site has been brought to a high state of improvement by the Mackinaw City and Wawatam Beach Improvement Association, and it was the sojourning place for several thousands of people this last summer. The popularity of Wawatam has just taken form and the future holds in store much prosperity for the beach, while Mackinaw City will be the leading resort center of Michigan.

During the early part of the summer 1916, a tour over the East Michigan Pike was arranged by the Detroit Board of Commerce and the Northeastern Michigan Development Bureau. The purpose of the tour was to stimulate interest in the building of good roads along the Lake Huron Shore -- roads which would be of benefit to the farmer and the tourist alike. At the same time those interested in the advancement of the West Michigan Pike, running between Chicago and Mackinaw City, were to make their annual tour. Mackinaw City was doubly interested in these movements and at once applied for opportunity to give assistance.

There are splendid opportunities for industrial propositions. Apply to Improvement Association for information.

State Ferries Terminal At Mackinaw City

from the
Mackinac Island News
August 2, 1941

The State Highway Department has worked unceasingly to make the auto ferries dock at Mackinaw City the last word in efficient traffic convenience. Work has been progressing for several years to convert the beach shore line into an ultra modern terminal.

The picture above shows the various lanes of approach and departure, the convenient and perfectly appointed waiting room, and the landscaped grounds. But the main theme was not beauty, but service to the thousands of automobiles which each month embark here for the scenic trips on the fleet of modern steamers which are in continuous service between Mackinaw City on the southern peninsula, and St. Ignace, gateway to the upper peninsula.

INDIANS AT MACKINAW CITY - MICH.

JOHNSON PHOTO
AT THE EAST & WEST MICH.
PIKE MEET JULY 14-16
MACKINAW, MICH.

EAST & WEST MICH. PIKE MEET JULY 14-16
MACKINAW MICH.
JOHNSON PHOTO

Monument at foot of Central Avenue commemorating the northern end of the Dixie Highway--now the site of the Rock Garden.

Monument with ice house and band stand in background.

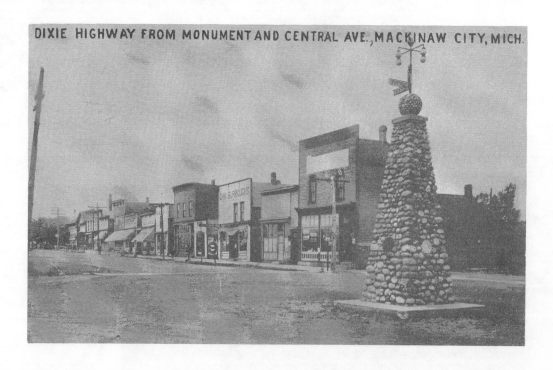

DIXIE HIGHWAY FROM MONUMENT AND CENTRAL AVE., MACKINAW CITY, MICH.

Chapter 11

Newsprint by Ruth Bauers

Mackinaw City
Traces a Great History
Back to 1712

May Be 2nd Oldest in Michigan

By Mrs. E. J. Bauers

Mackinaw City, northern most town located at the tip of the lower peninsula, is, strictly speaking, not a city, but a village of less than one thousand persons, except in summer, when hundreds of tourists and hay fever sufferers flock to the Northland for the relief which this climate affords them. Located on the beautiful Straits of Mackinac, one wonders if Longfellow could have been thinking of Mackinaw when he wrote "Here stands the forest primeval, the whispering pines and hemlocks"

Mackinaw City is thought by some historians to be the second the oldest. Its history dates back Michigan, Sault Ste. Marie being the oldest It's history dates back to the coming of Father Marquette and other Jesuit missionaries, who, undaunted by hardships of the trail, or the prospect of a slow death at the stake of savage Indians, slowly pushed their way through the trackless wilderness from Quebec to the Straits of Mackinac.

The community at Mackinaw was established by Fr Marquette in 1712. Before the coming of the white man this region had been the summer camp of Chippewa and Ottawa Indians and here Fr. Marquette found them and laid the foundation for a lasting friendship between the Indians and French. As early as 1673, French fur traders had attempted to set up a trading post in Mackinaw, but after having had trouble with Chief Cadillac about 1680, the Jesuits burned their chapel and returned to Quebec.

In 1714, a Fort was re-established by the French and friendly years of trading followed. Under French command the Indians roamed afar and warriors fought at Braddock's field and Plains of Abraham, where the English, through their victory over the French, gained possession of the vast Northwest Territory.

In 1761 the Fort at Mackinaw was taken over by an English garrison, but the Indians were discontented under their leadership. Under Chief Pontiac, an Ojibway Indian, plans were made to exterminate the English, and in 1762 the war hatchet was sent to all Indian nations. At a great Council meeting in the spring of 1763, the Chiefs assembled and pledged to take part in the war.

On June 4, 1763 the blow fell. Under cover of a game of La-Cross in old Fort Mackinaw, the Indians succeeded in massacreing most of the English, and a new page in the history of Mackinaw was written.

In October, 1764 the fort was again garrisoned by English troops and continued so until abandoned in 1781, when the English, fearing the fort could not be defended against another threatening attack by Indians withdrew to Mackinac Island, moving the fort with them. Lack of shipping facilities prevented the Indians from following them.

About 1909, the State Park Commission was persuaded thru efforts of the local Councilmen, to set aside twenty-two acres of land, including the site of the Old Fort, as a State Park. The Park was dedicated during the term of the late S. J. Smith, who served as Village President for several terms. One of the speakers on the dedication program was the Hon. H. F. Baker, State Representative and father of Tom Baker of Cheboygan.

The old French Fort was rebuilt about 1932, under the supervision of the late Chris Schneider, who was Superintendent of the Michilimackinac State Park for many years. Much excavating was done in order to determine the original location, size and shape of the stockade, so as to make it as nearly a duplicate of the original as possible. Inside the stockade area log houses such as were formerly occupied by soldiers and a monument bearing a plaque telling of the Massacre of June 4, 1763.

Little of Mackinaw history is recorded from 1763 until 1855, when a land firm in Cincinnati, Ohio, purchased most of the property in the Village. Chief owner and most influential in affairs of the Village was Edgar Conkling. Because of its location, geographically, he believed Mackinaw was destined to become a metropolis of a great commercial empire, with access to mineral trade, fisheries, furs and lumber.

Mr. Conkling made a plat of the Village and in 1857 it was surveyed by R. C. Phillips, from the plat. Little developed of importance until 1869, when Mr. Conkling made arrangements to build a dock and the contract was given to F. M. Sammons of Cheboygan.

In January, 1870, George W. Stimpson and his wife and family of four sons and two daughters, friends of the Conklings, arrived in Mackinaw from Maine, attracted by the wealth of timber land and prospects of lumbering. Mrs. Stimpson was the first white woman to have settled in the community and she spent the remainder of her life here, until her death in 1918, at the age of 90 years. Mr. Stimpson preceded her in death in 1885, at the age of 56. Death was caused by pneumonia.

The Stimpson's first home was a log house in a beautiful pine grove where the Sattler Hotel now stands. The house was later removed for the erection of the Hotel, which was known until recent years as the "Stimpson House."

It was in the Stimpson home that the first religious services of the Village were held and the first Sunday School organized.

A log school was built near the present site of the Buchmann home, with Miss Lydia Stimpson (later Mrs. E. C. Milliken, of Cheboygan), the first teacher, with an enrollment of seven pupils. Others who taught in the Village school were L. I. Willits, Miss Luella Smith, later Mrs. Stimpson Overton, and Miss Ella Eastman, daughter of pioneer homesteaders in the Bliss region, who later married Charles Stimpson. They were the parents of Mrs. Ruth Stimpson Barrett and Clarence Stimpson. In 1883, a site was purchased for a school for $170, and a building erected where the present school now stands. W. C. Thompson served as teacher of the grades with an enrollment of fifty pupils.

In 1882, it was thought advisable to organize under a Village charter. Accordingly, at a meeting of the Board of Supervisors in December, 1882, application was made for an order incorporating the described territory into the Village of Mackinaw City. The description included lots one (1) and two (2) of fractional section seven (7) and lots one (1) and two (2) of section eighteen (18) all in township thirty-nine (39) North, Range three (3) Cheboygan County Michigan. The petition signed by thirty-three citizens and the Board of Supervisors was presented to the Secretary of State and in 1883, the Village was incorporated by an act of Legislature, was approved in April 1882, under the law relative to Villages, passed in 1875.

The first charter election in the spring of 1883 resulted in the election of John Padden, President; E. M. Sutherland, Clerk; Samuel Chamberlain, Treasurer; and six trustees who were to serve as a Village Council. The first ordinance on record at the Village Hall was passed in May, 1901, and still remains in effect. At that time, all other ordinances on record were declared null and void.

The New York Central and Grand Rapids and Indiana railroads were extended to Mackinaw in 1881 and 1882 and in 1883, a number of buildings were erected and streets were graded. James Fox was the first New York Central Agent and Wilbur Robinson, the first railroad clerk. It was at that time that many new families moved into the Village, some in the employ of the railroads and others to make a living in a new and growing town. Among them were the families of James Ball, James Davenport, B. Kinsel, John Coffman, A. H. Buhler, David Wolford, David H. Smith, Chas. Dagwell and William Martin. Many of the descendants of these families still reside in Mackinaw.

The family of L. I. Willets came to Mackinaw soon after the Geo. W. Stimpson family arrived and became permanent residents. Mr. Willets purchased a lot and built a store where the L. H. Liebeck store now stands and continued to operate for many years. He also taught the Village school and was the first postmaster, when the post office was established in 1871.

In February 1870, Elder Riley of the Methodist Episcopal Church of Cheboygan preached in the home of Geo. W. Stimpson. A number of dock workers and others in the vicinity filled the house to capacity. After the dock was completed and the workmen left there were no church services until in the summer of 1881, the Presbyterian Church sent Dr. Cook from Harbor Springs to hold services once a month. Soon after a Church Society was organized and in 1883 a church built and dedicated.

In 1888 the Methodist Society organized with a membership of 18 persons. A site was presented by Geo. H. Todd, a citizen of Mackinaw City to the new organization and a new church was erected and named Ames' Memorial in honor of Bishop E. R. Ames.

In about 1908 the Roman Catholics organized and built a church and rectory on West Central Ave., but the buildings were later moved to their present location, which is more centrally located.

In 1871 application was made for the organization of a school district and in July of that year School District No. 1 was organized and the first meeting of District voters was held at the home of Geo. W. Stimpson on July 19 and three officers were chosen, William Wright, Moderator; Geo. W. Stimpson, Director; and Geo. Conrad, Assessor.

The first dock in the Village was built by Edgar Conkling in front of where the Straits Inn now stands. Thousands of cords of wood were cut within the Village limits and shipped from the dock for boats plying between Chicago, Buffalo and Lake Superior ports, as wood was used in those days instead of coal. Other docks were built in later years, the G R. and I. dock, the Citizens dock and the present Railroad dock.

The first Ferry boat, the "Algomah" was built in 1882, the engines being installed by the late Henry Ford. It towed a scow called the "Betsey" which had railroad track on it and carried five or six cars, which was adequate for the times.

The first ice crusher was the St. Ignace, and was followed later by the Ste. Marie No. 1 and later by the Chief Wawatam. The "Chief" has four tracks and a capacity of twenty-four standard freight cars. The engines and boilers were later taken from Ste. Marie No. 1, and placed in a new hull and named Ste. Marie No. 2, now used in cases of emergency or when the Chief Wawatam must go to dry dock for inspection or repairs.

The first Marine station in Mackinaw was operated by Forest Stimpson, son of Mr and Mrs. G. W. Stimpson. He built a home on "the Point" and had equipped one room for the station. His wife was the former Luella Smith, who also came from Maine, with her parents and had settled in Cheboygan. She was one of Mackinaw's early teachers. Children of the Forest Stimpsons were Margaret E., now Mrs. B. A. Parsons, who resides in the home built by her father and Lloyd Stimpson of Hollywood, Calif.

Forest Stimpson lost his life while delivering a message to a lake freighter and his body was never recovered. Several years later, his widow married John Overton, a Lighthouse Inspector for the government, who supervised the building of the present lighthouse.

Forest Stimpson also served as postmaster agent and telegraph operator for the New York Central railroad in the local office.

Geo. W. Stimpson, Jr., was probably the first veterinary surgeon in this community. He was an honor graduate of the Ontraio Veterinary College in Toronto, Canada and practiced in Qincey, Ill., before coming to Mackinaw in 1870.

Charles Stimpson, who owned the farm now owned by the Fred Grebe family, as a scientific farmer, and his farm was considered a model one in the early days. Nothing ever wasted on his farm, he never threshed grain, but cured as hay and fed it to his stock. He planned to sell at least 150 lambs each year, and raised Angora goats, which were an aid in keeping the grounds clear of weeds.

His son Clarence was a graduate of Michigan Agricultural College Engineering department and when World War I broke out was employed by the Pere Marquette Railroad as a civil engineer After several unsuccessful attempts to enlist in various cities, he was finally accepted by the examining board in Petoskey and joined the Sixth U. S. Engineers Corp. landing in France. He was wounded severely shortly after entering action and was the first Cheboygan County soldier to be wounded in France.

The David Smith family came to Michigan from Canada in 1871 and settled near White Cloud. A few years later they came to Mackinaw and purchased the Simpson Hotel which they and members of their family still own and operate and the name was recently changed to the Sattler Hotel. Included in the members of the David Smith family were S. J. Smith, Oscar Smith, Wm. Smith all prominent in the politics of the Village. S. J. served as State Representative of this District for several years.

Mackinaw has had two disastrous fires in its history. One, in March, 1900, when four business blocks were burned and one in June, 1916 when five stores on Huron Ave., were destroyed. Included in the 1916 fire was the drug store of J. H. Coffman and son, one of the Village's oldest stores, which was soon rebuilt and is now operated by George Coffman. This store has the distinction of being owned and operated by members of the same family on the same location since it was established in 1883.

In the 1916 fire , S. B. Chamberlain died from over-exertion while carrying merchandise from his grocery store. He was one of Mackinaw's older merchants having come here in 1883 from Plainwell.

In 1883 the Main Street of the Village was where Huron Avenue now lies. Stores were located in the block where the Coffman Drug Store is located and in the next block north. Other stores were Sutherland's Boot Shop, Barrett's Variety Store, a photograph shop, Zimmerman's Furniture Shop and Funeral Home, James Shepherd's grocery and feed store with offices upstairs and Richard's Grocery. Further up the block a very up-to-date hotel, the Mercier House, was located. It was burned in 1892.

Mackinaw has had several newspapers during its history. Some of these were the Mackinaw Witness, published by Rev. G W. and Geo. H. Wood and the equipment of which was burned in the 1916 fire; the Mackinaw Tribune, edited by S. G. Hosach in 1882, which was published each Thursday with the Cheboygan Tribune, and the Straits Journel, published in 1881 by George A. Mosher and in recent years one called the Ames' Journal published by Rev. Emerald B. Dixon, pastor of the Ames' Memorial Church in 1918-19. The prices of the early papers were $1.50 per year, payable in advance, but the Ames' Journal was 25c per year. Community is now served by the Cheboygan Daily Tribune, the Petoskey News and other down state dailies.

Mackinaw's first lighthouse was at McGulpin's Point, about three miles from the village. It was built in 1868 and the first lighthouse keeper was Thomas P. Dunn who served from 1868 until 1879 when he was succeeded by James Davenport who served as keeper for 27 years. In 1907 Mr. Davenport went to the Old Mission lighthouse, near Traverse City, where he remained until he retired in 1919.

One of Mackinaw's prominent citizens, of whom she is justly proud, is Frances Margaret Fox, noted author of children's stories. She was the daughter of the late Mr. and Mrs. James Fox and was born in Framington, Mass., in 1870. Educated in the Michigan Seminary in Kalamazoo she was Mackinaw's first primary teacher. Her stories were published regularly between the years 1900-1939 and she has been listed in the "Who's Who Among Northern American Authors" since 1929. For many years she spent her summers at her cottage in Mackinaw City and her winters in Washington, D. C. where she was one of the privileged few, having access to the Congressional Library. Because of the infirmities of age she is now cared for in the Arnold Home in Detroit, but her interest in Mackinaw and her friends of many years standing, still remains.

The first sidewalks in the Village were built by W. I. Ward of Cheboygan and later in 1904 Fred Black who had moved to Mackinaw from Essexville, and John Gowans from Gladwin, extended cement walks to all parts of the Village. Mr. Black served as Justice of the Peace in Carp Lake Twp.. being elected in 1906. He later went to Bay City, where he served as Justice for many years and was prominent in his department.

Three years ago he and Mrs. Black returned to Mackinaw and established their residence on West Central Ave. Because of his advanced age, Judge Black is unable to take an active part in the affairs of the Village, but he was recently elected as Justice of Wawatam Twp. and because of his thorough knowledge of state and federal laws is of much help to persons seeking authentic legal advice.

In 1912 six women of Mackinaw organized a study club for the study of Shakespeare. They were Mesdames Julia A. Inglis, Tena Barrett, Blanche Desy, Grace Robertson, Luella Overton, and Hattie R. Stimpson.

In 1913 they organized the Mackinaw Woman's Club and chose as a project the establishment of a library. Books were collected in a hand drawn cart and a library opened each Friday from 3 to 5 p.m., first in the town hall and later in a room in the school building, with volunteer librarians who were club members.

In 1923 two lots were purchased on Jamet St. and a library with club rooms was begun in 1931 and was completed and accepted in January 1932. Since that time the club has grown to a membership of 125. The library now contains more than 2,000 books. The Librarian is Mrs. E. C. Dagwell, who with her committee still continue to keep the library open Friday afternoons.

The Woman's Club meetings are held in the library from October through May. In addition to the library the club room is used by the staff in charge of the Clinic for Infants and pre-school age children once each month; and each church and organization are privilege dto use the building once each year, free of charge.

Twenty-one club members served as president of the organization, beginning with Julia A. Inglis, founder of the Study Club which later became the Woman's Club. Mrs. Inglis was a member of the faculty of Mackinaw School for 14 years and a member of the County Board of Education for four years before retiring in 1922. She was the mother of Mrs. Agnes Johnson of Mackinaw, and the late Mrs. Wm. Smith (Lucy), both well known residents.

Author's Note — In compiling the materials used in the writing of this history of Mackinaw City, the writer is deeply indebted and appreciative to Mrs. Margaret Stimpson Parsons and Mrs. Ruth Stimpson Barrett for valuable materials and photographs kept by their respective mothers and handed down for succeeding generations; also for a scrap book made by the late Hattie Richardson Stimpson and presented to this correspondent before her death as well as to other local citizens for information.

June 22, 1955.
Mrs. E. J. Bauers,

One of the First School Teachers

Luella Smith

Mackinaw City's first school was built of logs. One of the early teachers was Miss Luella Smith. She later married Stimpson Overton.

A Pioneer of Mackinaw City

George W. Stimpson

George W. Stimpson came to Mackinaw City with his wife and six children in 1870. He built the well known hotel that was widely known as the Stimpson House until renamed in recent years the Stattler. The first religious services in the community were held in his home.

Mackinaw's First Marine Reporter

Forest J. Stimpson

Forest Stimpson, son of pioneer hotelman George W. Stimpson, was postmaster agent and telegraph operator for the New York Central railroad at Mackinaw City. He was also first marine reporter, and lost his life delivering a message to a freighter.

Train Ferry Stuck in Straits, So Passengers Walk

The powerful ice-breaking train ferry Saint Marie was used by the State Highway Department to carry autos and passengers across the Straits in winter as the regular car ferries could not get through. But sometimes the train ferry got stuck too.

This photo was taken on Feb. 17, 1939 and shows the Sainte Marie icebound somewhere in the Straits. Bottom photo, the passengers get tired of waiting for release, and get out and walk to shore. How they would have welcomed the Straits Bridge.

Construction of the Coast Guard icebreaker Mackinaw in 1944 took the worry out of winter. The train ferries still get stuck once in a while, but the Mackinaw is able to arrive from Cheboygan and free them in comparatively short time.

(photos on following page)

Chapter 12

Wawatam Memories

from the Wa-Wa-Tam Association
August, 1958

George L. Kern--My wife Huldah and I always looked forward to coming to Mackinaw City via the Grand Rapids and Indiana Railroad. In the old days, the train often consisted of as many as 14 Pullmans and a diner. We enjoyed the picnics and trips on Roxy's boat. We especially loved the Beach in its wildness during the early days. My first visit to WaWaTam Beach was in 1911, and my cottage was completed in 1914. Much of the material used in the building was shipped up from Indianapolis. I even sent a carpenter along from home to take charge of the construction work.

Chester Allensworth--My first visit to the Beach occurred in 1922. Anna, my wife, and I stayed at the Inn operated by Mr. George Applegate. In 1923 I worked as bus driver for the Inn. Anna was also employed there.

Mrs. Marion Flaherty Bow--I remember the wonderful Beach picnics and parties at the Inn. The auction of lots around 1916 was a big event. Many people came. The auctioneer moved from lot to lot, followed by the crowd. In addition, there was a feast and a drawing where a member of the Wolff family won a Beach lot.

Robert Strider--I first visited Mackinaw City in 1922, accompanied by my parents, Bishop and Mrs. R. E. L. Strider of Wheeling, West Virginia. Our cottage, number 32, was purchased from the Pecks in 1923. In 1949 Dr. McKinney, of Saginaw, bought and completely remodeled it. In 1955 my sister, Mrs. Sidney Bullock of Charlestown, West Virginia, and my wife and I acquired the Warner cottage. With our four children, we plan to spend as many summers here as possible. Things I remember best: The old foghorn at the lighthouse. The evolution of the auto ferries from the little *Mackinaw City* and the *St. Ignace* to the *Vacationland*. The days when a bike could be ridden from McGulpin's to the State Park.

Dr. Douglas Steere--I remember the joy of the springhouses spaced all the way up the Beach where you could get a delicious drink of ice cold spring water, and the mysterious old Boat House at McGulpin's Point.

Claude W. Johnson--My mother, Mrs. Carrie Edmonds and Mrs. C. A. Roberts were sisters. Mr. Harding showed my mother the lot on which our cottage stands by the light of a lantern. She bought the lot at once, and I purchased the one directly west of it, but I sold this piece of property a few years later. At that time, 1911, there were no cottages from McKinney's corner to Mrs. Wolff's cottage, and there was no sidewalk. We used to come to Mackinac Island by boat, then via the old *Algomah* to Mackinaw City. It was a long walk to the cottage, as we had to go up Central Avenue to Pemot, down Pemot to McKinney's corner on a sidewalk and then through the sand back up the Beach to the cottage.

Mrs. G. G. Scott--I remember: Deer coming down to the lake to drink. A freighter grounded close to shore. An old English lantern found in the woods under several feet of underbrush. Digging for Indian graves. The dock at the lighthouse for landing sick seamen. Dinners, parties, teas, dances, etc., at the Inn. Playing tennis on the court maintained by the Association. Horseback riding at the Inn when Mr. Davies was the owner. Coasting with bikes down the old lighthouse road. Dances at Trail's End before the lodge burned down.

Mrs. Melvin Renkenberger--When our Beach was being promoted, Mr. Harding brought in a couple of auctioneers to conduct a huge sale of lots. These two men, wearing Prince Albert coats and big felt hats rode in an open carriage, stopping from time to time along the rutty old trail to sell a few lots. Quite a crowd of people came straggling along and each time the carriage stopped, the sale of lots was pressed. Quite a number of townspeople, as well as others, purchased lots at that time. Some of the lots in back of the present drive and west of the cemetery sold for as little as $15.00. Later, when more cottages had been built, Mr. and Mrs. Harding sponsored a baked whitefish dinner, served from tables constructed by Mr. Harding in the region of the present Curtis cottage.The whitefish were planked and cooked at an especially prepared fire. A pit was dug and big logs burned down to coals, then the planked fish were set up alongside and browned to tender flakiness. The Beach people were brought up to the picnic spot in motor boats owned by Mr. Wolff, Mr. Peck, Mr. Harding and Mr. Jackson. One year, after the dinner, Bishop Leete pronounced and we had an old-fashioned spell-down.

Mrs. Edwin Olds--When we were guests of the Davises in 1929, the Beach was wilder and less well occupied than now. There were plenty of lots which were not yet cleared. The concrete sidewalk which extended the length of the Beach was a popular and delightful promenade at any hour of the day or evening.

Mrs. W. B. Narrin--There was no electricity out at our end of the Beach when we built in 1937. While Mr. Narrin was President of the Association, he obtained releases for the power line right of way. By 1941,all cottages had lights.

Mrs. Herbert Asmus--I remember playing in the old sawdust pile near the side of the Voss cottage. I used to hunt Indian relics near the Fort. There was an old Indian trail behind the John I. Astrom cottage which ran back to Central Avenue. There was an old bench south of McKinney's corner which was placed there by Mr. Harding for people to rest on while walking to town. At one time, while of high school age, I waited on tables at the Inn.

John G. Astrom--When Fred Leete graduated from his bicycle mail delivery route for Beach residents, I took over this very lucrative business. We used to keep our car in the Inn's garage while staying in Mackinaw. It was a treat to have Sunday dinner at the Inn.

John Naill--I remember the good days, long since passed, of Tripoli, Pop Corn and the trimmings.

Nora Morr--Mr. and Mrs.   M. D. Renkenberger and I visited the B.E.Z. cottage of Vine Harding in July, 1915. Mr. Harding met us at the railroad station and took us to the New York Central Dock where he had his motorboat moored. Then he took us to WaWaTam Beach via boat. There were not many motor cars at the time. All along the Beach were docks and many motor boats.

Sidney Freeman--I have seen the water line range from fifty feet or more out from the present one to the high mark of 1953 and 1954. Trail's End Bay has been one of the best swimming spots and the ride to

Wilderness Park one of the prettiest. This park was the site of a CCC camp before the war. While there are still blueberries, blackberries and strawberries, they are not as plentiful as they were in the past. Thirty years ago there were raspberries and gooseberries as well. I remember one day, some few years ago, we went out in the late afternoon near the end of August to get blueberries. We found a very wonderful place with bushels of berries available. However, as it was getting near dark and we were in marshy land, we decided to go back the next day to pick several quarts of them. Mother Nature had other plans, though. A frost came that night and the next day there were no oerries at all, or rather they were there, but spoiled.

Mrs. Edward Carrington--The big dock in front of Wolff's was a popular place to go bathing.

Mrs. Claude Cox--Mr. Harding was very active in promoting a friendly, neighborly feeling among the summer residents. There were many picnics, beach parties, etc. I recall one of the many parties in Mr. Harding's house when there was a mock wedding ceremony. Mr. Harding, a very tall man, acted as the bride and Mrs. Jackson, a rather short lady, acted as the groom. There was always great fun at these parties.

Mrs. Theodore Marsh--When Mr. Marsh selected our lots he had to cut his way from the road to the water with an ax. The growth was almost impossible to penetrate. Our cottage was a Mershon and Morley ready made house from Bay City. With a crew from the factory, it went up in one day. Next day the roof was on and we moved in. We had kerosene oil lamps and a wood stove. We were pioneers.

Dr. Robert English--George McMillan, between the ages of about 12 to 18, used to deliver the mail by bicycle. Everyone had corn roasts in front of their cottages. In 1917 or 1918 my father and I, in front of our cottage, between the hours of 5 a.m. and 4 p.m. made the largest catch of perch ever recorded in northern waters--over 1100. The entire Beach had perch to eat for weeks. We listened to the Dempsey-Willard fight over the telegraph wire at depot. The whole town was there.In the big tennis tournament of 1930 I lost in the finals to a boy named Rocky, a singer who was a protege of Mrs. Hast. Dr. Carl Bradford, then a student at Wisconsin, was allergic to poison ivy. When he lost a ball over in the woods, we would all get new balls, purchased by him. Mr. Bowman had the first radio on the Beach. Three tubes and earphones. Vine Harding used to pick up people on the Beach and take them to the *Algomah* in his Model T.

Berniece C. Thomas--I came to Mackinaw City in 1924 and never missed a summer after that. Ihad a room and my meals with Mrs. M. A. Wolff on WaWaTam Beach until the fall of 1932 when I bought Mrs. Wolff's little cottage. My husband Harry and I remodeled it and renamed it "Justamere". I love WaWaTam Beach and have many happy memories that will be with me always.

Mrs. Myla Herrman Luessow--In 1925 my aunt and uncle, Mr. and Mrs. Julius Herrman brought me to Mackinaw for a visit at the Kern cottage. Mrs. Kern was my aunt's sister. The following summer, my parents, my brother and I rented the Claude Johnson cottage. Later, my mother purchased two lots and built the cottage we now own. My brother drove Mother up here during spring vacation one year and he wired the cottage for electricity. At that time the ice was piled so high on the shore that the fishermen's shanties out on the Straits could only be seen from the second story windows. The road in back of the cottages wasn't open and so they had to walk through the woods on top of the hard snow.

Wawatam Inn
Vine Harding standing near steps.

Auction of Wawatam lots
Mrs. Louis Liebeck in black hat and dress

Big Rock at McGulpins Point

Left to Right, Front Row -
   Helena Haw Guernsey, Peggy Owens Astrom, Barbara Owens Gard, Allison Haw Weeber, Dorothy Haw Scott, Roy Owens, Mrs. Owens.

Left to Right, Second Row -
   Ronald Ferguson, Llewellyn Owens, Thomas Haw III, Thomas Haw, Jr.

69

A Few Recollections
of the
Wawatam Beach Sidewalk

Robert E. L. Strider

I have many early memories of the sidewalk, from the first day that I looked out on the Straits, as a small boy of five, in 1922, in front of what became the Strider cottage, later owned by Dr. McKinney. As a young native of the land-locked state of West Virginia, I thought the expanse of the Straits and Lake Michigan to the west the most awesome sight I had ever seen, easily equal to what I imagined the ocean might someday appear.

As a growing boy I delighted in riding my bicycle from the area of the Fort (as yet totally unrestored, merely an expanse of sand and beach grass and one stone monument) to McGulpin's Point. The breaks in the sidewalk occasioned from time to time by winter storms were generally repaired, and there were many years in which the ride was uninterrupted. The first major break to remain unrepaired, it seems to my recollection, was at the bluff just west of Douglas Steere's cottage.

There were two springs along the shore protected by gazebos. There might have been a third, but my vision of it is pretty hazy, and it may exist only in my imagination. The first, and the one that lasted longest, was Harding's spring, at Harding Poing. The second, in an area now thoroughly inundated, was just beyond what we called Sunset Point, not far from where the easternmost of the pipe or cable crossings is now situated. To get a bucket of water from this second spring one had to skim off the algae, but Harding's Spring ran cold and clear. There were at least two other similar gazebos, neither of them covering a spring: one at the end of Leete's dock, the other just out on Sunset Point. I remember being embarrassed (and also convulsed) when an unmannerly hound dog of ours disrupted the peaceful sunset reveries of a couply of ladies sitting in that Sunset Point gazebo enjoying, until they were so rudely invaded, a box of chocolates.

A kindly lady who lived in Clearview Cottage, Mrs. Walters, used to pay me ten cents a week to bring her a bucket of water from Harding's Spring in my wagon, every evening before supper. The wage may seem niggardly, but my mother was opposed to my accepting money for any purpose from neighbors, and the ten cents was the result of considerable negotiation.

An occasional treat each summer was a quart of ice cream for dessert from Stom's store, and it would always be my happy duty to ride up the beach on the sidewalk to buy it and get it home before it melted. Once in a while I would be rewarded with an extra nickel, over and above the sixty cents, or whatever the cost of the ice cream was in those days, for a candy bar to munch on the ride back down the beach to our cottage.

My most unusual adventure along the sidewalk was one evening when, at about the age of twelve, I was riding along peacefully when a large dog emerged from the underbrush, along about in front of the Hathaway cottage, just east of Stom's store, lunged at me, got his teeth caught in the pocket of the khaki shorts I was wearing, and pulled them right off. He must have hit a vulnerable seam that ripped all the way out. As I retired discreetly to a clump of cedar, my companion, Ronnie Ferguson, holding his sides, rode home to get me another pair of pants.

Most of my memories of the sidewalk, however, are less lurid. There is one amusing historical note. In August, 1923, the news came that President Harding had died. Someone came to the house and mentioned the sudden and unexpected death of Mr. Harding. That morning I had seen the imposing figure of Vine Harding, an impressive man of about six feet six, walking along the beach. I knew him well, and occasionally he would drop by and chat with us, and once replaced a light bulb on the porch without even getting on a chair, a feat that was bound to impress a six-year old. When our visitor departed, I announced to the family that Mr. Harding couldn't possibly have died, for I had just seen him.

When I think of the Mackinaw sidewalk I think of innumerable walks past the cedars, balsams, spruces and birches, to and from McGulpin's and down to the Fort and back, during the day and long into many an evening. It is too bad that the depredations of time and the weather have destroyed so much of it.

An All Time Directory of
Wawatam Beach Residents
To 1957

Dates in parentheses show years
cottages were constructed.

4   Elizabeth Poppendick, Thomas Ward, Mrs. A. J. Fitzgerald (1913).

5   Dr. Carl Bradford (1950).

6   Dr. Carl Bradford, Dr. Hubert Slusser, Vera Duisen, Helen Kennedy, Percy O'Brien (1937).

7   H. T. Morgan, John and Helen Naill.

9   James T. and Nellie Flaherty, Marion Flaherty Bow (1914).

10   Ed Saulton, Goodloe H. Rogers.

11   Mrs. Margaret A. Wolff, Oliver Miller.

11½ Mrs. Wolff, Harry and Berniece Thomas, J. R. Childs.

12 Henry and Dot Isabelle Morlock, Mrs. Francie Yager, Blanche De Vries Bernard.

13 Frank and Emma Klauser, Mr. Brown, Mrs. M. E. Grah, Paul Voelker, C. W. Jones.

14 Russell Rogers.

15 L. D. Johnson, William E. Crane, Mrs. A. B. Crane, Edward Carrington, William E. Carrington (1915).

16 George and Huldah Kern (1914).

18 Frank E. Noblett (1956).

19 Mrs. Carrie Edmonds, Claude Johnson.

21 John and Louise Hermann, John A. Hermann, Erwin E. Luessow (1930).

22 Miss Wheeler, William F. Yeslin, Mr. Backie, Jerry Bonter, Oliver Miller.

22A H. W. Martin, C. P. Omohundro.

23 Melvin and Celia Renkenberger (1922).

23A Nora Morr (1924).

24 Mrs. V. Haecker.

25 John and Hattie Stimpson, Mr. Lockwood, Ethel Barnard (1912).

26 Mrs. Lena Martin, Blanche Zerkle, Grace Zerkle (1941).

26A Chester and Anna Mary Allensworth (1932).

27 John and Hattie Stimpson, Albert Cook, Ellsworth Jones.

28 John B. Hilliker, Goodloe Rogers, E. A. Deiss.

29 J. H. Goetz, E. H. Voss, David Voss.

30 William Richardson.

31 Dr. D. C. Weir, Robert Soest.

32 Glen Peck, Bishop R. E. and Eleanor Strider, Dr. A. R. McKinney.

33 Frank and Nellie Bosworth, Dr. A. R. McKinney.

33A Roy Ownes (1925).

35 Dr. J. L. Bullock, Roy J. Enos, William Coupal.

35A C. A. Roberts, Claude C. Cox.

36 John O. Brock, Thomas Haw, Gifford and Dorothy Scott.

37 C. A. and Cora Roberts, Mary and Martha Watkins, Mrs. Paul Fry (1909).

38 A. B. and Kathryn Wesler, Edith Dysinger, Verne Barnett (1911).

39 Mr. and Mrs. Poole, Mr. and Mrs. English, Dr. Robert English (1909).

40 Edward Finkbeiner (1956).

41 Mr. Merritt, Mr. Bowman, Dr. and Mrs. T. E. Howson, l. A. Pierce (1910).

41A Vern Wilson.

42A Vine Harding, H. W. Moore, Bernard Gunther, May Hall.

44 Vine Harding, Mrs. H. W. Moore (First cottage on the Beach).

45 Mr. Daugherty, Richard Warner, Jr., Robert E. L. Strider (1909).

46 George and Elizabeth Jackson, Donald and Lucy Gridley (1910).

47 Katherine Rexer, Ben C. Shull, Elizabeth B. Glore (1910).

48 Charles Brook, Herbert and Lillian Asmus (1908).

49 George MacDonald, Rudolph Dahlstrom, Beryl Dassow (1907).

50 C. E. Burrows, Mrs. Gordon Sattler, Raymond La Comb.

51 Rex Burrows, Nathan and Zella melhuish, Syble Melhuish, Hartland Smith.

52 Frank freeman, Sidney and Grace Freeman (1911).

53 Mrs. McCarthy, Mrs. Ivy Morgan (1909).

54 Rev. Gordon, H. C. Walters, Donald F. Jewell.

55 Ray Anderson.

60 Bishop F. D. Leete, Frederick D. Leete, Jr.

61 A. L. Roberts.

62 Mrs. Francis Brenner, T. W. Attwood, Betty A. Crandell.

63 Charles Volkman, charlotte O'Keefe, James A. Hathaway.

63A W. J. Davis.

64 W. J. Davis.

66 Guy Brown, Kyron Clune, John Clune.

67 Bert Downer, E. M. Williams.

68E½ Grace Hamilton Morrey, R. A. and Ina Stuckey, C. E. daugherty.

68W½ Mrs. Margaret Hast, Mrs. Alice Jones.

69 K. T. Freiburger.

71 John I. Astrom, Edith Astrom, John G. Astrom (1914).

73 Eugene Troendle, Hanna Troendle, Lyle Wheeler.

74 Mrs. Dora Krause, Mrs. F. G. Lubeke.

75 Miss Edith Davenport, Peter Alexander.

75A John Ball.

76 James Hathaway.

79 George Stom.

80 J. F. and Ella Walters, William Swetnam.

81 William A. Lewin, Dorothy McBride, Mrs. Louise McConnachie, Mrs. Marjorie Penn (1933).

84 K. C. Marston, Augusta Leatherman.

87 Lee Hoffman.

91 Edwin G. Olds (1953).

93 Mado Shore, Donald Dixon.

96 Ogden Nickerson.

97 Dr. E. D. Bixler.

100 M. R. Hardy.

102 Mrs. Berry B. Johnson.

108 T. W. Van Sickle, Chas. Corin, Donald Darrow.

112 Joseph Pettit.

113 Miss Schilling, Wilfred Weist (1939).

114 E. M. Davis, Dr. W. C. Donald.

115 Theodore and Elizabeth Marsh (1923).

116 Joseph McDonnell (1950).

120 Mrs. Wm. Karns, C. P. McGuire.

121A Lyman Hendrickson.

122 John Schramm.

123 James Steininger, C. P. McGuire.

124 W. I. Kinsey, Marion A. Bushanan (1928).

125 O. F. and Helen Poindexter.

125A William Uhl, Mr. Poindexter.

128 Fabian La Tocha (1955).

131 Miss Ellen olson, Miss Lillian Wagner (1926).
133 George and Christina McMillan, Carl and Louise
       More (1925).
141 Douglas V. Steere (1938).
144 Rudolph Dahlstrom, Ferris Coffman.
146 Robert and Thelma Sisson (1951).
149 A. F. Harnishfager.
150 W. B. Narrin (1937).
150A O. V. Davenport.
152 Jack Kirby, Elmer E. Walters.
152A Mr. Steinburger.
154A Mr. Wainwright.
155A Lloyd Desy.
160 W. W. Howard.
161 Mrs. Nora Wolf.
162 Mrs. Thelma Wolf Tam.
163 Mr. Wilson, Julius Vertes.
165 Nelson Reed.
169 Mrs. Lena Lake Forest, Miss Georgia Emery,
       Dr. J. K. Bell (1919).
170 Ed Curtis.
Light house U.S. Government, Charles Williams, H.
       E. Skinner, Ralph Shaw (1868).

Excerpt From The Minutes
of the
Wawatam Association

1921: On the evening of September 9, 1921, about 20
       Beach residents met at the Harding cottage
       and formed the WaWaTam Beach Improve-
       ment Association. Mrs. Van Sickle and Mrs.
       C. A. Roberts were appointed to draw up a set
       of rules and regulations.

1922: Three meetings were held in the State Park
       Pavillion. Dues were set at $5.00 per year.
       Beach members were informed that repairs to
       the sidewalk would have to be made at the
       owner's expense.

1923: A dance was held for the young people in the
       dining room of the Inn. The President
       requested that the parents urge their children
       to "wear tennis shoes when playing and not to
       play on the court when wet."

1925: Bishop Leete suggested that speeding on the
       alley be stopped. Mr. Doerfer was hired as
       caretaker for the following year.

1927: The Treasurer reported a balance of $98.25 in
       addition to the $77.48 retained by the
       Mackinaw Bank which had recently failed.

The Village Council planned to open an access
road near the cemetery, and also one about a
half mile to the west. This was to take place
after the grading of Central Avenue was
completed.

1931: The Secretary was empowered to place in the
       hands of the Conservation officer of Emmet
       County information regarding a man who had,
       on July 14, driven up to several vacant lots
       along the beach, filled his car to capacity with
       young trees and shrubs and driven off.

1932: The Village Council informed the Association
       that it could no longer be responsible for any
       part of the caretaker's salary, but that the
       Marshall would make regular trips up the
       beach. Bishop Leete was appointed Chairman
       of a committee to rid the beach of poison ivy,
       goldenrod and ragweed.

1933: There was a rising vote of thanks from Mrs.
       Pettit's son, who with the help of Bobby
       Dahlstrom, worked hard to put out a fire on
       the Beach. Hours later some of the cottagers
       found it necessary to add many buckets of
       water. Mr. Krueger, the Marshall, was sent
       for and came at once with pick and shovels to
       unearth the smoldering roots. For several days
       he kept a close tab on the area.

1935: A special assessment of $1.00 from each
       member was required to pay a reward of
       $50.00 to Mr. Dahlstrom who was instrumental
       in capturing a man who had broken into a
       number of cottages. It was voted to prohibit
       the sale or rental of lots or buildings on
       Wawatam Beach for places to dispense liquor
       or for any undesirable amusements. Dues
       were returned to the pre-Depression level of
       $5.00.

1936: Much to the disappointment of all who were
       present at the first meeting, the scheduled
       exhibition by the Mackinaw City Fire
       Department had to be postponed. A letter of
       appreciation was sent to the Village Council
       for the temporary repairs made on the
       sidewalk and work done on Cottage Avenue.
       According to Mrs. Wagner, "People along
       Wawatam Beach do not belong to the 400
       unless they have a garbage sign."

1938: The Association expresses its appreciation
       and gratitude to the members of the Village
       Council for the placing of speed limit signs on
       Cottage Drive. John Krueger started his first
       year as caretaker for the Association.

1939: An expression of appreciation was extended to

Mr. Narrin for his tireless efforts toward securing lights at the west end of the Beach. Mrs. Stimpson sent a letter thanking the group for helping the Women's Club. 119 people were present at the annual picnic. The Association went on record as being opposed to the widening of the boulevard, as this would destroy many trees.

1941: Lights for all cottages on the beach were installed this year. Mr. Bow attempted to get city water for those on theBeach who desired it. A letter was sent to the State Department of Health regarding the menace of the City Dump.

1943: John Kreuger took over the job of garbage collection as well as Caretaker.

1948: There were 110 cottages on the beach and 66 Association members. The annual picnic was held at Shaw's Lighthouse with 85 people attending.

1950: $25.00 was presented to the Lions Club to be used for High School band instruments.

1955: The Historical Committee and the officers of the Association appeared on a half hour program presented on WCBY, Cheboygan, and WHAK, Rogers City. Produced in cooperation with the Mackinaw City Chamber of Commerce, the broadcast dealt not only with the Association, but also with the history of the Mackinaw area. Entertainment at the annual meeting consisted of movies and slides showing Mackinaw in winter. Alice Asmus and Charles Asmus provided delightful piano and violin music during the evening.

1956: The members were requested to write the proper authorities expressing their approval of the construction of a small boat harbor in Mackinaw City.

1957: The Constitution was amended so that only those who own property on the Beach may become members of the Association.

Captain Roberts driving the Wawatam Beach float in a parade.

Boardwalk at Wawatam Beach.

Vine Harding's Mackinaw

by John E. Moore

Part One

He was a tall man, big-boned,
and he came out of California and,
Before that, the Yukon, where the gold was.
Around the turn of the century he showed up
here, at Mackinaw, to look over
his inheritance, three miles of wild beach
facing north where the winds came
and a cold he had learned in Alaska.

  The town of Mackinaw was already old
but after the railroads came there
in the eighties it built up around
one street and a scattering of houses
clear around to where the old fort
had crumbled into the sand dunes
along the Straits.

                    A newish lighthouse
marked what they called Old Mackinac
Point; the rest was cut-over land and
west by south, a trail to Cecil,
where they still lumbered by a bay
where they'd snaked a pier out
about a half mile into the westward bay.

  Harding rented a rowboat up town
and came by water to his inheritance;
there was no other way yet.

                    From the water
he saw a shallow bay open to the north
and in the center of this crescent
a small point where three great pines
towered over the scrub cedars and
the stony beach.

                    He put ashore here,
stumbling over the loose, limestone rocks
until he stood on the grass margin
under one of the old pines, a white pine
that loomed skyward and swayed softly
in the gentle wind.

                    For it was June
and the air was bright and warm,
midges and black flies swarming over
the brushy shoreline.

                    Inland
a small clearing waited for him,
a natural space where underfoot
the wintergreen and kinikinick grew,
a waiting space where he would build
his place.

                    Already in his mind
he could see the house, a lean-to
of one room, a hot-air stove
and a bed–little else.

  Later he rowed back to town,
bought the rowboat, and arranged
for lumber, a raft of it, to be

floated around to the beach, the spot
he had chosen.

  This was the beginning of that long affair
of the heart and mind and body, Harding
and his dream of a summer place, a beach
where people would find a peace and joy
they could find no place else.

  Harding had married my grandmother's sister,
a lovely but frail woman,
as soon as he had returned from Alaska.
Now they were staying with her people
in Grand Rapids.

                    In a fever of haste,
Harding put together the one-room shack
under the big pines behind the beach,
living in a pup tent the while.

                    As soon
as he had finished the building
he took the train south, gathered up
their belongings and returned to Mackinaw.
Proudly he carried his wife to the beach
from the rowboat, putting her down
under the great pine where she could see
the shack; she too loved the place on sight
and the love grew as the summer waned.

  Harding had brought his surveying instruments,
crude and clumsy; but he knew what to do;
with the deed in hand he began laying out lots;
he drew up a map of the whole beach
and began plotting out his dream.

  By the first frost he had visioned
the long sidewalk that would span the
whole length of the beach, following the curve
of the bay, always close to the water.
Its building would have to wait for spring;
as autumn came in the northwest wind
swelled in the night and roared through the pines
and hammered the waves against the rocky shore.
He cut stove wood; there was plenty
in the second-growth trees behind the shore.
They were snug in the little house,
waiting for winter, listening to the geese
and ducks going over, headed south.
Someday, if their dreams came true,
they too would head south come fall.

Part Two

  On a cold November morning
the smooth water of the bay turned
to a sliding sheet of bright ice,
too thin to hold anyone up,
only a whisper of what lay ahead.

  Before the month was out
Harding got a buck and they had
venison to go with the ducks
he had taken on the waters
out front.

                    And when the snows

came in the night and the wind
rose to a blizzard, they banked
the fires and settled in to winter.

On calm days they snowshoed
through the back woods to the town road.
Harding's eyes and mind were always
on the coming spring and what the breakup
would mean.

He was anxious for the new season,
the new time when he could get out plans
to work, could build his sidewalk
and start work on a bigger house.

It was a good waiting time,
the winter, the white country,
the white shore against the ice floes
that formed solid clear across
to the Upper Peninsula.

Dreams
seemed more real in winter,
closer than ever to the real doing,
the fulfilled plans.

So the shortened days
and weeks crept by and the shack
held the warmth they needed.

The shore ice held fast into April
but then one day in a mild rain and a high wind
the breakup came at last.

The main channel
went a sharp blue and the west wind
cleared the Straits of ice.

Working like one
driven Harding hired men and laid out
the long sidewalk, beginning at the east end
of the beach, the end dunes near the
plot of grass where the old fort was.
By the first of June the sidewalk was in;
people up town saw Harding as crazy,
but he didn't mind. He cleared a road
about a hundred feet south of the walk
and running along what became
the back of the beach lots--
a dusty narrow road.

And he saw
another road was put in to join
the long main street.

People and cars
could find the beach then and
become buyers of lots.

By July
Harding had hired two carpenters
and they began building a large cottage
next to their shack.

At the same time
he began their larger cottage, adding
a two-story frame building to
the lean-to shack, which became the kitchen.
And on the shore in front
he dug down until the water
bubbled up, a fine spring whose water
was clear and pure and cold; he caught

the water in an up-ended drain tile,
and over it he built a spring house
with pillars of untrimmed cedar
and rustic seats around the sides.
He found other flowing springs at block
intervals along the beach; for each
he built spring houses.

Before the summer was out
there were five more cottages
and more planned.

He hit on the idea
of auctioning off lots at cost, nearly,
if the buyer would build in a year.
The scheme worked rather well
and Harding prospered; early
in September that year he bought
a Cadillac brougham, loaded it
down with gear, and the two
drove over the rutty roads to Florida
where he bought a place, planted
some oranges, and began the pattern
of life that held for the rest of his life--
Florida in winter, Mackinaw in summer.

Part Three

Early the following spring, while the coreopsis
and ox-eyed daisies bloomed in the clearings
he built the Inn, a long two-story hotel
planted squarely in the center of the woods
a block south of Harding Point, the place
where his new big cottage was.

The Inn
opened in July of that year to a full house,
largely people who came for two weeks or more,
finding the food good and the Inn
quiet in the sweet air of pine and balsam.
There was a new tennis court behind
the beach road near the Inn, and a
cleared and grassy lawn for croquet.

There were some thirty cottage owners
by the end of that summer, enough people
to form the beach association, and for the ladies,
a bridge-playing group that met each week
at the Inn.

Harding bought a launch
that season and cleared out the shed
by the cottage to make a boat house.

But late that summer the big thing
was Harding's pier. There were many
short docks jutting north into the bay
and rowboats all along the shore.
But Harding's new pier was the best
and the longest, a log-crib dock
that thrust straight north from the beach
in front of the Harding cottage
almost a thousand feet to end
in an L-shaped crib making the east side
of the pier a shelter for the many boats

that could tie up there and be safe.
At the end of the pier the bottom was sandy;
Harding built here a diving tower, not too high,
but just about right for swimming.

Part Four

These were the summers I remember best,
the twenties and thirties.
We had a little place
across the beach road from Harding's.
August
of each summer found us there for my asthma;
the good air always cured me; I had my cousin
Dorothy to play with, Harding's only child,
older than I was by a few years.
That summer
we found the long Harding pier broken
in the middle; an autumn storm and winter ice
had torn through a section of the cribs;
the logs from the dock covered the beach.
We could still walk part way out, to the broken place
at least.
I remember we salvaged much of the timber
and built two rafts from the logs and played pirate
most of the time.
Harding never got around
to repairing the pier; eventually all that remained
was the end crib with the diving platform,
a forlorn reminder to that once great dock.
Of course, the boulders that had once
filled the cribs now scattered through the shoals
of that shallow point. About all the good that came
of it was the myriads of leeches under those
scattered boulders; we collected them
and in September when the perch ran
off the piers up town, we sold them for bait.
I remember
that fishing, sitting on a bollard on
the railroad dock and hauling in
pound-sized yellow perch.
Harding
preferred lake trout; he had lots
of heavy line and lots of feathered spinners
he used trolling from his launch,
back and forth at about the drop-off
in front of the cottage.
Once I rowed
a heavy boat he had, long after
he had sold his launch. I remember
how sore my back got, how painful
a thing it was, all that rowing
as fast as I could to keep the spinner
about a foot off the bottom; trout
fed about that deep in September.
In the early times
lake trout had been plentiful there, but
by the late thirties they were scarce;
I remember Harding getting but one

in those years, though I wasn't always
along with him.
And I remember that as a kid
I loved to go along in his old Cadillac
when we went for wild huckleberries
on the sand dunes by French Farm Lake,
or we went for the same afternoons
to Wilderness Park, ten miles west,
where we followed a narrow trail
through the pines, by a marsh,
back to a fire tower where we most often
saw deer.
And I remember early mornings
when I'd see Harding taking
his early dip out front; he looked
like a walrus, breast-stroking along,
sometimes swimming the whole length
of the beach, out where it was blue and deep.
I tried to copy his form but I never quite
managed it. And on quieter times
when I'd be watching him putter around
fixing the roof of the cottage or repairing
the spring house out in front, I'd try
to get him to tell me about the Alaska
or the Gold Rush. He'd show me
the gold nugget he wore on his watch chain,
but he didn't tell me much. He'd
got his fill of trying to pan for gold,
so he and his partner bought a boat
and went into a good business,
freighting in supplies for the miners.
This would be in the late twenties;
all of a sudden the land boom in Florida
broke and Harding lost most of what
he had once held there. Before the bust
he had done well and made almost a fortune.
Then, after 1929, things grew harder for him;
but he held on to the Mackinaw land.
He belonged to that generation
that believed in land as the only wealth,
so as he grew older and poorer
he used every means he could to hold
to the land at Mackinaw, that is,
what remained of the beach still unsold.
Before the Depression there were
probably close to a hundred people
in the association, and the beach
was lined with cottages.
I think
that his life was a success, as far as
we can tell; surely he filled out
the dream he had held; surely the beach
today lasts as a kind of memorial
to him; my generation is the third
to have known the summers at Mackinaw
and to have felt it to be really home.

Part Five

He died in Florida that early spring
and they brought him home to bury him
in the Wayland cemetary, a few miles
from the little town of Bradley, where
he had grown up.

The old farm was farther east,
near Gunn Lake and Indian Hill,
where Harding had been the only one
to climb that twisty road on a high wheeler
in the days just after the Civil War.

I drove around that way later
in the summer and then visited the cemetery.
He sleeps next to his father, Josiah,
on the west side of the cemetery, the older part
where all the early settlers lie under
the huge elms and maples.

I think
he would have preferred to rest in
the little cemetery behind the beach
at Mackinaw.

I thought last of him
one day this last summer when the leaves
of the locust trees near our lot blew
softly in a west wind, and far over the
waters of the Straits the far shore
seemed near and the air was ripe
with the balsam smell he always loved.

Surely few men have loved a place
as Vine Harding loved his Mackinaw.

The Word, Mackinac

from the
Mackinac Island News
August 2, 1941

The word "Macki-
nac" has had as many
changes in spelling as
have most names de-
rived from Indian
languages.

Today the straits
connecting Lakes Michi-
gan and Huron are
called the Straits of
Mackinac, pronounced
as if ending in "aw".
Adding somewhat to the
confusion, Mackinaw
City is pronounced the
same way, Mackinac
Island is also pro-
nounced as if ending in
"aw", never as if ending
in "ack".

There was a time
when it was spelled
with an "ack" ending.
The spelling of the name
has gone through myriad
changes.

In the days when
explorers, fur traders
and Jesuits passed this
way in their canoes the
term Michilimackinac
was applied variously to
the Island, to the region
drained by the Great
Lakes to the fort at St.
Ignace, the fort at
Mackinaw City and to
the country of the straits
and the eastern portion
of the Upper Peninsula.

In Indian the word
Michilimackinac means
"The Big Turtle."

First mention of
Mackinac Island was
made in 1670 by Father
Allouez, who spelled it
"The Island of Michili-
mackinac." Father
Dablon spelled it "Mis-
silimackinac," dropping
the final "k" while
Cadillac varied the spel-
ling with "Missilimac-
kinack." Charlevoix
added an extra "l"
making it read "Michilli-
mackinac."

Chief Wawatam Hid His Blood Brother In An Island Cave Filled With Skulls

from the
Mackinac Island News
August 2, 1941

There are some
people who are not
aware of the many
significant facts and
legends surrounding
Skull Cave, one of the
points of interest on
Mackinac Island.

The cave, imbedded
in a shell shaped lime-
stone rock, is situated
about four hundred
yards north of historic
Fort Mackinac. It may
be reached either by
walking a winding path
from Arch Rock or by
riding a roadway over-
arched by beech and
maple trees.

Its historical signifi-
cance goes back to
1763. Wawatam, an
Indian, befriended
Alexander Henry, an
English fur trader.
Wawatam at the time of
the massacre of old
Michilimackinac located
the cave as a place of
refuge for this young
adventurous traveller.

Henry entered the
three foot wide by ten
foot high opening. It was
night. Henry was sleepy
and dozed off into sound
slumber. Upon awaken-
ing in the morning he
discovered that he had
been sleeping on a bed
of human bones. He was
terror stricken, but war-
fare demanded he re-
main in the habitat of
dead men for three
more days.

Many reasons have
been put forth in
explanation of the bones
in this cave. Alexander
Henry, in his writings,
seeks to establish their
origin. He cites the
belief that some natives
perished there as the
waters once overflowed
the Island. Then too, the
bones may have been
those of some Sioux
Indians who hid in the
cave when pursued by
the Ottawas. A very
logical conclusion is that
the cave was a recep-
tacle for the bones of
prisoners who were
sacrificed and devoured
at war feasts. The
Indians revered the
bones of their sacrificed
victims and Skull's Cave
may have been the
sanctuary of the mar-
tyred dead.

Chapter 13

A Reporter at Large:
A Little Journey
To Mackinaw

by John Moore

John Moore, professor emeritus, the University of Montana, is a Michigan native and continues to be a permanent summer resident on Wawatam Beach after first coming here in 1919. He is a poet and novelist with both academic honors and publishing credits.

It used to begin this way. When hay-fever summer came, August fifteenth always, we got out the big trunk, and my dog stayed close and knew what was in the air, and I sneezed more than I had to. The train was a night train, leaving Kalamazoo about ten-thirty, whistling once after it stopped for the north yards, gathering speed through the celery marshes where out the window the lights grew fewer and smaller and the smell of the marshes died out and the cinders sifted in and that sharp soft coal engine smell wrapped around me and I thought of the dog up ahead in the baggage car, the muzzle tied to her collar (only if the hard-boiled baggage man was on, she would have to wear the thing, something she despised from the bottom of her heart). And then the woods by the river, dark of course, though I knew they were there. Cooper's Glen (For James Fenimore, who was thought once to have communed with something or other in those beeches and maples), where the dutchmen's breeches and trilium and mayflowers grew before the gravel company bit into the hills and only stones and steam shovels remained; then Plainwell, where I had some cousins, and on beyond, the first hour or so waiting for Grand Rapids, where there was a train shed and the lights came up and there were porters and switch engines and the fine right sense of being still up in the middle of the night, going somewhere. Trains were still trains then and even the Pullman was a thing of only partial privacy, a thing of shared intimacy where the smell of the asafoetida bag someone wore to alleviate the asthma was as sharp and fine a thing as the green curtains swaying as the train wound through the hills north of Grand Rapids and straightened out for the long stretch through all those darkened station houses--Cedar Springs, Sand Lake, Paris, Reed City--all the rest of them, while the whistle moaned and shrieked as only those old steam passenger engine whistles on the Grand Rapids and Indiana Railroad could do it, echoing back from the scrub woodlots and the pine barrens and the sand hills around Cadillac, where the engine changed and a new crew came on. I was always, I think, awake there and looking out of the raised crack of the shade into the cones of light around the station, hoping to see the little lake beyond, the clump of trees, northern trees, and the band stand, hoping to smell something that was north too.

Beyond Cadillac was the north then, the hills where the trees stood in scrubby clumps with a few forgotten white pines rising up grandly on the ridges. And the lakes with the summer resorts and the fishing, the sleepy cars waiting, three men getting off with their creels and tackle boxes and carefully wrapped fly rods. They'd be on Fife Lake in the morning, watching the red sun clear the marshes and hoping for the bass that waited along the lily pads in the far-off coves. But I slept some of the time, not wanting to, wanting always to hold both at once, the awful hurry to be there, the awful pain at that land slipping by in the darkness where all that it was lay hidden and waiting.

Really I was waiting for Petoskey, where the train found at last the big water and where it was already light, pale and promising heat later in the day. And the dining car waiter would come through somewhere before then, somewhere around Walloon Lake with the first call for breakfast, and already there were people robed and sleepy weaving down the green corridor to the rooms at the end of the car. I could dress in something under three minutes then, even in an upper berth, moving eelike into my pants, waiting until later to tie my shoes. Then I could watch. Often it was going down Boyne Hill (the Valley of the Boyne--and it was years before I knew of the other Boyne and the blood and all) when I looked out into that fresh mist of sunrise, the caught and held leaves of the maples, the thrust of the cedars as we wound along the stream and the low marshes where the night fog rose and undulated and revealed once and once only the dark waters roiling around the bends where the cattails grew and a lone crow rose and flopped in the heavy air. Those were long miles down that stream, since beyond, through a rift in the hills, lay Petoskey and the waters of Little Traverse Bay, and that was the real beginning, the real north. There were old lumber mills first, their scalloped dead chimneys rusting away, their roofs rotted in; and rows of old company houses, and then the first of the streets where the crossing bells dinged higher and higher and then lower and lower as we passed, slowing now, the station just ahead.

And then the Bay. Just beyond the station and the highway, down the long sharp fall of the shore, it waited. (I always figured it was waiting for me--no one else ever saw that bay, no one.) And the sun, somewhere behind the hills to the east, would catch those far waters and there would be wind out there and white caps and that marching fresh coolness of water coming in, washing away the night in its coming, filling the whole bay with blue and light and the sense and deep feel in the stomach that no one had ever been here before; it was untouched, untouchable. (We move to water always, the deepest urge we have.)

Surely there must have been mornings when the sun failed to cut the fog, mornings when rain streamed down the windows and drove the train smut to the window sills in little dirty puddles and far off the hills above Harbor Springs were gone in the greyness and no bay at all was there, only the grey vacancy and the drip of water from the long overhangs of the station and the hiss of steam as the engine panted and throbbed, and the old high taxicabs hissed up and stopped, their brakes squealing and their tires making lighter marks on the black slick station platform. Surely this was so. I can't remember it, though; I don't want to remember it, of course. Blue is the color of memory and all the suns always rise and the wind comes fresh from the northwest in that north country and the smell of balsam is everywhere.

Thirty-seven miles to Mackinaw. The train, one lost summer, made the side run around the bay to Harbor Springs, and I hated it, all that time wasted, all that sweep of bay to be covered and the stops made where the fashionable hotels were. But Harbor Springs was worth it--that finest of bays and deepwater harbors in all that land. A New England kind of town with towers and white paint and sailboats held to their shadows as they rode at anchor in that greenwater. I looked, of course, and then had breakfast, for the folks were up by then. I never figured then how parents could sleep so late (seven o'clock) and have those most wonderful of breakfasts in the diner, and all so matter-of-fact. Where, I wonder, is the oatmeal so creamy or the sugar so near being powdered or the cream so much or so thick as on those diners when I was a boy? What have they done to them?

North of Petoskey the land rises and the railroad winds through the hills, along the shores of Crooked Lake where the station was white in those days and gingerbread about the deep overhangs and set in the greenest of grass plots where the petunias bled in the morning sunlight. But I was in a hurry then and the

train dragged, gained speed, slowed for the little towns, Alanson, Pellston, Levering, the flat center part of the Peninsula coming toward its final and unbelievable end at Mackinaw. This is cut-over land now, where the aspens grow and the soft woods take over and the scrawny fields lie all summer in mullein and milkweed and the old apple orchards gnarl up and die slowly. Then the woods close in and open out and it's Carp Lake, the last stop before Mackinaw, the lake glimpsed to the east, flat and still in the morning, the rowboats fixed there beyond the hotel piers, all headed the way the wind comes, all waiting on that glassy water.

Those last six miles were the best and the worst, full of the long sitting with the bags ready and the coat over the plush back of the seat and my eyes watching, ticking off the landmarks--the dune to the west that showed for but a second over the trees, marking French Farm Lake, the sandy ruts of the road westward that died in the deep aspens near an old clearing where the blackberries were thick and brambly in September. And, at last, the slow fall of the tracks cutting down the last glacial lake level to the flat where, with the suddenness of a dream, the train swung the wide curve into the first siding and there ahead was the wedge of lake and the old depot beside the row of poplars. I was in the vestibule then, of course, smelling the rich soot of the engine and the sharp metal-cutting smell of the brakes grabbing the wheels, and over all the remembered early morning freshness that comes now but once in a great while--the water smell unlike the salt oceans, compounded of sand and bunker coal and pine woods and the bottoms of old rowboats where the fish worms dry out and wither.

And in that first split moment, before the movement began again, our movements now, not the train's, all of the past summers came together and all the urgency to see it all at once, how the land had changed (and the fear that it had changed and wasn't the old dream anymore) and how the cottage looked and where the water level was this year--everything and everything....

It was wonderful and slow and needful--a whole ritual that my father loved, but which for me was wasted time. Even so, nothing was changed here, not along this one main street that had been here for years, plotted out to be more than it was, the street wide, stores on the north side only and across from it the stretch of grass and old poplars and the depot. The stores were the same, beginning at the corner with the old hotel with the wide porches and the spittoons and the hard chairs where the railroad crew stopped over and already, since it was hay-fever season, the regulars were planted, still with handkerchiefs and red noses and the drawn-out speech of Indiana. Then the drug store, the Liebeck's, then the hardware, then the gap where the old theatre had been (it burned down when I was about seven or so), then a bar, a restaurant where one summer the Greyhound buses stopped and became a part of the town, then a gift shop and another grocery, and the end of the street. At this end, the east end, was the old marker, a stone pile with a bronze plaque, that marked the end of the old Dixie Highway--Miami to Mackinaw. And beyond, the water reached eastward, fading far off to the green line of Bois Blanc Island and the open waters of Lake Huron.

No, nothing had changed the town. I checked off that in my mind, as though I were some inspector-general or other, full of the needful accounting of this place which I possessed as much as it possessed me.

We went westward, down the main street, beyond the garages, the isolated gift shops, the scattering of old houses, and the roundhouse where already our engine had been put away and was smoking easily through the square chimney on the roof. Central Avenue, they called this street (part of an older dream), and on west it was in fact an ungrown boulevard, with the weeds and thistles marking the parkway in the center and the right hand part of the road a sand rut. We followed the other one, rutty too and dusty even this early in the morning. Always as I remember it that road was dry, the hard fine limestone covering white with dust, the later blooms of asters and goldenrod along the edges dusted and pale. But north behind the trees was the place, through that cover of pines and scrub cedars and spruce and aspen where the paths were and where all the dreams lurked. We turned that way at last, down a road that tunnelled toward the single square of bright water, down by the road to the Inn, turning west again along the little road behind the cottages, the Bullock's, the Robert's, the Wexler's, the English's--and ours at last, where the road curved and a yellow pine stood tall and waiting, almost in the way.

That's the way it was, the getting there, the fine fuss and the waiting, the ride that was all rides I ever wanted or had, so it seemed then. Maybe the train did it, though coming now in June with an even greater freshness still on the whole land and water, sneaking into town unannounced by the brave blowing of the train whistle, unbothered by the trunks and the dog on the leash and the bags and suitcases and picnic basket of leftovers from the icebox at home--this was somehow different, less important. Even so, coming in from the south on the highway, I remember where the rise is and how the view suddenly opens and there it all is, the smoke of the ferries at the State Dock, the spire of the radio mast by the old lighthouse, the water, looking infinitely narrow and like a lake you could swim across, before you slope down to the reality of it. That's good, too. But I think the train is better.

Or was. For now the trains are all gone, save for a few lost freights that roll into Mackinaw at night, pulled by a noisy deisel switcher, reeking of oil smoke and the scum that brings to everything.

It was surely better long ago, when my father slipped the dollar to Johnny and his old Maxwell trembled and coughed under the yellow pine. I ran around the cottage through the rough dried grasses of August, the dog ahead of me, to find the old spring house on our beach and the magic water of the Straits lying there waiting with my whole magic summer ahead of me.

The dog was all tail and body like a snake filled with gladness, the leather muzzle hanging awkwardly on her collar, the leash tight and bothersome. The trunk would wait on Johnny's truck and come down later, but we got in Johnny's old Maxwell taxi and pulled away, while I tried to look every way at once. East the railroad went on, straight to the end of the pier where the *Chief Wa-wa-tam* waited for the North Shore cars, which she would ferry across the Straits to St. Ignace. And on the other side of the pier the old *Algomah* rose high and white in the new season's paint, her black thin stack mounting even higher and rolling out the smoke rich and wonderful. She went to the Island; and before we left the station our train had gone on out the pier and the people, rich ones mostly, going to the Island, were going aboard, their golf bags and softly tanned luggage following. But that was another world and mine lay in the waters beyond and around, in the town that lay north of the depot, where we went now, stopping for the groceries at Liebeck's, stopping at the post office in case there was mail already, stopping at the drug store next to Liebeck's to leave word for the woman at the phone exchange that we were there and that we would want ice delivered (she got the word to the fish house where the ice was and George would pass the word on and the ice would come.)

Chapter 14

The Depths of The Straits

Straits Divers Locate Mystery Ship, Schooner

Petoskey News-Review, July 1967

Dick Campbell and Fred Leete III, history diving enthusiasts from Mackinaw City, have come ashore with positive identification of two more ancient ships.

They were located over last weekend when members of the First USA branch, British Sub Aqua Club were diving in making surveys for the planned August expedition of that organization.

On July 2 they brought ashore the 2,000 pound anchor from the sailing steamboat Fred McBriar. Their further findings last week verified the location and names of the two additional wrecks.

The schooner Northwest has been located in 90 feet of water west of Mackinaw City while the schooner M. Stalker was located in 120 feet of water east of the Straits Bridge. Diving at these depths is greatly limited in respect to the amount of time each diver can spend without danger of the bends.

In the last several days, Leete and Campbell have both required extensive decompression times after diving at depths of the wrecks as long as navy tables permit. They must hold at 30 feet or 10 feet beneath the surface for long periods of time before they can bring their discoveries to the surface.

Among the artifacts recovered from the Northwest have been the captain's pistol, his figured clay pipe and a whiskey bottle. Other artifacts are a cooking stove, special galley pots and pans and English ironstone china. Of particular interest to Leete was the china which was manufactured by the J. and G. Meakin Company of Hanley, England. Leete has also recovered ironstone ware from the W.H. Barnum, the schooner Northwest and the Fred McBriar.

Rare China

The famous English pottery is still in existance having celebrated the 100th birthday in 1951. The company originally went into business to deal with the colonies and tremendous amounts of ironstone china traveled westward with the growing America. He said the historical significance of these finds is tremendous.

Last Friday the officers of the British Sub Aqua Club in the United States were granted a hearing before the Mackinac Island State Park Commission to present their report of the exploritory work done in the Straits of Mackinac over the past six years. They also presented their definite proposals to the commission regarding future work and a recommendation of the establishment of a completely restored ship in a maritime museum at Mackinaw City. The commission is studying these proposals along with the feasibility of accomplishing them.

A.T. Lange flew to Mackinac Island from Indianapolis to assist. Leete in the presentation before the commission.

Research indicates there were more than 1,500 small steamers operating in the Great Lakes in 1890. These vessels averaged 240 tons as compared with the tremendous capacities of modern cargo ships. Many of these early vessels were passenger ships in comparison with less than a handful of passenger ships left on the Great Lakes today. For this reason today somewhere there lies over 1,500 old vessels powered by steam not to mention the thousands which carried sail exclusively.

Of course, many of these vessels were burned or wrecked in shallow waters on reefs and shoals where they were torn apart eventually by wind and waves or demolished by tremendous pressure of ice in the winter. The great value of the wrecks located by the BSAC is that they lie deep enough in the water not to be damaged by ice but they are not too deep to be reached by qualified and well trained divers.

Mystery Solved

George Coffman of Mackinaw City told Leete and Campbell together with Dick Race of Chicago and John Steele of Waukegon, Illinois a tale of a schooner which years ago sailed away from Mackinaw City one night on a light southwesterly breeze and the vessel never reached a port. The following day the crew came ashore near Fly Point, southeast of Mackinaw City with a tale of being rammed by another vessel and sunk.

Because the schooner had laid in at Mackinaw City for several days with no urgency of getting under way and then sailed away at night, there was speculation that the captain and the crew had deliberately scuttled the vessel and sunk it in a deep hole between Mackinaw City and Mackinac Island. Whatever the cause of the sinking, the vessel did not settle into deep water but instead hung on a shoal where its masts could be seen the following day.

The crew of the vessel stayed in Mackinaw City until the evening train arrived, hoping the captain would pay them off so they might depart. However, the captain kept putting the men off until they went to him in a body, demanding their money. They threatened to tell what they knew if they were not paid in time to catch the next train. Somehow, the captain raised the money to pay off the crew and that was the last that was known of them.

81

The name of the vessel was unknown until last Sunday when Leete and Race each brought up to the surface one of the carved wooden name boards from the quarters of the vessel, M. Stalker, and there is still paint in the deeply carved letters. Ornate iron pieces decorated the ends of the nameboards.

Captain Dana Thomas Bowan, author of several books including Shipwrecks of the Great Lakes, Lore of the Lakes and Memories of the Lakes, reported the Stalker was built in Milan, Ohio about 1860.

Vessels built in Milan had to be negotiated through a canal of several miles length to the Huron River and thence into Lake Erie.

Lore Important

As members of the Little Traverse Historical Society, Campbell and Leete are interested pointing out that "these shipwrecks on our doorstep belong to our children and grandchildren as part of Michigan's History.

"As others come and take away the wrecks piece by piece for their own personal profit, they destroy the value of the future and make both recovery and restoration impossible. Efforts are being made to devise some means of guarding some of these interest-ing and historic wrecks so that they may be recovered intact and used in the proposed museum," Leete said.

He said the wrecks can be restored in much the same was as in the Mystic Museum in Connecticut, the USS Constitution in Boston and the USS Constellation in Baltimore.

"A significant maritime museum in this area would draw and hold thousands of summer tourists and also if research facilities are available, scholars would come on a year around basis to study the items in the museum," Leete concluded.

Raise Historic Anchor From 100 Feet
Anchor, Articles for Mackinaw Museum

4-PETOSKEY NEWS-REVIEW, Thursday, July 6, 1967

Part of a dream came true for members of the First U.S.A. Branch of the British Sub-Aqua Club Sunday when a large anchor was raised from the wreck of the "Fred McBrier" and placed on shore at Mackinaw City. Weighing almost 2,000 pounds, the $8\frac{1}{2}$ feet long iron anchor is resting now in the waterfront park while permanent display is planned.

Dick Campbell and Fred Leete, III of Mackinaw City have been working on the project of creating a complete marine museum in the area for several years and actively promoting the project in talks before service clubs and the Little Traverse Regional Historical Society. Last year a ten day expedition of the British Sub-Awua Club in the Straits area was highly successful in detailed exploration of another wreck believed to be the "Minneapolis," lying in 120 feet deep water near the Mackinac Straits Bridge. Another 10 day expedition, devoted to recovering historic objects for the people of northern Michigan will be conducted this August by the B. S-A.C.

The British Sub-Awua Club has given the time and equipment and talent of 18 qualified divers to the hoped- for establishment of a proper museum which would preserve the history of this area. Over the past four years the value of the expeditions which have been sponsored by the B. S-A.C. has been placed at approximately $20,000. No member of the organization receives any compensation for his time and services. The equipment alone, not including boats and support gear, is valued at $4,600.

"The job has just begun" says Dick Campbell. "We must find a way to protect these valuable his-toric wrecks from people who want to take them away, piece by piece". One of the anchors from the McBrier was removed last week while we were actively working on it, and it could easily be sold for $500 to a collector or for display at a business place, Campbell said.

This week the officers of the B. S-A.C. have been granted an opportunity to appear before the Mackinac Island State Park Commission at their monthly meeting and explain the results of their work and their proposals for raising and displaying one of the underwater treasures of Emmet county.

Leete reminded people that "raising 2,000 pounds (a ton) of dead weight from over 100 feet in open water is a dangerous procedure and should not be attempted by amateurs! Even the diving to depths of 100 feet is not advisable without thorough training, practice, and safety procedures," he warned.

Fred praised the help of John Steele, Waukeegan, Ill. and Dean Deliyanides of Mackinaw City and Grand Rapids. "Dean drove out the shackle pin when we removed the huge anchor from its chain-down at the 100 feet depth-and when he gave the last blow the chain literally jumped backwards about three feet and could have seriously injured an in-experienced diver!"

It took two great lifting tanks to raise the anchor. "It was a beautiful sight when it rose to the surface", said Campbell. But it took about six hours to slowly tow the rig into Mackinaw City from the location nine miles west of the Bridge.

Jack Paquet donated the ser-vices of his large wrecker truck to raise the anchor from the wat-er at the city dock, and with the guidance of City Superintendent George Parker it was placed in the waterfront park.

Another diver who has aided materially in the historical work is Dick Race of Chicago, Illinois. Dick's boat Neptune and John Steele's Lake Diver are equipped with sophisticated wreck locating equipment-electronic machinery similar to Navy sonar gear. With this, it is possible to search large areas around the surface search ship as well as the bottom directly under the ship.

Mackinaw City Diver to Get Coveted Award 1973

MACKINAW CITY – Richard A. Campbell of Mackinaw City has received notice from the London Headquarters of the British Sub-aqua Club that he has been promoted to first class diver.

This is the highest rating in the world-wide organization, and he thus becomes only the second American in history to receive the coveted award.

To achieve the award, Campbell spent several years in lower class diving and in the study of various diving courses, such as life saving, diving theory, underwater safety procedures, and physiology of diving under all conditions. Examinations were given in each class graded by a team of English experts.

Fred Leete, III, of Mackinaw City and Indianapolis, is the only other American to have received the award, which is given only once a year.

Campbell is employed by the Mackinac Bridge Authority in inspection and maintenance of the underwater portions of the bridge. He will be officially awarded the distinction at the Fifth Conference on Underwater Education to be held in Toronto on September 7-9 of this year.

MACKINAW CITY - Proud divers show the giant anchor and other findings brought from 100 feet of water for a planned museum here. From left: Fred Leete III, John Steele, Dick Campbell, Dick Race.

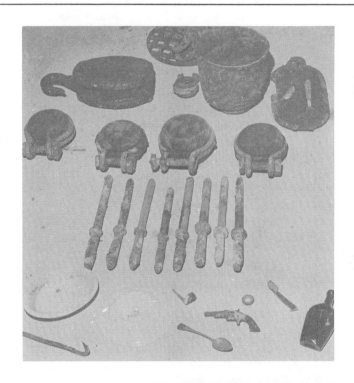

Articles recovered from shipwrecks of the Straits

"McBrier", "Stalker", "Northwest", "Minneapolis" and "Barnum."

Chapter 15

Chris Schneider
And His Park

by Judy Ranville

When Edgar Conkling planned and surveyed Mackinaw City, he saw the need of a place for recreation and designed an area for a park. The following is a quote from his publication, titled *Mackinaw City*, dated 1857. "The Park now laid off, embraces the ground of Old "Fort Michilimackinac", sacred in its history of the country. These grounds, now in their natural condition, are unequalled for beauty of surface, location, scenery, soil, trees, etc., by any Park in any city in this country; and when the skillful hand of the horticulturist has marked its outline and threaded it with avenues and footpaths, pruned its trees and carpeted its surface with green, it will present the very perfection of all that constitutes a Park delightful."

In 1904 the city turned control of the park to the State of Michigan, and it thus became Michilimackinac State Park. Mr. John Stimpson was named the first park caretaker, and he remained at that post until 1921, when Christian Schneider came and began his duty in guiding the long range development of the park.

At that time there was just a one-lane cinder road to the lake at the foot of County Line Road, now Nicolet Street. There was a flag pole, a few cement benches and picnic tables and a large cannon near the entrance. Later an outdoor kitchen was built and the picnickers and campers both cooked there. It had a roof, but no sides--a long table and benches and a large stone stove and later a very large restaurant-style wood-fired cook stove.

Later the Pavillion was built, and the townfolk as well as the campers enjoyed dances and parties there. The Hayfever Association also held their meetings there.

With the coming of the Bridge, the Pavillion was moved and made into a park residence, presently the home of Mr. and Mrs. Reynold Schneider.

The first park entrance was made of metal, but when cars became more numerous it had to be taken down because it wasn't strong enough to take being backed into so often! It was replaced with a massive stone arch--the pride and joy of Chris Schneider. It was topped by a large painted Indian.

The park street was paved around 1928-29 and the registration office was built in 1930. To the left of the entrance was a bandstand and restroom buildings.

There was no limit on the length of time you could stay in the park, and at first 200 camps a year was a busy year. Later as many as 200 camps per day were registered--no one was turned away; they were given a corner somewhere to pitch their tent.

The first trailers to come into the park were homemade, and people called them boxcars. There were also trailers called covered wagons that had the door in the back end. The first manufactured trailer was brought into the park by a man named Tony Wagner, and it was quite a curiosity; many came to look at it.

Another attraction in the park was the zoo. The animals were all locally collected. There were black bears--Maggie and Jiggs, owls, raccoon, bobcats and fox. One fox was so tame that he followed the park employees around like a dog and rode in the trucks with them. Maggie and Jiggs were tame enough to be let out of their cages on chains and didn't bother the men when they cleaned their cages.

When the Bridge was under construction, the increased noise and activity made the animals restless and they had to be taken away. Maggie and Jiggs were 25 and 30 years old and were turned over to the DNR, and what happened to them is unknown. Many of the young folk in town grew up being friends of Maggie and Jiggs, and those two old black bears were missed.

The Park Manager, Christian Schneider, was a very unusual man--he was a friend to each of his campers and he never forgot a face or a name. If you camped here one year and came back two years later, he knew you by name. People liked this personal touch.

Chris Schneider was born in Cross Village, the son of Dr. and Mrs. Christian Schneider, in 1886. Dr. Schneider was a typical country doctor who often was paid for a house call in butter, milk or eggs.

Chris grew up in Cross Village and married the local school teacher in 1912. Chris and Emma had one son, Reynolds, who followed his father's footsteps in park management.

Chris was a friend to everyone--a good listener--and no one will ever know those he befriended. People who stayed in "his" park came back every time they were near to see him.

Having grown up in Cross Village, Chris learned to speak the Indian language and knew hundreds of Indian legends and tales and always had a ready audience to listen to them.

When the Memorial Day Pageant had its beginning in 1934, Chris was Park Manager and worked very closely with Roger Andrews, then chairman of the MISP Commission in planning the program. The replica of old Fort Michilimackinac had been constructed by the W.P.A. as a work program, and the townfolk wanted to dedicate it.

People lent their cars, and they were driven to Cross Village to transport real Indians to Mackinaw. It took three days to bring them all in. They set up their camps inside the Fort and entertained the onlookers with dancing, basket making, stories and just parading in their native costumes.

Chief Thundercloud was very impressive in ceremonial dress complete with headfeathers. In late afternoon before the "re-enactment" was to take place, the sky filled with clouds and it looked as if rain would ruin the next day's program. In the conversation on the possibility, Chris spoke to the Chief in Indian, and he answered, "Me fix it."

He was smoking a large cigar, so he puffed it, blew the smoke skyward, waved it in the air, danced a little, buried the cigar ashes in the ground and repeated this act a few times, and as if by magic the clouds rolled away and the sun came out--the threat of rain had vanished. Whether this was merely a coincidence or not, Chief Thundercloud's audience was enthralled and no one could have convinced them that he didn't have a supernatural power bestowed on him by the "Rain God".

With the weather in good hands, the parade started the next day at the State Dock, and the soldiers, resplendent in their red coats, and the trappers in buckskin, marched with their flags and muskets to the Fort.

Governor and Mrs. Comstock were here and rode in the parade.

During the "attack" put on by the soldiers and Indians, Walter Peppler, who was bald, had his head painted red under a wig, and he was to get scalped. The attacker had had a little fire water prior to the program and somehow in the excitement had mislaid his soft rubber tomahawk and hit Walt with a real stone club. Walt collapsed and no one knew what had happened to him. He was hauled in and had a knot on his head about the size of an egg. It was quite a realistic show, and Walter thought so, too!

One British soldier had also shared the "spirits" and somehow had gotten a scratch on his face that bled a little. He was sprawled out under a tree, and when people came by and saw him they thought he had been killed for sure and some women fainted.

It was quite a day--fun for many--and interest in the Fort was created, but as the Depression progressed, it dwindled until the present Fort was built under a new program.

Mrs. Emma Schneider who for 13 years worked in the Mackinac Island information booth in Mackinaw City.

Chris Schneider - a remarkable man. With his passing in December, 1952, much knowledge of Indian lore was lost.

Michilimackinac State Park, Mackinaw City, Mich.

Michilimackinac State Park, Mackinaw City, Mich.

CANNON IN CITY PARK, MACKINAW CITY, MICH.

225 Year Old Map of Mackinaw City Fort Located

Cheboygan Tribune

LANSING-- A 225 year-old map is being called "the greatest find of the year" by historians and archaeologists at Fort Michilimackinac.

For 15 years, historians at the fort, located in Mackinaw City, have been searching for a French map of the area.

Recently, a visiting Canadian historian, George Ingram, showed Dr. David Armour, Assistant Superintendent of the Mackinac Island State Park Commission, a copy of a hand-drawn map which had not been identified but which he thought could be of Michilimackinac.

Dr. Armour recognized it immediately as being of the fort area. The fort was smaller than later maps but the basic shape was correct.

The clincher was the names on houses in the fort. Langlade, Amiot, Ains, Blondeau and Chevalier were Michilimackinac residents whose births, marriages and burials are recorded in the parish register on Mackinac Island. Now, for the first time, it is possible to tell where they lived within the fort.

The Church, Jesuits' house, Blacksmith Shop and other places including the Powder Magazine, which park archaeologist Dr. Lyle M. Stone is excavating this summer, are clearly marked.

Outside the fort the stables of Monsieur Langlade, several bake ovens and an ice house are indicated.

The original of the map is in the Public Archives of Canada in Ottawa. It is filed in the collection of Michel Chartier, Marquis de Lotbinier, a French engineer who made a journey to Michilimackinac in 1749 and undoubtedly drew the map at that time.

A copy of the map is now on display for visitors to the fort.

In recent years, reconstruction of Fort Michilimackinac was based on three English maps from the 1760's and a meticulous archaeological program.

Prior to British occupancy the French founded the fort as a major fur trading post in 1715 and held it until 1760 when the English conquered Canada.

The fort is being reconstructed by the Mackinac Island State Park Commission to the period of the American Revolution, 1776.

Upon his return to Canada historian Ingram instructed the archivist to write "Michilimackinac" on the folder. The Public Archives of Canada have identified their mysterious map and Michigan has its "find of the year."

* * *

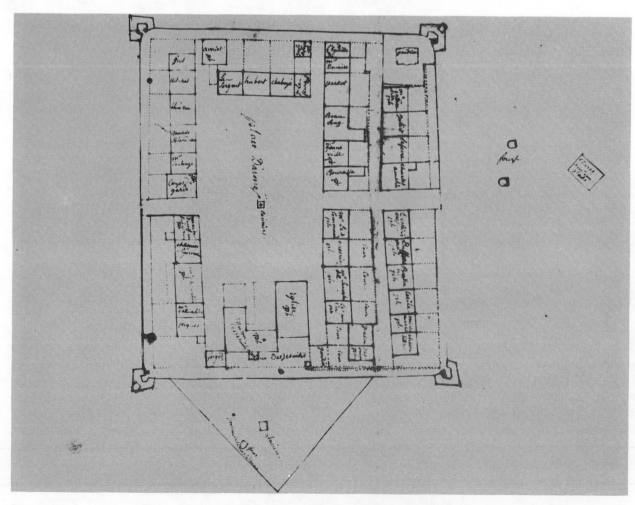

Orders For
Fort Michilimackinac -
July 4, 1776

Collections of the State Historical Society
of Wisconsin, Vol. 18

1776: WESTERN INDIANS REINFORCE CARLETON

(Letter from Maj. A. S. De Peyster to Charles Langlade; reprinted from De Peyster, *Miscellanies*, p. lxix.)

To Monsieur Langlade   Orders
MONSIEUR—You will take command of the savages of this post that consist of People of several nations and some Canadian volunteers, with these you will undertake your journey in order to join the superintendent of Indian affairs in the neighborhood of Montreal or the officer that commands the troops of the King in that Quarter from whom you will receive your orders.72

You will do your best to harass the Rebels wherever you may encounter them, and in all matters you will conduct yourself with your customary prudence and Humanity.73

[DE PEYSTER]

AT MICHILIMAQUENAC, July 4, 1776.

72 News of the American revolt must have reached Mackinac in 1775, by way of Montreal and Detroit. Henry Hamilton, who came up from Canada in the autumn of 1775, as lieutenant-governor of the latter place, had already seen Montreal in the hands of the American troops, and Sir Guy Carleton, the British governor, escaping to Quebec; see *Mich. Pion. and Hist. Colls.*, x, p. 267. He would seem to have brought orders for Indian auxiliaries to be sent to Carleton in the spring. But by that time, affairs had changed in Canada. Montgomery had fallen before Quebec; Arnold's ineffectual siege had been raised by the coming of a large force of British and Hessian troops; the Americans had been defeated at the Cedars (April 19, 1776), and their army had finally evacuated Montreal and retreated toward Lake Champlain. June 25, Carleton wrote De Peyster, countermanding his order for Indian auxiliaries—see *Wis. Hist. Colls.*, xi, p. 174; but it was too late to reverse the order. Before Carleton's note reached Mackinac, Langlade had already (as per this document) received orders to command the reinforcement. A part of the Indians must either have gone in advance, or made a very quick passage, for they were in Montreal by July 19, when they were dismissed with presents and compliments, and orders to be in readiness for the next season's campaign; see *Mich. Pion. and Hist. Colls.*, x, pp. 262, 263.

The superintendent of Indian affairs at that time was Guy Johnson, Sir William's nephew and son-in-law; the former's chief deputy way Daniel Claus, his brother-in-law. They held numerous councils with the tribesmen in 1775 and 1776, and induced many to take the warpath against the Americans.—Ed.

73 Langlade probably joined Carleton at Isle aux Noix, and although ill during the summer (*Wis. Hist. Colls.*, viii, p. 406), performed his duties with satisfaction to the commander-in-chief; see Carleton's testimonial in *Id.*, xii, pp. 39-41. Carleton's letters at this date (Oct. 6, 1776) were written just before the naval battle of Valcour Island, on Lake Champlain. The lateness of the season made it necessary that Langlade should return to Mackinac before that engagement. He went via Niagara and the lakes, as per next document.—Ed.

Fort Museum Has
LaCrosse Stick Used In
Pontiac Massacre, 1763

from the
Mackinac Island News
July 26, 1941

One of the most interesting relics in the free museum on Old Fort Mackinac, and truly the only one of its kind in the world, is a la crosse stick used in the game to gain entrance into old Fort Michilimackinac and massacre the British garrison in 1763.

The history of this 178-year-old stick is authentic. It was handed down by Indians from one generation to another as a souvenir of the bloody victory until nearly 60 years ago, when an aged Indian gave it to Tony Eccous, then a boy living in a settlement near Cross Village, a short distance from Mackinaw City. The old Indian, who was very fond of the little white boy, one day said to him, "I give you something to remember." He then took the la crosse stick hanging on the wall and presented it to him.

While holding it in his hand he told the story of the massacre, occasionally striking it through the air to illustrate how the game was played. Then he handed it to the boy, telling him to always keep it, as it had been in his family "a long, long time."

Eccous became caretaker of one of the large summer estates on Mackinac Island. In

1934, when the ter-centennial of Jean Nicolet's landing on the Island was celebrated, the Mackinac Ialand State Park Commission also promoted an elaborate Historical Fair in Old Fort Mackinac. Thousands of dollars worth of relics were loaned for the occasion, some presented to the Commission for permanent keeping in the Fort Museum.

Shortly after the opening of the Mackinac Historical Fair, Eccous came up to the fort with the la crosse stick. He told its story and said he would like to give it to the Commission for display in the Fort Museum, where visitors could see it and ponder its thrilling history.

The type of stick shows its antiquity, also that la crosse players in those days must have been highly expert with its use. It is about four feet long, made of hickory, and the loop is only six by four inches whereas the modern la crosse stick is five feet long, the loop is eight to ten inches wide and 18 inches long. Into the edges of the loop is strung a bagnet, loose enough to hold a ball in the crotch where the base of the loop joins the stick.

The ball must be carried in the net while the player runs with it or hurls it from the net to another player on his team, who must catch it in his net, and so on until there is a favorable opportunity to "shoot goal". The ball may be intercepted by a player on the opposite side by catching it in his net, and passing it on to his teammates. The ball also may be knocked out of the net by an opposing player with his stick.

The trick of catching the ball in a modern net 10 by 18 inches is difficult. To catch a ball in midair in a little loop only four by six inches required greater skill and a keener eye. Later la crosse sticks used by Indians show they gradually increased the size of the loop. When it became a popular game among white men, particularly in Canada, the loop was increased to its present size.

It is not only a highly skilled game but very fast and requires lithe athletes, fleet of foot. It is also very rough, many injuries being inflicted in the course of a game by accidental (?) blows from the heavy hickory sticks and collisions in scrimmages.

It was a great day of celebration in Mackinaw. The battle was so real in appearance that some women in the audience fainted. Local men were the actors and those identifiable are:

Front row: Everett Desy, Howard Wehner, Clark Trumbull, Jack Shields, Otis Smith.

Second row: Unknown, Fred Wallin, Fred Doner, George Carlton, Unknown, Unknown, Charles McVey, Unknown, Roy Darling.

Top Row: Bob Pierce, Unknown, Unknown, Guy Wolford, (?) Cosens, Harold Nau, Unknown, Jim Desy, Frank LaWay with flag.

First pageant, 1934.

ANNUAL

Re-enactment PONTIAC Massacre

OF 1763

at

OLD FORT MICHILIMACKINAC

MACKINAW CITY,

MICHIGAN

JUNE 30th, 1934

Large Cast of Real Indians in Their Native Regalia Protraying in Six Acts. British Possession of Fort, Conspiracy of Pontiac, Gathering of Indians, Game of Bagattawa, Victory Dance and Grand Victory Feast. Under Direction of Indian Missionary Fr. Aubert.

A Realistic Portrayal of this Historic Event, Played by the Native Indians as only they can play it. Be sure to see— Massacre of the Red Coated Haughty British Garrison.

Distinguished Guests To Be Present.

Gov. W. A. Comstock, Sec. State, F. D. Fitzgerald, Cong. P. M. Brown

and Other State and National Officials.

Program of Events of the Day

Col. JOHN G. EMERY - Marshal of the Day

Flag Tournament	9:00 A. M.
AT MACKINAW HEADLAND GOLF COURSE	
Ball Game	10:00 A. M.
WILDERNESS CCC Camp vs MACKINAW CUBS	
Band Concert, Reception for Gov. Comstock and other Officials	11:00 A. M.
AT HOTEL HOWSON	
Parade Starting at Intersection of U S 23 and U S 31	1:00 P.M.
OTHER CITIES AND RESORTS OF MACKINAW REGION WILL BE REPRESENTED.	
Re-Enactment of Pontiac Massacre . . .	2:30 P. M.
BY LARGE CAST OF NATIVE INDIANS AT OLD FORT MICHILIMACKINAC	
Boat Races and Other Sports at State Dock . . .	5:00 P. M.
Band Concert - Street Dancing, Cheboygan Band . .	7:30 P. M.
Boxing Matches at City Park . . .	9:00 P. M.
C C C CAMPS - WILDERNESS PARK - WOLVERINE - CHEBOYGAN	
Dancing at Michilimackinac State Park Pavilion .	9:30 P. M.
MUSIC BY ORCHESTRA OF CHARLEVOIX	

CELEBRATION

Mackinaw City, July 1st, 1930

PROGRAM

Opening of Golf Course, Municipal Airport, Howson Hotel, Sid's Place, and Lake Huron Beach Camp.

1:15 p.m.   Michilimackinac State Park, speaking by the Hon. Fred R. Ming, Representative; and Mr. Frank Kenyon, Supt. of Michilimackinac and Mackinac Island State Parks.

1:45 p.m.   Sid's Place—Howson Hotel—Lake Huron Beach Camp, where we will get acquainted with and look over the properties of the enterprising owners who believe in our town. Rev. Vern W. Butler, Speaker.

2:30 p.m.   Golf Course dedication.   Where fitting ceremonies will be held commemorating this most important addition to Mackinaw City.   Dr. A. C. Tiffany, Speaker.

3:30 p.m.   Municipal Air Port Dedication.   We should all feel a pride in this new commercial enterprise. Prosecuting Attorney Ward I. Waller, Speaker.

4:00 p.m.   Ball Game at new ball park on Central Avenue. Mackinaw vs. Cheboygan.

6:30 p.m.   Banquet at Wa-Wa-Tam Inn on the beach.

9:00 p.m.   Dance at State Park Pavilion.

A splendid band has been secured, which will start at the town hall at 1:00 p.m. and march to the State Park and furnish music for the afternoon.   Let all the Citizens and Visitors of Mackinaw turn out in full force, thereby showing our appreciation to the men who are building up our town and making this a more worth-while place to live in.

CHAMBER OF COMMERCE.

BOOST   YOUR   HOME   TOWN

Official Program

- Opening Old -

Fort Michilimackinac Stockade

Mackinaw City -- July 1st, 1933

**BAND CONCERTS During the Day by
BOYS MILITARY BAND OF MENOMINEE,
and CHEBOYGAN CITY BAND**

9:00 A. M. Flag Tournament, Mackinaw Headland Golf Club.

10:00 A. M. Base Ball game, Cheboygan Macks vs the Mackinaw Hill Billies.

11:00 A. M. Band Concert, Cheboygan Band, Ball grounds

12:00 to 1:00 P. M. Lunch Hour.

1:30 P. M. Historical Parade to Michilimackinac State Park.

2:00 P. M. Opening Ceremonies of Old Fort Michilimackinac at Band Stand in State Park.

Speaking by GOV. COMSTOCK, Attorney General O'Brien, Hon. Prentiss M. Brown, Father Paul, Hon. S. J. Smith, Capt. C. A. Roberts, Dr. J. T. Craddock, President Board of Commerce.

3:00 P. M. Indian Pageant, re-enactment of Massacre of 1763 at Stockade.

4:00 P. M. Base Ball game, American Legion Junior teams of East Jordan and St. Ignace.

5:00 P. M. Band Concert, Boys Military Band of Menominee at State Dock.

6:00 to 7:30 P. M. Dinner Hour.

8:00 P. M. Band Concert and Street Dance. Boys Military Band of Menominee.

CASE OF RAIN, PROGRAM WILL BE HELD JULY 2nd.

Early entrance to Michilimackinac State Park as it looked when Chris Schneider came to Mackinaw.

94

Fort Michilimackinac at the time of the 1934 "Re-enactment" pageant.

Relic Hunting
at the
Old Fort.
Mackinaw City,
Michigan

Bear Pen
"Maggie", or is it
"Jigs"?

Chapter 17

Dagwell Marine
Reporting Station

Nancy Dagwell Campbell

The traditional tooting of steamer whistles in the Straits of Mackinac have disappeared. Cottagers and travelers across the Straits heard for years a sort of Morse Code from freighter whistles as they passed Mackinaw City. These seemingly unscheduled and haphazard sounds, accompanied by puffs of white steam drifting across the Straits, had a purpose; they were identifying themselves to the Marine Reporting Station. In 1960, after 62 years of service, the Dagwell Marine Reporting Station closed, and another phase of Great Lakes shipping ended.

In 1893, Charles T. Dagwell established a weather reporting station on the Straits of Mackinac and five years later established the Marine Reporting Service which operated until the closing of the shipping season in December 1959. From 1932 until it closed, the station was operated by his son, Elton C. Dagwell.

The work of the station, which operated 24 hours a day, consisted of furnishing reports of vessel passages through the Straits of Mackinac to newspapers and various vessel owners and agents. Reports of vessel passages to the owners gave name of vessel, direction of passage and weather conditions at time of passage. Steamship companies thus knew when their boats could be expected to reach Great Lakes ports. These lists not only were important to marine officers, but were read avidly by sailors' families, who liked to keep in touch with their men.

Before the establishment of a signal code for identification of ships, Charles Dagwell went out in a small boat to meet all ships and identify them. He also delivered mail, groceries and change of shipping orders to the passing ships. In rough weather, this was often an unpleasant ordeal. The small boats used by Charles Dagwell were the now famous Mackinaw boats, which he not only sailed but also built in a workshop next to his station.

After identifying the vessel, the passage was then relayed to the owner by Postal Telegraph or Western Union. In 1910, ship companies devised a code system which consisted of long and short blasts of the ship whistle. Each steamer was assigned its own code letters preceded by the code letters of the company which owned her. For example, the company fleet code for Boland & Cornelius was one long, one short, one long and one short blasts. If this was followed by three short blasts, this would signify that the vessel was the *Adam E. Cornelius* of that fleet. When atmospheric conditions made the whistles hard to hear, a 46 inch telescope was used to identify the ship's name and the company was identified by the company insignia on the smokestack.

Vessel passages were furnished daily to ten newspapers and 38 companies or vessel agents employed this service. Vessel owners and newspapers receiving these reports were located in New York City, Buffalo, New York, Cleveland, Ohio, Detroit, Michigan, Chicago, Illinois, Fort William and Toronto, Ontario. In addition to the marine work, the station acted as weather observer for the United States Weather Bureau. A 75 foot weather tower stands next to the marine station and weather flags are displayed from it. There is also an anemometer which records wind speeds. This weather service is still active today, and furnishes reports every six hours to the Weather Bureau in Sault Ste. Marie, Michigan and lake ice reports, during late winter, to the Detroit office of the Weather Bureau.

This business was unique as it was a family enterprise and supported two generations of the Dagwell family. The Marine Station, along with the railroad, was a major factor in the establishing of the Western Union business in the Mackinaw-Cheboygan area. All reports by the Marine Station were forwarded by Western Union Telegraph. In most cases, reports to owners were within the minimum of ten words, but reports to newspapers consisted of 135 to 160 words per message. Ten newspaper reports were sent daily. Vessel passages through the Straits of Mackinac ranged from 8000 to 10,000 vessels per season of navigation, with the same number of reports sent.

In the early years of the Marine business, the Western Union office in Mackinaw City was open 15 hours a day and employed three operators during the navigation season, but with the Depression and the decline of the railroad, the hours were cut to eight a day and two operators. In the early 1950's, with a further decline in the railroad business, the Mackinac City Western Union office was closed and became an agency office. The Marine Station then had to install a teletype at the station and forward their reports through the Cheboygan and Detroit Western Union offices. After the Marine Station closed in 1960, the Cheboygan Western Union office did not handle enough business to maintain an office and closed and became an agency office.

The Marine Reporting business was an economic factor in this small area and its closing affected several people, but progress was also affecting its usefulness. During World War II and the Korean War, vessel passages were banned from the newspapers; by the middle 1950's, most ships were equipped with ship-to-shore radios and talked directly to their companies, and larger and fewer ships are plying the lakes today. The closing of the Marine Reporting Station marked the end of an era in lake history. An era of providing vital service to fleet owners, marine offices and sailors' families.

EPILOGUE:

This article is an excerpt from a paper written in 1962 for a graduate course at Michigan State University. The weather station run by Elton C. Dagwell closed in 1969. The weather tower and Mackinaw boat mentioned in this article are now on display at the Marine Museum at Michilimackinac State Park at Mackinaw City.

Charles Dagwell - Marine Reporter. Mackinaw City 1898-1927 - in Mackinaw Boat.

Marine Reporting Service Ended by E.C. Dagwell 1960

Elton C. Dagwell declared today that he has "retired" from the marine reporting business which was operated by the Dagwell family at Mackinaw City for the past 61 years

"I am 65 years of age," said Mr. Dagwell. "It is retirement age, and I have decided to retire."

The work of reporting ship passages 24 hours a days has become too much of a chore. The work was divided between him, his wife and his children. The children now are gone or have other interests.

A son Robert is employed by the Mackinac Island Ferry Company. A daughter living in Mackinaw City is Mrs. Richard Campbell. The other children are Mrs. Clara Ecklund of Flint and Mrs. Gerald Erspamer of Livonia.

The Dagwell Marine Reporting station reported ship passages at the Straits of Mackinac to over 30 shipping lines and newspapers.

With retirement of Mr. Dagwell, Mackinaw City is left without a marine reporter. The Cleveland Plaindealer recently appealed to the Cheboygan Chamber of Commerce for aid in locating someone who might be interested in doing this work.

The work involved identifying ships by their whistle signals, according to a code which identifies the ship by line and name. Mr. Dagwell has a huge list of ships and their code blasts. In a years time he would report from 9,000 to 10,000 ship passages.

The marine reporting station was started by his father, Charles T. Dagwell in 1898. When the father died in 1927 his wife continued the business. Elton Dagwell took it over in 1932, and has operated it ever since.

He admits his work is easy by comparison with early years when his father started the business. At that time the marine reported had to go out in a small boat to meet all ships. In rough weather, this was often an unpleasant ordeal.

Mr. Dagwell is supervisor of Mackinaw township. He was chairman of the Board for five years.

Mr. Dagwell said the first vessel to go through last year also made the trip on April 4. That time the ship was the Standard Oil tanker Robert Stewart.

He, Dad Log Straits Weather for 70 Years

August 31, 1968

Weather Bureau Honors E.C. Dagwell

MACKINAW CITY--On Friday, Eldon C. Dagwell, 73, received an award from the U.S. Department of Commerce for 36 years of voluntarily operating a weather reporting station here.

The citation on the award read: "for unexcelled service to marine interests and unusual deligence in reporting timely ice information from Mackinaw City, Michigan."

The weather service here was first begun by Dagwell's father in 1898. Eldon took over in 1932 and has been on the job ever since.

His responsibility is to report wind direction and velocity, cloud cover, visability, and duration and height of seas. In addition, Dagwell displays small craft and storm warnings on a 75-foot tower which the federal government erected in his back yard back in 1908. In the spring, he reports ice conditions along with his regular observations.

Reports are called in four times a day, at six hour intervals, to the U.S. Weather Bureau station at Sault Ste. Marie. Once the U.P. station receives them, they are consolidated with other area reports.

Dagwell operates the weather service from February 15 to December 15 each year. His compensation is $1.60 a day---not the kind of wages to get rich quick on.

Now retired, he once made a living reporting vessel passages through the Straits to ship owners and various newspapers.

Although his wife died in 1959, the long-time weatherman still has four children and 10 grandchildren whom he visits during the winter months and entertains at his Straits home in the summer. Always active in his community, he has served on both the local school board and the city council and is now in his 27th year on the County Board of Supervisors.

August, 1975

E.C. Dagwell Passes Away Yesterday

Mr. Elton C. Dagwell, age 80, of Mackinaw City, former marine reporter and civic leader, died Tuesday at Little Traverse Hospital.

Mr. Dagwell was born February 28, 1895 in Mackinaw City, the son of Charles and Norah Dagwell. He was married to Genevieve Weber of Chelsea, Michigan on February 14, 1917. She preceded him in death in 1959.

Mr. Dagwell worked for the Pennsylvania Railroad until the death of his father at which time he took over the marine reporting business. He held this position and also worked for the U.S. Weather Bureau for 30 years until his retirement in 1960.

Mr. Dagwell was a former member of the Mackinaw City Village Council and served as its president for several years. He was former Mackinaw City Fire Chief, and a member and president of the Mackinaw City School Board. For 26 years he was supervisor of Mackinaw Township and for five years, he served as chairman of the Cheboygan County Board of Supervisors. He was also a former member of the Mackinaw City Lions Club. He had received the John Campanius Holm Award from the United States Department of Commerce for meteorologists. Survivors are three daughters, Mrs. Richard Campbell (Nancy) of Mackinaw City, Mrs. Ray Tollefson (Peggy) of Livonia, Mrs. Clare Eckland (Betty) of Flint, a son, Robert of Westland, Michigan, two sisters, Mrs. Jane Olson and Mrs. Cletus Supinger and a brother Ted all of Midland, twelve grandchildren, and one great-granddaughter.

The family will receive callers this evening at the Nordman Funeral Home from 7 until 9 o'clock, and on Thursday from 2 to 9 p.m. Friday morning the body will be moved to the Church of the Straits at Mackinaw City and will lie in state there from noon until 2 o'clock.

Funeral services will be held at 2 p.m. and Rev. Raymond C. Provost, Jr. will officiate. Interment will be in Lakeview Cemetery in Mackinaw City.

* * *

Elton Dagwell (center) receives award from Norton Strommen (R), state climatologist of East Lansing, and Fred Day, official in charge of the U.S. Weather Bureau at Sault Ste. Marie. (NEWS Photo by Jim Lutzke). Petoskey News-Review.

Chapter 18

Lighthouses of the Straits

Chapter 3 of Lighthouses of the Great Lakes
By Eric J. Campbell, Mackinaw City High School 1974

FORWARD:

The lighthouses of the Straits of Mackinac area are of personal interest to me as my uncle helped to build one of them; my grandfather, John Campbell was the last lighthouse keeper at Old Mackinaw Point; my other grandfather, Elton C. Dagwell was a marine reporter at the Straits, and my father, Richard, lived in several lighthouses for the first twenty years of his life.

Grays Reef Lighthouse, twenty miles west of Mackinaw City, is one of several stations erected in recent years to facilitate the highly specialized traffic of the Great Lakes. It is situated on one of the principal routes from lower Lake Michigan ports to the Straits of Mackinac, and marks a new channel dredged through the shoals at this point. The lighthouse is built upon a stone and concrete filled wood crib sunk below the surface of the lake. Above the crib is a heavy concrete deck from which rises a steel superstructure. In this superstructure is housed the machinery for operating the fog signal and the radio beacon, and the living quarters for the keepers. On top of this is the tower from which the light is displayed. This type of station, standing in deep water, close to the track of vessels, is effective as it offers a definite mark for which vessels can steer directly. This lighthouse replaced one of the last lightships to be maintained by the United States upon the Great Lakes.

From both an engineering and architectural point of view, one of the most noted lighthouses on Lake Michigan is White Shoal, established in 1910. As early as 1878, the Chicago Lumbering Company stationed a water-logged vessel over White Shoals to mark this dangerous reef. The lighthouse was the first fixed structure built on any of the dangerous reefs and shoals which had formerly been marked by lightships. The structure consists of a timber crib, seventy-two feet square and eighteen feet high, resting on a level mattress of gravel on the shoal in twenty feet of water. The concrete deck of the pier supports a conical-shaped tower topped by an aluminum lantern.

This tower contains the crew's living quarters and the machinery and equipment necessary to operate the light.

In 1890, Congress appropriated $5500 for the building of a complete fog signal station at Old Mackinaw Point. Old Mackinaw Point was constructed in 1892 to replace McGulpin's Point Light, which is just west of Mackinaw City. In 1928 electricity was installed and the oil lamp era of lighthouses ended. This occasion was witnessed by the keeper and his family, who were assembled on the lawn to watch the first switch pulled. The lighthouse contained the signal light and living quarters for two families. A separate building contained the fog signal and radio beacon. Old Mackinaw Point Lighthouse was disestablished in 1957 when the value of its service depreciated because of the completion of the Mackinac Bridge. The Lighthouse was replaced by a series of lighted sound buoys and private aids to navigation. The lighthouse and station property were turned over to the State of Michigan for use as a Historical Museum in 1960.

Before "turning the Point" and telling of the Straits Lighthouses in Lake Huron, there are two lighthouses of the Straits which have not been mentioned: one is a private home and the other lies in ruin. McGulpins Point Light was Mackinaw's first lighthouse and is about three miles from the village. It was built in 1869 and the first lighthouse keeper was Thomas Dunn who served from 1869 to 1879 when he was succeeded by James Davenport. This lighthouse was replaced by Old Mackinaw Point Light in 1892 and is now the private home of Mr. and Mrs. Ralph Shaw. They have restored it and kept the structure as it was originally built.

The Waugoshance Light was put in commission in 1856. This lighthouse was situated in an area of many reefs and was a dangerous passage into the Straits area. This lighthouse was put out of commission when the new White Shoals Light was built, about four and a half miles to the west. Waugoshance still stands, although in ruin, as it was used as a bombing target during World War II.

The Round Island Lighthouse was commissioned by the U.S. Government in 1896 and for fifty-two years guided sailors through the Straits of Mackinac and the treacherous Round Island passage. Its first beacon was a white kerosene lamp with a pendulum device that flashed red every twenty seconds. It also contained two foghorns and was manned by a crew of three. In 1924, the lighthouse was furnished with an automatic light. In 1948 a new automatic beacon was built near the Mackinac Island breakwater and the Round Island Light was abandoned. The lighthouse, a three-story brick structure, stands within the boundaries of the Hiawatha National Forest on Round Island's 329 acres and was recently named a national landmark. The structure is slowly crumbling into the Straits, as over the years, wind, ice, waves and vandals have damaged the structure. Efforts by a private group of citizens are now trying to raise funds to preserve this structure.

In Lake Huron stands one of the world's most famous lighthouses. All of the forces of ice, wind and pounding waves have not succeeded in demolishing Spectacle Reef lighthouse. This light is celebrating its 100th birthday this year. An extraordinary feat of engineering and construction made possible the building of this lighthouse. It stands in eleven feet of water on a submerged limestone reef off the eastern end of the Straits of Mackinac. The nearest land is Bois Blanc Island, ten and a half miles away. The engineer-architect was Major D. M. Poe, who was General Sherman's chief engineer on his march through Georgia. Work on the lighthouse began in May 1870, but was not completed until June 1874. The years between yielded only twenty months of work, because the icefields that surround this exposed place prevented work in the winter. The structure, 82 feet high, rises from a man-made island whose main purpose is to protect the tower against direct ice pressures. The first thirty-four feet of the tower are solid granite, each layer of blocks cut so that it locks into the one above and below. Above that height rise five round rooms with diameters of about fourteen feet. The walls are five and a half feet thick. When the keepers returned to the newly completed tower in 1874, ice was piled against it to a height of thirty feet, seven feet above the top of the doorway. They had to cut away the iceberg before they could enter.

There are many more lighthouses on the Great Lakes, each well known and having their own fascinating history. The lighthouse, beacons and buoys of the Great Lakes have saved many a sailor's life since the first light was constructed. But the storms of the inland seas have claimed many lives, despite all the navigational aids that man has been able to devise.

BIBLIOGRAPHY

Adamson, Hans C., *Keepers of the Light*. New York, N.Y.: Greenberg Publishers, 1955.

Beers, J. H., *History of the Great Lakes*, vol. I. Chicago, Ill.: J. H. Beers & Company, 1899.

Hatcher, Harlan, *A Pictorial History of The Great Lakes*. New York, N.Y.: Bonanza Book Co., 1963.

Johnson, Arnold, *The Modern Lighthouse Service*. Washington, D.C.: Government Printing Office, 1890.

Lewiton, Mina, *Lighthouses Of America*. New York, N.Y.: Criterion Books, 1964.

United States Coast Guard, *Historically Famous Lighthouses in the United States*. Washington, D.C.: U.S. Government Printing Office, 1939.

Greys Reef Lighthouse

Old Mackinaw Point, Mackinaw City.

Waugoshance Pointe Lighthouse

John P. Campbell, Last Lighthouse Keeper, Old Mackinaw Point.

Old Mackinaw Point Lighthouse, Mackinaw City.

Chapter 19

McGulpin's Point

The Davenport Family

McGULPIN'S POINT

I don't know who this McGulpin was
to have a point named for him; I only know
his point, where the water goes a fathom deep
six feet off shore.
       And his light house
built in 1868, no longer used; it sits
on top of the bluff in a clearing.
The woods crowd around.
       From the platform
where the light once sat, you can look out
today into a blue distance, water and sky,
or near at hand the tops of beeches
and the pointed tips of firs.
       In this loud silence
the summer holds high court and later
grows regal as the leaves turn and fall.
       This is a place of vast distances
and lonely silences, where even a landsman
can find the far waters waiting
peaceful and always serene.

John E. Moore

McGulpin Point Lighthouse

Term Paper For Extension Class
By Launa Barrett
of Mackinaw City

The "Old Lighthouse" located at McGulpin Point, about two miles west of Mackinaw City, is one of the oldest landmarks still existing in that vicinity. It was built in 1848 even before there was any town at the present site. It is located on a bluff about fifty feet high, overlooking the Straits of Mackinac.

The road to the Old Lighthouse wound through the woods – cedars, spruces, Norway pines and hemlocks standing tall and straight along the roadside -- when suddenly appeared cedar bars and a white picket fence surrounding a big green clearing. In this sun-bright clearing on ten acres of ground, stood the McGulpin Point lighthouse, built of cream-colored brick, with its round tower on the north side toward the water that lay beyond and far below. A long and steep stairway built into the bluff led down into the woods and into the shore where the government rowboat was tied to a small dock.

The interior of the lighthouse was much the same as that of other houses. The living quarters comprised a story and a half with five large rooms on the main floor and three bedrooms and a hall upstairs. The bedrooms were by far the most interesting rooms because they were reached by means of the winding stairs of the tower. The basement was divided into three rooms, two under the living quarters, and one under the tower, which was used as a storeroom for supplies in connection with the keeping of the light.

The tower itself was forty-eight feet high and, being circular, was reached by winding stairs. At the top was the marvelous room where the light was placed, to shine through most powerful lenses out over the Straits and guide the crews of the many ships. At that time such guidance was given by a single large kerosene lamp which was supplied with fuel by means of a tube leading from a near-by storage tank. This storage tank was filled daily from the store room beneath the tower. It was the duty of the keeper's children to make this daily trip up the long winding stairs carrying the pitcher-shaped container filled with kerosene, so the beacon would never cease to shine. The lamp at that time was much different from those of today, for it was stationary and it shone out through the immense lenses which must be cleaned and polished every day so as to not interfere even the least bit with the clearness of the light. The lamp was lighted every night at sunset and threw its welcome rays continually over the surrounding territory until sunrise the following morning.

Thomas P. Dunn was appointed the first keeper of the lighthouse and he, with his family, came from Detroit to take over his duties. The second keeper was a Mr. Louisignau who came from Mackinac Island and the third a man named Bourisaw. Among these three men they diligently cared for the lighthouse and traffic on the Straits for thirty-one years. No records being available, nothing that happened during that period is known. However, the next keeper and his family I have known ever since I could walk. They have been close neighbors of ours for more than thirty-five years and it is from them I have obtained the facts used in this theme.

James, or "Pap" Davenport, as everyone in our town knew him, was an honest, upright citizen of whom any community could be proud. He was a Frenchman and with his wife and nine children moved to the McGulpin Point lighthouse from little Point Au Sable in 1879. They made the trip with all their belongings in a sailboat. At the time they settled in their new home, Mackinaw City was getting the first railroad in its history. The Michigan Central was extending its system to this point in lower Michigan, using a box car for a station.

Many are the stories related by members of the Davenport family concerning life at the Old Lighthouse. For instance, they recall one spring when twenty-seven sailing vessels were all stuck in the ice at one time, directly opposite the lighthouse. Of course, in those days there were no ice cutters to release them, so they had to wait until a shift of wind would move the ice floats and allow them to proceed on their way.

Perhaps the most vivid impression made upon the minds of the children during their life in that locality was when a steamer caught fire as it was traveling through the Straits. This happened several years after their installation on the new job, and by this time steamers were beginning to take the place of the old sailing vessels. Imagine the excitement as well as fear and alarm of the nine children late one afternoon in early December as they spotted a steamer ten miles up the Straits headed full speed for McGulpin Point and on fire! Especially distressing was such a happening when they realized their father had gone to town, and the passing years had brought death to their beloved mother, so they were left alone to take any necessary action. What a job the older children had trying to quiet the younger ones, who were almost frantic with fear when they were scared to death themselves! But they finally succeeded, after a fashion, and were able to begin making preparations for the care of the survivors, should there be any. As the boat drew closer, with the whistle blowing full blast, they could distinguish members of the crew -- a gruesome sight -- literally fighting for their lives, silhouetted against the raging flames. There was little that could be done except pour water dipped from the Straits upon the flames with as much speed as possible and trust to luck. In those days they couldn't use wireless and immediately have boats from the various ports rushing to their assistance. They were strictly on their own and were headed for shore and the nearest available help. It took quite a while for the boat to make it to shore, but it came steadily on with every man on board still at his post. By this time the residents of the town had been attracted by the

spectacle and many of them hastened to the Point to aid in rescue work, if possible, and also out of curiosity. Best of all, for the children alone at the lighthouse, their father had returned and they felt secure once more. As the boat neared the shore, it rammed into the shallow water at full speed and it was up to the local people to carry on. The lifeboats of the crew had already been burned and there was only a single rowboat on shore. Using this, continuous trips were made between the boat and the land, bringing only two men to shore each time. However, this was kept up until the entire crew of seventeen had been brought safely ashore.

Brought safely ashore! The Davenports recall the near-dead condition of these men as they were once more placed on land. Being so late in the fall the water had already begun to freeze and pile up roughly along the shore. Each time the rowboat approached the ice willing hands reached out for the men and as they were hauled out of the boat and over the edge of the ice many of them slid along like dead weights. They were so completely exhausted that they could not make another move to help themselves further. What a time there was at the lighthouse for the next few days! Even the tiniest Davenport made himself useful in running errands and trying to add to the comfort of the sick and injured men.

The boat, Waldo A. Avery, had been loaded with corn which of course was useless as such, after the terrible drenching and scorching. Worst of all, the insurance had expired the previous day, as insurance companies set a certain date when navigation is officially closed and no claims after that date will be considered. So the cargo was sold to a company in Canada who salvaged what they could during the winter, and shipped it to a starch factory.

When the Davenports had completed twenty-seven years at the McGulpin Point Lighthouse the new building was erected at Old Mackinaw Point which is within the present village limits. This meant that the operation of the Old Lighthouse was to be discontinued.

For many years the building remained open to the public and soon became the most popular picnic site of our community. How well I recall the good times we had as children in our excursions to the Old Lighthouse. We would pack a lunch and start out in the morning, arriving in plenty of time for our noon-day meal, and then spend the afternoon in playing. With so many interesting things to do the time passed much too quickly. First of all, we always went to the lighthouse and climbed the tower; then still in the climbing mood we would test our bravery on the surveyor's observatory. This was constructed of steel much like the fire towers of today, and although it was about the same height as the lighthouse tower it took much more nerve to ascend even part way because this climb was up a nearly perpendicular steel ladder placed on the outside of the framework. When we would tire of this procedure we would climb down the bluff, always stopping at the old well to make a wish, because to us it surely was a wishing well. This well was seventy-eight feet deep and the water was secured by lowering a bucket with a rope. From here we would go down to the shore to wade in the water and make islands of the large flat stones a few feet from shore. As the sun began to set we would start our hike back home, tired, but as happy as though this had been our very first trip to this historic spot.

Two Sturdy Island Pioneers

from the
Mackinac Island News
July 26, 1941

One of the very oldest French families to settle on Mackinac Island when it was inhabited almost entirely by Indians was the McGulpin family. They are proud of the Indian blood that has been mixed with the French blood in their veins.

William McGulpin moved from Quebec to Mackinac before 1812, and his oldest daughter was born here in 1812, under the British flag. His son Benjamin was born in 1827, one of ten children. He was a baker and contracted with the government of the United States in 1817 to furnish bread to all federal and military personnel here. He held an 1812 land grant issued by James Madison, President of the United States, for block 296 here. The old grant is printed on parchment. McGulpin's Point near Mackinaw City was named for Benjamin, who once owned the property including that area. He operated a dray line on the island until his death in 1910 at the age of 84. His wife, the former Elizabeth Boyd, died in 1915 at 85.

Sellew G. McGulpin, son of Benjamin and Elizabeth, is the senior Island representative of the family now. He was born here in 1876, and has lived here all his life.

Bill Chapman was a famous expert carpenter and cabinet maker.

McGulpin Point Lighthouse
James ("Pap") Davenport and Children

No. 1

United States of America

to

Patrick McGulpin

Patent
Dated June 1, 1811
Rec'd June 22, 1881
Liber 8 Page 520

Description: Beginning on the South border of the Straight of Lake Michigan, thence South 5 degrees East 112 chains 5 links to a pine tree, thence North 85 degrees East 60 chains 5 links to a pine tree, thence North 85 degrees East 60 chains to a cedar tree, thence North 5 degrees West 93 chains 17 links to a post standing on the border of Lake Huron, thence along the border of said Lake North 66 degrees West 19 chains 64 links, thence North 74 degrees West 36 chains 50 links to the Cross Cape, thence South 62 degrees West 9 chains 50 links to the place of beginning. Containing 640 acres.

(Note: Includes abstracted property, except that part of land abstracted lying in Sec. 14, T. 39 N. R. 4 W.)

Issued under an Act of Congress entitled *An Act Regulating the Grants of Land in the Territory of Michigan.*

No. 2

Patrick MacGulpin (signs Patt McGulpin)

to

George McGulpin, son of the said Patrick McGulpin

Deed (copy)
Dated Sept. 3, 1818
Ack'd Sept. 3, 1818
Rec'd June 13, 1916
Liber 63 Page 96
Consid: Natural love & affection & divers other considerations

Description: Land abstracted with other land, except that part of land abstracted lying in Sec. 14, T. 39 N., R. 4 W.

Certified June 10, 1916 by the Register of Deeds of Mackinaw County, Michigan. Taken from deed recorded June 28, 1882 in Michilimackinac County, Michigan.

No. 3

We have examined the records of the Judge of Probate and the Register of Deeds, Emmet County, Michigan, but fail to find anything in the matter of the estate of George McGulpin, deceased.

Nancy McGulpin and Francois McGulpin

Quit Claim Deed
Dated Nov. 16, 1853

to

George T. Wendell and J. A. T. Wendell

Ack'd Nov. 16, 1853
Ack'd Nov. 18, 1863
Rec'd Nov. 18, 1853
Liber 1 Page 343
Consid: $1-

Description: Land abstracted with other land, except that part of land abstracted lying in Sec. 14, T. 39 N., R. 4 W.

Known as the Old George McGulpin place.

Appears to have been transferred from Mackinac County Liber H, pages 6, 7 and 8, but no certificate of transfer annexed.

No. 5

Nancy McGulpin and Francois McGulpin

to

George T. Wendell and J. A. T. Wendell

Quit Claim Deed
Dated Nov. 16, 1853
Ack'd Nov. 16, 18, 1853
Rec'd Nov. 8, 1855
Liber 1 Page 352
Consid: $1-

Description: Land abstracted with other land except that part of land abstracted lying in Sec. 14, T. 39 N., R. 4 W.

Acting Register of Deeds of Emmet County, Michigan, certifies that this instrument is a true transcript from the records of Cheboygan County.

No. 6

Nancy McGulpin

to

Edgar Conkling

Deed
Dated Sept. 2, 1865
Ack'd Sept. 2, 1865
Rec'd Sept. 7, 1865
Liber B Page 480
Consid: $25 to her in hand paid and the further sum of $200 to be paid as per written agreement on the perfection of the title hereto to the grantee by Edgar Conkling

Description: All her right and interest of whatever nature now or hereafter acquired in and to all that certain section of 640 acres of land on which she long resided with her parents and which was given her by her mother some six years before her death and known as McGulpins Point about two miles west of Old Mackinaw on the straights of that name now in Emmet County, Michigan and more particularly described in American State papers Vol. 1 pages 374 and 375 giving the decision or award of the United States Commissioners in 1808 in favor of the claim numbered 335 to Patrick McGulpin for said land and by said Patrick to his son George McGulpin the father of said Nancy by deed dated September 3, 1818 Record A, p. 49 Michilmacinac County Mich. patented June 1, 1818, recorded June 28, 1822.

Covenants to warrant and defend against own acts.

Constitutes and appoints the said Edgar Conkling her true and only lawful attorney irrevocable for her and in her name to do whatever may be deemed by him necessary in any court of law or otherwise in order to fully acquire a peaceable possession of the said property hereby approving of sustaining and defending any and all of such acts as freely and perfectly as done by herself.

No. 7

Affidavit	Affidavits
by	Rec'd (no date given)
Joseph Pyant and Alexander McGulpin	Liber B Page 481

(From these affidavits it appears that the Wendells were to support Nancy McGulpin and her mother Francois McGulpin as a consideration for the conveyance of the land abstracted with other land.) The affidavit of said McGulpin has no date of execution, that of Pyant September 8, 1865.

No. 8

Affidavit	Affidavit
by	Rec'd Feb. 2, 1866
Alexander McGulpin	Liber B Page 493

(Denies some of the statements made in affidavit at Instrument No. 7.)

Subscribed and sworn to February 2, 1866.

No. 9

Affidavit	Affidavit
by	Rec'd Feb. 3, 1866
	Liber B Page 548
Joseph Pyant, Register of Deeds	

That subject matter at Instrument No. 7 is heresay and does not have personal knowledge of the same.

I would further state to do justice to all parties concerned that I was told by J. A. T. Wendell of Mackinac that they had purchased the property out and out and paid for it at the signing and acknowledging of the deed and that they were not obligated directly or indirectly to pay the said McGulpins one cent for their support or in any other way and it was so explained at the time before witnesses and perfectly understood by all the parties, for the said McGulpins Claim at the time of purchase was worth nothing as the property was forfeited previously by Mortgage Deed to the late Michael Donsman of Mackinac which was and is still on Record by the late George McGulpin, husband of Francois and father of Nancy McGulpin and also Samuel McGulpin, a supposed heir if then living to the half of the property and that she, Nancy, had no right to deed away his interest if he was still alive and that the said Nancy and Francois told them at the time of sale before witnesses that the late George McGulpin, her father, told her and her mother and others on his death bed that the said tract of land belonged to Michael Donsman of Mackinac and that Francois, her mother, answered at the time "Then we have nothing and we will be out of doors." That the late Michael Donsman commenced suit immediately after against them for the possession of said property and that they - to employ counsel to endeavor to defend it and finally purchased by advise of counsel the Donsman right to it from the Donsman Estate.

Subscribed and sworn to February 3, 1866.

EMMET COUNTY ABSTRACT & TITLE CO.

James Davenport and grandson Lloyd Desy.

THE DAVENPORT FAMILY

By Melinda Beyne
(great-granddaughter of Lizzie)

It has been more than 180 years since the Davenport family settled in the Straits area. Major Davenport was posted on Mackinac Island. There, he fell in love with a young Indian girl, but was refused permission to marry her by his post commander and sent back to England. Major Davenport returned to Mackinac Island when his tour of duty ended and resumed his courtship of the young Indian girl, followed by marriage vows.

Through the years, many children and grandchildren were born in the Davenport family. One of the most noted was James Davenport, lovingly known as "Pap" by relatives and family friends.

James Davenport was born on Mackinac Island in 1847 and was one of a family of fourteen children. For a time, he sailed the Great Lakes on various schooners, but it was not long before his sailing career was cut short by his marriage. He was married on April 18, 1870, to Madeline Lasley, whose father was James Lasley, Postmaster on Mackinac Island and later to become one of the first Assistant Postmasters of Chicago.

The year 1871 was a busy year for James and Madeline Davenport. At this time, they made their move to the Village of Mackinaw, and it signaled the beginning of a career with the Department of Commerce and Labor that lasted forty-seven years.

James Davenport was appointed Assistant Keeper of the Lighthouse at Waugoshance Point on April 19, 1871, at a salary of four hundred dollars a year. It was the first year of his appointment, and Captain James Davenport was alone, for the first time, at the Waugoshance Lighthouse. A fierce wind was blowing the smoke of a Chicago fire over Lake Michigan, creating a dense fog. It was during this lonely vigil that a schooner piled up on Waugoshance Reef, and the crew swam ashore. In the harrowing three weeks following the wreck, the rations consisted of a meager diet of beans, their hunger perhaps somewhat abated by Captain Davenport's accomplishments on his violin, the sounds blending in with the turbulent waters of Lake Michigan. Years later, he was to meet one member of this surviving crew and overheard him relate his experience to a fascinated logging crew. When he described the very young lightkeeper, Captain Davenport then identified himself as the "long ago, young lightkeeper."

Captain James Davenport was Assistant Keeper at Waugoshance Lighthouse for three years, then was appointed, on January 5, 1874, Keeper of Petite Point Au Sable Lighthouse. He served at that post until 1879. At this time, he was transferred to Old McGulpin Point Light and was positioned there until March 13, 1907.

There is a prevalent story connected with McGulpin Point that is worth repeating because it is linked closely with the early Mackinaw City settlers whose ancestors are still to be found here.

So the story goes, the schooner California was wrecked near McGulpin Point. Many lives were lost and as the bodies floated ashore they were stripped of their valuables.

Since that night, it is said, a mysterious light appears each year off the shores of McGulpin Point.

His last appointment, ending a long and satisfying career, was as Keeper of Mission Point Light Station, Old Mission, Michigan. He was positioned at Old Mission from March 13, 1907 to the year 1918. His pay was five-hundred and forty dollars a year, with house and grounds. It was supplemented by his abilities as a carpenter and cabinet maker. Many of the oldest homes in Mackinaw City were built by him. His first venture in building was the Davenport family home, located on Sinclair Street. It was constructed from the wood of ships wrecked on the Straits of Mackinac.

His years of service were punctuated by both happy and sad events. During these years his wife Madeline bore him ten children. She died on March 18, 1891, giving birth to her tenth child. The baby died three days after the date of birth. It was Madeline's last wish to be buried on Mackinac Island, so James bundled the bodies of wife and child onto a sled as the griefstricken children lined up on the bitter cold shores of Lake Huron to mournfully watch their father's departure. Stately and imposing was the tall and austere figure of James Davenport and his young daughter Edith, pulling the dead mother and child across the frozen Straits of Mackinac to be laid to rest on the Island.

After Madeline Davenport's death, her sixteen-year-old daughter Edith assumed the household duties and helped her father rear her brothers and sisters.

Captain James Davenport died at the family home in Mackinaw City at the age of eighty-five on March 18, 1932. He was survived by sons Harry, Joseph, Overton and James (Bud) and daughters Edith, Lizzie and Louise. Three of Captain Davenport's children preceded him in death: his daughter Gracey, his son Frank and his daughter Rachel.

The crumbling headstones at Lakeview Cemetery in Mackinaw City record the death of many Davenports. As of June 1975, there are two direct descendants living in Mackinaw City, Lloyd Desy, son of Rachel, and Clifford W. Burroughs, son of Lizzie.

Charlie Burroughs, husband of Elizabeth Davenport, father of Clifford.

Clifford (Gib) Burroughs and wife Mabel. Gib is a grandson of "Pap" Davenport.

Prof. H. A. and Frederick Davenport, Champion Rope-Walkers of the World, brothers of James (Pap) Davenport, great uncles of "Gib" Burroughs.

Davenport sisters (top to bottom) Elizabeth, Edith, Rachel, Louise (known as Todd). Elizabeth is the mother of Clifford Burroughs. Rachel is the mother of Lloyd Desy.

Margaret Lasely
sister of Mrs. James Davenport

Chapter 20

Ralph Preston's
Railroad Memories
Of 1924

By Judy Ranville

I started working for the Michigan Central Railroad in Bay City, Michigan in 1918 and worked there for five years, transferring to Detroit, where I worked for one year. I was then sent to Mackinaw City as a car foreman. We arrived in Mackinaw on August 12, 1923, with our three-year-old son Robert. I recall it took us 12 hours and seven blowouts to drive from Bay City to Mackinaw. Our two younger children, Pauline and John, were born here.

When I started working for the railroad, I began at twenty-eight cents per hour, and when I received a raise to thirty-three cents, I purchased a home and was able to pay for it.

In 1924 Mackinaw was a rather small town, and I remember there were only 12 telephones. For my work I needed a phone, so I applied for one and was told it would be at least a year before I'd get one. The State Dock had just been built a year before and there wasn't a building on the lake shore from the dock, south, to the one mile crossing, except one house where the Plaunts lived and fished.

In spite of its smallness, Mackinaw had more activity and men employed at that time than one would ever believe because we had nine passenger trains coming in here, two on the DSS&A (Duluth, South Shore and Atlantic), four on the Pennsylvania and three on the Michigan Central. We had nine trains in and nine trains out daily, as well as the freight trains.

Mr. Herbert Galbraith was the Michigan Central agent at the time, with his office in the depot. Over at the freight house he had a chief clerk, Charlie Fulmer, and a private stenographer, and there were also 8 or 10 clerks in the office, also car checkers and such. He also had transport men who would unload the smaller capacity cars belonging to the DSS&A onto the transfer platform and then load it onto larger Michigan Central cars and move it all out of here in one car instead of several smaller ones. They could then return the DSS&A cars to the Upper Peninsula.

There were three clerks in the ticket office to sell tickets, send and receive messages. The baggage department employed three men, there was a janitor, and a hotel and dining room also in the depot. This was managed by Harry Whitehead, and employed numerous clerks, cooks, waitresses and chambermaids.

Thirty-seven men, including myself, were in the car department. This included car cleaners, clerks and inspectors.

The locomotive department had thirty-one men working. They were machinists, hostlers, coal shovelers and cinderpit men.

Bill Wilkes was section foreman for the Michigan Central. He had six men who did nothing but care for the yard and dock tracks. Tom Flynn and a crew of six cared for the tracks between the south end of the yard and Freedom.

In the Building Department, the foreman was Dan McIsaac. Later years, Ted Morris was foreman. They and their crew were responsible for repairs to buildings, platforms, the dock, and any repairs from here to Grayling.

The Signal Department was run by Roy LaCombe. He had charge of all communication equipment between here and Grayling.

Art Buehler was agent for the Pennsylvania and Elton Dagwell was chief clerk. They employed six men to work in the office and to check cars. Fred Bowmen was section foreman, and he and six men cared for the tracks between here and Carp Lake.

Ice was cut from the Straits in the winter and put in the large ice houses and the refrigerated cars and car air conditioners were all serviced with this ice. Men iced the cars by hand. Coal was also shoveled into the buckets, which were dumped into tenders of the locomotives, as we had no coal dock at the time. Also in the winter months we had two stationary boilers in the round house that provided all the steam for heating of all buildings and coaches. This required three extra men, one for each "trick" (shift). We burned a carload (50 tons) of coal each day.

In the winter extra men were hired to shovel snow. In 1927, eleven carloads of logs were on the No. 11 track and were completely covered with snow. One hundred extra men were hired to shovel snow onto cars that were then taken away from the yards and unloaded. It took two weeks of steady shoveling to rid the yard of snow.

In those days the *Chief Wawatam* operated 24 hours per day and often times the *Sainte Marie* would run as well. I remember one time when there were 3000 cars loaded with forest products sitting on side tracks waiting to be hauled south across the Straits. That time the *Sainte Marie* ran two weeks straight with the *Chief* to get caught up.

These were for the most part good years, but there were also unpleasant times too. We had a number of derailments and accidents, the worst being the "Birchwood" derailment at Mullet Lake on January 2, 1942. The fireman, Fred Berry, was killed.

I was made equipment foreman in 1942, and retired in 1955 after having a serious heart attack.

My son John has made railroading his life's work and is now equipment foreman for the Southern Railroad in Tucson, Arizona.

Old handcar.

A run of half an hour from Cheboygan, and the traveler by the Michigan Central is at Mackinaw City, where a connection is made with the staunch and elegant steamer, *Algomah* under command of that veteran of the lakes, Captain Hiram Ames, for Mackinac Island, Point St. Ignace, and the upper peninsula. The sail across the north channel to the island requires but thirty minutes, and every minute affords a new view of scenes as grand and beautiful as tourist's eye ever beheld, or tourist's heart could ever wish to feast upon. At Mackinaw City, under the management of Albert Maxwell, is one of the finest railroad hotels and eating houses in the United States. It is called, in honor of the late general passenger agent of the Michigan Central Railroad, the "Wentworth House", and is finished, furnished and conducted in as elegant style as the most fastidious and epicurean tourist could ask or wish. It contains ticket offices, waiting rooms, parlors, suites of apartments and a grand dining hall, with every convenience and comfort that ingenuity and taste could suggest or money procure.

Taken from the 1883 Michigan Central Railroad tourist guide, *Mackinac Island*, by P. Donan.

Mrs. Murray - Charlie Gwilt   Car Cleaners
Mrs. Murray is the mother of Clayton Murray --
killed in World War I and after whom the local
American Legion Post was named.

from the *Cheboygan Daily Tribune*
January 8, 1936

The last smoke-snorting iron horse has been dragged from Mackinaw City, towed away over the New York Central lines as one more unit in a string of freight cars hauled by two Diesel engines.

112

Steam, Switch Engine prior to 1920. (Left to right): Sunday Desy (father of Lloyd), Charlie McVey (father of Mickey), unidentified, Chet Rouche, engineer (father of Fred), Bill Martin.

Ludwig Millhausen, Vern Niles, Frank Duffina, Ralph Preston, Sr.

Unidentified fireman in photo (above) was my father John Harper who was killed in the railroad yards in Mackinaw about April 1917 at the age of 37. He had resided at 108 E. Jamet. He left his wife Sarah Isabelle Harper and a daughter and 3 sons, who later moved to Saginaw. His death was caused by electrocution. On a cold, rain and sleety morning he picked up a power cable which had fallen across the tracks in front of the engine. I remember being told the town closed down for his funeral.

--Wallace Harper, Saginaw, Michigan

Railroad Roundhouse.

G.R.&I. Roundhouse - stood in back of where IGA now stands.

Mackinaw City Depot, year 1888.

Bell Stack Steam Locomotive, 1890.

Chapter 21

The History Of
Transportation Across
The Straits of Mackinac

A THESIS SUBMITTED TO THE GRADUATE SCHOOL
OF THE UNIVERSITY OF HAWAII IN PARTIAL
FULFILLMENT OF THE REQUIREMENTS FOR THE
DEGREE OF MASTER OF ARTS IN HISTORY
AUGUST 1963

By
William Henry Barrett

Thesis Committee:

James M. McCutcheon, Chairman
Cedric B. Cowing
Ramon H. Myers

PREFACE

The author's interest in this topic of transportation across the Straits of Mackinac developed from his family history. The author's great grandfather was George W. Stimpson, the first settler in Mackinaw City in 1869. Mr. Stimpson left behind him many stories and records of the harrowing experiences he and his sons witnessed while transporting passengers and freight across the Straits by sailboat and sleigh. Therefore, from the pride and interest in family history developed an enthusiasm for the challenge of the Straits of Mackinac. The author felt the awareness of this challenge through his own lifetime, as he witnessed man's later attempts to conquer the Straits with a dependable year around means of transportation. He saw the greater part of the State Ferry era, and eventually the building of the Mackinac Bridge, which was the final solution to the challenge of the Straits. This was the same challenge his great grandfather had first attempted to meet, by transporting goods and passengers across the Straits in a small sailboat during the summer and in a sleigh, across the frozen ice, during the winter.

Chapter I

BACKGROUND AND EARLY HISTORY OF THE
STRAITS OF MACKINAC

The Straits of Mackinac region was first claimed and settled by the French. After the French and Indian War, 1763, the Straits became part of the British domain. The region next came under the rule of the Thirteen Colonies by the terms of the 1783 Treaty of Paris, which brought an end to the American Revolution. The British did not actually turn the region over to the American authorities until 1796 when the British evacuated Fort Mackinac.[1] Michigan became a territory in 1805 and a state in 1837. However, it wasn't until Michigan became settled in the northern peninsula that a transportation and supply problem arose and the Straits of Mackinac became a barrier to inter-peninsular transportation.

The Straits of Mackinac is five miles wide at its narrowest point and runs east and west, connecting Lake Huron and Lake Michigan. It is known as an unpredictable stretch of water owing to its strong currents and winds. It is common for these waters to change, within fifteen minutes, from glass calm to a rough sea with four foot waves. Swells over twenty feet high have been known to funnel through the Straits when a severe storm sweeps in from one of the two lakes. The area is known for its generally windy condition. In fact, seldom are the waters calm, except during the winter when its entire five mile width is frozen. The thickness of this ice averages from two to three feet, but when heavy storm winds force ice into the Straits from one of the lakes, a funneling condition is created, causing the ice to pile up along the shoals and shore, sometimes to a height of forty feet. This pile-up is most likely to occur in the Spring when the ice begins to break up. In the deeper parts of the Straits the ice is usually forced under, or piles up and then settles. This action creates a jagged, rough appearance with large ice windows.[2] When this occurs, the true depth of the ice, possibly forty feet, is not, of course, apparent.

The name Mackinac came from the Ojibway word Michilimackinac, which means "Great Turtle".[3] The

"Great Turtle" being an island that is situated at the northeast end of the Straits. Lake Huron borders the northern side of the island and the Straits border the southern side. The island is extremely high, with cliffs rising from its shores to a height of two and three hundred feet; thus, from a distance, giving it the appearance of a turtle.

During the French and British rule in the Seventeenth throughout most of the Eighteenth Century, the Indian word, Michilimackinac, was used indiscriminately for the present locations of Mackinaw City, St. Ignace, Mackinac Island and the Straits of Mackinac. During the latter part of the Eighteenth Century the "Michili" was dropped and the name Mackinac was used to distinguish Mackinac Island and the Straits of Mackinac. The name St. Ignace was given to the tip of land touching the northern part of the Straits where the present city of St. Ignace is located. Mackinaw, which has replaced the general name of Michilimackinac, is used for the tip of land which borders the southern edge of the Straits of Mackinac where Mackinaw City is now located. It should be noted that Mackinaw City is spelled with a final "aw" instead of "ac". The reason for this is that Mackinaw City was founded by Englishmen in 1869, and thus it was spelled in the English language and pronounced as "aw". The name of Mackinac with a final "ac" is French, but the "ac" ending is also pronounced in French as "aw" in English.

The French were the first to claim and settle the region. The first white man to catch a glimpse of the Straits of Mackinac was probably Jean Nicolet, a Frenchman sent by the governor of New France in 1634 to search for the non-existent passage to Asia. The first settlement on the Straits appeared when Father Marquette built his mission, St. Ignace, on the northern shore in 1671. This is the second oldest settlement in Michigan, the oldest being Sault Ste. Marie, located fifty miles north of St. Ignace where Lake Superior meets the St. Mary's River. The French soon saw that a fort placed at St. Ignace would give them control of a key water route; and in 1690, Governor Frontenac decided to establish this fort which was named Fort de Baude.[4] In 1701 the fort was abandoned and the garrison moved to the banks of the Detroit River establishing there a fort to stop the British from moving into the area of Lake Erie and Lake St. Clair.[5] By 1715 a new fort was established at the Straits of Mackinac by the French. This time it was constructed on the southern side where Mackinaw City today stands; and it was called Fort Michilimackinac.[6]

The French and Indian War finally brought an end to the French rule over the Straits of Mackinac. France lost her North American Empire to the British during the war. When the British captured Quebec in 1759, Fort Michilimackinac could no longer be supplied. The French evacuated the fort in the fall of 1760, taking the garrison into the Mississippi region. The British took command the following summer.

The British ruled the Straits area until 1796, when the Thirteen Colonies gained control as a result of the American Revolution. The British did not maintain the popularity with the Indians as did the French; and in 1763, the British garrison at Michilimackinac was massacred as part of the famous Pontiac Conspiracy. The conspiracy was brought under control within a year, and the Straits region was not disturbed until the American Revolution broke out. The success of George Rogers Clark in the Ohio Valley made the British fearful of an attack; therefore, they moved the fort to Mackinac Island where they felt a stronger defense could be maintained. According to the Treaty of Paris of 1783, which brought the war to an end, the colonies were to receive Fort Mackinac and the Straits region. England kept her garrison at the fort until 1796. At that time, she agreed in the Jay Treaty to give up the forts along the Great Lakes.

The Straits of Mackinac was valuable to the French and British because it held one of the strategic keys to the fur empire. With a fort in the area, they were able to control the traffic between Lake Michigan and Lake Huron. They also regulated the St. Mary's River which empties into Lake Huron only a few miles away; and from this river came all the furs from Lake Superior. Around the Straits of Mackinac were settlements of the Ojibwa, Ottawa and Huron tribes. The Ottawa village of L'Arbre Croche near the Straits was one of the largest Indian villages in the northwest. The reason so many Indians settled in the area was because of the plentiful fish supply found in the waters around the Straits. This, too, was to the advantage of the French and the British because the more Indians there were the more furs there would be to purchase; thus they would increase the wealth of their empire. For these reasons, the French and British considered the Straits of Mackinac as an asset and not as a barrier.

During French and British control of the region, almost the only means of crossing the Straits of Mackinac was by birch-bark canoe. These canoes were usually about thirty feet long and four and a half feet wide. Seven or eight men would paddle one; and a total load, including men, equipment and furs, would often be around four tons.[7] One of the main reasons why the canoe was used more extensively than sailing vessels, was because the canoe was more adaptable to the Ottawa-Nipissing route. This route started at Montreal where the Ottawa River empties into the St. Lawrence River, followed up the Ottawa River west to Lake Nipissing, then down the French River into Lake Huron, and across to Mackinac. This route was used because it was shorter and quicker than the Lake St. Clair, Lake Erie and Lake Ontario route. The Ottawa-Nipissing route could be covered from Montreal to the Straits of Mackinac in eighteen days, even though there were many difficult portages along the route. The light birch-bark canoe was very adaptable to such a river voyage with many portages.

Sailing vessels did not come into common use until the British took over the French Empire in 1763. Under

French rule the Great Lake forts were supplied from Quebec by way of the Ottawa-Nipissing route, thus canoes had to be used. When the British gained control of the Great Lakes region they also supplied the post from Quebec, but they used the route coming by the way of Lake Onterio, Erie, St. Clair and up Lake Huron. This route was vulnerable to rough seas; therefore, the sailing vessel was more practical for supplying the posts than was the canoe. Thus after 1763 the schooner became a common sight upon the Great Lakes, but by no means completely replaced the canoe as a common means of travel because the Indians and fur traders continued to use them extensively for their travel.

The first ship to pass through the Straits of Mackinac was probably LaSalle's *Griffin*, in August, 1679. This ship was lost at sea the same year after leaving Green Bay on Lake Michigan with a load of furs. The first two ships to appear on the Great Lakes after the *Griffin* were the British schooners, *Huron* and *Michigan*, placed in service in 1763 to supply the ports in the Great Lakes region.[8] From 1763 on, more schooners were built and placed in service on the Great Lakes.

During these early colonial days there was little fear or hesitation in crossing the Straits in a canoe; it was an everyday occurrence. The sudden winds were always a danger in such a small craft; yet, the inhabitants accepted this danger with a certain amount of indifference. This indifference was not complete since the Indians, as well as the traders, became alarmed if caught in a sudden storm while on the waters. The Indians were sure that such a storm was caused by the angry gods and often a dog, tobacco, or something of value was sacraficed overboard to appease them.[9]

The colonial inhabitants accepted the unreliability of transportation as a part of life that should be taken in stride. Storms and heavy winds would often suspend all possible traffic across the Straits for several days during any time of the year. Travel was made difficult during winter because the inhabitants had to walk across the frozen Straits, encountering many spots of jagged ice pilings which often formed. In the early spring traffic would be prohibited by fields of floating ice. These inconveniences were accepted as part of daily life. It wasn't until the Upper Peninsula became settled that a demand developed for reliable year-around transportation across the Straits of Mackinac.

When the British finally evacuated the Straits of Mackinac in 1796, the region was placed under the government of the Northwest Territory. In 1803, it became part of the Indiana Territory and in 1805, the Straits became part of the newly organized Michigan Territory. Few people had yet settled in Michigan--the territorial population was only a little over 3,000. However, by 1837, with a population of about 175,000, Michigan became the twenty-sixth State of the Union.

The old colonial and Indian concept of letting nature govern movement across the Straits of Mackinac gradually gave way to a demand for a reliable transportation. This change intensified as the Upper Peninsula developed its mining industries, and these industries drew an increasing number of settlers into the region each year. During the early years of the Upper Peninsula's development, the settlers and industries received their supplies and shipped out copper and iron ore by the water routes exclusively. The major fault with these routes was that they were inaccessible during the ice-locked winter months. Although horse and sleigh and dog teams were first used to meet the problem of winter isolation, they were highly inadequate for supplying the needs of the growing population. Few supplies could be carried by such conveyances, and certainly, no ore and ingots could be exported from the region. In 1840, just before the first mines began operating, the population of the Upper Peninsula was 1,457. Each decade the population doubled, until in 1890 there were 180,533 people in the area.

The mining of copper was the first major industry in the Upper Peninsula. It had been no secret that there was copper there; the Indians had used it for weapons, the French knew of its existence in 1636, and the British had attempted to exploit it in the 1770's. But few realized how valuable the deposits were. In 1837, the same year Michigan became a state, the state legislature appointed Douglas Houghton as state geologist and instructed him to survey mineral resources of the Upper Peninsula. His first report, made in 1841, indicated that there were deposits of iron, copper, lead and silver in the area. The copper deposits were located mainly in the Keweenaw peninsula, extending west into Ontonagon County and east to Baraga County. The Federal Government owned all this land at the time and began leasing it to mining companies in 1844, and later, in 1847, sold it outright. The mining companies boomed; Michigan became the leading state in copper production for the next forty years.

The mining of iron ore paralleled that of copper, and also became a major factor in developing the Upper Peninsula. The first iron ore mine was opened in 1845; and, by 1846, there were 104 companies organized with locations secured.[10] The Marquette range was the first range to be developed. The Menominee range was exploited next, followed by the Gogebic range.

These early mining companies found it impossible to supply industries with copper and iron ore during the winter months, and this supply problem helped to create a demand for reliable transportation across the Straits. When the mining companies first began in the 1840's, the ores were processed into ingots at forges and kilns set up throughout the mining areas. Thus compacted, the metal was easier to ship. These ingots coming from the copper range and those from the Marquette iron range were shipped in barrels by boat across Lake Superior to Sault Ste. Marie; here the ingots had to be transported by land around the St. Mary's rapids and reloaded on another ship to continue their voyage to the industrial cities in the lower Great Lakes regions. This time consuming and expensive method was soon superceded in 1855 when the Sault Locks were opened, allowing ships to sail on a continuous voyage from Lake Superior through the St. Mary's River to Lake Huron. This improvement greatly encouraged the mining industries. The shipment of iron ore in 1855 was around 1,500 tons; by 1860 it had increased to 114,000 tons.[11] Although most copper and some iron ore were still smelted into ingots for shipment after 1855, itbecame progressively more profitable and convenient to ship the raw ore to lower Great Lakes industrial areas for processing. When winter arrived ore shipments would be held up for four months due to the freezing of the Great Lakes. This created a problem because industries on the lower Lakes could not stockpile enough ore for winter operations. This was true until the decade of 1910 when the large, new steel freighters were able to build up a sufficiently large winter stockpile. Occasionally, between 1840 and 1882, copper ingots would be transported through the Straits by sleigh and then to the lower lakes industries, but the resulting freight costs were beyond reason. No iron ingots or iron ore are known to have been shipped by sleigh during the winter. By 1882, the railroads had answered the shipping problem by completing their lines from Southern Michigan to Mackinaw City and across the Upper Peninsula to St. Ignace. The only breach in this new ore shipping route was the Straits of Mackinac. If the railroads could supply this missing link, they would be able to supply the lower-lakes industries with their winter supplies of ore; otherwise, the ore would have to be shipped by a longer and more costly railroad route around the Great Lakes. The railroad companies set out to establish a ferry system which would be able to transport railroad cars across the Straits throughout the year.

Another contributor to the industrial development of the Upper Peninsula was lumbering. The industry was limited to the demands of the local market until after 1850. Soon timber products were shipped from the northern area to different points of the nation. By 1880 Menominee ranked sixth among the nation's lumber-producing points.[12] Lumbering continued to be

a major industry of the Upper Peninsula as it still is today, and thus added greatly to the transportation needs between the two peninsulas.

The third and least of the industries of the area was fishing. Lake trout, white fish and herring were found in the northern Great Lakes in large quantities. Fishermen in the Upper Peninsula were quick to take advantage of this natural resource, and in 1860 there were 32 fishing concerns, employing 130 people out of a total population of 1,011 in Mackinac County in the Upper Peninsula.[13] John Stimpson's records give an excellent picture of the region's wealth in fish. He told of his father employing men to lift two large pot nets one July day; the yield from these nets was 8,200 pounds of white fish.[14] In the 1800's catches were

shipped from the area in barrels after the fish had been salted. The industry declined during the early 1900's due to the lamprey eel and over-exploitation by the fishermen. Today, the industry is almost completely gone. However, the point here is that in the 1800's fishing was an important Northern Michigan industry which contributed greatly to the products to be shipped across the Straits to the southern markets.

Mining, lumber and fishing were the major industries of the Upper Peninsula. With the development of these industries came the increasing population, and with the population came a demand for a reliable year-around transportation across the Straits of Mackinac in order to sustain the economy. This demand was slowly met, first by the guide service of private citizens living in St. Ignace and Mackinaw City, and then by the railroad companies who initiated a ferry service across the Straits. Next, came the Michigan State Highway Department's State Ferry Service, and finally, the Mackinac Bridge gave the people of Michigan a year-around, dependable service across the Straits of Mackinac.

TABLE I

POPULATION GROWTH OF THE UPPER PENINSULA

1840	1,457
1850	5,743
1860	21,414
1870	43,700
1880	85,030
1890	180,523
1900	261,172
1910	325,628
1920	332,556
1930	318,696
1940	323,544
1950	302,258
1960	306,084

(FOOTNOTES)

1 F. Clever Bald, *Michigan in Four Centuries* (New York, 1954), pp. 90-92.

2 Ice windows are large sheets of broken ice protruding upright into the air.

3 Alexander Henry, *Travels and Adventures*, (Montreal, 1809), p. 37.

4 Willis F. Dunbar, *Michigan Through the Centuries* (New York, 1955), I, 59.

5 Roger Andrews, *Old Fort Mackinac on the Hill of History* (Menominee, 1958), pp. 22-23.

6 Ibid., pp. 29, 32-33.

7 Henry, op. cit., p. 13.

8 Dana T. Bowen, *Lore of the Lakes*, (Daytona Beach, 1940), p. 6.

9 Henry, op. cit., pp. 174-84.

10 Dunbar, op. cit., I, 223.

11 Bald, op. cit., p. 245.

12 Dunbar, op. cit., I, 327.

13 Ibid., I, 222.

14 John Stimpson, phonograph recordings, side 8.

Chapter II

THE STIMPSON FAMILY'S PART IN STRAITS TRANSPORTATION

From around 1850 until 1882 mail, goods and passengers were transported across the Straits through the efforts of people living in the Straits area. The sailboat was their main means of transportation during the summer, while the horse and sleigh was used during the winter. Primarily men from St. Ignace provided this early service mainly because St. Ignace was the oldest settlement in the area, dating back to French colonial rule.[1] Mackinaw City citizens did not take part in such services until after 1869. Yet, one of the best known records of the methods and conditions of early Straits transportation came from the papers and records of a Mackinaw family.

Among the many who contracted with the Federal Government at different times to carry the mail across the Straits were members of the Stimpson family, the first white family to settle in Mackinaw City in 1869.[2] The Stimpsons are of special interest here because their family papers have been preserved and the last family surviver, John Stimpson, made notes and phonograph recordings of their experiences in transporting mail and passengers across the Straits during this early era in Michigan history.

It is important to note here that the railroad did not get to Mackinaw until 1881. Therefore, until 1881, Mackinaw was isolated from any major land travel. In 1882, the steam ferry *Algomah* was put in service by the railroad companies to transport mail, passengers, and railroad cars across the Straits of Mackinac. Throughout the winter months the *Algomah* was often stuck fast in the ice. As a result, it often became necessary for people to hire the Stimpsons to guide them across the Straits, a service the family continued to perform until 1888 when the railroad companies replaced the steamer with a more dependable ship. Obviously, the Stimpsons' help in Straits transportation from 1870 to 1888 was of considerable value.

The Stimpson family came to Mackinaw primarily to build a refueling dock; guiding and transporting across the Straits became a secondary task. In 1854 a group of businessmen purchased the southern tip of the Straits region.[3] Edgar Conkling from Cincinnati owned the largest share in this business, a business of establishing a city at this location–Mackinaw City. The opportunity for the establishment of Conkling's city occurred when the need arose for a refueling station where ships could stop during their voyage through the Great Lakes. At that time the steam ships burned wood; and, as a result, required more refueling stops. In 1870, Edgar Conkling gave George Stimpson a contract to come to Mackinaw, cut timber and build a refueling dock.[4]

George Stimpson had settled in Cheboygan, Michigan, in 1867, where he worked as a lumberjack.[5] In the fall of 1869 he took his oldest son, Charles, age 18, and several workmen to Mackinaw. They began to cut timbers for the dock, bunkhouse and cabin which was to shelter his wife, Elvira, and his five younger children: Lydia, age 17; Ida, 15; Forrest, 11; George Jr., 10; and John, 7.[6] The cabin was ready for the family by February, 1870, when he moved the family from Cheboygan to Mackinaw. The family traveled by sleigh along the shore on the ice, for there were no roads or trails to Mackinaw at the time. The dock was completed during the summer of 1870, at which time Conkling persuaded George Stimpson to stay at Mackinaw and take care of the Conkling interests which included running the refueling station.

During the navigation months on the Great Lakes, the Stimpsons kept the dock loaded with piles of four foot logs. A steamer would pull in and clear the dock of wood, taking forty to sixty cords. It would take three to four hours to load the steamer, after which the dock would again be loaded, ready for the next ship. When winter returned, the Stimpsons would start cutting and hauling wood, replenishing the supply for the next summer. A winter's cutting averaged from twelve to fifteen thousand cords of fuel.[7]

The first ten years the Stimpsons lived at

Mackinaw, there were few routes into the city, although during the summer of 1871, a state road was cut from Cheboygan to Mackinaw. George Stimpson's receipts show that a man earned two dollars a day while constructing this road. [8] This road, incidentally, was rarely used because it was almost impassable. The most convenient way to get from Cheboygan to Mackinaw was still by boat in the summer and by sleigh, traveling along the shoreline, in the winter.

The Stimpson boys played an important part in the transporting of passengers and freight across to St. Ignace, as well as from Cheboygan to Mackinaw and Harbor Springs to Mackinaw. In 1875, George Stimpson acquired a five-year contract to carry the mail between Mackinaw and Cheboygan for the sum of one hundred and fifty-six dollars a year. [9] Contracts of this type were issued to the lowest bidder. The mail was delivered once a week, and it was George W. Stimpson, Junior, who carried out the contract. Between 1875 and 1888 Forrest and John Stimpson had, at various times, government contracts for carrying mail. They had a one-year contract to carry the mail between Mackinaw and Harbor Springs. This particular trip was made on horseback because the amount of mail was seldom over fifty pounds. [10] Another mail run they had for just one year was between Mackinaw and St. Ignace. The year of this contract appears to have been around 1876. John and Charles were proud of the fact that they never missed making a trip, even under harrowing conditions.

When Forrest was seventeen, he acquired a twenty-five foot sailboat and was always available to take passengers and freight across the Straits to Harbor Springs or to Cheboygan. The amount he received for transporting a barrel of goods across the Straits was one dollar, a very sizable amount for that time. In the winter, the boys would be available to guide travelers across the ice, traveling by horse and sleigh, or by skating, pulling mail, baggage and passengers on a large hand sleigh.

The remainder of this chapter includes accounts and experiences of John, Charles and Forrest when they transported passengers, freight, and mail across the Straits. These anecdotes have been taken from the phonograph recordings and writings of John Stimpson, written and recorded shortly before his death in 1942.

From early spring until late fall the trip across the Straits was made by sailboat, even in very rough weather when many lake ships would be anchored in the sheltering harbor of Mackinaw waiting out a storm. In early winter the boat would turn into a sheet of ice; deck, sails, and even the men's yellow slickers would be covered with ice. The man at the tiller, under such conditions, would often find his face cut and bleeding from ice flaking off his slicker during the crossing.

The year John and Forrest Stimpson had the government mail contract for crossing the Straits, they made the last boat trip on a Saturday, breaking ice almost all the way back to Mackinaw. On the following Monday, the two men skated across, pulling the mail on a hand sleigh. The ice was about an inch and a half thick and they did not dare stop for fear their concentrated weight would break through the ice.

When the ice on the Straits became three inches thick, a team and sleigh were then used to transport passengers and freight. The team would take off from Graham's Point and run straight across to Gros Cap Point on the St. Ignace side. A road was built upon the ice because the team crossed constantly over the exact spot, packing down the snow on the road while the loose snow was blown away. When Spring came the road would be about two feet above the ice. As the ice would thaw, large air holes would appear on either side of the road; when the weight of the team traveled across the ice, water would slosh and spout through these air holes. Under such conditions, once a team started across, there was no turning back. If they did, they would have to get off the narrow road onto the thawing and weak ice where breaking through was almost a certainty.

The trip across the Straits by team would take from fifteen to thirty minutes, depending upon the ice and weather conditions. Often there would be large cracks in the ice. Some days a crack would close so tight the ice would buckle and pile. In this case, the team would wait until the men chopped a way through and cleared the road. On other days, the same crack would be open to water, four to six feet wide. A plank would be placed across the opening for the passengers to cross and often some of the baggage would be taken across the plank in order to make the sleigh lighter. Next they would back the team up about thirty rods, and then the horses with the sleigh still attached behind would be whipped into a gallop and jump the crack. The Stimpsons boasted that they never lost a horse on the ice during all their years of transporting.

When the *Algomah*, the first steamship to run between Mackinaw and St. Ignace, was stuck in the ice, the Stimpson boys would go down to the railroad depot and earn ten to fifteen dollars a day guiding people across the ice. On one of these occasions, sometime between 1882-1888, Forrest Stimpson guided a group across the Straits. When he arrived a United States representative and the editor of the Sault Ste. Marie paper wanted to hire him to help two other guides take them over to Mackinaw. A storm was moving in, and Forrest insisted they move immediately if they wanted to get across. The two passengers and baggage were loaded upon a hand sleigh and the three guides with skates, two pulling and one with a pole pushing from behind, began the passage across. When the group left Gros Cap Point, the snow was coming down hard; they had to run by compass. The wind increased, cracks began to rumble and zigzag across the ice, the guides were aware of the danger and increased their speed when suddenly a huge span of open water loomed before them. The sleigh was quickly swung around and back, coming to a slow stop. They were now floating up the lake. The guides left the sleign and skated in different directions hoping to find an escape route. Forrest returned and said that he had found a place that would do if they moved fast. They went to a spot where there were many large floating ice cakes jammed together which were also moving up the lake. They ferried the passengers across one by one until they were again on solid ice. They loaded up the sleigh again, skating as fast as three men could skate in a race against death, for they knew the ice would soon break all the way. When they neared the shore another danger met them. The ice was piling up ahead of them about ten or more feet high along a shoal not far from shore. The men had to wait their chances and scramble over the moving ice mass one by one. The hand sleigh was to be the last to come, but a large cake of ice rose into the air and came crashing down upon it, destroying everything. However, the men had reached safety, and just in time, for within fifteen minutes the Straits was a wide open span of angry dark water.

Around 1874, George Stimpson built a hotel by adding a large building to his log house. He named it the Stimpson House. This hotel provided accommodations for travelers who were forced to wait several days before the Straits of Mackinac became passable. Mrs. George Stimpson always cooked for the large numbers of people stopping at the hotel. She would bake in one day a bushel of doughnuts, twenty loaves of bread, and a dozen mince pies; plus getting the regular meals. The price for one night's lodging was one dollar and fifty cents, including meals. Mrs. Stimpson had to have all the winter's supplies shipped in by boat during the fall, for once winter settled over Mackinaw, there would be no more supplies. If an item was not ordered or the supply ran out, there would be no choice but to go without.

That the people received their supplies by ship was typical of pioneer life in northern Michigan, and helps to emphasize the fact that land travel was limited which in turn created a relatively small demand for transportation across the Straits until the late 1800's. Land travel did not develop until the 1870's and 1880's when the railroad reached the northern regions; then the demand for transportation across the Straits of Mackinac began to intensify.

Around 1884 a group of immigrants, who were on their way to help build a railroad in the upper peninsula, were staying at the Stimpson House waiting to cross the Straits. The *Algomah* was stuck in the ice and yet the ice was not thick enough for a team and sleigh. The Stimpsons became appalled over their unruly conduct and drunkenness. After they were at the Stimpson House three nights, George Stimpson told John to get them across the Straits that day, even if he had to drown the team in doing it. The sleigh was made ready and the party of about twelve men were loaded aboard. When they reached the Straits, they found the ice only three inches thick. Under such conditions, the sleigh could not be stopped, because the weight could cause a breakthrough. As the team sped across the ice,

rumbling sounds occurred as the ice cracked under the weight of the sleigh. This caused considerable uneasiness among the passengers. They were in the middle of the Straits when a large gap of open water appeared. John knew he didn't dare stop, so he turned the team and followed the gap several miles until it narrowed down to about three feet. He then whipped the team across the gap, hoping the horses would not trip. They made the crossing safely to St. Ignace. John did not waste any time in starting his return trip because a northwest wind was developing, and he knew the ice would soon break up. He kept the team at a full trot all the way. During the last mile, he saw the ice piling along the shore line, so he knew the ice field was moving down the Straits. However, he got to the Mackinaw side with no time to spare. When stopping to check a cut one of the horses acquired from the jagged ice, he looked back and saw the open waters of the Straits.

These anecdotes serve to give us a vivid picture of the hazardous and unreliable conditions confronting transporting across the Straits of Mackinac during the early 1800's. These conditions make it easier to understand why a need for a reliable transportation developed as the northern region grew in population and in industry.

1 Edwin O. Wood, *Historic Mackinac* (Boston, 1918), I, 80.

2 John Stimpson, phonograph recordings, side 2, 1940.

3 Abstract, lot 3, block 69, Mackinaw City.

4 E. Conkling and G. Stimpson contract, Jan. 3, 1870, George W. Stimpson papers.

5 John Stimpson, recordings, side 2.

6 Family Bible, George Stimpson papers.

7 John Stimpson, recordings, side 2.

8 Receipt, July 7 to Sept. 1, 1871, George Stimpson papers.

9 Contract from U. S. Post Office Department, March 8, 1875, George Stimpson papers.

10 John Stimpson, personal writings.

Chapter III

RAILROADS AND THE RAILROAD FERRIES

The railroads were slow to develop in Michigan. By 1882, two railroads had reached Mackinaw from the southern part of the state, and one had connected St. Ignace with northern Michigan. A transportation company was organized by these three lines to provide a railroad ferry service across the Straits of Mackinac. This brought the three railroads together into a fairly reliable and scheduled service between the two peninsulas.

The first major step in Michigan's railroad building came in 1837 when the legislature voted unanimously in favor of state built and operated railroads. The state program lost popularity when the internal improvements bill rose to over four million dollars; also private roads were launching a successful attack against state ownership. The result was that the state sold, in 1847, all its lines to private companies for two and a half million dollars.[1] During the 1850's, construction greatly lagged. Apparently, some stimulus was needed. This came in 1856, when the United States' Congress passed a bill granting to each state a large amount of public lands to be given to railroads. Three sections on each side of the track were to be given for every railroad mile constructed.[2] Even with these generous grants, a total of only 779 miles was under operation by 1860.[3] Furthermore, all this mileage was located in the lower part of the state. It wasn't until the late 1860's that the railroads began pressing steadily north, toward the Straits of Mackinac. There were 1,638 miles of railroad under operation by 1870, and over three million acres of state and federal land had been granted to Michigan lines by 1872. The 1880's were the boom years in Michigan railroad construction because over four thousand miles were constructed during that decade.[4] There was little construction after 1900.

The construction of railroads into Northern Michigan was encouraged by the possible profits of lumber, mining, farming and other industries. The railroad that approached Mackinaw City from the southern part of the state closely followed the lumbering industry. The railroad owners hoped that, as the timber was cut, farmers would move in and thus agricultural products would replace timber shipments. This concept did not develop because the northern part of the lower peninsula proved to be generally poor farmland, and only a limited amount of profitable farming developed. Farming in the Upper Peninsula is rare due to extremely poor soil and a short growing season. Therefore, the railroads in the Upper Peninsula drew their revenue by shipping supplies into the area and taking the raw materials, ore and lumber, to the southern markets. This service was most important during the winter months when water transportation was halted because of ice.

The first railroad to Mackinaw was the Michigan Central in 1881. This railroad became the largest in Michigan and was later absorbed by the New York Central system. The Michigan Central's first main route came from Detroit to Jackson, from that point to Owosso, from there to Saginaw, and then to Mackinaw. As a subsidy for construction, this company received over seven-hundred thousand acres of government land, the second largest amount granted to any Lower Peninsula line.[5] In 1881 when the Michigan Central completed its line into Mackinaw, George Stimpson had the honor of driving the last spike. There was a large public bonfire to celebrate the completion of the railroad.[6] Much of the celebration centered around the only tavern in town and a wild brawl occurred. A fight developed, and when dawn broke the following day, the tavern was in shambles; the front window was broken, the bar mirror was smashed, broken glasses, bottles and furniture were strewn all over the tavern and onto the street.[7]

The second railroad to Mackinaw was the Grand Rapids and Indiana, which gave the city access to the western part of the state. The road started at Fort Wayne, Indiana, and ran to Grand Rapids, Michigan. In 1867, the company started construction north from Grand Rapids. The system was completed to Traverse City in 1871, Petoskey in 1874, and Mackinaw City in 1882.[8] The government granted this railroad over 850,000 acres of land in Michigan. The line later became a part of the Pennsylvania Railroad system. Of the two railroads, this one was most active in advertising the northern region to tourists and hay fever sufferers. The company annually published a guide to northern fishing lakes and resorts, and as a result, this railroad often called itself the "fishing line."[9]

The first railroad into St. Ignace was the Mackinac and Marquette Railroad Company which started from St. Ignace and eventually extended to Marquette by December, 1881. This line was incorporated into the Duluth, South Shore and Atlantic Railroad Company in 1887, and plans were made to extend the road to Duluth.[10]

The effect these railroads had upon both St. Ignace and Mackinaw was noticeable. New stores and businesses opened up, new families came to live in the communities, and a need for city government developed. Both settlements applied for local rule around the same time, Mackinaw City becoming incorporated as a village in 1882 and St. Ignace becoming an incorporated city in 1883.

In 1881, the three railroads that had service to the Straits of Mackinac formed the Mackinac Transportation Company. The company's major task was to provide reliable and scheduled ferry service across the Straits. The first ship they had built was the Algomah.

The Algomah was built at Detroit in 1881. One hundred and twenty feet long, thirty-three feet at beam, and four hundred eighty-six gross tons, it was constructed of wood.[11] One feature the Algomah had which made her different from the average ship in the Great Lakes was a pointed bow which flattened out near the water line. This design enabled her to ride upon the ice, forcing it down and breaking it with the ship's weight. The Algomah had the distinction of being the first known ice breaker of this kind.[12]

As an ice breaker, the Algomah was an

improvement. This ship could negotiate thicker ice than the pointed bow ships, even though they might be heavier. Therefore, she could move through ice better than the average ship of her time. Yet, though she was an improvement, she was not a complete success since the ship could not completely master the thick ice during the height of winter. When ice became two and three feet thick, she often became stuck. The *Algomah* was occasionally ice-bound for weeks at a time; and, on occasions, she was carried away by large ice fields which were shifted by the winds. During one winter, she became stuck and couldn't be moved until spring. On this occasion the freight aboard the *Algomah* was taken off and transported the remainder of the way by horse and sleigh. Such occurrences made it obvious that a larger and heavier ship would be necessary to negotiate the thick ice throughout the winter.

The *Algomah* towed a scow called the "Betsy" which held about four railroad cars, and it was through this towing method that the first railroad cars were carried across the Straits of Mackinac.[13] During the first years of operation, it became obvious that the *Algomah*-"Betsy" combination had several limitations. It was impossible to cross the Straits in severe, rough water with railroad cars on an open scow. Also, the *Algomah* found it difficult to tow the scow when there was any ice, regardless of how little there might be. Therefore, it became evident that a ferry was needed which could place the railroad cars on its lower decks. Thus, the *Algomah* was replaced in 1888 by the ferry *St. Ignace* which was heavier and could hold railroad cars upon its lower deck.

However, for many years after this replacement, the *Algomah* played an important role in the Straits of Mackinac, for the ship was sold to a private line which transported goods and passengers to and from Mackinac Island during the summer. Because the *Algomah* was an ice breaker and could successfully break ice if it wasn't too thick or if it softened by the spring thaw, she was often hired to break the spring ice through the Straits, the St. Mary's River and the Sault Ste. Marie Locks. The papers reported in 1923 that the *Algomah* was engaged by the steel companies to free twenty-three ships imprisoned in the Straits' ice off St. Helena Island.[14] The captain of the *Algomah* at that time was William Schepler of Mackinaw City, who served as the ship's captain until she was retired in 1938. The ship then remained in the Cheboygan harbor until she sank. During World War II, the city of Cheboygan raised the ship in order to clear the harbor. She was towed to Mackinaw City where she was filled with rocks and then sunk so as to make part of a breakwater for small boats. This breakwater, now known as Schepler's Dock, runs off Central Avenue. The engine from the *Algomah* is now in the Ford Museum at Dearborn, Michigan, because Henry Ford helped to install it when he was a young machinist.[15]

The new ice breaker, *St. Ignace*, was put in operation in 1888 and represented progress in the Straits transportation system because it combined new, improved features together with some of the old ones used in the *Algomah*. This new ship was made of wood and designed by Frank Kirby, a naval architect. The *St. Ignace* was two hundred and fifteen feet long and could carry, depending upon their size, twelve or more railroad cars.[16] This ice breaker, like its predecessor, had a flat bow so it could ride upon the ice, forcing it down by the ship's weight. This was an extension of the flat bottom bow principle used in the *Algomah*, except the *St. Ignace* did not have a point on its bow at all, but was a flat-nosed ship. In fact, it came to be called a "spoonbow". About eight feet before the bow reached the water, it cut back, thus giving the ship great ability to ride upon the ice and force it down. Another new feature was that it had a forward propeller which would create a vacuum by drawing the water from under the ice so it would be easier to force the ice down when the ship rode upon it. The propeller also helped to cut the large chunks of ice as they passed under the bow, forcing them under the ship and out the stern. At the same time, the forward propeller gave the ship more forward power.[17]

There are several opinions concerning who developed the forward propeller principle. The most recited account gives the credit to Commodore Lewis R. Boynton of St. Ignace. In 1872 or 1873 the city of Alpena was sealed in by an early ice formation. No railroad had been extended to Alpena at that time and so all its supplies had to arrive by ship. Boynton, who was manager of the "People's Line" which consisted of the ships *St. Paul* and *St. Joe*, was asked to get provisions to the city. He started out with the two ships loaded with the needed goods. However, when he got to Thunder Bay, he found it choked with ice, blocking his approach to the city. Upon surveying the situation, he lashed the two ships side by side, but facing in opposite directions. Thus the stern of the *St. Joe* rode upon the ice, its propeller in reverse creating suction and helping break up the ice as the weight of the stern broke it down. At the same time, the *St. Paul* used its forward power to help, and the two ships reached their destination in this manner. This account was written by Oliver C. Boynton, son of Commodore L. R. Boynton, in 1945 and published in 1948.[18]

Another account is given by John Stimpson. In the early 1870's, a steamship company from Chicago was always one of the first to send ships through the Straits of Mackinac in the spring. They would send two sister ships, and upon reaching the ice-plugged Straits, they would lash them together, one ship in reverse, the other applying forward power. An account of this company's development of the stern method is also given in a farm journal article in Ruth Stimpson's scrapbook, but it gives no dates.

Both reports are correct, but as to who was the first to use the method is not determined. However, from the two incidents, we can obtain a good picture of how the "spoonbow" and forward propeller method was developed.

The riding upon the ice to force it down had been used well before the 1870's.[19] An example of this method being used in the Straits is described in Forrest Stimpson's journal, dated 1874. Three ships, *Japan*, *Blanchar*, and *Ocean*, worked together in late March to forge a channel through the ice-choked Straits. The cargo of the *Japan* was shifted aft to raise the bow so it could ride more easily upon the ice in order to force it down. The *Blanchar* then placed its bow against the *Japan's* stern and they began forcing their way through until both became stuck. Then the *Ocean* moved in line and pushed upon the *Blanchar's* stern. With their combined efforts, they broke a channel through the Straits of Mackinac.[20] No doubt this ability to ride upon the ice was kept in mind when the *Algomah* was designed and again later in the design of the *St. Ignace*.

The *St. Ignace* was the first ice breaker to combine the principles of both a "spoonbow" and a forward propeller. Both of these principles were developed through the years by trial and experience; they were not the product of one man.

The success of the *St. Ignace* as an ice breaker was impressive, and yet, the ship could not completely master the ice which often became over two feet thick. She would become stuck several times during the course of a winter. It also became apparent that the ship's wooden hull was not holding up too well against the heavy ice. Still, even with these faults, the *St. Ignace* was a marked improvement over the *Algomah*.

It soon became evident that a larger and more powerful ship with steel plating would be more efficient. Thus, the ice breaker *Sainte Marie* was built in 1893 to supplement the *St. Ignace*, the *St. Ignace* remaining on the route until 1913. About 1900, when the *St. Ignace* was still in service on the Straits, she keeled over at the dock when heavy cars carrying ore were loaded on just one side.[21] The extent of the damage and how she was recovered is not recorded. In 1913 the *St. Ignace* was sold to another railroad company and later was destroyed by fire.[22]

In 1893, the *Sainte Marie* was built for the Mackinac Transportation Company to serve at the Straits. This ship was constructed of wood with steel plates, a "spoonbow", and forward propeller. The ship was three hundred and thirty-five feet long and had a capacity for eighteen freight cars.[23] The *Sainte Marie* did most of the hauling, with the *St. Ignace* in reserve. Since railway traffic steadily increased in the 1890's it was common for the two ships to carry a total of two hundred and fifty railroad cars in one day.[24]

During the winter of 1900-1901 Admiral Makaroff of the Russian Navy and his aide, Captain Mellen of Finland, were guests of the Mackinac Transportation Company. They spent the winter observing the success of the two ice breakers and studying the ship's construction. From their observations, these men drew plans and constructed a similar ice breaker to connect both ends of the trans-Siberian railroad across the 300 mile long Lake Baikal.[25]

In 1911, the *Chief Wawatam* was built for the Mackinac Transportation Company and was quickly recognized as being the most capable of the ice breakers. This ship held the claim of being the world's greatest ice breaker for many years. The major advantage this vessel had over the *St. Ignace* and *Sainte Marie* was that she was a ship constructed entirely of steel. Experience has proven that the strain caused by the heavy ice was too great for a wooden ship. Even the all steel *Chief Wawatam* had to have yearly repairs to her steel bow, because the constant banging of the breaking ice would loosen and break rivets. This ship was three hundred and fifty-two feet long, with a draft of twenty-six feet and a capacity for twenty-six railroad cars.[26] Shortly after this new ship's appearance, the old *Sainte Marie* was scrapped; and, in 1913, a new steel *Sainte Marie* emerged, using the engines from the first *Sainte Marie*.[27]

The sister ships, *Sainte Marie* and *Chief Wawatam*, battled the ice for about fifty years. Under normal winter conditions with the ice close to three feet thick, these railway ferries had little difficulty moving through the ice. It was the winds and strong currents that created the navigation hazards by carrying the ships out of their channels in huge ice drifts, or causing the ice to pile, making it difficult to break through. The ice in the Straits has been known to pile ten and twenty feet high and extend to a depth of forty feet. The two ships would attempt to clear a channel, to keep it open, and to use the same route all winter, but winds and shifting currents often closed this channel. It was only with great difficulty that they could open a new channel.

The months of January, February and March tend to be the hardest on the ice breakers. During these months many occasions have been recorded of the ships getting stuck. The most difficult year in breaking ice occurred during the winter of 1921-22 when heavy winds piled the ice in the Straits high and deep, forty feet deep in places.[28] During that winter the *Chief Wawatam*, captained by W. P. Robertson, was stuck for five days. The efforts of the *Sainte Marie* to rescue her were in vain. The ship's crew went out on the ice to clear the rough jagged pieces which piled up. Passengers were paid one dollar if they wanted to help. Clearing the ice enabled her to move some but not enough to completely free herself. Aboard the *Chief Wawatam* were one hundred and seventy passengers. On the third day, fifty-six of them walked across the frozen mass of ice to St. Ignace; on the fourth day, thirty more left; and on the fifth day, twenty made their way to shore. It was difficult walking because the ice was piled in jagged pilings ten feet high or more throughout the area.

Finally, a crew of railroad men came from

Mackinaw City with five hundred pounds of dynamite. They drilled holes in the ice, placed some dynamite and discharged it, raining upon the ship a shower of ice. The jolts and flying ice from the explosions broke an estimated forty windows in the ship. More provisions were brought to the ship by hand sleigh in order to feed the remaining passengers and crew. Everyone was properly fed and cared for at no extra charge. The ship's officers gave up their staterooms to the women and children, while the rest slept in the lounge. On the morning of the fifth day the *Chief Wawatam* gained headway after the ice was loosened by the dynamite blasting. She worked her way to the St. Ignace dock by early evening, thus ending the longest stranded ship episode on the Straits. The two ships continued having difficulty in the ice throughout the remainder of the winter of 1922. [29]

The two boats were seldom stuck for more than one day again, with one exception. On January 30, 1937, the *Chief Wawatam* was crossing the Straits in a blinding snow storm when it was blown off course in an ice flow and was run aground on North Graham Shoals. The ship was laden with twenty-one freight cars and a crew of forty-five, but with no passengers. The bow of the ship was forced up five feet above its regular water line. The *Sainte Marie* tried for two hours to pull her off, but finally gave up and took over the *Chief Wawatam's* transporting task. [30] The Mackinac Transportation Company requested the Coast Guard cutter, *Escanaba*, to help two tugs from Rogers City make their passage to the Straits so they could pull the *Chief Wawatam* off the shoals. [31] Neither tugs nor the cutter showed up, and finally, after the fourth day of being stranded, the *Chief Wawatam* backed off under her own power when a rise in the water occurred. Since her forward propeller was damaged, she left the next day for River Rouge, Michigan, to undergo repairs. [32]

The incidents just presented were given in order to show the difficulties confronting the ferries in transporting across the Straits of Mackinac. It is important to note that the railroad ferries gave a service much more reliable than ever before. Yet, it was not perfect because a severe storm or heavy ice conditions could stop traffic and temporarily sever the transportation between the two peninsulas. The fact that the ferries did not provide an absolutely reliable and immediate service was a factor which led toward the bridge development.

During many years of service these two railroad ferries transported a variety of products between the two peninsulas. The goods shipped north into the Upper Peninsula were general consumer goods, food products and mining equipment. There were no major shipments passing through the Straits and on to the Pacific coast. One of the few products shipped north that went beyond the Upper Peninsula was burlap to be used for grain and flour-sacks in the Minneapolis region. Shipment coming from the Upper Peninsula were mainly iron ore, copper ingots, timber products, fish and flour. All these products, with the exception of flour from Minneapolis, came from the Upper Peninsula. The flour shipments decreased in the first decade of 1900 when it began to be transported by way of Chicago to the eastern market. During the late 1800's iron ore was the major product shipped south across the railroad ferries; it began to decline in the early 1910's, when large, new steel freighters began stockpiling the ore. Finally, ore shipments by rail stopped completely in 1930's. Copper shipments declined to a trickle after World War I as did the fish shipments which had stopped completely by the 1930's. Today, the only major product shipped by railroad across the Straits is timber.

The railroad ferries also played an important role in inter-lake navigation. The Straits of Mackinac opened for inter-lake navigation in late March or early April. At such times the *Chief Wawatam* and *Sainte Marie* were often hired by different shipping companies to help their ships through the ice-choked Straits, Sault Ste. Marie locks and St. Mary's River, just as the *Algomah* helped in the earlier years. The shipping companies were usually eager to start navigation as early as possible in order to supply their industries, especially the steel companies. The records and papers are full of accounts telling about the number of freighters stuck while trying to attempt an early passage through the Straits.

For example, in 1872, during the last week in March, there were 20 steamers and 75 sailing vessels stuck throughout the Straits area. [33] At that time there were no ice breakers to help them, and so they had to work their way out or wait until the ice broke up. The ships at that time were constructed of wood, making it risky to try to fight the ice without damaging the ship. Just such a case was that of the *Nashua* in 1872 when it sprung a leak. The captain solved his problem by ordering 50 barrels of flour thrown overboard to bring the leak above the water line. [34] Years later, the problem was partly resolved when the *Algomah* appeared upon the scene. She helped in getting the ships through, as did later the *Chief Wawatam* and *Sainte Marie*.

During World War II, the demand to get the large steel constructed ore carriers through at an earlier date resulted in a long line of stuck freighters, with the *Chief Wawatam* and *Sainte Marie* busy trying to free the ships and transport war freight across the Straits at the same time. This pressing condition prompted the Federal Government to build a Coast Guard ice breaker to serve the region. The result was the construction of the greatest ice breaker ever placed upon the Great Lakes, the *Mackinaw*.

The *Mackinaw* revealed the evolution of the ice breaker. The ship was 290 feet long and 74 feet abeam. She had six Diesel engines capable of producing 10,000 horsepower, a forward propeller 12 feet in diameter, and two after screws of 14 feet in diameter. One of her newest features was her ballast tanks, which enabled the ship to rock out of heavy ice. The ship could move 150 tons of water forward or aft through these tanks in 16 minutes, and 400 tons could be pumped port to starboard twice in four minutes.[35] Another development was that the ship had no rivets in her hull construction; single bead welding was used. In this way one of the defects inherent in the steel railroad ferries was avoided in that their rivets would work loose and break due to the constant pounding of the ice.[36] The *Mackinaw* was commissioned December 20, 1944, which event completed the long development of the long development of the ice breaker, a development which began with the small wooden *Algomah*.

The *Mackinaw* was placed under the command of the U. S. Coast Guard and was used to open the shipping channels in the spring, and also to keep the Straits open during the winter. This improvement gave more reliability to the railroad ferries, because if they became stuck, the *Mackinaw* was available to break the channel and free the ships. Since the *Mackinaw* was a government commissioned ship, she was not, of course, used as an interport transport ship.

The *Sainte Marie* and the *Chief Wawatam* serviced the Straits until declining railroad traffic caused the Mackinac Transportation Company to discontinue the service of the *Sainte Marie* in the fall of 1961. The automobile led to the decline of the railroad, and after World War I, miles of railroad track were abandoned each year.[37] Railroad traffic declined. In 1949 the Pennsylvania Railroad discontinued its passenger runs between Cadillac and Mackinaw City. Then, in 1953, the New York Central stopped its passenger service except for a weekend special during the summer. Soon, there was only sufficient freight traffic to require the service of one ship. Also, because the Mackinac Bridge was opened in 1957, the *Sainte Marie* was no longer chartered by the Michigan State Highway Department to carry automobiles during the winter when the regular ferries were laid up. Nor was she being hired by shipping companies to clear channels in the spring, because the ice breaker *Mackinaw* had taken over that task. Thus, in the fall of 1961, the *Sainte Marie* sailed forever from the Straits of Mackinac. The *Chief Wawatam* continues to handle the small amount of remaining railroad traffic.

The decline and shift of the mining industries created much of the decline in the railroad traffic crossing the Straits. For over forty years, since 1847, Michigan was the leading state in copper production, but Michigan's copper industry began to decline rapidly in the 1920's because it could not meet the competition of the Rocky Mountain copper mines. The price of copper fell from 55 cents a pound in 1864 to 4.9 cents a pound in 1932. The population of Houghton, Michigan's major copper area declined steadily, from 88,098 in 1910 to 47,631 in 1940.[38] This decline in population decreased the demand for consumer goods which hurt the railroads; and, at the same time, the shipments of copper to the southern industries diminished. The mining of iron ore shifted from the Marquette range to the Menominee and Gogebic range. The two latter ranges were in the western part of the Upper Peninsula where iron ore was shipped by rail down the west side of Lake Michigan and then east to the industrial areas. This development caused fewer and fewer shipments of iron ore to be sent through the Straits route until there were no more ore shipments by the end of the 1930's. The last shipments of iron ore going through the Straits were shipped to a foundry in Mancelona, Michigan; this foundry closed down during the depression of the 1930's. Another reason why iron ore was no longer shipped across the Straits was because the large steel lake freighters had the capacity to stockpile hugh amounts of ore which lasted the industries through the winter. During the 1890's the total number of railroad cars carried daily by the railroad ferries averaged from 300 to 350 cars. Today, the average is from 30 to 50 cars. The coming of the automobile has also played a major part in the decline of railroad traffic crossing the Straits.

1 Bald, op. cit., p. 225.

2 Willis F. Dunbar, *Michigan Through the Centuries* (New York, 1955), I, 310.

3 Ibid., I, 310.

4 Ibid., I, 310.

5 Dunbar, op. cit., I, 109.

6 Ruth Stimpson, scrapbook, I, 23.

7 John Stimpson, recordings, side 8.

8 Dunbar, op. cit., I, 311.

9 Ibid., I, 110.

10 Emerson R. Smith, *Before the Bridge*, (St. Ignace, 1957), p. 66.

11 Notes on photograph, Edward T. Brown Collection.

12 Edward T. Brown Collection.

13 Ruth Stimpson, op. cit., I, 253.

14 *Cheboygan Tribune*, May 2, 1923.

15 Ibid., Feb. 8, 1924.

16 Ruth Stimpson, op. cit., I, 3-4.

17 *Cheboygan Tribune*, March 6, 1948.

18 Ibid., March 6, 1948.

19 Forrest Stimpson, journal.

20 Ibid.

21 E. Smith, op. cit., p. 72

22 Ibid., p. 71

23 Ruth Stimpson, op. cit., I, 34, 172.

24 Ibid., I, 174

25 *Cheboygan Tribune*, Mar. 8, 1958.

26 Ruth Stimpson, op. cit., I, 174.

27 E. Smith, op. cit., p. 71.

28 Ruth Stimpson, op. cit., I, 245-7.

29 Ibid.

30 *Cheboygan Tribune*, Jan. 30, 1937.

31 Ibid., Feb. 3, 1937.

32 Ibid., Feb. 4, 1937.

33 Forrest Stimpson, journal.

34 Ibid.

35 *Inland Seas*, Apr. 1945, p. 38.

36 Ibid., p. 38.

37 Dunbar, op. cit., I, 310.

38 *Michigan Manual*, 1961-1962, p. 376.

Chapter IV

MICHIGAN STATE FERRIES

Another form in transportation across the Straits of Michigan, which paralleled the railroad ice breakers, was the Michigan State Ferries under the direction of the Michigan State Highway Department. The development of the automobile as the major means of transportation created a demand that the State provide a ferry service connecting the highways of the upper and lower peninsulas. This ferry service started in 1923 with one small ship. Automobile traffic across the Straits increased each year, forcing the Highway Department to expand its service until there were five ships and a total capital investment of over fifteen million dollars by 1953. The ferries did not pay for themselves and ran into debt each year. Also, this service did not always provide immediate transportation across the Straits because heavy traffic for a total of about twenty days during each year created a long lineup of autos, some waiting as long as ten hours to board the ferries. These faults plus the fact that a bridge would help develop and bring the two Peninsulas closer together, created a demand for the building of a bridge to replace the State Ferries.

Highway development was an important factor in creating the State Ferries. If the Highway Department were to link the state through a system of highways, it would be necessary to connect, in some way, the highways between the two Peninsulas. Also, as highways improved, more people, mainly tourists during the summer, found their way to the north region, thus increasing the demand to cross the Straits of Mackinac.

Roads were slow to develop. In the early years, up to 1905, the townships and counties were responsible for all road construction. They were dirt and gravel roads, built to be used by wagons. The automobile created a demand for better roads, ones which would permit greater speed. In 1905, the Michigan Highway Department was created with Horatio S. Earle as State Highway Commissioner. [1]

The department was given $20,000 to distribute to counties as rewards for road construction. In 1913, trunk line routes were mapped out and counties were given double reward money if they constructed these routes according to State specifications. [2] Two of these trunk lines, one from the west side of the state and the other from the east side, terminated at Mackinaw. A federal government act passed in 1916 gave federal aid to state highway construction in a matching fund system, which stimulated construction in Michigan. [3] These first trunk lines were gravel roads. It wasn't until the 1920's that the State started to push asphalt and concrete construction. [4] The first concrete highway into Mackinaw City was completed in 1928, coming in from Cheboygan. [5]

In 1913 the first "pike" trip was made, in which a large caravan of cars left St. Joseph and drove in a group to Mackinaw City, taking four days for the journey [6] "Pike" trips were organized by private auto clubs who made the trips for adventure and vacation. These "pike" trips became an annual affair and were carried on until 1919. Such trips were also made by groups from Detroit, coming up the eastern route. These auto caravans received a great deal of publicity helping to create an interest in auto travel to Northern Michigan.

When this heavy auto traffic appeared in the northern regions, it was found that many travelers wanted to cross the Straits of Mackinac. However, the only transportation service across the Straits at that time was railroad ferries belonging to the Mackinac Transportation Company. If a person wanted to take a car across on these railroad ferries, he had to first drain all the gas from the car and then to roll the car upon a railroad flat car. In due time, the flat car was put aboard the ferry. The most discouraging factor in transporting a car in this manner was the charge of forty dollars for a one-way trip. [7] As time progressed and more cars appeared, the fee decreased to fifteen dollars a car and it was possible to drive it aboard rather than to load it upon a flat car. One man arrived with a large G. M. truck and was charged eighty-seven dollars to transport it across the Straits. He paid it, but his loud public protest to the American Automobile Association was a moving factor in the growing demand for the State to establish a ferry service. Under such conditions, it is easy to see why more and more citizens of Michigan began to pressure the State to provide a cheaper ferry service across the Straits of Mackinac.

The Michigan State Ferries were created by an act of the Legislature in April 1923, and placed under the direction of the State Highway Department. Highway Commissioner Frank Rogers announced during the late winter of 1923 the department plan to secure a State ferry service across the Straits of Mackinac. [8] He sent Edgar French to the Straits to make a special investigation concerning the possibility of establishing such a service, and to secure options on possible docking accommodations. [9] He secured an option on the Chambers dock with 215 feet of water frontage in St. Ignace, which frontage was later purchased for ten thousand dollars. [10] No dock was available for sale on the Mackinaw City side. There was talk of restoring an old dock three blocks north of the railroad dock, but this plan did not develop. [11] Finally, arrangements were made for the State to rent part of the Mackinaw City railroad dock for $150 a month. [12] Introduced by Senator Bohn of Newberry, the bill which created the State Ferries was passed through both houses by April 26, 1923, with no major opposition. [13] The act allowed the Highway Department to set aside $150,000 of its funds for the purchase of docks and ferries.

The first ferry purchased was the small wooden Ariel. The State bought this ship from the Walkerville Ferry Company for $10,000. [14] The Ariel was built in 1881 and serviced the Walkerville (now part of Windsor, Ontario) -Detroit run until sold to the Highway Department. [15] This ship had a capacity for 16 to 20 vehicles, depending upon their size. The first trip across the Straits of Mackinac was on August 2, 1923, the ship leaving St. Ignace with three cars aboard. [16]

The Ariel, which was under the command of Captain May, was built to navigate calm rivers and not the rough Straits. Her car deck was about four feet above the waterline extending about four feet out from the regular freeboard. This protruding car deck created considerable difficulty in rough waters

because huge waves would slap under this ridge and shake the ship. Her first rough sea test came on August 12, when rough seas came close to capsizing the little ship. The Ariel was forced to tie up until the Straits calmed down. [17] Whenever a wind as high as 30 miles an hour swept the Straits, the Ariel had to stop her runs and wait it out.

During the first year of operation the gross was $27,906.25, and the Ariel transported 10,351 vehicles across the Straits of Mackinac. [18] The State did not receive a profit during the first year of operation, nor did it in years to follow. The policy of the department was to provide a reasonably cheap transportation across the Straits for the citizens of Michigan. The Ariel suspended service for the first year when she went into winter quarters at Cheboygan on November 20.

When the ice cleared in the spring she renewed her service; the traffic, in the interim, was handled by the railroad ferries. The railroad ferries would carry automobiles after 1923 for about five and six dollars each, although the service was still secondary to the railroad traffic.

The Ariel served the Straits until 1926 when she went into operation between Port Huron and Sarnia until the Blue Water Bridge was opened. Finally, she was taken to Detroit and scrapped in 1948 after five or six years of idleness. [19]

Eventually the state built a dock on the Mackinaw City side. The State Ferry Department purchased 115 feet of water frontage about a block south of the railroad dock, for the sum of $550. [20] Through the summers of 1923 and 1924 a dock was built which was of a rock-filled concrete construction extending 1,400 feet from the shoreline until it reached a natural depth of 14 feet. [21] This dock was 25 feet wide with a 20 foot road and a five foot sidewalk. [22] Only one ship at a time could be loaded here. The cost of this dock was approximately $120,000 and it was put into general use in 1925. [23]

The Ferry Department realized that a more durable ship than the Ariel was needed. In October 1923, the Highway Department was given approval to purchase two ships from the federal government. [24] They were the Colonel Pond and the Colonel Card which were renamed the City of St. Ignace and the City of Mackinaw. These ships had been built by the federal government for service in New York harbor during World War I at the cost of $300,000 each; however, the state paid only $30,000 each for them. [25] In January, 1924, contracts were awarded to the Great Lakes Engineering Company to lengthen the ships from 130 feet to 180 feet, giving them a capacity of about 40 vehicles. [26] The cost for this lengthening was $115,250 more than the State paid for the ships. The ships had a 25 foot beam which was increased by adding eight feet to each side. This second alteration was done during the winter of 1925-26 at a cost of $113,830 for both ships. [27] After that, the ships were able to carry 55 to 60 cars. The last change made on these ships was designed to further increase their capacity, and it took the form of the addition of an upper forward deck where 20 cars could be placed by a dock elevator which was constructed in the early 1930's. [28] Even with these new additions, the ferries could not meet the demand created by the increasing traffic across the Straits.

The next addition to the State Ferry fleet was the *Straits of Mackinac* in the summer of 1928. This ship was built for the state by the Great Lakes Engineering Works at a cost of $327,176, [29] and was placed in service on July 1, 1928. [30] In 1929 an upper forward car deck was placed upon her so she could carry still more cars. [31] Years later, in 1943, this upper car deck was removed when the elevator became obsolete.

In June 1930, contracts were awarded for the building of an extension to the docks in Mackinaw City. The Mackinaw City dock was to have a triangular landing area added to the old dock, thus having landing faces of 284 feet, 300 feet and 375 feet. The St. Ignace dock, which was constructed in 1932, was to have three landing faces. [32] The St. Ignace dock was greatly enlarged, being reconstructed as a solid stone-filled dock, surrounded with iron sheet piling and covered with concrete. Upon both these docks was constructed a two-car capacity elevator tower of 60 feet. [33] These elevators were used to put cars on the upper deck of the three ferries.

These new facilities greatly improved the efficiency of the three small boats. The major improvement being the ability of three ships to load and to unload simultaneously, thus saving any waiting period when docking. The elevators were not as successful as hoped for, since only one ship could use them at a time. If all the ships were to use them, then they would create the old problem of ships waiting. The loading of cars upon the upper deck was very time consuming; furthermore, the loading of this deck was not done in rough weather. During World War II the elevators were left out of general use and were never used again. Except for about twenty rush days in August and during the November deer season, the three small ferries were able to handle each season's traffic with little trouble until the late 1930's. During the late 1920's, the total number of vehicles transported increased by about 20 per cent annually, until the 1929 season's total was 130,942. [34] No additional state ferry service was needed in the early 1930's because of the sudden drop in traffic accompanying the depression. The lowest ebb was reached in 1932 when the total traffic carried was down to 99,121 vehicles. By 1934 it was again increasing, until it reached a 206,087 vehicle mark in 1936. [35] Again the ferry facilities became pressed throughout the season, creating a need for additional ships and docking facilities.

As a result, the *City of Cheboygan* was added to the Straits' fleet in August 1937. The Highway Department purchased the ship from the Ann Arbor Railroad Company for $25,000 in May 1937. It was formerly the *Ann Arbor IV*, a steel ship, built in 1906,

270 feet long, and had a capacity for 85 automobiles. [36] The ship already had a noted history. For years it was on the Manitowoc-Kewaunee-Frankfort run. The *Ann Arbor IV* had twice run aground on the rocks at Kewaunee, wrecked on the piers at Frankfort, capsized at Manistee, and wrecked on the south Frankfort breakwater during an 80 mile an hour wind. [37]

When purchased by the state, the ship was taken to Cheboygan to be remodeled. The vessel was a stern loader, but the state did not have a dock for stern loading; therefore, four side ramps, two on each side, had to be cut so she could be loaded from the side and thus use the same docks as the other three ships. The cost for remodeling the *Cheboygan* was approximately $75,000. [38] The ship was christened the *City of Cheboygan* amid a general celebration on August 7, 1937, at the Cheboygan dock. [39] The following day the ship began its duties in transporting across the Straits of Mackinac under the command of Captain S. M. Frey. [40]

Again in 1937 and 1938 the state expanded its docking facilities in Mackinaw City and St. Ignace. Two main improvements were made: a large parking area was created so cars would not have to wait on the highways for the ferries, and a channel and dock was made for a stern loading ship. Before the end of the 1937 summer, the state had provided for approximately 17,500 square feet more of parking space on the St. Ignace side by taking over the area once occupied by a curio shop and a barber shop located on the northwest end of the dock. [41] In the fall of 1937 the state announced its estimated $530,000 plan to enlarge the docks. The Mackinaw City dock would be made 275 feet wider, rock-filled and capped with concrete, creating parking space for about 1,100 cars. [42] Also, an end-loading dock would be built which would be used by the *Cheboygan*. In St. Ignace, the plan would have the coal dock improved so it could be used as a stern-loading base. The work on these improvements was started in the fall of 1937 but was not completed until late summer 1938. [43]

Throughout the 1936 transporting season, the ferries carried 206,087 vehicles, a figure which jumped to 274,749 in 1937. It was extremely difficult for the ferry service to handle this mounting traffic, and so Highway Commissioner M. B. Van Wagoner pushed a plan for a new ice breaker ferry. Van Wagoner proposed a 372 foot Diesel ice breaker with a 150 vehicle capacity at a cost of $700,000. [44] He tried to have it built with P.W.A. funds, but failed to get federal approval. The plan was then revised with the idea of constructing it as a state project. [45] This plan failed also because the bids were too high. The contractors wanted over a million dollars to build the ship, both in 1936 and 1937 when bids were taken. [46]

With this program defeated, Van Wagoner turned to other means to strengthen the ferry service. One was to buy an additional ship; another was to lease the *Sainte Marie* from the Mackinac Transportation

Company to carry cars for the state during the ice-locked months when the regular ferries were laid up, thus giving the public a year-around State Ferry service.

The new State Ferry was the *City of Munising*. This 339 foot ship was formerly the *Pere Marquette No. 20*, a railroad ship running out of Ludington.[47] The thirty-five year old ship was purchased for $60,000 in February 1938. From her dock in Ludington, where she had been laid up for several years, the *Pere Marquette No. 20* was taken to the Manitowoc Shipbuilding Company dry dock at Manitowoc, Wisconsin, where the ship was reconditioned at a cost of $125,540.[48] After the ship was reconditioned and remodelled, she was taken to Escanaba. There, before a great crowd, Mrs. John Hannah, wife of the mayor of Munising, christened the ship the *City of Munising*.[49] During the last of June, 1938, this 120 car capacity stern-loading ship joined the fleet at the Straits of Mackinac.[50]

In October 1940, the state sold for $75,000 the *City of Mackinaw* and the *City of St. Ignace* to the Federal Government. The Federal Government wanted these ships as part of the national defense build up prior to our entering World War II.[51] Renamed the *General William E. Horton* and the *General Arthur W. Yates*, these ships were assigned to the New York Port of Embarkation.[52]

At the same time, October 1940, that the state sold these two ships, the Highway Department was authorized to purchase as soon as possible a large ship to replace these two ships. Thus, for $65,000 the Highway Department bought the *Pere Marquette 17*, a train ferry operated by the Pere Marquette Railroad Company.[53] The reconditioning and remodeling of the ship was done at Manitowoc, Wisconsin. There was a rush to get the ship ready in time for the deer season traffic, and so the formalities of christening the ship were omitted. The ship was named the *City of Petoskey* and reported for service November 19, 1940, adding her 105 car capacity to the fleet in time to help with the heavy traffic created by the hunting season.[54]

World War II reduced the traffic from 372,844 vehicles carried in 1941 to 121,596 vehicles transported in 1944.[55] This was due mainly to gasoline rationing. Obviously the ferries had little trouble in handling the traffic during the war.

When gasoline rationing was lifted, Straits traffic boomed once again. In 1946, 440,321 vehicles were transported; the ferry facilities were pressed once more. Again the Highway Commissioner looked for ways to increase the efficiency of the ferries and expand facilities so the Department could take care of the increasing traffic.

During the winter of 1946-47 when the ferries were in winter quarters, the *Cheboygan*, *Munising*, and *Petoskey* had their bows cut down and a forward loading ramp built.[56] This was done by the De Foe Boatworks in Bay City for $229,531.[57] Now the three

ships could save 10 minutes on each trip because they did not have to perform the time-consuming task of backing into the dock.

In 1947, Highway Commissioner Ziegler proposed, once again, the plan to build a large ice breaker ferry with a capacity for 150 vehicles. This time the proposal was vetoed by Governor Kim Sigler.[58] However, the plan for a four and a half million dollar ice breaker was finally approved in 1949.

The opponents to the building of the ferry were mainly supporters of the Mackinac Bridge project. They felt the Bridge would soon be approved; and, if so, the state would be stuck with a four and a half million dollar ice breaker that had been used for only a few years. Highway Commissioner Ziegler was in opposition to building a bridge and in strong favor of expanding the ferries to meet and fill the traffic demands across the Straits.[59] He seemed to be of the opinion that a new ice breaker would take care of the increased traffic and provide an efficient year-around service, thus obviating the need for a bridge. Also, the people of the state would not be so inclined to support a bridge project after having spent four and a half million dollars for an ice breaker plus another three million for new docks.

The new ice breaker was approved, built and named the *Vacationland*. The ship was built by the Great Lakes Engineering Works in River Rouge, Michigan, launched in April 1951, and completed for service by January 1952. The 150 vehicle capacity ship was one of the most powerful ships on the Great Lakes with its four Diesel engines generating 10,000 horse power. Its total length was 360 feet with a 75 foot beam. Twin propellers were installed both fore and aft, and a pilothouse constructed on each end thus enabling the ship to travel either way with equal ability. This, of course, eliminated the time-consuming task of turning around. The *Vacationland* was fireproof, had two large lounges, a ship-to-shore radiophone, and could travel 15 miles an hour.[60] The ship made its first trip across the Straits carrying autos on January 13, 1952.[61]

In 1950, the state undertook the project of constructing a new dock near St. Ignace. The dock was constructed one and one half miles south of the city. By locating the dock there the department was able to cut two and one half miles per round trip off the ferrying route. A large parking area to accommodate several hundred waiting cars was part of the new dock project. This new St. Ignace dock cost $1,960,381.[62] It was opened for general use in late summer 1951. On the Mackinaw City side, a new docking slip was constructed for the *Vacationland* since the regular slip was much too narrow for the new ship. Also, large oil tanks were constructed on the shore where the fuel for the Diesel *Vacationland* would be stored. The cost for these projects at Mackinaw City was $938,080, to bring the total for both docks, at St. Ignace and Mackinaw City, to $2,999,472. These new docking facilities plus the

Vacationland greatly incrased the efficiency of the State Ferry Service by requiring less time to cross the Straits and being able to transport a greater total of cars in one day. Now close to nine thousand cars could be transported in a twenty-four hour period.

The ferry schedule has varied throughout the years and seasons. In 1923, when the *Ariel* started to make its regular trips, there were only four round trips a day.[63] The ferry began its season's service on August 2, 1923, and laid up for the winter on November 21. It took the *Ariel* about an hour to make a one-way trip, including docking. The first trip of the day began at 6 a.m. and the last trip at 9 p.m. with no trips made at night. This same schedule was maintained until 1928 when the *Straits of Mackinac* was added to the fleet, allowing hourly service during the summer months between 6 a.m. and 9 p.m.[64] In 1928 the ferries made a stop on each trip at British Landing, Mackinac Island.[65] This stop was made regularly during 1928. The year in which this service discontinued is not certain, but it was definitely not carried out in 1931. In 1931, trips were made hourly, generally between 6:30 a.m. to 11:30 p.m. with a trip at 1:30 a.m. and at 4:30 a.m.[66] This schedule was called the summer schedule, June 1 to September 18, and was maintained with few exceptions from 1931 to 1957.

A trip every one and one half hours was generally maintained for the Spring and Fall, except during hunting season. The trips were made between 6 a.m. and 10:30 with a trip at 1:30 a.m. and 4:30 a.m.[67] This schedule was maintained between April 16 through May 31 for the Spring and from September 19 to November 30. This basic Spring and Fall schedule was maintained from 1931 to 1957.

There was no winter schedule from 1923 until 1936.

The Michigan State Ferries did not have an ice breaker, and so the service would be discontinued from December 1 to April 15 when the Straits was locked by ice. Traffic crossing the Straits during winter had to travel on the railroad ice breakers which adjusted the automobile schedule around the priority of railroad traffic. In the fall of 1936, the state was able to lease the ice breaker *Sainte Marie* from the Mackinac Transportation Company because railroad traffic had greatly decreased and the ship was falling into general disuse. The winter schedule varied from year to year; generally four round trips were made each day with no trips at night.[68] The *Sainte Marie* stayed under lease year around and was used as a supplementary ship during the rush seasons in the summer and during deer season. In 1952, the *Vacationland* appeared as the ice breaker for the State Ferries and the service of the *Sainte Marie* was discontinued.

The crossing time for the ferries was gradually cut down through the years. It took the *Ariel* about an hour to cross the Straits. When the large boats came into the picture, between 1937 and 1940, they were able to make the crossing in 45 minutes. In 1947, when the *Cheboygan*, *Munising* and *Petoskey* had bow ramps built on them, so they would not have to turn around and back into the dock, the trip could be made in 35 minutes. When the St. Ignace dock was relocated, cutting two and a half miles per round trip from the route, the passage could be made in a half hour or a little less. Of course, the times taken to cross would vary according to the weather conditions.

In 1937, the special truck trips were initiated during the summer months. Before this service, it was common for buses to be thrown off schedule and for truckers to fail to meet a contract because of a traffic tie-up at the Straits.

One of the greatest problems of the State Ferries was to cope with the seasonal fluctuation of traffic. Table No. II gives a good picture of this problem. Over fifty per cent of a year's traffic came during the three summer months of July, August and September. During certain weekends, holidays, and before deer season, the traffic would be so heavy that large line-ups would occur because the ferries could not accommodate the sudden traffic jams. Under such conditions, the ferries would operate a free schedule by loading and moving across as fast as possible. The three days before the Michigan deer seasons were always the days of the greatest traffic line-ups, because the upper peninsula had become noted for its wooded area and its plentiful deer. Even with a capacity on the Mackinaw City dock to hold about 1,100 waiting vehicles, the line would extend seven or more miles along the highway resulting in waits of six to twelve hours for a ferry.[69] The line-up also usually occurred during the 4th of July weekend, Labor Day weekend and four or five weekends in between, a total of about 18 to 20 days. Other than these times, the State Ferries had no trouble in taking care of the traffic. In 1952, five ships were in operation during these periods; but during the rest of the months, one or two ships could easily handle all the traffic. This situation would leave at least three ships idle for the greater part of a year. Such imbalance created a problem because a certain segment of people wanted the ferry system extended to take care of the rush periods, and yet to do so would be uneconomical because it would involve an increased capital investment in still more ships which would also be idle during the greater part of the year. The added idleness would increase the taxpayers' burden just to provide immediate transportation for 18 or 20 days. This difficult problem must be kept in mind as one of the arguments in favor of building a bridge across the Straits of Mackinac.

The toll charge for the ferries was first determined by a vehicle's wheel base length.[70] When the *Ariel* first started in 1923, the charge for cars was $2.50 per car and up.[71] The act which established the Michigan State Ferries authorized the tolls to be fixed on the basis of cost, interest and depreciation. At the beginning of the season in 1926, the rates were

TABLE II   SEASONAL FLUCTUATION OF TRAFFIC

Month	Vehicles 1939	Per Cent of Year	Vehicles 1949	Per Cent of Year	Per Cent Increase
January	4,017	1.4	9,839	1.6	145
February	2,445	0.9	8,650	1.4	254
March	3,933	1.4	12,543	2.1	219
April	7,301	2.6	20,183	3.3	176
May	15,000	5.4	37,868	6.2	152
June	25,498	9.1	56,890	9.4	123
July	63,258	22.6	130,573	21.5	106
August	71,796	25.6	141,602	23.4	97
September	35,611	12.7	72,545	12.0	104
October	15,537	5.5	40,339	6.7	160
November	26,491	9.5	59,075	9.8	123
December	9,356	3.3	15,866	2.6	70
Total Year	280,243	100.0	605,973	100.0	116

lowered to $2 per car and up, depending upon the overall length of the vehicle.[72] From 1928 through the winter of 1935-36 the state arranged with the Mackinac Transportation Company to carry vehicles on the *Chief Wawatam* and *Sainte Marie* during the winter seasons for the same prices that the State Ferries carried them in the summer. The state paid the difference between the lower state toll and the higher toll demanded by the Mackinac Transportation Company. In 1933, the Michigan Legislature amended the original State Ferry Act so that the rates were established on operating cost. The charge for a car went down to $1.25 or $1.50, according to the length of the vehicle. The majority of passenger autos in the 1930's were at the $1.25 rate; whereas, in the 1950's, the majority crossed at the $1.50 rate.[73] The toll for trucks and buses ran from $2 to $3, and $1 to $1.50 for trailers. The charge for all vehicles included transportation for the driver. Additional adult passengers were charged 25 cents, and children 10 cents. There were no round-trip rates.[74] The rates

just given remained the same from 1933 to 1953. In June 1953, the ferry rates were increased considerably: passenger cars, $2 and $2.50; trucks, $2.50 to $8; trailers, $1.75 to $3.25; buses, $4 and $5. These rates included the driver with a 35 cent charge for each additional adult passenger and 10 cents for children.

There were two possible reasons for this sudden increase in rates. One was to help meet the seven million dollar cost of the *Vacationland* and the new dock built in St. Ignace. The other reason was in connection with the passage of the Mackinac Bridge Bill in December 1953. The state was aware that tolls for crossing the bridge would have to be much higher if they were going to meet the payments on the bridge bonds. Therefore, the state felt it would not cause as much alarm if they raised the ferry rates in 1953 and then set the bridge toll higher in 1957 when the bridge went into operation. This gradual rise would be better than to have rates jump from $1 to $3.50 at one time.

The Michigan State Ferry program did not operate

with the intention of making a profit but rather as a service in connecting the highways of Michigan. It was the decision of the Highway Department to keep the rates low so it would not deter people from crossing.[75] This possible deterrent was always a major concern of the people of the upper peninsula who had become more and more dependent upon the tourist trade. Due to inflation and the increased number of ships, the yearly State Ferry deficit was $167,349 and by 1952 it was around three quarters of a million dollars.[76] The cumulative capital investment stood close to three million in 1939.[77] By 1953, the capital investment in the State Ferry System climbed to over fifteen million dollars.

The number of men employed varied according to the seasons, but the State Ferry System was always an important means of livelihood for the people of the Straits area. Each of the large ships required a crew of approximately 36 men; and, on the docks on each side, 60 men were employed, 20 on a shift, to direct traffic and dock the ships. The total payroll amounted to over half the total yearly expenditures. For example, in 1946 the total expenditures for the ferries were $1,006,312 of which $591,152 was for labor.[78] By 1954 the amount spent for employees' salaries was $1,414,403.[79] After World War II the ferry employees were unionized as the United Public Workers of America, Local 707, of the C.I.O.[80] Only two short strikes were recorded, one in 1953 and another in 1955.[81]

During the 34 years the State Ferries were in operation few accidents occurred. The most noted occurred in July, 1937, during a heavy fog when the City of Cheboygan collided with the Straits of Mackinac, resulting in several injuries to passengers. The only death in this accident resulted from a kettle of boiling soup which fell over the cook who was aboard the Straits of Mackinac. Seven cars were damaged aboard the Straits of Mackinac. The Cheboygan sustained very little damage, whereas the Straits of Mackinac was broken open, but luckily the break was above the water mark and the calm condition of the Straits allowed her to return safely to the Mackinaw City dock. In 1949 the Petoskey collided with the steamer Robert L. Ireland close to the docks at St. Ignace during a fog. No damage was done to the Petoskey, but the Robert L. Ireland owners later filed a claim against the state for $20,147 damages.[82] There are three occasions recorded where the Vacationland sustained damages to herself and the docks when she missed her slip and struck the dock due to high winds blowing her off course.[83]

Weather conditions occasionally hampered ferry travel. The St. Ignace docks were fairly well protected from the high seas by protecting lands, but the Mackinaw City dock was extremely vulnerable to the heavy seas during an eastern storm. Huge waves would hit against the dock, making it impossible for the ferries to dock. Under such conditions the ferries would tie-up on the St. Ignace side and wait out the storm. Such a situation occurred about once in two years. As for the ferries navigating the Straits during a storm, none had any trouble except the small Straits of Mackinac which was not used unless necessary. At one time a large A & P truck toppled over on the Straits of Mackinac during a severe storm. In March 1957 when the ice was breaking up, a heavy east wind piled mountains of ice in front of the Vacationland's dock at Mackinaw City, making it impossible for her to dock. Only after 22 hours, during which time the ice breaker Mackinaw gave aid, was the ship able to dock.[84]

The movement to replace the Michigan State Ferry System with a bridge began in 1934 and was culminated in late 1953 when the bridge bill was passed. One of the major leaders in defense of the State Ferry System was Highway Commissioner Charles Ziegler who was in office from 1943 to 1957. His arguments against the bridge were: one, 99 million dollars was too much to pay for a bridge when the state already had 15 million invested in the ferries; two, the toll for the bridge would have to be four times the ferry toll, this large increase would discourage people from going to the Upper Peninsula and as a result hurt the area's industries; three, the ferries could handle traffic with little waiting except for about twenty days of the year, thus it would be foolish to spend 99 million dollars for a bridge just to give immediate transportation for twenty days; and four, the high winds and heavy storms would prevent traffic from crossing the bridge just as it often prevented the ferries from running.[85] Another outstanding argument in favor of the ferries was their sentimental value; many people went north just to ride the ferries and greatly enjoyed the boat trip across the Straits. These arguments were presented after the feasibility of a bridge was certain in the late 1940's. Before that time the question of the feasibility of the bridge was enough to stop any definite movement towards its construction.

Ziegler continued to push for the development of the State Ferries, even when the bridge became inevitable. It seems rather ironic that he succeeded in getting a seven million dollar program passed in 1949 to build an ice breaker and a new dock in St. Ignace. These additions were put in operation in 1952, and just one year later, 1953, the bridge bill was passed which eventually canceled the entire State Ferry System. Thus the seven million dollar investment was only put to use for five years, or until 1957 when the bridge was opened to the traffic and the ferries were laid up to be disposed of later.

The 15 million State Ferry System was disposed of after 1957 to private business interests and city governments. Mackinaw City acquired the dock on the south side of the Straits. The city then leased the dock to private ferry companies taking passengers and goods to Mackinac Island. The three docks on the St. Ignace side were turned over in the same manner. The five State Ferries were one by one sold to private

TABLE III   YEARLY FERRY TRAFFIC, 1923-1956

Year	Total Vehicles	Per Cent Increase over Previous Year
OPERATION SUSPENDED IN WINTER		
1923	10,351	
1924	38,468	280.0
1925	59,484	54.6
1926	75,179	26.4
1927	92,963	23.7
1928	107,516	15.7
1929	130,942	21.8
1930	132,633	1.3
1931	129,858	- 2.1
1932	99,121	- 23.7
1933	107,170	8.1
1934	138,302	29.0
1935	164,848	19.2
1936	206,087	25.0
OPERATION TWELVE MONTHS OF YEAR		
1937	274,749	33.3
1938	255,068	- 7.4
1939	280,243	9.9
1940	296,762	5.9
1941	372,844	25.6
GASOLINE RATIONING		
1942	261,398	- 29.9
1943	105,211	- 59.8
1944	121,596	15.4
1945	216,783	78.3
NO GASOLINE RATIONING		
1946	440,321	103.1
1947	501,109	13.8
1948	552,404	10.2
1949	605,973	9.7
1950	604,612	- 0.2
1951	683,814	13.1
1952	694,516	16.1
1953	900,782	13.3
1954	853,318	- 5.2
1955	907,643	6.3
1956	890,671	- 1.0

companies. The *Straits of Mackinac*, smallest of the fleet, was sold to the Mackinac Island Transportation Company, and thus was the only one of the ferries to remain in the Straits region. The *City of Cheboygan* was sold to Edward Anderson of Chicago where the ship was used as a floating potato warehouse at Washington Island in Lake Michigan.[86] The *City of Munising* and *City of Petoskey* were purchased by the Crosslake Transportation Company who used the ships to transport trucks and trailers between Milwaukee and Muskegon, Michigan.[87] Later, in 1961, the *City of Petoskey* was scrapped. The four and one half million dollar *Vacationland* was sold for one and one half million dollars to a Canadian firm. It was renamed *Pere Nouvel* and now serves the 50 mile run between Rimouski and Baie Comeau at the mouth of the St. Lawrence River.[88]

1 Frank F. Rogers, *History of the Michigan State Highway Department* 1905-1933, (Lansing, 1933), p. 31.

2 Ibid., p. 90.

3 Ibid., p. 98.

4 H. D. Dillman report, Feb. 1926, Records of the State Highway Department.

5 *Cheboygan Tribune*, Mar. 9, 1928.

6 Rogers, op. cit., p. 155.

7 E. Smith, op. cit., p. 8.

8 *Cheboygan Tribune*, Mar. 1, 1923.

9 Ibid., Mr. 13, 1923.

10 Rogers, op. cit., p. 146.

11 *Cheboygan Tribune*, Mar. 13, 1923.

12 Rogers, op. cit., p. 146.

13 *Cheboygan Tribune*, April 26, 1923.

14 Rogers, op. cit., p. 146.

15 Report, Marine Historical Society of Detroit Inc.

16 *Cheboygan Tribune*, August 2, 1923.

17 Ibid., Aug. 13, 1923.

18 Rogers, op. cit., p. 145.

19 Report, Marine Historical Society of Detroit Inc.

20 Rogers, op. cit., p. 146.

21 Ibid., p. 146.

22 Ruth Stimpson, op. cit., II, 58.

23 Ibid., II, 58.

24 *Cheboygan Tribune*, Oct. 17, 1923.

25 Ibid.

26 Ibid., Jan. 31, 1924.

27 Rogers, op. cit., p. 147.

28 Ruth Stimpson, op. cit., II, 58.

29 Rogers, op. cit., p. 148.

30 *Cheboygan Tribune*, June 26, 1928.

31 Rogers, op. cit., p. 148.

32 Ibid., p. 152.

33 Ruth Stimpson, op. cit., II 58.

34 Report on Traffic and Revenues, Dec. 10, 1953, Coverdale and Colpitts. Hereafter cited as Coverdale and Colpitts Report.

35 Ibid.

36 *Cheboygan Tribune*, May 4, 1937.

37 Ibid., May 14, 1937.

38 Ibid., May 4, 1937.

39 Ibid., Aug. 7, 1937.

40 Ibid., July 9, 1937.

41 Ibid., June 11, 1937.

42 Ibid., Sept. 1, 1937.

43 Ibid., Oct. 27, 1937.

44 Ibid., Oct. 21, 1937.

45 Ibid., Aug. 10, 1937.

46 Ibid., Oct. 21, 1937.

47 *Cheboygan Tribune*, Feb. 8, 1938.

48. Ibid., Mar. 15, 1938.

49 Ibid., June 27, 1938.

50 Ruth Stimpson, op. cit., II, 35.

51 *Cheboygan Tribune*, Oct. 16, 1940.

52 Ferguson to Royall, Apr. 19, 1946, Records of the Michigan Highway Department. Hereafter cited as Highway Records.

53 *Cheboygan Tribune*, Oct. 16, 1940.

54 Ibid.

55 Coverdale and Colpitts Report.

56 *Cheboygan Tribune*, Apr. 17, 1947.

57 McDonald to Woodfill, Mar. 6, 1950, Highway Records.

58 Ziegler to Dell, Nov. 21, 1950, Ziegler Papers.

59 Ibid.

60 *Cheboygan Tribune*, Jan. 9, 1952.

61 Ibid., Jan. 14, 1952.

62 Foster to Ziegler, Aug. 10, 1950, Highway Records.

63 *Cheboygan Tribune*, Aug. 2, 1923.

64 Coverdale and Colpitts Report.

65 Log Book, *City of St. Ignace*, 1928, Highway Records.

66 Coverdale and Colpitts Report.

67 Ibid.

68 *Cheboygan Tribune*, Dec. 17, 1937.

69 Ibid., Nov. 13, 1937.

70 Rogers, op. cit., p. 147.

71 *Cheboygan Tribune*, Aug. 5, 1924.

72 Rogers, op. cit., p. 147.

73 Coverdale and Colpitts Report.

74 Ibid.

75 Ziegler to Dell, Nov. 1950, Ziegler Papers.

76 Financial Statement, 1946 and 1952, Highway Records.

77 Don Kennedy, State Ferry Report, Highway Records.

78 Financial Statement, 1946, Highway Records.

79 Budget Report, 1955, Highway Records.

80 Bentgen to Ziegler, Aug. 8, 1946, Ziegler Papers.

81 Ziegler notes, Ziegler Papers.

82 Ziegler to Sept. of St. Ferries, Dec. 15, 1949, Ziegler Papers.

83 McDonald to Ziegler, Feb. 17, 1953, Ziegler Papers.

84 *Inland Seas*, Summer, 1958.

85 Ziegler to Dell, Nov. 21, 1950, Ziegler Papers.

86 *Inland Seas*, Spring, 1959, p. 66.

87 *Inland Seas*, Summer, 1959, p. 145.

88 *Presque Isle Advance*, Feb. 1, 1962.

Chapter V

THE MACKINAC BRIDGE

The long evolution of transportation across the Straits of Mackinac came to an end with the erection of the Mackinac Bridge across this natural barrier which had long severed the state. The Mackinac Bridge became the world's largest suspension bridge when it was completed in 1957. Once again man conquered the elements of nature; no longer could raging seas and ice-locked waters stop transportation between the two peninsulas. The two sections of Michigan became closer economically and politically when man was able to cross the Straits at his own convenience, with few exceptions, and not at the convenience of nature. The building of this bridge took only four years. The engineering feasibility of building such a bridge was assured two decades before its construction. The greatest obstacles to getting the bridge built proved to be economic and political. The program to build this bridge moved slowly from 1934 until 1953 when the last political and economic obstacles were overcome and the green light was flashed for the construction to begin. The engineers then set forth to prove their pledge that the bridge could be built. On November 1, 1957, the first traffic crossed the completed structure and thus ended the Era of the State Ferries and began the Era of the Mackinac Bridge.

It would be impossible to credit any one person with the idea of building a bridge across the Straits. As early as the 1880's men wrote down their suggestions that such a bridge might be possible. It could easily be that their enthusiasm was fired by the completion in 1883 of the Brooklyn Bridge, which was America's first suspension bridge. In 1922, Michigan's first Highway Commissioner made the statement that a bridge could be built or a floating tunnel constructed.[1] As time passed more people suggested such a bridge. As the years advanced into the late 1920's it became definite, from an engineering standpoint, that a bridge could be built. It would have to be a powerful structure to stand against the strong currents, heavy winter ice and treacherous winds, but it could be done.

The first big step towards the Mackinac Bridge reality came in March 1934 when Governor Comstock signed a bill creating the Mackinac Straits Bridge Authority.[2] To be chairman of the Authority, the

Governor appointed G. Donald Kennedy who proved to be an able and progressive leader in promoting the bridge. The Mackinac Straits Bridge Authority was given the power to investigate feasibility, issue and sell bonds, build a bridge, and fix and collect tolls.

The Authority recommended that the bridge follow an island-hopping route from Cheboygan, Bois Blanc, Round and finally to St. Ignace. They applied to the WPA for a grant to build according to this plan, but were turned down in 1934 and again in 1935.[3] Professor James H. Cissel, head of structural engineering at the University of Michigan and first secretary of the Authority, persuaded the Authority to change the island route to an angular route from Mackinaw City to St. Ignace utilizing the shoals for major footing.[4] Cissel traveled throughout the state promoting the bridge by giving talks to organizations and clubs. His promotion of the 32.5 million dollar bridge began to arouse enthusiasm. The Authority once again submitted the plan for financing the bridge through the WPA in 1937, and again it was turned down.[5] This plan was turned down because the cost was too high and the feasibility of it was questioned by the WPA.

During this time George T. Horton created interest in constructing tunnels, instead of a bridge across the Straits, when he read a paper to the American Society of Engineers in July 1937. Horton felt that two tunnels, composed of 30 foot tubes 3.7 miles long could be built for $29,400,000 across the Straits. The tunnel plan did not agree with Cissel's thinking, but it was investigated. The plan was rejected because of the expense and maintenance costs. The tunnels would have to be at least 350 feet deep and six miles long.[6]

The Bridge Authority proceeded to remove the question of the feasibility of building a bridge. They contracted with the construction company of Modjeski & Masters in Harrisburg, Pennsylvania, in 1937 to make a survey of the economic and engineering feasibility of the bridge.[7] The survey was to find the water depth, pressure, strain of ice and types of soil in the Straits, to determine also the best route, the cost, maintenance, and if there would be enough traffic to pay for its operation and upkeep. The survey got underway in the summer of 1938, and the full report was submitted to the Authority in July, 1940.[8] The estimated cost of this survey was $180,000.[9]

The Modjeski & Masters Report was good ammunition for those who favored a bridge. It recommended a bridge built straight across the Straits, rather than Cissel's plan of utilizing the shoals. The bridge would be a suspension bridge with a 5,500 foot approach causeway extending from the northern shore; no causeway would be used as an approach on the south side. The structure would have two main spans, 4,600 feet and 2,950 feet. The estimated cost was $26,740,000. The report estimated that according to their studies on Straits traffic, $950,000 revenue would be taken in during the first year of operation, and the annual operation and maintenance cost would

be around $765,000. They recommended the immediate construction of the 5,500 foot causeway on the St. Ignace side because it could be used as a ferry dock, shortening the ferry route while the bridge was under construction.[10]

The Authority had to receive permission from the U. S. Congress to construct a toll bridge. This request was granted in August, 1940, after it had been denied the year before. The Authority also had to receive permission from the War Department, inasmuch as the bridge would be over navigable waters.

The Authority had been turned down three times in attempts to receive WPA grants for constructing the bridge, and so a new plan was adopted in which the Highway Department would ask the WPA for a grant to build the $825,000 causeway on the north side of the Straits.[11] This causeway would serve a dual purpose; first, as a temporary ferry dock to be used until the bridge could be completed. This would cut ferry trips from 9.4 miles on the northbound route and 8.4 mile on the southbound route (routes that are necessary because of shoals) to 4.6 miles on a straighter line from dock to dock. Second, this causeway would eventually become the approach to the Mackinac Bridge. The plan was approved by the WPA, and construction was underway during the summer of 1941. Plans were being made for financing the remainder of the bridge through the Reconstruction Finance Corporation when World War II erupted, killing any hope of a bridge at that time. The Authority became defunct because its members were occupied with war efforts; and in 1947, the State Legislature officially abolished the Mackinac Straits Bridge Authority.

A new Mackinac Bridge Authority was created in 1950 by the State Legislature. It was to be a seven-man board, six appointed by the Governor and the seventh was to be the Highway Commissioner, acting in an ex-officio capacity. Governor Williams appointed the following men to the Authority: Prentiss M. Brown as chairman, former U. S. Senator from Michigan and one-time resident of St. Ignace; George A. Osborn, editor of the Sault Ste. Marie newspaper; Charles T. Fisher, Jr., who was a Detroit banker and member of the famous "Fisher Body" family; Fred M. Zeder, a Detroit automobile executive; William J. Cochran, an automobile dealer from Iron Mountain; and Murray D. Van Wagoner, who had been State Highway Commissioner and Governor of Michigan. The Highway Commissioner at that time was Charles Ziegler who was the ex-officio member.[12] Mr. Zeder later died and Governor Williams appointed Mead L. Bricker. It is important to note that this Authority had less power than the first Authority, created in 1934. The Authority created in 1950 had only the power to investigate the feasibility of the bridge; whereas the 1934 Authority had power to investigate, issue and sell bonds, build a bridge and fix and collect tolls.

The 1950 Authority wasted no time in retaining three of the top bridge engineers in the country: David

B. Steinman, Glenn B. Woodruff and Othmar H. Ammann. These men were to give the program a thorough examination and determine the physical and economic feasibility of a bridge.[13] The Authority also acquired the services of Coverdale and Colpitts, traffic engineers, to survey the financial probabilities of the structure.[14] By January, 1951, the engineers presented their favorable bridge plan. The bridge was to run on a straight line from Mackinaw City State Park across to the northern peninsula. As a northern approach, the planned bridge would make use of the causeway built in 1941. The plan included only one major span rather than two as in the previous plan. The estimated cost for the bridge had jumped to $87,000,000.[15] Because the Korean War had begun in the summer of 1950 and no steel was available for building such a bridge, once again the development of the bridge project was temporarily side-tracked by a war.

At that time the opposition began to work for the defeat of the bridge project. One of the main reasons why there was more opposition to the bridge in 1950 than in 1934 was because of the differences in financing. In 1934 there was a good possibility of getting a grant from the Federal Government through the WPA, in which case the people of the state felt that they would not be paying the whole cost of the bridge. Also, the building of the bridge at that time would have created employment for people in the Straits area. In 1950, these advantages were lacking and the cost of the bridge had risen to $87 million, which amount many people felt was to come out of the state's taxes. These reasons, plus many others, gave rise to a strong opposition towards a bridge.

A main reason, which seemed to be the major one, for not wanting a bridge was because the state had already invested millions of dollars in the State Ferry System. A bridge would do away with this investment.[16] The opposition strengthened their hand when they acquired the *Vacationland* plus the new docks in 1952. These additions cost the state over seven million dollars and at the same time greatly improved the service across the Straits. The opposition knew that the people of the state would be reluctant to dump this investment for a bridge.

The reason Ziegler led the Republican opposition is rather hard to determine. When one reads the Commissioner's papers, they seem to reveal in Ziegler a sincere belief that developing the ferry system was the best answer to the Straits transportation problem. However, it was obvious, too, that some of his opposition was political. The State Ferries provided many positions for political appointment, and as Highway Commissioner, Ziegler had control of these appointments. The opposition for a bridge came mainly from the Republican party, although not all Republicans in the State Legislature were against it. Those from the Upper Peninsula were certainly in favor of this proposal. Generally, then, the opposition was centered around a group of Republicans with

Ziegler as their unofficial leader.

One argument used by Highway Commissioner Ziegler was that the Straits of Mackinac had winds between 50 and 80 miles per hour some 37 days each year between April 1 and November 1, as reported by the captains of the ferries who kept records of the wind condition.[17] These have never been made public, but any citizen of the Straits area would know they are false. Very few times a year does a wind ever hit over 50 miles per hour, not over ten times a year. Lighthouse records showed that around twenty-five days during a year does the wind reach a velocity of 25 miles an hour or over.[18] The highest wind ever recorded in the region was 78 miles per hour. The reason Ziegler presented such a report was that he wanted to convince the people that wind conditions would stop traffic from crossing the bridge just as wind conditions had stopped the ferries, and thus a bridge would not be a great improvement over the ferries. This argument was convincing and very few people knew it was wrong.

The most effective argument against the bridge was the prediction that bridge tolls would be so high that traffic across the Straits would decline and, in turn, would cause an economic slump in the Upper Peninsula. Ziegler reported that a driver and car crossing the bridge would have to pay $5 while the car and driver paid $1.25 crossing the ferry; a trucker would pay $18 while he had paid only $4.50 on the ferry.[19] The estimates were based upon the interest to be paid on the bonds and the estimated amount of traffic that would cross the bridge. This proved to be wrong, but it did cause a great deal of concern, especially in the Upper Peninsula.

The Bridge Authority spent an amount of time reporting to the people that tolls would not be four times as great, but only slightly above the rate charged by the State Ferries, and that the reliability of a bridge would increase the total amount of traffic, enabling the Authority eventually to lower the toll rates. The Authority was right only in part. When the bridge was opened, the toll for a car and all passengers was $3.25; traffic did greatly increase, but in 1961 the tolls were raised to $3.75, rather than lowered.

Other arguments against a bridge were: the rock under the Straits was full of caves and would collapse under the weight of a bridge; the bridge just couldn't be built; the ice and winds would tear the structure down; and the State Ferries held a sentimental value to many people. These were among the major arguments and obstacles that the Authority had to meet and overcome.

The Authority believed that a bridge, being more dependble, would entice more people into the Upper Peninsula and thus help its economic growth. A bridge would bring the two peninsulas closer together, not just economically, but politically, industrially and socially. The bridge would not be a service just to Michigan but to the whole Midwest. The bridge would give people a ten-minute trip, and they could cross at their own convenience and not at nature's. This element of reliable quick passage from peninsula to peninsula was one of the most convincing points of all. The ferries, even if there waiting, could not transport vehicles across in less than thirty minutes. Then time had to be allowed for loading and unloading which would make the time around fifty minutes. Furthermore, the shortest schedule had a ferry leaving every hour, and so this could make the waiting and crossing time one and one half hours. Finally, people planning to cross could get caught during a rush weekend, such as the Fourth of July, and have to wait over seven hours before getting on a ferry. All this delay would be eliminated with a bridge.

In 1952 the Authority asked the State Legislature to grant them more power, to employ an engineer of their coice, issue revenue bonds, build the bridge and levee and collect tolls. A law was passed to this effect and signed by Governor Williams in April, 1952.[20] The Legislature granted the Authority the right to build but made it clear that the Legislature would not back the financing of the bridge; the Authority would have to build and pay for the structure itself.[21] This provision was the product of a somewhat anti-bridge Republican Legislature. The result was that the bonds had to carry a higher interest rate because the faith and credit of the state were not behind them. State backing would not have cost Michigan a cent, would have saved millions in interest and made the bonds easier to sell.

Before the sale of the bonds, contracts for the bridge construction had to be negotiated. Before they invested their money, possible buyers of the bonds wanted to be sure that the bridge could be built for the amount of money raised. Two major contracts were negotiated: one for the substructure was awarded to Merritt-Chapman & Scott Corporation for the sum of $25,735,600; the second contract went to the American Division of the U. S. Steel Corporation for the sum of $44,532,900 for the superstructure construction.[22] These contracts were without escalator clauses, which made them slightly higher. Several smaller contracts were obtained also.

The bonds were revenue bonds, to be paid off solely from tolls expected from the bridge traffic. Interest on the bonds and other obligations during the building of the bridge had to be paid from the original loan, as there was no income during the construction period. The Authority attempted to sell the bonds in late 1952, but were unsuccessful. There was no market at the time for such a sizeable bond issue.[23]

The Authority launched a plan to make the bonds more attractive. They proposed to the Legislature that the state pay annually $500,000 to the Authority for bridge maintenance. This would come from the Highway Department's funds because the bridge would be five miles of state highway, which the department should maintain. Also, the department's State Ferries were losing three quarters of a million

dollars a year. The bridge would free the highway department from this annual loss; therefore, the department would not experience any new hardship by paying $500,000 for maintenance.[24] If this annual amount was awarded, it would free all toll revenue for bond and interest payments. It would show that the state was behind the Authority and, in turn, would greatly help the sale of the bonds because it would make them a safer investment. The State Highway Department fought such a proposal, but the Legislature passed the bill granting the annual payment—cut, however, to $417,000 a year. The bridge opposition in the Legislature was able to attach a rider to the $417,000: If the bridge bonds were not sold by December 31, 1953, the appropriation act would expire at that time. The bill was passed in May; only a little over six months was available to float the bond issue.[25]

During the summer of 1953, the members of the Authority traveled widely in an attempt to sell the bonds. The situation looked poor, and the Authority was thinking about having the people of Michigan approve a bond issue at the next election. Then the situation brightened in October when a New York insurance company executive, Stuart Silloway, financial vice-president of Mutual Life of New York, made a secret tour of the Straits and Upper Peninsula area. He told the Authority that the investment looked sound and that his company would purchase some of the bonds. He would also help line up other companies.[26]

Silloway suggested that the bonds be sold on a take-down basis -- in other words, provide the construction money as it was needed. This plan was not accepted by some of the other companies who persuaded the Authority to accept a plan (which would cost $10,000,000 more in interest) to divide the bond issue into $79,800,000 of first lien bonds at four percent interest, and $20,000,000 of second lien bonds at 5¼ percent.[27] The bond issue totaled $99,800,000 which was in excess of the 1951 figure. This excess was not due to a rise in materials and labor, because the total construction cost was kept within the engineers' original 1951 estimate of $76,300,000. The increase in the bond issue developed from the difficulty in getting the bonds sold, in the discounts on the bonds and in interest to be paid during construction.[28]

By December 8 all banking houses concerned had agreed to the plan. According to law, the bridge bonds had to be advertised for public sale for seven days. This was started on December 10 and the date for opening the bids was set for December 17. The bond sale, according to law, had to be approved by the State Administrative Board, but the Board would meet on December 15, two days before the bid-opening day.[29] The Board was persuaded to recess until December 17. Everything seemed to be in order.

Two elements of opposition were yet to appear.

The first was the disapproval by Republican State Treasurer D. Hale Brake, who was a member of the State Administrative Board, of the extra $10,000,000 interest cost. He suggested the Authority wait and try to get the approval of the people in a vote, and then the State Legislature might put its backing behind the bond issue. This suggestion was not accepted by the Board or Authority.[30] The other obstacle was the attempt, on December 16, by State Senator Haskell Nichols of Jackson to get the Michigan State Supreme Court to forbid the Administrative Board to approve the sale of bonds. The Supreme Court did not issue the restraining order at that time, thus giving the Administrative Board the clearance to approve the bonds' sale on December 17, 1953. The restraining order was issued after December 17, and a month later the Supreme Court upheld the legal position of the Mackinac Bridge Authority.[31] The long hard financial struggle to have a bridge built across the Straits of Mackinac had finally ended in victory. The bridge would be built.

The ground-breaking celebration occurred May 7, 1954, on the St. Ignace side, and May 8 on the Mackinaw City side of the Straits of Mackinac. The main speakers in the Mackinaw City ceremony were Governor G. M. Williams, Dr. David Steinman, Prentiss Brown, U. S. Senator Charles Potter, and U. S. Representative Victor Knox. The day's program included a large parade and an Indian pageant.[32] Official construction of the bridge began in the spring of 1954.

A large armada of construction vessels pushed their way to the Straits of Mackinac to participate in the construction. Many came by the way of the Mississippi River-Illinois canal route. By mid-summer the bridge construction was utilizing the largest marine construction fleet ever assembled--an estimated ten million dollars worth of marine equipment.[33]

Six sea-based and eight land-based survey towers were constructed in the Straits area. From these towers the surveyors located the thirty-four units of the submarine structure which had to be placed within a fraction of an inch because the superstructure was prefabricated and had to fit in place on the piers.[34]

The priority task for the first construction season was the placement and construction of the major foundations of the bridge, mainly the two circular steel caissons used to support the towers' piers. These caissons were 116 feet in diameter, prefabricated steel sections, floated to the site, welded securely, and then filled with rock that was infused with a concrete mixture. This mixture forced the water out and formed a solid mass of concrete around the rock. As the weight forced the caissons down, new sections were floated out and added on. Each caisson had an eighty-six foot diameter dredging well in its center. Through bucket dredging, jet pressure (water piped under high pressure to wash away and loosen the overlay), air-lifts (pumping soil and water from

bottom), and dynamite, the overlay was loosened and taken out from under the caissons through the dredging wells, thus enabling the caissons to settle. When Merrit-Chapman & Scott stopped construction in the middle of January, the caissons were close to bedrock and secure from ice damage during the winter. The following season saw both caissons resting firmly on bedrock: the south caisson was down 201.9 feet below.[35] Then stone and concrete were filled into the dredging wells to secure them. In all, over 500,000 barrels of cement went into the two caissons.[36]

During the construction year of 1955, the mammoth bridge foundation, which included the minor piers approaching from each side to the anchorage, was completed by the Merritt-Chapman & Scott Corporation. The steel workers arrived and started work on the superstructure. By mid-summer the two main steel towers were under construction. These towers were prefabricated, assembled on the mainland, and then floated to the location to be riveted into place. The close of the construction season saw the two towers completed, standing 552 feet above the water. The truss spans were put together in St. Ignace, and before winter closed down the year's work, two of them were floated out and settled into place, one on each side of the anchorages.[37]

The main tasks scheduled for the season of 1956 were the spinning of the cables and the extension of the truss spans from both mainlands to the anchorage piers. Before the cable could be spun, two catwalks were laid, extending from one anchorage to the other, passing through the tops of the towers, and following the exact suspension curvature of the future cables. Constructing these catwalks was extremely hazardous, and two lives were lost during this phase of the construction. After completion of the catwalks, the spinning wheels began shuttling back and forth between suspension towers laying four strands of 0.196 inch wire each time they crossed the 8,614 foot gap. Each wire was then tested for tension, adjusted, and attached to the anchorages in a fanning-out system, later to be secured with concrete. The cables contained over 41,000 miles of wire when they were completed, and each attained a twenty-four inch diameter.[38]

The weather prevented the placement of the last spans from the mainlands to the anchorages before the close of the 1956 season of construction. As these truss spans were completed, the highway construction workers of both the Garvaglia Company at the north approach, and the Johnson-Greene Company at the south approach, began pouring concrete onto a temporary steel re-enforced plywood floor, making a roadway six inches thick.[39] Thus, before the 1956 season closed, a portion of the bridge roadway was completed, stretching towards the anchorages.

The construction season of 1957 saw the completion of the Mackinac Bridge. The truss spans to the anchorages were first completed. Next, the truss spans which were to be attached to the suspension cables were floated out and hoisted into place. A favorable summer enabled the workers to make up for time lost during the previous year.

On November 1, 1957, on schedule, the bridge was completed and opened to traffic, just in time to meet the flood of deer hunters crossing the Straits for the annual season in upper Michigan. The great dream was now reality. Across the Straits of Mackinac was the largest bridge of its type in the world. The bridge was formally dedicated on June 27 and 28, 1958, amid a great celebration and nationwide publicity. A federal stamp was issued commemmorating the occasion.

During the first complete year the bridge was under operation, 1,390,390 vehicles crossed the Straits, as compared to 907,643 vehicles crossing duringthe last complete year of the State Ferries. This great increase was due mainly to the flood of people who wanted to see and cross the bridge for the first time. Since the first year the number of vehicles crossing the bridge has declined; until only 1,098,828 crossed in 1961. The year 1962 showed an increase of about 50,000 vehicles over 1961.

When the bridge first opened, the toll for a passenger car was $3.25, and increased to $10 or more for large trucks, depending upon the number of vehicle axles. In 1961 the rates for passenger cars were increased to $3.75 with a similar increase for trucks. Many people strongly feel that the rates are too high and have hurt the development of Upper Michigan. They feel that the yearly percentage traffic increase has not been what it was hoped to be. Yet many believe that the convenience of the bridge has been a great asset to the state.

Today it is possible to stand in the reconstructed Fort Michilimackinac and catch in one glimpse the fort and the Mackinac Bridge, each representing an era of the long struggle to conquer the Straits of Mackinac. The picture marks a contrast of the long road until man overcame one more obstacle of geography.

1 Earle to Coffman, Nov. 12, 1922, Coffman papers.

2 *Cheboygan Tribune*, Mar. 28, 1934.

3 Ibid., Aug. 21, 1937.

4 Ibid., Jan. 23, 1937.

5 Ibid., July 13, 1937.

6 Ibid., July 27, 1940.

7 *Detroit Free Press*, Dec. 31, 1937.

8 *Cheboygan Tribune*, July 29, 1940.

9 Ibid., Oct. 19, 1938.

10 Ibid., July 29, 1940.

11 Ibid., Aug. 10, 1940.

12 *Michigan Manual*, 1951.

13 *Cheboygan Tribune*, Jan. 18, 1951.

14 Coverdale and Colpitts Report.

15 *Cheboygan Tribune*, Jan. 18, 1951.

16 Ziegler to Dell, Nov. 21, 1950, Ziegler Papers.

17 Ibid.

18 Mackinaw City Lighthouse, weather records, 1940-55.

19 Ibid.

20 *Cheboygan Tribune*, Apr. 30, 1952.

21 David B. Steinman, *Miracle Bridge at Mackinac*, (Grand Rapids, 1957), p. 27.

22 Prentiss M. Brown, *A Dream Comes True*, St. Ignace Kiwanis Publication, (1957), p. 6.

23 Steinman, op. cit., p. 29.

24 Brown, op. cit. p. 5.

25 *Detroit Times*, May 4, 1954.

26 Ibid.

27 Ibid.

28 Steinman, op. cit., p. 31.

29 *Detroit Times*, May 4, 1954.

30 Steinman, op. cit. pp. 32-33.

31 *Detroit Times*, May 4, 1954.

32 *Cheboygan Tribune*, May 10, 1954.

33 Gregg Smith, *The Mackinac Bridge Story*, (Bay City, 1956), p. 5.

34 Steinman, op. cit., p. 52.

35 Ibid., pp. 79-92.

36 G. Smith, op. cit., p. 8.

37 Ibid., pp. 1-5.

38 Steinman, op. cit., pp. 115-147.

39 G. Smith, op. cit., p. 28.

State Ferry Dock, Mackinaw City

S.S. Straits of Mackinac, Mackinaw City, Michigan

State Ferry Dock - Mackinaw City

Parade - day the soil was turned to begin building Mackinac Bridge - 1954.

Bridge Dedication - Governor G. Mennen Williams, Prentis M. Brown, David B. Steinman

"Big Mac"

State Boats

"City of Petoskey"

"Vacationland"

Railroad Boats

LOADING TRAINS ON RAILWAY FERRY "CHIEF WAWATAM" MACKINAW, MICH.

Island Boats

Island Boat at Mackinaw City

Algomah I

Algomah I
at St. Ignace, Mich.

Algomah II

Chippewa

S. S. Chippewa of the Arnold Line.

The Islander

ELVA

The *Glad Tidings* was built at Miller's dry dock at Chicago in 1889, having an overall length of 80 feet and an 18 foot beam. Captain Henry Bundy sailed his "gospel ship" into many Lake Michigan and Lake Superior ports. Once docked, he would preach from the dock to an assembled crowd or go ashore spreading his message to anyone who would listen.

When age finally caught up with the 79-year-old Captain Bundy, he was forced to give up his ministry after 1905. He died the next year. The *Glad Tidings* was purchased by the Arnold Transit Company and rechristened the *Elva*. She was renamed in honor of the wife of F. K. Keightley of St. Ignace who was associated with the Arnold Line. Her new owners converted her to a passenger ship that ran between Sault Ste. Marie, DeTour and the Les Cheneaux Islands until 1938.

Keith Widder
Mackinac Island State Park Commission

BIBLIOGRAPHY

A. Manuscripts.

George Coffman Paper, 1880-1950, Mackinaw City.

Coverdale and Colpitts, Reports on State Ferry traffic and Revenues, Dec. 10, 1953.

Mackinac Bridge Authority, letters from, 1960-2.

Michigan Highway Department Records, group 58-5, Lansing Archives.

Michigan Historical Commission, letters from, 1960-2.

Mrs. Ella Stimpson Letters, 1873-1916, Mackinaw City.

Forrest J. Stimpson Journals, 1871-1888, Mackinaw City.

George W. Stimpson Papers, 1870-1885, Mackinaw City.

Mrs. Hattie Stimpson Scrapbook, 1920-1948, Mackinaw City.

John B. Stimpson Phonograph Recordings and Writings, 1940, Mackinaw City.

Miss Ruth Stimpson Scrapbook, 2 Vols, 1890-1940, Mackinaw City.

Charles M. Ziegler Papers, 1943-1957, Lansing Archives.

B. Legal Documents

Abstract, lot 3, block 69, Mackinaw City.

C. Photographs.

Edward T. Brown Photograph Collection, Lansing Archives.

D. Newspapers.

Cheboygan Tribune, 1916, 1960, Cheboygan.

Cheboygan Weekly Times, 1872, Cheboygan.

Detroit Free Press, 1916-1960, Detroit.

Mackinaw Witness, 1892-1902, Mackinaw City.

New York Times, 1958, New York.

Presque Isle Advance, 1962, Rogers City.

The Republican, 1888, St. Ignace.

E. Pamphlets.

Prentiss M. Brown, A Dream Come True, 1957, St. Ignace.

Edgar Conkling, Title to the Lands of the Mackinaw City Co., 1857, Cincinnati.

F. Periodicals and Magazines.

Readers Digest, Oct., 1956.

Fortune, Oct., 1956.

Inland Seas, Apr., 1945.

G. Diaries.

Stimpson, Mrs. George, 1881-1886.

H. Monographs and Special Studies.

Larzelere, Claude S. "The Red Man in Michigan," Michigan History Magazine, XVI, (1933), 344-376.

Walker, Charles. "Father Marquette and the Early Jesuits of Michigan." Michigan Pioneer Collection, VIII (1907), 368-395.

I. General Works.

Andrews, Rogers. Old Fort Mackinac on the Hill of History, Menominee, 1938.

Bald, F. Clever. Michigan in Four Centuries, New York, 1954.

Bowen, Dana. Lore of the Lakes, Daytona Beach, 1940.

Dallas, James M. Missions at Old Mackinaw, Ancient and Modern; including the Story of the Fort and Massacre. Mackinaw City, 1902.

Dunbar, Willis F. Michigan Through the Centuries. 4 vols. New York, 1955.

Henry, Alexander. Travels and Adventure in Canada and the Indian Territories between 1760 and 1776. Toronto, n. d.

McCoy, Ray. The Massacre of Old Fort Mackinac. 7th edition. Bay City, 1950.

Rogers, Frank F. History of the Michigan State Highway Department 1905-1933. Lansing, 1933.

Smith, Emerson R. *Before the Bridge*. Bay City, 1957.

Smith, Gregg. *The Mackinac Bridge Story*. Bay City, 1957.

Steinman, David B. *Miracle Bridge at Mackinac*. Grand Rapids, 1957.

Wood, Edwin O. *Historic Mackinac*. 2 vols. Boston, 1918.

and, having neither wife nor children, his generosities spread far and wide to those less fortunate than himself. He lived an upright Christian life, and it is a privilege to honor his splendid record.

The engine of the first *Algomah* was installed by a young Detroit mechanic, Henry Ford, and that same engine is today a prized exhibit at Mr. Ford's historical Greenfield Village, having been bought by him two years ago.

Henry Ford Built The Engine; Joe Fitzpatrick The Good Will

from the
Mackinac Island News
July 26, 1941

There is history, drama and pathos in the story of the original Island Transportation Company, the successors of which are now operating the *Algomah II*, between Mackinaw City and Mackinac Island. This boat was purchased a few years ago to take the place of the old *Algomah*, which was bought in 1881 by L. R. Boynton and the late J. F. Keightley. The details are a bit vague of the progressive events. Joseph Fitzpatrick later acquired enough of the stock to hold a full half interest, after serving for years as purser of the line, never operating but the one boat.

The original *Algomah*, 130 feet overall, with a beam of 33 feet and a 1000 hp. engine, appeared in 1881 as the first of the famous ice crushers which have bucked the mountainous ice of the Straits of Mackinac during the winter months. The *Algomah* towed barges, carrying freight cars, from Mackinaw City to St. Ignace long before the *S.S. Wawatam* and *S.S. Sainte Marie* appeared on the scene. After these latter giants had taken over regular car ferry work, the *Algomah* began summer service between Mackinaw City and Mackinac Island, the kindly, generous and efficient Captain Joe Fitzpatrick in charge as purser. Today he is still living, but in broken health and requiring constant care. He retired from active work several years ago. Captain Joe was ever a friend where friends were needed

LAKESIDE HOTEL, MACKINAW CITY.

This cosy hotel has many advantages not shown in the picture. The principal of these is the lovely Straits of Mackinaw, the beach of which comes within a few feet of the additions in the rear of the hotel. From any window on the side of the building during the summer, you may look out over the white crested waters, and see long processions of sailing vessels and gigantic steamships carrying grain, coal, lumber and the products of the world's markets across the Great Lakes. A view from Lakeside Hotel is delightful, beyond imagination.

A short distance down the beach is the site of old Fort Michilomackinac, now completely obliterated, and covered by a growth of pines, The steamboat landing is within a stone's throw, where the largest ships of the lakes make a landing.

In the warmest of weather the nights are as cool as they are up at an elevation of ten thousand feet in the Rocky Mountains, while the air at all times of the day is cooled by continuous breezes.

Mrs. M. Clark, the proprietor, an estimable lady, has been a resident of Mackinaw City for ten years, seven of which she has put in at the hotel business. The Lakeside Hotel, over which she so ably presides, contains 20 rooms, which are furnished in an unusually pleasing manner. The table service is second to no hotel in Michigan. There is a homelike hospitality about the place, that satisfies the most forlorn individual, and persons desiring a rest find it fully up to their utmost desire. This season there have been people from Kentucky, Ohio and the southern part of Michigan, who spent their entire outing at the Lakeside, preferring it to Mackinaw Island, which is but a short distance away by ferry boat. So popular has the house become, with commercial travelers as well as tourists, that Mrs. Clark will build an addition before next season, capable of accommodating the large number of people that next summer will find seeking apartments at the Lakeside, over this season's business. Rates at the Lakeside are: $1.50 and $2.00 per day, and $7 a week.

Later the Windermere Hotel.

Chapter 22

Protestant Churches

Presbyterian Services Were Begun in 1881

This history written for the Cheboygan County Centennial.

by *Cheboygan Daily Tribune*

A glimpse into the early years of the Mackinaw City Presbyterian Church. Taken from first minutes recorded by Dr. Henry Conkling and a brief history of the first fifty years by Miss Alice Marsh, daughter of the first Pastor, the Rev. Mr. A. Marsh.

The first mention we have of the Presbyterian Church in Mackinaw City is from the minutes written by Dr. Henry Conkling dated Sunday May 28, 1881. He writes, "Presbyterian preaching this day in a G. W. Simpson Hotel, Mackinaw City, Michigan, by Rev. J. J. Cook a missionary of the Grand Rapids Presbytery. His residence about seven miles from Harbor Springs, Herman Post Office, Emmet County. This was the first Presbyterian sermon in this place. Fourteen persons were present. The Rev. J. J. Cook came monthly until the fall of 1881 and held services. Meetings were discontinued through the winter. In the spring of 1882 he came once or twice to preach and then discontinued his labors at this place."

The next preacher to come was Rev. A. B. Peebles sent here by Rev. T. D. Marsh, Synodical Missionary of the Presbyterian Church in Michigan. The Rev. Mr. Peebles was from Oberlin, Ohio as a supply preacher and preached his first sermon on May 28, 1882 in Shepherd's Hall.

Church Is Organized

On July 11, 1882 (Tuesday at 3 p.m.) organization of the First Presbyterian Church of Mackinaw took place in the office of Dr. Henry Conkling in a building erected for a store house at the south west corner of Central Ave., and First Street. This was the first church organization of any denomination of Mackinaw City.

The meeting was conducted by the Home Missions Committee of Grand Rapids Presbytery, Rev. Augustus Marsh of Cadillac presiding as chairman. Others present representing of Ionia, Rev. John Redpath of Boyne Falls, and Elder J. J. Hood of Boyne Falls. Rev. John Redpath acted as clerk of the meeting and Rev. Mr. Jewell preached the sermon from Romans 12:1.

Dr. Henry Conkling and his wife Matilda presented letters from the 2nd Presbyterian Church of Bloomington, Ill., and George Gane and his wife Sarah presented letters from the M. E. Church of Clam Lake, Michigan.

Upon reception into the church membership Mr. Gane and Dr. Gane and Dr. Conkling were elected elders and were regularly ordained by the laying on of hands and installed into office, after which the First Presbyterian Church of Mackinaw City, Michigan was duly organized.

Church Site Given

Two lots for a church building were offered by Dr. Conkling, gifts of himself and his brother James of Springfield, Ill. Rev. T. D. Marsh reported a gift of $100.00 and an additional pledge of $50.00. Rev. Peebles donated an organ, after which the congregation sang, "I Love Thy Kingdom Lord," and was dismissed by the benediction.

Through the spring and summer of 1882 "Meeting and Sabbath School" were held in a passenger coach of the GR & I R.R. and later continued through autumn and winter in a building on the south west corner of Central Ave., and First Street.

In November of 1882 a manse was built described as size 16 x 22, 1½ story with small room at west side.

The First Pastor

In May 13, 1883, Rev. Marsh of Cadillac held services in Shepherd's Hall, and again on June 3, 1883. On June 17 Rev. Mr. Campbell of Spring Lake, Michigan, held services, and on June 24, Rev. Marsh came as the first pastor of this church.

The erection of the church building was begun in April, 1883, and the first service was held in it on a rainy Sunday morning August 12, 1883. September 26, 1883, marked the Dedication Sunday with Rev. L. M. Schofield of Grand Rapids preaching the sermon and the dedication by Rev. A. Marsh, the pastor.

From this point the church moved forward in its witness of God to the community, state, nation and the world.

The Church of the Straits

(Methodist and Presbyterian)
Mackinaw City, Michigan

by
Maribeth Barnett
April 18, 1967

INTRODUCTION

Since the founding of the city of Mackinaw is so closely tied to the construction of its churches, it seems impossible to write this history without first giving a brief description of the early beginnings of the town.

"Reverend Dr. Morse, father of the inventor of the telegraph, was one of the first protestant ministers to visit the region in 1820. He preached on Mackinac Island."[1]

One must realize that, due to the moving of the fort from Mackinaw City to Mackinac Island in 1781, the main civilization in the Straits Region at this time was concentrated on Mackinac Island.

The first records we find on the city of Mackinaw are about the year 1857. These documents show Mr. Edgar Conkling and his associates of Cincinnati, Ohio, having purchased the area from the government, were the sole owners of the lands of Mackinaw. Edgar Conkling was believed, by many of his friends, to be a visionary and a dreamer. He was convinced that Mackinaw City was very adaptable to settlement; and was soon to become a thriving, growing community. With these ideas in mind, he had the ground surrounding the old fort surveyed and platted for a town. The following are excerpts taken from that survey which seemed to at least support Mr. Conkling's theory that the lands of the village were very acceptable for settlement:

"Gents: Having completed my surveys of Mackinaw City and the surrounding lands belonging to your company, at your request, I herein embody briefly the result of my observations. Mackinaw City, situated on the south side of the Straits, and upon the northern extremity of the Southern Peninsula of Michigan, occupies a position at once admirably adopted to the conveniences and necessities of a great city, and susceptible of easy and commensurate improvement.

"...Upon the whole, I can not but congratulate your company on the site you have been so fortunate as to possess for a prospective city, affording, as it does, almost unexampled facilities for settlement and improvements. While at the same time its commercial advantages, being at the center of an immense agricultural and mineral district, with many other minor pursuits inviting to human industry, give ample promise that in the onward development of the mighty north-west, it must become a great Central Metropolis."[2]

During the years immediately following the survey, it appeared that Edgar Conkling's dream was a fantasy. For thirteen years the lands of Mackinaw lay dormant. Then in 1870 the first inhabitants arrived in the village. These were workmen who boarded in a log shanty and were employed by Mr. Conkling in building a dock. Soon after the construction of the dock, settlers began arriving in the area. The first homesteaders were Mr. and Mrs. George W. Stimpson, who erected a log house located where the Sattler Hotel now stands. Mr. and Mrs. L. I. Willits operated the first general store at the site of what is now Dann's Market.

Thus before his death in December 1881, Edgar Conkling had the opportunity of seeing his greatest ambitions becoming a reality.

THE PRESBYTERIAN CHURCH

Early in the history of the village of Mackinaw it was agreed by the residents that a church was a definite need if the town were to attract worthy settlers.

From some early church records written by Dr. Henry Conkling, a brother of Edgar Conkling who was the founder of Mackinaw City, we learn that the first Presbyterian service was held May 22, 1881, in the G. W. Stimpson Hotel. Fourteen people attended the service which was conducted by Reverend J. J. Cook, a missionary of the Grand Rapids Presbytery, whose residence was in Harbor Springs. Reverend Cook made trips monthly as long as weather permitted and then again for several months in the spring. Not long after this Reverend Cook discontinued his labors here and Reverend A. B. Peebles, an unordained minister from Oberlin, Ohio, replaced him. Reverend Peebles' first service was held on May 28, 1882 in Shepherd's Hall which was located where the Albert Silfven residence now stands.[3]

In July of the same year, a meeting of the committee for the organization of churches in the Grand Rapids Presbytery was held at Mackinaw. This meeting was conducted in the office of Dr. H. Conkling at the site of the present Dixie Tavern with the following men present: Reverend T. D. Marsh, Synodical Missionary of Grand Rapids, Reverend Agustus Marsh of Cadillac, Reverend D. A. Jewell of Ionia, Reverend John Redpath of Boyne Falls, and Elder J. J. Hood of Boyne Falls. Reverend D. A. Jewell delivered the sermon which was taken from Romans 12-1 and during the meeting the First Presbyterian Church was duly organized. At this meeting letters were presented by Dr. H. Conkling and his wife from the Second Presbyterian Church of Bloomington, Illinois, and by George Gane and his wife from the Methodist Church of Clam Lake, Michigan, dismissing them from said churches. They were then officially united with the Presbyterian Church of Mackinaw. At this time Dr. Conkling and George Gane were ordained as Elders of the church.

There being no other place available, church meetings and Sabbath School were held for several weeks in a passenger coach of the Grand Rapids and Indiana Railroad. As fall and winter weather set in, services were conducted in a storehouse erected by Dr. Conkling at the southwest corner of Huron and Central Avenue where the Village Hall now stands. Average attendance at church services was forty and at Sabbath School twenty-five.

September 17, 1882, found the papers for the church being officially recorded in the County Court House in Cheboygan and the following trustees being elected to serve the church: Dr. Conkling - three years, George Gane - two years, and Charles Stimpson - one year.

On Sunday, October 29, 1882, the regular service and the first communion services were given by Reverend W. S. Potter of Petoskey with ten persons partaking of the sacrament.

By this time, having held services in a hotel, a railroad car and a storehouse, the congregation very much desired a church of their own. Dr. Henry Conkling and his brother, James C. Conkling of Springfield, Illinois, graciously donated to the church lots fourteen and fifteen of block seventy. During the fall of 1882 a manse was built on lot fifteen, and the following summer a church was commenced on the remaining lot. The building committee consisted of James Shepherd, Henry Conkling, George Gane and S. B. Chamberlain signed an agreement on April 5, 1883, with contractors Robert Basset and John Padden to erect the building. [4]

About a month before the church was completed several items were placed in a tin can and deposited behind the wainscoting in the southeast corner of the building. These items consisted of a history of the church organization, the names of the first pastor, the members, the elders, and the trustees. Also included was a copy of the newspaper *Interior* and the pamphlet, *Title to Mackinaw City*, the latter being the survey which Edgar Conkling had made in 1857.

On a rainy Sunday morning of August 12, 1883, the bell on the newly erected church was rung for the first time, calling about thirty people to worship. The church windows were unfinished at this time and the openings were closed with pieces of muslin. Reverend Agustus Marsh, who had replaced Reverend Peebles, conducted the service.

During the official dedication service, which took place in September 1883, many visitors were present to hear Reverend L. M. Schofield of Grand Rapids deliver the sermon. At this time numerous gifts were donated to the church, among them the following windows:

"Sabbath School of the Presbyterian Church - Springfield, Illinois; Sabbath School of the Presbyterian Church - Grand Rapids, Michigan; Sabbath School of the Presbyterian Church - Mackinaw City, Michigan; Ladies Foreign Missionary Society - Sturgis, Michigan; Ladies Home Missionary Society of the First Presbyterian Church - Springfield, Michigan; Reverend A. B. Peebles - Salt Lake City, Utah; Employees of the Michigan Central Railroad (two windows)" [5]

A circular memorial window adorning the front of the church was given by Dr. H. Conkling and James Conkling in memory of their brother Edgar. [6]

The next few years saw a considerable increase in the church membership. This being the only religious institution in the area, people from many denominations (Methodist Episcopal, Baptist, Lutheran, Congregational) were united with this church.

The first baptism of the church was that of John Henry Buhman, infant son of Peter Buhman in June 1884.

Reverend Agustus Marsh remained in Mackinaw until 1887, at which time he was succeeded by Reverend O. J. Roberts. Then on Sunday, October 4, 1891, the congregation called Reverend James Thompson, a minister from Belfast, Ireland, to serve as their pastor at a salary of $450 per year. Reverend Thompson served the church faithfully until the fall of 1893 when he found it necessary to spend the winters elsewhere due to ill health.

One of the first organizations of the church was the Willing Workers Society organized about 1888. The women of this association were staunch pillars of the new church and raised money to aid in paying the pastor's salary, decorating expenses of the church and manse, and for various items of furniture for the sanctuary and kitchen. The next few years found a Northern Lights Mission Band, a Woman's Christian Temperance Union, a Women's Missionary Society, and a Young People's Society of Christian Endeavor being organized. The Willing Workers was the only society still functioning at the time of the merger.

The ensuing years witnessed a never-ending struggle of the church to survive. Ministers of the Presbyterian churches are not appointed by Presbytery, the governing body of the churches, as they are in several other denominations, but are interviewed by a pulpit committee and then voted on by the congregation. Therefore, when a pastor leaves, a congregation can find itself without a minister for an indefinite period, sometimes as long as several years. The Mackinaw church was no exception and in the 1920's they were without a pastor for some years. During these difficult times, many of the congregation, having been invited by the Methodists, worshipped in the Methodist church which was just a block away. As years went by many friendships developed among the members of the two congregations. Finally in 1929 Reverend Verne Butler was called as pastor of the church and accepted the call.

On August 5, 1932, the fiftieth anniversary of the organization of the church was celebrated. A delicious supper was served by the Willing Workers, after which Mrs. Luella Overton acted as chairman of the program. At the following Sunday worship service an interesting church history was read by Miss Alice Marsh, daughter of Reverend A. Marsh who served the church in its infant years.

Reverend Joseph Ryan was the pastor in the 1940's and during his ministry he served the Presbyterian Churches of St. Ignace, Rudyard and Hessel in the Upper Peninsula.

In 1958 the congregation was still being faced with the problems of pastoral supply. It was decided at this time to explore the possibilities of a joint parish with St. Ignace. After much discussion and several trips across the bridge, Reverend James Coombes was called in 1960 as pastor of the church in conjunction with the St. Ignace church. The membership of the church at this time was approximately fifty-three.

The following is a list giving as accurate an account as possible of the ministers who served this church:

Reverend J. J. Cook 1881
Reverend A. B. Peebles. 1882
Reverend Agustus Marsh. 1883-1887
Reverend D. J. Roberts 1888-1890
Reverend James Thompson 1891-1893
Reverend H. Wilson. 1894-1900
Reverend James M. Dallas 1901-1907
Reverend E. C. Rust. 1908-1910

Presbyterian Church

Street showing the First Presbyterian Church, Mackinaw City, Michigan.

The "Willing Workers" Society of the Presbyterian Church around 1905. Some of these ladies are Anna Buhler, Aggie Robinson, Mrs. Howard Born, Eloise Stringham and Mrs. Ball.

Reverend S. J. S. Moore 1911-1913
Reverend Joseph Klearkopes 1914-1917
Reverend W. J. Cross 1918-1919
Reverend Verna Butler 1929-1930
Reverend R. V. Chapin 1932-1940
Reverend J. D. Ryan 1941-1946
Reverend Earl Harris 1947-1949
Reverend N. Sichterman 1953-1957
Reverend Wm. Harmon 1958
Reverend Harold Bedient 1959
Reverend James Coombes 1960-1961

THE METHODIST CHURCH

The honor of holding the first protestant services in Mackinaw City belongs to the Methodists. In the year 1870 Reverend Elder Riley, desiring to be the first minister to preach in the new frontier town, arrived from Cheboygan and held worship in the home of George W. Stimpson. This was the only dwelling at the time in the village.

A few days after Reverend Riley's visit, Reverend J. A. VanFleet, a Methodist Episcopal minister from Mackinac Island, came with the same intentions as Reverend Riley. Finding he could not perform the first worship service, he did, however, consent to conduct several services in the old dock house.

Although the missionaries of the Methodist Episcopal denomination were the first in the field at Mackinaw, no attempt toward establishing an organization was made until 1888.

As has been previously mentioned, by this time most Protestants had already found a home in the Presbyterian Church.

About the year 1887, with denominational lines becoming stricter, the Methodists began aspiring toward a church of their own. In 1888 the Methodist Society was fully organized and met for a time in the village schoolhouse. Reverend E. Marble was secured as the first minister in March of that year and on March 19th, eighteen persons attended worship services.

A beautiful site, on a small bluff overlooking the blue waters of the Straits and in view of all passing ships, was presented to the church by George H. Todd, a citizen of the community. On this site, with a gift of $200 and a $200 loan, the Methodist Episcopal Church was started.

The lumber for the building was bought from the Wm. Callam Lumber Co. of Cecil Bay, which was located on the northeast shore of Lake Michigan about eight miles west of Mackinaw. Captain Ed Laway, who was about ten years old at the time, said his father received $1.75 per thousand board feet of lumber for shipping this material to Mackinaw by schooner. The lumber was transported to the shore at the site of the present Elton Dagwell residence where it was then dragged up the beach by Ed and his father to the building site. [7]

In January 1893 when construction of the church was nearing completion, *The Mackinaw Witness*

listed the names of those donating stained glass windows:

C. D. Todd - Santiago, California
G. H. Todd - Mackinaw City, Michigan
Mrs. M. Bissell - Grand Rapids, Michigan
Methodist Episcopal Church-Mackinaw City, Mich.
Mrs. A. Cater in memoriam of her father, Marcus D. L. McMaster
Ladies Aid Society - Mackinaw City, Michigan
George Fuller - Adrian, Michigan
Mr. and Mrs. Wm. Allman - Sturgis, Michigan
Methodist Episcopal Sunday School - Mackinaw City, Michigan

There were also two windows bearing the names of Dr. Harvey P. Smith and his wife Kate and a large circular window with the name Reverend T. J. Leek, Harrisburg, Pennsylvania, inscribed thereon. [8]

The new structure was named Ames Memorial Methodist Episcopal Church in honor of Bishop E. R. Ames and the first service in the new building was held on January 6, 1893. Three of the charter members were J. G. Richards, owner of a grocery store, C. H. Zimmerman, owner of a lumber business, furniture store, and livery stable, and B. Fairchild, a justice of the peace.

New seats for the church arrived and were put together and arranged in time for the dedication services which were scheduled for Sunday, February 19. *The Witness* reported the dedication services in its issue of March 4, 1893:

Sunday, February 19, was a day that will long be remembered in the annals of church history in Mackinaw City. It marked the completion of the church enterprise that has been in progress for some time past. It was the culminating point, and had been anxiously awaited by many in mingled hope and fear.

Early on the morning of dedication a storm began, and by the opening of the love feast a regular Mackinaw blizzard was raging without. Despite the unfavorable weather the house was comfortably filled by the time for the beginning of the regular service at 10:30.

Bishop Ninde seemed to be at his best, and preached a soul-stirring sermon from John 10, which for simple earnestness and market effect we have seldom seen excelled. He clothed the great sublime foundation of doctrines of the gospel in simple language that any child could understand. The only criticism we have heard of the sermon was that there was not enough of it.

After the sermon the pastor produced a large anchor which was covered with slips ranging from $25 to 50c. Dan Willits and Professor V. J. Hooper assisted and the work of liquidating the debt began. After a short silence the responses began to come in, and soon it became evident that the people meant business. In a few minutes the tide of enthusiasm reached its height, and responses from all quarters poured in with such rapidity as to tax the ability of the pastor and his assistants to record them. In less than thirty minutes the board with its silver texts was swept clear of the last dollar and when the pastor announced that $725 had been raised there were many surprised looks, even among those who had been most hopeful.

Another stirring sermon full of gospel was preached by the Bishop in the evening, followed by the dedication ceremony and the second quarterly communion service completed the day so full of satisfaction and blessing to all. The Bishop expressed many times his surprise and gratification of the beautiful appearance of the new church, and the hearty way in which the Mackinaw people responded to the financial call.

Brother J. Thompson, absent in the South, sent his congratulations.

Sunday School was an integral part of the church almost from the beginning. *The Mackinaw Witness* of October 1892 listed the following classes and teachers:

Bible Class . . . . No. 1 . . . J. J. Richards
Bible Class . . . . No. 2 . . . Reverend N. P. Brown
Intermediate Class . . . . No. 3 . . . Mrs. N. Harrison
Intermediate Class . . . . No. 4 . . . A. E. Smith
Primary Class . . . . No. 5 . . . W. Willits
Primary Class . . . . No. 6 . . . J. E. Wilson

Other organizations of the church were an Epworth League, a young people's organization, which was started in 1893, and a Ladies Aid Society organized about the same time. The name of Ladies Aid Society was later changed to The Women's Society of Christian Service. The ladies of the society held ice cream socials, suppers, and teas to raise money and were very influential in assisting with church expenses and spiritual guidances.

Some of the sermons delivered in the new church during its infant years were: *Motive Power of Religion, What It Is to Be a Christian, The Unknown God, Christ the Divine Potter,* and *The Story of Ahab and Jezebel.* [9]

In 1902 the records of the Ames Memorial Episcopal Church listed thirty members of whom the following were trustees: J. G. Richards, R. Neil, W. Durha, W. S. VanHelen, A. D. Marks, and D. Willits.

The purchase of the house which resided on the same lot as the church was completed in 1925. This house, which was bought from C. H. Zimmerman, made the church the sole owner of the triangular shaped plot of ground overlooking the Straits.

The house, when not needed as a parsonage, was rented and brought in additional revenue for the church.

The next few years saw several changes taking place in the church. In the early years of her life she had been Methodist Episcopal. Then in 1940, after many years of pondering and study, it was decided by the governing body of the Methodist faith that all branches of the Methodist denomination would be reclassified as solely Methodist. This, of course, meant some changes as far as discipline was concerned and was a hard pill for many congregations to swallow. It was, however, quite readily accepted by the Mackinaw congregation.

The financial burden of the church became greater as years went on, and during the years from 1934 to 1950 the church became one of several on a circuit. Carp Lake, Levering, and at one time Pellston was included in this circuit. This tended to ease the financial problems somewhat, as each charge contributed to the pastoral expense.

Mrs. Ruth Bauers recalls that in 1939 she was asked by the District Superintendent to conduct a survey among the members of the congregation to gain their reactions to a possible merger of the Methodist and Presbyterian Churches. Most responses were favorable, but when the pastor learned of her endeavor, he was very indignant and told her so in no uncertain terms.

By the year 1950, the church felt that it could again support its own minister, and Reverend L. S. Reed came to Mackinaw. While Reverend Reed and his wife were getting settled in the parsonage, an oil stove exploded, causing a fire which destroyed the entire interior of the residence as well as the church records, which were housed inside.

Her early years saw the church serving the religious needs of lumbermen, fishermen and sailors. Several times when the Presbyterians were without a pastor, she ministered to that congregation as well as to their children at Sunday School.

Gradually, the principal industry of Mackinaw became the tourist industry. The church, while still being faithful to her year-round congregation, became the vacation home of prominent ministers, educators and businessmen, as well as the itinerant tourists. Many times such prominent men as Bishop F. D. Leate, Reverend J. S. Steininger and Dr. Douglas V. Steers occupied the pulpit on a summer Sunday morning.

The Ames Memorial Methodist Church is very proud, as she rightly should be, of the fact that she never once closed her doors during the many years she served her congregation.

During the years just preceding the merger her number of members had grown to approximately eighty-one.

The following is a list of all the pastors who served this church:

"Reverend E. Marble 1888
Reverend L. Blanchet 1889
Reverend E. Marble 1889-1890
Reverend George Brown 1890
Reverend Irwin Engle 1890-1891
Reverend D. A. Ball 1891-1892

The sermon topic Sunday morning is' "A Perishing People." Come out and enjoy gospel preaching.

A story is going the rounds of a poker game where two men each held four aces. And it was not in some far off city but our own local town.

Marvyn Lowry arrived home this week beating his welcome by a small margin.

If the Madden Bill passes, mail clerks will get a thirty five per cent increase. So hurry up, Burly, we expect you to prevent it.

The Methodist Sunday School is getting ready for a whopping picnic.

T. M. T. M. Garden Club was entertained Friday at Newlands with story telling by Miss Fox, the children's friend.

Dr. Jonh Dystant, Bay City District superintendent, will hold the fourth quarterly conference of the Ames Memorial Methodist Episcopal Church Saturday night at the church.

Mrs. Frank Glympse flew through town Thursday.

The subject for last Thursday's prayer meeting was "The Unexpected in Life" and sure enough the Presbyterians came over and had a fine time. Next Thursday evening the subject will be "The Teach Me's." This might prove helpful to you.

Miss Norva Dagwell is having her piano recital in the church Saturday afternoon.

Corporal Sam Sprague was in town this week with another of the state police. Fifteen are stationed in Pellston patrolling forest fires.

Many questions are being asked, ' What's the matter with the Ladies' Aid?"

How many windows were broken in the school-house? We think of a little poem that may explain:
The schoolboy isn't vicious but
He thinks with wistful yearning
Just now what joy 'twould be to him
To see his schoolhouse burning.

Personal liberty in action is what blew up the munition factories and what is running Russia today.

The AMES JOURNAL

MACKINAW CITY'S LITTLE WEEKLY

Vol.1 No.37 Issued Every Friday. Aug. 1,'19

Major Andrews consents to speak Sunday Evening!

CHAUTAUQUA ADVERTISING

Thursday, the advance man of the Chautauqua hit town and liberally dosed us with advertising.

Now it is time for everyone to begin talking Chautauqua and not stop until every last seat in the big tent is full and we are assured a yearly one.

The program continues for five days beginning August twentieth and contains some fine numbers.

OLIVE SHEPLER REPORTED BETTER

A telegram arrived Thursday night saying that little Miss Olive Shepler was very low.

Father and mother hastened to Petoskey by auto.

As we go to press we hear that she is a little better.

WENT OVER WITH FIRST DIVISION

WON DISTINGUISHED SERVICE CROSS HONOR

A great patriotic meeting will be held on next Sunday evening, August 3, at the Methodist Church when Major M. M. Andrews will give the principle address.

Major Andrews went across with the First Division and saw most of the American fighting as he was with the 26th Infantry.

For bravery he was given the coveted Distinguished Service Cross.

Major Andrews said he saw more Christianity practiced in France than he ever saw before.

No one can really afford to miss this opportunity to hear this great and distinguished man. Service men are especially invited.

Ames Memorial Church
North Huron Avenue

The AMES JOURNAL

Jamet St. Mackinaw City Mich.

"Entered as second-class matter November 1, 1918, at the post office at Mackinaw, Michigan, under Act of March 3, 1879."

EMERALD B. DIXON
Editor and Publisher

Subscription Price 25 cts a year

Don't let kind words die.

No man receiveth the love of God to himself alone.

In getting ready for heaven practice enjoying the presence of little children.

Some folks who cry for better sermons are already overfed but underworked.

I must meet my obligation to the church if I would have the church meet its obligation to the world.

WHAT DO YOU THINK?

That wonderful two miles of sidewalk needs repairing and cleaning. Everyone loses because of it.

What would you think, beach and town people, of having a bee one day and see what we could do with it?

NEWS

Here is some news that may surprise some folks: there are enough people in Mackinaw City who stand for better things (higher schools, sewerage, water works, civic pride, law enforcement and Christianity) to make this a decent place to live.

But they have acquired a habit that almost becomes a sin — that of keeping quiet, sometimes to the extent of giving a wrong impression of their views.

To them we would say, "Stand up, speak out and bravely, in God's name."

SENSE

"Where can I safely invest my money?" was once asked of a wealthy and liberal man of God.

He answered. "Give to God's Cause, where I have put thousands. I find the interest due is promptly paid and the investment is perfectly safe. I shall meet it beyond the river and enjoy it forever."

CARD OF THANKS

We wish to thank our many kind friends and neighbors, who, through their thoughtfulness helped to brighten the many dark days we have passed through.

Their many expressions of love and sympathy were greatly appreeciated by us.

Sincerely,
Samuel J. Smith and Family.

Reverend George Kard 1941-1943
Reverend Kermit Mier 1943
Reverend Dorr P. Garrett 1943-1946
Reverend Lloyd M. Schloop 1946-1949
Reverend Leon Shaffer 1949-1950
Reverend L. S. Reed 1950-1956
Reverend Brad Stanton 1956
Reverend LaVerne Steele 1956-1959
Reverend R. R. Terwilliger 1959-1960
Reverend Colby Johnson . . . . 1960-1962"[10]

The problems facing the Methodist and Presbyterian congregations of Mackinaw City were certainly not unique. These problems are often found in small communities where there are churches of several denominations with small memberships. These churches find that there aren't enough members to do the jobs and that the financial burden is too great.

The year 1960 found the Methodist and Presbyterian Churches being served by two young ministers—Reverend Colby Johnson in the Methodist Church and Reverend James Coombes in the Presbyterian Church.

The Methodists, finding their church inadequate during the summer months, were contemplating the construction of a new building.

The Presbyterians had solved, at least for the present, part of their problem by entering into a joint parish with St. Ignace.

However, on the recommendation of these two young pastors, it was decided by the congregations to study the possibility of a merger between the two churches. After winning the consent of the superiors of both denominations, a Joint Discussion Committee was organized. According to church record, this committee consisted of eight members, four Presbyterians—Kenneth Teysen, Clara Waara, Walter Melms, Amelia Cole, and four Methodists—Jane Bradford, Ruth Klingler, Stanley McRae, and Bill Newsome.[11] The committee was requested to meet once a month for approximately a year to study all phases of the problem and to set up articles under which the proposed unified church would be governed.

The first steps taken by the group were to determine similarities and differences of the two churches and then to contact any churches which were known to have merged successfully in hopes that they could offer some suggestions. By December of 1961 the committee had met three times, and it was with regret that both congregations learned of the intention of Reverend Coombes to leave Mackinaw. It was then decided by the group to hold joint services during the remainder of the winter with Reverend Johnson conducting the services.

Meanwhile, Joint Discussion Committee meetings progressed and by April 17, 1962, the name, The Church of the Straits (Methodist and Presbyterian), had been selected for the proposed church. The Articles of Federation had been drawn up and were mailed to each member in preparation for the final vote of the congregations.

On May 14, 1962, at 7:30 p.m., members of both congregations gathered in the Presbyterian Church to decide an important issue of their lives. Each congregation met separately for a short time, the Methodists with their District Superintendent, Reverend Heath Goodwin, and the Presbyterians with moderator, Reverend Dan Axt. A joint discussion period followed, after which a vote was taken. Of the 51 votes cast, forty-nine were in favor of the merger and The Church of the Straits came into being. It is of interest to note that once before, some eighty years earlier, these churches had had a unified congregation.

The first pastor of the new church was Reverend George Start, a young Methodist minister who had just finished his schooling in Denver, Colorado. Reverend Start and his wife Ellen seemed to have unlimited energy, for guiding the marriage of these two churches was a never-ending task.

One of the biggest problems facing Reverend Start was the crowded condition of the church during the summer. The winter months saw a small congregation of approximately 100 people but as warm weather arrived the congregation swelled from 350 to 450 people. An immediate attempt at solving the problem was the organization of three Sunday morning services. This eased the situation somewhat, but at the 11 a.m. service many people were still turned away.

A personal recollection is of an 11 a.m. service one Labor Day weekend. By 11 o'clock, the sanctuary, vestibule and fellowship room in the back of the church were completely filled and still the crowds kept arriving. Finally, as a last resort, the ushers placed some folding chairs outside and many people sat or stood and listened to the service through the open windows.

In the fall of 1962 a building committee was appointed to begin coordinating plans to build a new church. One of the first decisions this group reached was that of erecting the building on the triangular shaped piece of land then occupied by the Methodist Church and parsonage. This, as you will recall, was a site that offered an excellent view of the Straits and also of the "Mighty Mackinac Bridge".

During the next three years, the building program was besieged by many setbacks.

Then in 1965, with the new building still in the planning stages, Reverend Start was sent to Cadillac and the congregation was left without a pastor. It was decided by the Board of Governors, local governing body of the church, as recommended by the Articles of Federation, to try to obtain a Presbyterian minister.

Reverend John J. Buchanan, interim pastor from Maryland, filled the pulpit for the summer and in October, Reverend Raymond Provost of Cleveland, Ohio, was elected by the congregation to serve as the next pastor of the church. Reverend Provost is a Presbyterian minister who has recently returned to this country after seventeen years as a missionary in Korea.

Under his able leadership, the plans for the new church once more moved ahead. The spring of 1966 saw construction crews on the job and the project underway.

The laying of the cornerstone for the church took place August 15, 1966. A sealed container holding records of both Methodist and Presbyterian churches was enclosed in the cornerstone. By the end of the year, the new building was completed and the first service was held in January, 1967.

The union of these two churches is still in infancy but the future of The Church of The Straits looks very bright and promising.

The following were members of the building committee for the new church:

Donald Bell, Chairman
Keith Darling
Dorothy Darrow
Judith Leete
Roger McCormick
Bud Miller
John Scherf
Kenneth Teysen
Betty Teysen

Church of the Straits

FOOTNOTES

1 James M. Dallas, *Missions at Old Mackinaw, Ancient and Modern, including the Story of Fort and Massacre,* p. 35.

2 R. C. Phillips, *Title to Mackinaw City,* quoted in the *Cheboygan Daily Tribune,* August 13, 1966.

3 George Coffman, an interview, February 14, 1967.

4 *Records,* First Presbyterian Church of Mackinaw City, 1883.

5 Dr. Henry Conkling, Records of First Presbyterian Church of Mackinaw City, 1883.

6 Ibid.

7 Ed Laway, an interview, February 26, 1967.

8 *The Mackinaw Witness,* January 7, 1893.

9 Ibid., July 14, September 23, October 21, 1893.

10 Ruth Bauers and Joan Cosen, *Church Messenger,* 1954 p. 3.

11 Records, The Church of the Straits, 1961-1962.

BIBLIOGRAPHY

Bauers, Ruth and Cosens, Joan, *Church Messenger,* 1954.

Cheboygan Daily Tribune, July 2, 1955, and August 13, 1966.

Conkling, Dr. Henry, *Records* of the First Presbyterian Church of Mackinaw City, 1883.

Dallas, James M., *Missions at Old Mackinaw, Ancient and Modern, including the Story of Fort and Massacre,* 1902.

Phillips, R. C. *Title to Mackinaw City,* 1857.

Records, First Presbyterian Church, Mackinaw City, 1882-1961.

Records, Ames Memorial Methodist Church, Mackinaw City, 1888-1961.

Records, the Church of the Straits, Mackinaw City, 1962-1967.

The Mackinaw Witness, October 1892, January 7, 1893, February 4, 1893, July 15, 1893, September 23, 1893, October 21, 1893.

INTERVIEWS

Mrs. Ruth Bauers, February 20, 1967

Mr. and Mrs. George Coffman, February 14, 1967

Mr. Ed Laway, February 26, 1967

Church of Straits To Burn
Church Mortgage Sunday

May 1971

REV. CARL OSWALD

Now that the debt on the new church building has been completely paid, The Church of the Straits in Mackinaw City intends to celebrate and give thanksgiving with a special worship service to burn the mortgage.

On Sunday evening at 7:30 a special program is being planned by the pastor, the Rev. Raymond C. Provost, to mark this historic date. The featured speaker of the evening will be the Rev. Carl Oswald,

pastor of St. Paul's United Methodist Church of Cheboygan. The actual burning of the mortgage will be conducted by Donald Bell, chairman, and other members of the building committee which has now completed its assigned responsibilities. Special music will be presented by the Straits choir under the direction of Stanley McRae and the organist, Mrs. Jane McLott.

The burning of the mortgage is the lastest milestone for this historic church on the Straits of Mackinac. The First Presbyterian Church of Mackinaw City was organized in 1882. The Ames Memorial Methodist Church was organized in 1888. Together they represented the Protestant witness in this area serving the lumbermen, sailors railroad men, farmers and many others who pioneered here The first services were held in empty boxcars, vacant buildings or any other place suitable to accomodate a gathering of people.

The Christian love and hard work that went into the building of these two churches has been both the heritage and strength over the years. The lumber from which the two buildings were made was brought here by sailing vessels from the forests near Cecil Bay, a few miles west of Mac-

kinaw City.

On July 1, 1962 following a year of intensive study by a joint committee, the two churches federated to become one-- The Church of the Straits (United Methodist and United Presbyterian.) That the union has been successful is evidenced by the steady growth of the Christian witness in the Straits area.

The sanctuary and the Roger McCormick Fellowship Hall were completed on August 15, 1967. A pastor's residence was built a year later. Since then memorial gifts of pews, a carillon, a pipe organ, sanctuary skylight, and both an exterior lighted cross on the tower and an interior chancel cross as well as carpeting and drapes provided by the Women's Association have added to the physical plant.

Spiritually, the Church of the Straits serves regular members from St. Ignace to the north to the central portions of both Cheboygan and Emmet counties to the south. During the summer thousands of visitors attend from every state of the union and from many foreign countries.

Everyone is cordially invited to share with members of the church on this happy historic occasion.

- -

Mackinaw City Bible Church. Founded by Rev. Lyle Hoover, who established a church in Mackinaw City in 1960, holding services in Wawatam Town Hall for 8 years. Present edifice was built in 1968.

Chapter 23

The Catholic Church
in Mackinaw City

by Margaret A. Paquet

INTRODUCTION

Mackinaw City and the entire Straits area has the most colorful and exciting history of any part of our state of Michigan.

A person entering this area for the first time and viewing the beautiful waters of the Straits, the re-constructed Fort Michilimackinac, and the several museums located in the region must become aware of the fact that this area played a significant role in shaping the destiny of this state.

As in most areas, religion played an important role in the growth and development of the Straits region. In writing this paper, I intend to trace the development of the Catholic Church in Mackinaw City, from the time of the arrival of the first missionaries in the 17th century to the present day.

The location of our state, with its Great Lakes waterways and the abundance of fur-bearing animals, made Michigan a leading center for the early fur trade.

Wherever the fur trader went, the Jesuit priest followed, for both were interested in the savage, one seeking him for his peltries, and the other for the salvation of his soul. [1]

When the Sioux Indians in Canada pushed the Ottawas and Ojibways down into the Straits area in 1669, they settled at Michilimackinac, or the Pointe, which is now St. Ignace, Michigan. Pere Jacques Marquette, a Jesuit priest, came with them. He built a mission and a church on what was known as the Pointe. [2]

While building the church and establishing his mission at the Pointe, we know that Father Marquette visited Mackinac Island. He and his immediate followers spent some time in the central village of the Ottawa Indians, L'Arbre, which meant Crooked Tree. This is now known as Cross Village. Father Marquette had great dreams and desires for educating the Indian people. He had even hoped to establish an Indian college at St. Ignace, but these dreams ended with his death in 1675. Other missionaries carried on the work of Father Marquette, but their job was a most difficult one.

With the end of the seventeenth century, the story of the territory of Michilimackinac became a divided one. Antoine de la Mathe Cadillac, commandant of the garrison at the Pointe, quarreled bitterly with the Jesuits over his reckless exploitations of the Indians in his ambitions to increase the fur trade. Cadillac's conflicts with the Jesuits began soon after his arrival there about 1695.

The Jesuit priest at Michilimackinac at this time was Etienne Carheil. Father Carheil bitterly opposed the brandy traffic, which brought displeasure from Cadillac and the fur traders in this region.

In 1701, Cadillac moved his garrison to his new fort in Detroit. He invited the Indians to the north and west to settle around the new fort, and soon the fur trade began to flourish there, unhampered by the scruples of the Jesuits. [3]

Whether the savage was willing and happy to go to Detroit has been questioned, nevertheless he went. Fur was king. His love and devotion to the forest commerce were stronger than his piety, so that by 1703, Father Carheil was forced to leave, as his little flock had deserted him for Cadillac and the fur trade of Detroit. [4]

Father Carheil's writings gave a gloomy picture of Michilimackinac at that time. In the days before Cadillac's arrival, the missionary had some influence with the traders, but now he had none, as the traders knew that regardless of what he did, the commandant would back him up. The soldiers and Cadillac violated the very laws they were there to enforce, participating in illegal trading, gambling and selling brandy to the Indians. With this state of affairs, it is no wonder that Cadillac and Father Carheil came to a parting of ways.

Although the commandant, soldiers, Indians and Jesuit priest had left Michilimackinac, it was not entirely abandoned. There were fourteen or fifteen Frenchmen, some wanderers and traders who stayed in this area, so we know that trading continued to take place.

The Jesuits had worked long and hard for their slow progress in the north and appealed to the governor of Canada for another post at the Straits. The French, at second glance, realized that it was necessary to re-establish a post on the Straits lest they lose both Indians and precious furs in this whole upper region to the English. In 1715, Fort Michilimackinac was built on the south shore of the Straits, where Mackinaw City is now located. [5]

The colorful history of Fort Michilimackinac, on the south shore of the Straits is well known. This is a sacred site, as well as historical, because during the half century from 1715 to 1765, the light of Christianity was brought to the pagan world through the devoted labors of many missionaries, successors to Father Marquette, who pioneered at the earlier mission across the waters, in St. Ignace.

We know from the record books that a church was built in the fort when it was re-established about 1715. A second church was built about 1741. Some of the missionaries and visiting missionaries recorded in the records were:

```
1708 - ?   Reverend Father J. Marest, S.J.
1741 - 53  Reverend Father J.B. Lamorenie, S.J.
           (visit)
1741 - 65  Reverend Father DuJaunay, S.J.
1742 - 44  Reverend Father C.G. Coquarz, S.J.
           (visit)
1753 - 61  Reverend Father M.L. LeFranc, S.J.
1768-75    Reverend Father Gibault, Vicar
           General of Illinois (visiting)      6
```

Father DuJaunay, as the records show, spent a considerable period of time at Old Mackinaw, as the south fort was called. He left here shortly after the massacre of 1763, where his influence had been responsible for saving the lives of many of those Englishmen who were not struck down in the first bloody days of the massacre. Thereafter, but for three brief visits from Father Pierre Gibault of Illinois, Fort Michilimackinac was without the services of a priest. Many of the inhabitants, including an outstanding man of Jewish faith, Ezekiel Solomon, petitioned the British government to exert its influence to try and get a priest assigned to their St. Anne's parish, but in vain.

In the winter of 1781, the British garrison moved Michilimackinac's church over to Mackinac Island, realizing that the French inhabitants would follow only if their church was transferred to the Island.

The logs that composed its walls were taken down and dragged across the ice to the Island, where with reverent care, it was re-erected. For a period of almost one hundred years after the removal of the fort and chapel, Old Mackinaw was little better than a wilderness. A few Indians and traders came through then, but the center of activity remained at the Island.

In the year 1857, the lands of Old Mackinaw were in the hands of Mr. Edgar Conkling and others in Cincinnati, Ohio, who sometime previously had purchased them from the United States government. During the summer of 1857, Mr. Conkling had the ground adjoining old Fort Michilimackinac surveyed and plotted for a town. [7]

Mr. Conkling had dreams of a great town. He believed that this could be the Detroit of the north, due to its access to the waterways and its direct routes to the south for the inevitable railroads. The land of Mackinaw City slopes gently to the waters edge, and Edgar Conkling could almost see a booming town located on these banks along the Straits of Mackinac.

For thirteen years after Mackinaw City was surveyed, the site remained an unbroken wilderness. In 1870, Mr. Conkling built a dock, and the workmen who boarded in a small log shanty were the first inhabitants of the village. [8]

Roman Catholics were the first to hold religious services in Mackinaw City. In the year 1870, during the building of that first dock by Edgar Conkling, a priest came up from Cheboygan and conducted services for the benefit of the workmen, who were mostly of that faith. [9]

The following account of the Mass, performed in the boarding house, is from the pen of Edgar Conkling:

Mackinaw City, Michigan
February 27, 1870 Sunday

Reverend Charles Decunick, Catholic priest of Cheboygan, Michigan, preached in the boarding house of Patrick Manion at 10:00 A.M. in English, to sixty persons (fifty men, ten women and children) and performed Mass and explained it. After noon he preached in French to forty persons, thirty-two men, eight women and children. Four women had infants, carried half a mile in a dreadful snowstorm and drift, which lasted all day and night before.

He promised his people to erect a meeting house for them next summer, on ground I promised them, and I also promised them all the ground for a college, etc., their church needed.

He stayed Saturday afternoon and all Sunday until Monday morning with me in my storeroom, and boarded at my cost. But for the wind and snow, many more would have come from the surrounding country.

February 11, 1870, Friday - Reverend C. Decunick baptised one child (boy) of P. Manions and gave out his above appointment for the 27th of February.

(signed)
Edgar Conkling
10

In December 1881, the iron horse reached Mackinaw City. There was much rejoicing, as the arrival of the railroads opened communication by land as far south as Detroit.

The priests of St. Mary's Church in Cheboygan took charge of this district. Among these were Fathers De Smet, Alois Webeler, Edward Caldwell, Karen Whelen, Dennis Malone and Albert Dequoy. [11]

The visits of a priest to Mackinaw City were few until the railroad connected the village with towns to the south. From 1881 to 1910, the priests from Cheboygan came on the train to say Mass. There was no church building during these years, so services were held in various homes and buildings.

Captain Ed LaWay, who came to Mackinaw City as a young boy in 1885, recalls that Mass was said in his home on several occasions. Captain LaWay, who lived at Big Stone Bay on the Lake Michigan side of Mackinaw City, said that parishoners gathered in his home for the service, with a wooden table serving as the altar.

The *Mackinaw Witness* of June 26, 1897, noted: Reverend Father Caldwell of Cheboygan was here Tuesday morning and said Mass in Shepards Hall. He baptised the infant child of Mr. and Mrs. George Cantile. Mr. Caldwell will be here again July 20. Shepards Hall was located on the site of the present home of Mr. and Mrs. Al Silfven.

When St. Charles parish was formed in Cheboygan, Father F. Magnan visited Mackinaw City for Mass and instructions.

Until the first church was built, Mass continued to be said in the homes of parishoners, such as the homes of the LaWays, Paquets, McIsaac's, and John Hayes. Services were also said in the schoolhouse, Masonic Hall, Macabee Hall, Merciers Hotel, Shepards Hall and the Town Hall.

Merciers Hotel, which was located on the approximate sites of the Tower and George Hayes homes, burned down in 1893.

Mr. George Coffman, who came to Mackinaw City as an infant in 1883, recalls that the Mercier Hotel was a large two-story building, with a large dormer or cupola forming part of a third floor and that Mass was said in this top story. A statue of the Blessed Virgin Mother was placed in the cupola. He remembers that at the time of the fire, people were yelling and screaming and pointing to the upper floor. Seeing the statue through the smoke and flame, they thought someone was trapped in the burning building.

The daily newspaper, *The Mackinaw Witness*, gave the following news items of Father Magnan's monthly visits:

February 23, 1899: Reverend Father Magnan of Cheboygan was in the city Tuesday, holding Mass with his flock in the forenoon, and a childrens' service in the afternoon.

March 23, 1899: Father Magnan of Cheboygan was in town Tuesday, conducting his monthly service.

April 20, 1899: Reverend Father F. Magnan of Cheboygan was here Tuesday and yesterday saying Mass with his flock.

The children were given instructions by the visiting priest, but when it was time for their First Holy Communion, they had to take more instructions in Cheboygan. Mr. Martin A. McIsaac, who now lives

in Mackinaw City, recalls that he and his brother, Floyd McIsaac, took the train to Cheboygan on Saturday morning, had their special instructions that day, spent the night with family friends and received their First Holy Communion at Mass the following morning, in Cheboygan.

A visit from the Bishop was a very special occasion. He came on one occasion for a Confirmation service, and was served dinner in the home of Dan McIsaac. Their family considered this an honor and for years after, the chair the Bishop used was referred to as "the Bishops' chair."[12]

The faith of these parishoners was strong. Many of them lived outside of the town, but braved many stormy days to attend Mass whenever it was held.

Mrs. Francis Cox Marshall, has lived in Mackinaw City since 1915, moving from Carp Lake, six miles south of Mackinaw City. Mrs. Marshall recalls that her father and brother walked from Carp Lake to Mackinaw City, following the Pennsylvania Railroad tracks, for Mass, regardless of the weather.

In 1903, at the suggestion of Father Magnan, the Catholic people of Mackinaw City purchased from Clinton L. Conkling, trustee under the will of Mercie A. Conkling, deceased, lots one (1), two (2), three (3), eighteen (18), nineteen (19) and twenty (20) of block thirty-five (35), Village of Mackinaw City, County of Emmet, State of Michigan. The deed was executed September 19, 1903, consideration one hundred and sixty-five ($165.00) dollars. [13]

On October 3, 1905, Henry Joseph Richter, Bishop of Grand Rapids, wrote the following to Father Magnan:

Reverend Dear Father:

Permission is hereby granted you to erect a new church at Mackinaw City according to the dimensions given in the Seminary Report for 1902 as appropriate for country places. No debt. however, may be incurred.

Yours sincerely in Christ,

Henry Joseph
Bishop of Grand Rapids, Michigan [14]

In 1907, Father Magnan began the erection of the first Catholic Church in Mackinaw City.

The parishoners worked hard to raise the building funds for their church, to add to their regular church collections. Suppers were held in the town hall, which was a two-story building located where the village hall now stands. A St. Patrick's day supper was an annual affair and all the townspeople looked forward to that date in March. The ladies of the Altar Society held their meetings in different homes and a luncheon was served to raise funds for the new building.

In 1909, the Bishop appointed the parish committeemen. They were Louis J. Gehl, John Hayes, A Desy, Dan McIsaac and Peter Duffins.[15] This group of faithful men, along with the other parishoners, worked long and hard until their dream for a church of their own became a reality.

In June of 1909, Reverend John McDonald was appointed assistant to Reverend Alois Webeler at St. Mary's Church, Cheboygan, and Mackinaw became a mission of that parish. Under Father McDonald's supervision, the church, with a seating capacity of one hundred and twenty-five people, was finished in June, 1910.

A bell for the new church was purchased in April of 1910. The bell, which weighed six hundred and eight pounds, was bought from St. Boniface Catholic Church, Bay City, Michigan, for one hundred and fifty dollars. It rang a few minutes before each Mass, welcoming those in church and telling the late-comers to hurry along. One Sunday morning, as Chris Plaunt was scurrying towards the church, the bells rang, but not as long as usual. He stopped, looked up towards the steeple and said, "ring, dame ya, ring. I've got two bucks in ya." This, indeed, was a humorous kind of pride, but a genuine one. [16]

On Saturday, July 2, 1910, Right Reverend Henry Joseph Richter, Bishop of Grand Rapids, blessed the church building and placed it under the patronage of St. Anthony of Padue.

The statue of the Blessed Virgin Mother, which is in the church today, was purchased by the children of the parish, who received their catechism instructions from Father McDonald in 1909-1910.

On August 4, 1910, Father McDonald was transferred from St. Mary's, Cheboygan, to St. Joseph Church, East Jordan, Michigan, and Reverend George L. Nye succeeded him.

Father Nye made frequent trips to Mackinaw City, saying Mass in the new church and giving catechism instructions. The Cheboygan priests also traveled to their missions in Wolverine, Alverno and Afton.

St. Anthony's parish grew in size, along with the town. Three years after the church was completed, the bishop granted permission for the erection of a rectory. Plans for the building were made by A.J. White and Sons of Big Rapids, Michigan. The work began in October, was under roof in November and completed for occupancy in 1914. The rectory was located in the lot adjoining the church building.

On December 29, 1914, Reverend Father George L. Nye was appointed first pastor of St. Anthony of Padus Church and the missions of St. Aloysius, Wolverine, and St. Monica's in Afton, Michigan.

Shortly after his arrival in Mackinaw City, a man hurried to the rectory, pounded on the door, and breathlessly told Father Nye, "come to the Point at once!" Father Nye was baffled, and asked, "come to the point of what?" The message was finally interpreted for him, and he found out that there was a sick person at Fly Point, which was an Indian settlement about three miles from town, on the Lake Huron shore, and he was being asked to make a sick call at the Point! [17]

The parishoners were good workers and continued their activities to keep their parish from debt. The ladies Altar Society met regularly, sponsored dinners and bazaars for fund-raising projects. There were approximately thirty families in the parish at this time.

The people of the parish always felt that the church and rectory were built "out of town", as there were no other buildings in that section of town yet. The bishop evidently felt the same way, because on July 12, 1920, Reverend E.D. Kelly visited St. Anthony's and directed that a new location be obtained so the church would be in town. On October 19, 1920, lots eight (8), nine (9) and ten (10) of block sixty-nine (69) were purchased from Charles Stimpson, consideration eight hundred and fifty dollars ($850.00). [18]

Julius Hudson and crew, of Cheboygan, began the work of moving the church building on June 9, 1921. Mass was said at the new location on the Feast of St. John the Baptist, June 24, 1921. Hudson and Company moved the rectory by July 19, and the foundation work was completed on August 8, 1921. The church and rectory were now located in the center of the town, on the corner opposite the schoolhouse.

On November 8, 1921, Father Nye was appointed pastor in Holland, Michigan, and was succeeded by Father J. Bernard Hanskneckt, an assistant at St. Mary's Church of Bay City, Michigan. Father Hanskneckt continued the parish and mission and was well liked by all the people in town.

The parish purchased lot seven (7) of block sixty-nine (69) from Charles Stimpson on November 28, 1923, for the sum of two hundred seventy-five dollars ($275.00). Church property then consisted of the four lots, on the northwest corner of block sixty-nine.

In June of 1925, the mission of Afton was detached from the parish of St. Anthony's and attached to the parish at Onaway. The parish of Alverno was then made a mission and attached to the parish of Mackinaw and remained a mission church until 1937.

Father B.G. Winowecki succeeded Father Hanskneckt at St. Anthony's. The parish continued to grow, and when Father Andrew Bieniawski was appointed pastor in 1928, there were fifty families in the parish.

Father Bieniawski served his parishoners at St. Anthony's for the next thirty-three years. He was well liked by all and became known in all the surrounding cities. Father Bieniawski had an exciting background, which showed his great love for Christ and His church.

Father Bieniawski was born in 1874, in Poland, and entered the seminary when he was eighteen. The seminarians felt the Russian persecution, and while they were studying, the seminary was raided and closed by the Russians. They escaped and were hidden inbasements, barns and attics by friends. At the invitation of Pope Leo XIII, they continued their studies in Rome. While he was studying there, Father Bieniawski met Bishop Henry J. Richter of the Diocese of Grand Rapids, Michigan, and accepted his invitation to go to Grand Rapids when his studies were completed. Father Bieniawski was ordained in Grand Rapids on December 7, 1897, and served the following sixty-four years in various parishes in the Diocese of Grand Rapids.

The church building served its need through the 1930's and the war years, but it then became evident that a larger church was needed. The summer tourist season boomed, and the church could not accommodate the visitors, even though six Masses were said on Sunday during the summer months. The building was getting old and was in need of repairs. When the bell was rung, the whole building would tremble. The sacristy was inadequate, confessionals were unhandy and the heating a problem, as anyone knew who attended Mass during the winter months.

A building fund had been in existence for many years, but it was not until 1958 that definite plans were made.

The members of the building committee were: Raymond Desy, Sr., chairman, James B. Marshall, Lloyd Desy, Leo Vachow, Louis Kelso, William Paquet, Robert Beaufhamp, James McMillin, Charles Carty, Thomas Alexander and Joseph Pajot. [19]

Plans for a new church and rectory were designed by Mr. Ted AuClaire of Petoskey. The architecture was typically "northern Michigan" with its high wood trusses and cement block design.

The property for the new buildings was purchased from Mrs. Anna Biggs, and consisted of lots one to eighteen, inclusive, Block 21 of the original plat of Mackinaw City, according to the plat recorded in the Emmet County records.

The following bids were accepted: Peterson and Westberg - General Contractors, $110,901.00; Hector Bourrie and Sons - Plumbing and Heating, $14,475.00; and Henderson Brothers - Electrical, $10,059.00, for a total cost of $135,435.00.

In July of 1958, each parishoner received a letter from Father Bieneawski asking each to make a substantial and sacrificial gift to the church and accept his share of the responsibility. The committeemen called on each home and the people responded generously with pledge donations. At this time, there was approximately $25,000.00 in the building fund, and the rest was to be borrowed and paid back in ten years.

Ground breaking ceremonies were held in late November of 1958. This building project included the new church, a rectory attached to the church, church furnishings and a full basement with complete kitchen facilities. The church building, to seat four hundred, is one hundred and ten feet long and forty-eight feet wide. The attached rectory is sixty-eight by fifty-two feet. When the church was completed, in the Spring of 1959, the total cost was $180,000.00, including loan interests.

The first Mass in the new St. Anthony's of Padua Shrine was said on July 3, 1959, at 7:30 in the evening, with parishoners and many other townspeople in attendance.

Father Bieniawski continued as pastor until his retirement on June 23, 1961. He was pastor at St. Anthony's for thirty-three years and perhaps the oldest priest in the state to undertake a building program and see its completion.

Father Linus Schrems was appointed pastor on June 23, 1961. Father Schrems was born in Saginaw, Michigan, on September 20, 1899. He was ordained by Bishop Edward D. Kelly in St. Andrews Cathedral, Grand Rapids, on February 2, 1926. Father Schrems served in various diocese parishes, and in September of 1943, entered the United States Army as a chaplain, serving in England, France and Germany. He returned to civilian life in May, 1946, and served as pastor of St. Mary's, Lake Leelanau, Michigan, before his assignment to St. Anthony's in Mackinaw City.

Father Schrems served as pastor until September, 1972. He was transferred to St. Joseph's Church, in Traverse City, Michigan.

He was succeeded by Father Herman Kolenda, who served as pastor until October, 1973. At this time, Father Donald Saliskar became the pastor, and served the parish until September, 1975. Father Joseph Kluonius became the pastor on September 3, 1975, coming to St. Anthony's from Skidway Lake, Michigan.

The men and women of the parish work for their church through the Men's Usher's Club and the Ladies Alter Society, respectively. The high school children are given catechism instruction from the pastor, and the grade school children receive weekly instructions from lay teachers.

St. Anthony's parish continues to grow in size and spirit. There are approximately one hundred thirty-seven families in Mackinaw City and thirty-one families from Carp Lake who are listed as parishoners.

Edgar Conkling's dream of a great, large city at the Straits has not come true, but if he were alive today, he would be proud of this village of nine-hundred thirty people, which he founded one hundred six years ago.

The members of St. Anthony's parish are strong in faith and spirit, and with their pastor's guidance, they are continuing to keep the light of Christianity burning in the land of Old Mackinaw.

FOOTNOTES

1. Reuben Gold Thwaites, *Jesuits Relations and Allied Documents* (Cleveland 1896-1901), P. 189.

2. *Collier's Encyclopedia*, "Jacques Marquette", Volume XIII, (New York 1954), p. 193.

3. Ethel Rowan Fasquelle, *When Michigan Was Young* (Grand Rapids, Michigan 1950), p. 28.

4. Ida Amanda Johnson, *Michigan Fur Trade* (Lansing, Michigan Historical Commission 1919) pp 52-53.

5. Fasquelle, op. cit., pp. 28-29.

6. Dwight H. Kelton, *Annuals of Fort Michilimackinac* (1883) p. 62.

7. James M. Dallas, *Missions at Old Mackinaw - Ancient and Modern* (1902), p. 27.

8. Ibid., p. 28.

9. Ibid., p. 28.

10. Ibid., p. 33.

11. *Historical Paper*, St. Anthony of Padua Catholic Church, (1957).

12. Interview with Mrs. E. D. Ackley, Mackinaw City, Michigan (February 24, 1967).

13. *Records*, St. Anthony's Parish, Mackinaw City, Michigan.

14. Ibid.

15. Ibid.

16. Interview with Mr. Martin A. McIsaac, Mackinaw City, Michigan (February 27, 1967).

17. Ibid.

18. *Records*, St. Anthony's Parish.

19. *Historical Paper*, St. Anthony of Padua Church.

BIBLIOGRAPHY

Church Records, St. Anthony of Padua Catholic Church, Mackinaw City, MI

Collier's Encyclopedia, Volume XIII, New York, 1954.

Dallas, James M. *Missions at Old Mackinaw - Ancient and Modern*, 1902.

Fasquelle, Ethel Rowan, *When Michigan was Young*, Grand Rapids, MI 1950.

Historical Remarks, Dedication ceremony of St. Anne's Church, Fort Michilimackinac, May 31, 1964.

Johnson, Ida Amanda, *Michigan Fur Trade*, Lansing, Michigan Historical Commission, 1919.

Kelton, Dwight H. *Annuals of Fort Michilimackinac.* revised edition 1883.

Thwaites, Reuben Gold. ed. *Jesuit Relations and Allied Documents.* Cleveland, 1896-1901.

Personal Interviews:
Mrs. E.D. Ackley, February 24, 1967
Mr. George Coffman, February 18, 1967
Captain Ed LaWay, February 26, 1967
Mrs. Frances Marshall, February 6, 1967
Mr. Martin McIsaac, February 27, 1967
Mr. O. F. McIsaac, March 5, 1967

St. Anthony's Catholic Church, W. Central Ave. - later moved to Henry Street.

Mackinaw City

Mrs. Judy Ranville, Correspondent   May 1971

St. Anthony's Church Retires Debt and Burns Mortgage

Sunday afternoon at five o'clock following the Benediction at St. Anthony's Church in Mackinaw City, the Rev. Fr. L. Schrems gave a short talk on the sacrifices the membership of the church has gone through during the past twelve years in building the new St. Anthony's church and retiring the debt.

Following his talk the building committee was invited to come forward for the mortgage burning ceremony. Robert Beauchamp, who was Superintendent of Schools while he resided in Mackinaw City, was asked to light the mortgage. After the burning the congregation joined in singing "America The Beautiful."

Those in attendence then retired to the church basement where they enjoyed a delicious pot-luck dinner.

Father Schrems read a church document that had been written by the late Father Andrew Bienowicki which stated that each and every member of the parish would have to sacrifice for the next twelve years to help in building the new church. This they have done with the generous help of summer residents and visitors ... their project has been completed. The parish is grateful for the generosity of these visitors.

Father Schrems invited Mr. Beauchamp to say a few words. He told of the many blessings he and his wife and family had received while working on the church project.

Raymond Desy, who was building chairman, told of the congenial co-operation among all the members of the parish and the building committee. He also gave due credit to the summer visitors and thanked them for their generous donations to the retirement fund. He remarked on the rarity of the day. "Where else would you find a small community with two churches burning their mortgages on the same day," he said. This was a very special day for both the Church of the Straits and St. Anthony's Church of Mackinaw City.

When St. Anthony's new building was started, many thought it was too large, but over the years the attendance has increased until during the summer months it has become necessary to hold six masses each Sunday to accomodate the worshipers. An invitation is extended to everyone to worship each week at St. Anthony's.

* * *

St. Anthony's Catholic Church and Parsonage - corner of Jamet and Henry Streets.

Chapter 24

The History of the
Mackinaw City
School System

by Judith Oliver
April 1967

INTRODUCTION

The little red schoolhouse is well known in song and story. The first schoolhouse in the Village of Mackinaw City was not a little red schoolhouse, for it was built of logs. Some of the earliest laws of the state of Michigan dealt with the organization of school systems. They provided for the establishment of school districts in each township. Each district was to have a moderator, a director and an assessor. Each township was required to elect a board of school inspectors consisting of three members. The laws did not make it mandatory for schools to be established; the initiative was left to the people of each township. [1]

THE MACKINAW CITY SCHOOL SYSTEM

Early settlers of Mackinaw City, in 1871, initiated an application for the organization of a school district. On July 9, 1871, School District No. 1 of Inverness Township was organized. At the time present Mackinaw City was in Inverness Township. Three weeks later the first meeting of district voters was held at the home of George W. Stimpson. Officers chosen at this meeting were William Wright, Moderator, George W. Stimpson, Directors, and George Conrad, Assessor.

Once the school district was organized and a board of directors elected, a log school was built near the present site of the Buchmann home. Mr. Edgar Conkling built the school, a building about sixteen feet wide and twenty feet long. It lacked a ceiling and was roofed with cedar bark instead of shingles. The cost of this building was between fifty and ninety dollars. Its furnishings were very plain. Students' desks and benches were homemade.

The first teacher was Miss Lydia J. Stimpson (the late Mrs. E.C. Milliken of Cheboygan). A term of three months was maintained that fall for the seven pupils enrolled. Miss Stimpson received a salary of twenty dollars per month.

Others who taught in the building, commonly called "The Village School", were L.J. Willits, Miss Luella Smith (Mrs. Stimpson Overton), and Miss Ella Eastman (Mrs. Charles Stimpson), daughter of pioneer homesteaders in the Bliss region. [2]

In this one room log school the students, ranging in ages from four to five to sixteen or older, recited their lessons. Pupils were usually supplied with a spelling book, a reader, an arithmetic book and a geography book.

School was held in the log building for approximately twelve years. In 1883 the district appropriated $170 to purchase a site for a new school building. A frame building was erected on the Northwest corner of Henry and Jamet Street, where the present elementary school now stands in Mackinaw City. The new two-story building had two classrooms, one on each floor. [3] The building was about twenty-five feet wide and sixty feet long. Each room was heated by a pot belly stove. [4]

The village school was of interest to everyone in the community. Many of the community's social gatherings and meetings were held in it. Indeed it was something of a neighborhood center. Each month a report on the progress of the scholars was published in the local newspaper. At this time Mackinaw City had its own weekly, *The Mackinaw Witness*. The monthly school report listed the scholars who passed their examinations. It also listed those who had been neither absent nor tardy, as well as those who had earned the largest number of perfect grades in daily lessons.

There were eighty-eight students enrolled in the two room school on September 24, 1892, fifty in the primary room and thirty-eight in the grammar room. [5] Ruth Bell was the primary teacher. Professor V.J. Hooper was principal of the school. The residents of the village were extremely well satisfied with the progress of the school under his principalship. An article in the *Mackinaw Witness* stated, "Even the pupils seem to be taking more than usual interest in their studies this year." [6]

The population of Mackinaw City was increasing rapidly as new families were moving in, thus causing the school enrollment to increase. By the spring of 1893 there were 130 pupils enrolled, fifty-one in the upper room and seventy-nine in the lower room. [7]

Due to the overcrowded condition some action had to be taken to remedy the situation. For a period of several months the following notice was published in *The Mackinaw Witness*:

NOTICE

A special board meeting of the legal voters of School District No. 1 in the township of Mackinaw called by the board of trustees of said district will be held at the school house in Mackinaw City on the 20 day of May A.D. 1893 at 7 P.M. for the purpose of voting to bond said district for one thousand dollars (1000) for building proposed and other necessary improvements.

By order of the Board of Trustees
E.M. Sutherland, Secretary [8]

The election, held on May 20, 1893, was successful and the bond issued. Several weeks later another notice appeared in the local newspaper:

NOTICE

To Contractors and Builders
Sealed proposals for the furnishing of material and building an addition to the school house in Mackinaw City, Michigan, will be received at the store of J.J.G. Richards in Mackinaw City until July 15, 1893. Said addition to be 26 feet by 28 feet and two stories high. For particulars regarding plan and specification apply to J.J.G. Richards, Mackinaw City. The board reserves the right to reject any or all bids.

By order of the Board of Trustees
E. M. Sutherland, Secretary [9]

S. S. Thuma was granted the contract to build the addition on the school house. Work was pushed rapidly on the addition, as the building was to be ready by the time school met in September. By August the building was enclosed and partly finished inside. [10]

When school began that fall, the village school had progressed from a one-room log building in 1871 with an enrollment of seven to a four-room frame building with over a hundred students.

Soon the school board felt the need to increase the efficiency of the school; it authorized, therefore, the adoption of a new course of study. The course of study, beginning that fall, would extend through a period of ten years. Each year was called a grade, with four primary grades, four grammar grades, and two high school grades. At the close of each school year examinations were to be held, the students to be promoted by classes. Students completing the course

of study were to be granted diplomas signed by the Director, the Moderator, and the Principal. Also, all students were to take part in rhetorical exercises, unless excused by the principal. With the adoption of the new graded system regularity of attendance was earnestly recommended, the board feeling that although attendance was important in any school, in a graded school it was essential. Pupils who were irregular in attendance would become confused and soon lose interest in their studies. [11]

The high school (grades 9 and 10) department was divided into three terms: fall, winter and spring. Specific courses were required each term. Ninth grade students were required to study Arithmetic, Grammar, Psychology and United States History in the fall. Algebra was added in the winter term. Concentration was placed on Michigan History, Composition and Botony in the spring. Tenth grade students studied Algebra, General History, United States Civil Government, and Geography in the fall. A class in bookkeeping was added in the winter term. Physical Geography and Rhetoric were included in the spring. Each term was approximately three months long. [12]

Miss Bell had charge of the grammar department and Miss Clementine Sommerville, of Newberry, was hired for the primary department. [13]

B. Fairchild and S.S. Thuma were elected to the board on September 9, 1893, to replace G.H. Todd and D.A. Trumpour whose terms were ended. [14]

Visits to the school by interested parties were not uncommon. Many people dropped in to see how things were progressing. One afternoon Reverend James Thompson visited the lower room and called the students' attention to a swarm of bees he was interested in. "Be obedient," he advised. "Be earnest, be truthful, be kind, be first with your lessons, and be never behind." [15]

Changes also took place in the spring of 1896. John Vickery was elected truant officer. [16] S.J. Smith was elected to the board in place of B. Fairchild. Professor Woolpert agreed to be principal for the coming year. [17] The third grade was transferred from the primary room to the intermediate room as there were too many students in the primary room. The sixth grade was transferred to the high school room. Jake Carlson took the place of Isreal Pendensen as janitor. [18]

Few teachers had any training beyond a high school education. They were required to take an examination given by the State Superintendent of Schools. During the summer of 1896 Reverend G.W. Wood was at the Cheboygan Central School for the purpose of conducting a one-month summer school to assist teachers or others interested in teaching in preparing for their examinations. A fee of six dollars per person was charged. Those who passed were qualified to teach that fall. [19]

Many social doings were held in the school house for the purpose of raising money to help purchase some of the school equipment. The first piano was bought with money earned from ice cream socials and other entertaining activities.

Basketball was the favorite sport of the students, the girls having a team as well as the boys. Games were played with teams from neighboring towns. Home games were held in the upstairs of the town hall. Travel to out of town games was by train. [20]

Most students remained in school only until they were sixteen, as required by law. Those who wished to earn their high school diplomas had to attend school in a district which had twelve grades, the closest being Pellston and Cheboygan.

In 1910 only two students completed the tenth grade, Delia Plaunt and Elton Dagwell. Mr. Dagwell recalls that he traveled to Pellston to study his last two years. He told how he would board the train on Monday and return on Friday to spend the weekend at home. During the week he would board with a family in Pellston. [21]

By 1912 the Mackinaw City School had all twelve grades. Four years later ten students graduated from high school. Graduation exercises were held in the theater, called The Old Casino, located where the Dairy Queen now stands. [22]

In addition to being overcrowded, the frame building was in need of major repairs. Two alternatives were proposed—add on to the old building or build a new school. After the situation was thoroughly analyzed the best plan was to build a new school. An election was held and the bond isssue passed.

Ground was broken in the spring of 1921. Warren Homes, an architect, designed the two-story red brick building. E.E. LaRue, a contractor from Midland, erected the building for approximately $60,000. Built to accommodate all twelve grades, classrooms were large and comfortable. Two classrooms, a gymnasium with a stage, and lavatory facilities were located on the main floor. The upper floor contained six classrooms and a large assembly room. The Chemistry and Biology laboratory was set up in one of the upper classrooms leading off the assembly room.

While the new building was being completed, classes went on in the old school. Graduation ceremonies for the class of 1927 initiated the completed building. [23]

The old four-room frame schoolhouse had outlived its usefulness after having housed hundreds of students for over thirty years. It was purchased by George Michica of Cheboygan, moved to a site near the Dan Elliot's residence in Mackinaw City, and converted into a hotel. The building burned a short time later.

Landscaping the grounds of the new school was completed during the summer of 1930. J.G. Kruger built a sidewalk from the south side entrance to the street. A Merry Whirl swing, bought by the P.T.A. with some assistance from the school board, was placed on the playground. The students as well as its eight teachers enjoyed working in the new school.

Financial problems struck in 1933. Teachers' salaries were paid up to March 16, but after that date there was no money for further operation. An application for state aid was tendered by C.K. Fulmer, Secretary of the Board of Education. The financial situation remained critical for the next several years. The teachers and the janitor agreed to a twenty per cent salary cut in order to keep the school from closing. The following year all school employees were offered and accepted blank contracts to be filled in at a later date. [24] Within the next few years the financial burden was eased and the future of the school began to brighten.

Salaries varied a great deal. Women teachers received less than the men teachers, and teachers in the elementary department were paid less than those in the high school. At one time the janitor's pay was higher than that of many of the teachers.

Some of the neighboring country school districts began closing about 1937, indicating a wish at that time to annex with a larger district. When the Freedom School located in District No. 2 Mackinaw Township closed, the district requested permission to send three students to Mackinaw City. The school board agreed but decided not to charge tuition that year. Later, when other districts closed, tuition was charged their students until definite annexation took place. Eventually school District No. 2 Mackinaw Township, Hebron Township No. 1, and Carp Lake Township No. 1 Fractional joined the Mackinaw City School System.

The school bought its first bus in the fall of 1950 to handle transportation for students living at least one and one-half miles from school. At the present time the school maintains two busses, one with a sixty passenger capacity and the other with twenty.

Total enrollment, kindergarten through the twelfth grade, reached 264 students by the fall of 1952. The building was so overcrowded that it was apparent that additional classrooms were needed. Several classes were held in the basement, but this was not too successful as the furnace blower made much noise and every time the janitor stoked the furnace fires it caused interference. For the fourth time since the beginning of the school district, the people were faced with the need for a larger school.

Land for a possible site was purchased on the corner of Central Avenue and South Pemot Street across from St. Anthony's Catholic Church in Mackinaw City. The board discussed various possibilities to ease the situation. It could build an entire new elementary school; it could attach a new wing to one side of the old school; or it could build a high school on the Central Avenue property. The decision was to build a new high school.

School board members traveled to other cities and toured new high schools which seemed to fit the plans the building committee had in mind. Photographs and sketches drawn up by salesmen from building companies were studied. Thrum of Lansing was employed as legal advisor for the building program and bond issue. The bond issue was set up for $268,000. [25] Through the efforts of the Board of Education, administration, faculty, student body, and interested citizens of the community the bond issue providing for the new high school successfully passed on March 3, 1956. The five to one vote was indicative of the sincere interest the people in the community had in education.

The final plan was drawn up and explained in detail by architect Paul Hazelton of Traverse City. After it was approved by the Department of Public Instruction, bids for construction were received and reviewed by the board and the architect. A construction bid of $169,927 from Cheboygan Construction Company was accepted. The electrical bid from the Lancaster Electric Company of Gaylord for $18,378 was accepted. L.J. Deming Company of Cadillac was hired to do the plumbing, heating, and ventilation work for $46,238. [26]

The floor plan included science laboratory, library, commercial rooms, general classrooms, music room, shop, gymnasium, locker rooms and offices.

The opening of the new high school was truly a milestone in public education at Mackinaw City. Many changes had taken place throughout the years, including the name of the school. A request was made in 1955 to change the school, then known as Mackinaw City District No. 1 Fractional, Mackinaw and Wawatam Township, Cheboygan and Emmet Counties, to Mackinaw City Public Schools, School District, Cheboygan and Emmet Counties. The request was approved and the distinctive name adopted in April of that year. [27]

Many persons in Mackinaw may fondly recall the little frame school house which they attended. The pot-belly stove roasted the nearest pupils and permitted those farthest away to shiver from the cold. They may also recall the open water bucket with a dipper floating on top and the harried teacher endeavoring to instruct pupils of several grades and ages. Today, besides reading, writing, and arithmetic, there are numerous other subjects and activities offered which are geared to the interest and abilities of the pupils.

At the present time there are 308 students enrolled in the Mackinaw City School System, 160 in grades kindergarten through six in the elementary school, and 148 in grades seven through twelve in the high school. Fourteen teachers are employed, seven teaching in the elementary school and seven in the high school. Class loads are relatively small with an average of twenty students per teacher. Summer school courses are offered for students interested in music, mathematics and reading.

Athletics play a major roll in the lives of the students, as well as interested parents and friends. The school is a member of the Northern Six Football Conference and the Northern Lakes Basketball Conference for Track and Basketball.

The citizens of Mackinaw City from the very beginning of the village had the education of their children at heart, as can be seen when the history of the school system is traced down through the years. Each and every year improvements were made, and it is almost certain that further improvements are in the offing.

FOOTNOTES

1 Dunbar, Willis F., *Michigan*, (William B. Eerdmans, Grand Rapids, 1965), pp. 399-400.

2 Centennial Issue, *Cheboygan Tribune*, Cheboygan, Michigan, July 2, 1955.

3 Ibid.

4 Interview with George Coffman, February 2, 1967.

5 *The Mackinaw Witness*, Mackinaw City Michigan, September 24, 1892.

6 Ibid, November 11, 1893.

7 Ibid, June 8, 1893.

8 Ibid, May 13, 1893.

9 Ibid, July 8, 1893.

10 Ibid, August 19, 1893.

11 Ibid, Spetember 9, 1893.

12 Ibid.

13 Ibid.

14 Ibid.
15 Ibid, December 3, 1892.
16 Ibid, February 8, 1896.

17 Ibid, May 30, 1896.

18 Ibid, May 16, 1896.

19 Ibid, July 4, 1896.

20 Interview with Launa Barrett, February 20, 1967.

21 Interview with Elton Dagwell, March 1, 1967.

22 Interview with Launa Barrett, February 20, 1967.

23 Interview with Launa Barrett, February 23, 1967.

24 School Board of Mackinaw City, *Records*, December 1, 1931.

25 Ibid, July 24, 1956.

26 Ibid, August 7, 1956.

27 Ibid, April 13, 1955.

BIBLIOGRAPHY

Dunbar, Willis F., *Michigan*, William B. Eerdmans Publishing Company, Grand Rapids, 1965.

Centennial Issue, *Cheboygan Tribune*, Cheboygan, Michigan, July 2, 1955.

The Mackinaw Witness, Weekly Newspaper, Mackinaw City, Michigan, 1883-1899.

School Board Records, Mackinaw City Public Schools, 1929-1960.

Interview with Launa Barrett, February 20, 1967.

Interview with Elton Dagwell, March 1, 1967.

Interview with George Coffman, February 2, 1967.

First school site of the present elementary school.

Mackinaw City High School, now elementary school.

Listed are names of some of the students shown in this 1911 school picture.
Max Pierce, Bernard Brady, Masten Spencer, Joseph Conloyue, Donald Luden, Fern Jensen, Thelma McGreggor, Marian Walters, Myrtle Wheeler, Helen Duffina, Marie Patrick, Cecelia Paquet, Lynette Robertson, Dorothy Ranville, Carl Desy, Catherine Patterson, Mildred Hilliker, Clara McCormick, Nina McGreggor, Fred Doner, Pearl and Exilda LaMoyne, Dorothy Irwin, Gertrude Sommers, Delva Deitz, Doris Smith, Victoria Weisner, Leona Niles, Louise McGinnis, Elmer Walters, Alvin Hoot, Clifford Burroughs, Leonard Walters, Phyllis Robinson, Laurence Desy, Marcella Wolford, Beatrice Potter, Irene Lane, Morrill Sisters, Donna Survois, Rayma and Virginia Smith, Helen McVey, Iva Burroughs, Lizzie Duffina, Clarence McGinnis, Russell VanHelen, Russell LaVan, Ellis Eastman, Rose and Pearl Zimmerman.

Teachers - Mrs. Ingalls, Carrie White, Maude Clark, Mr. Allie Wickett.

My Beginners

by Marie Fry

You are such tender blossoms rare,
Delicate, unspoiled by earth's
Defiling odorous aged Curse
Tender gentle fragile flowers.

Innocently you look to me
As a light that you may see
All life offers which is ours.

Sometimes I pray in
quiet hours that God will
guide me on to be
A little more like you
have tho't of me.

In all your springtime bowers,
I pray that you may all remain
The unaffected souls you are
That through the years
Your fortunes gain
In knowledge paths a reaching
Far untarnished clean
Unto the end
Until for you the Master sends.

Mackinaw City

Friday, June 4, 1971

Judy Ranville, Corres.
Phone 436-5340

2 Retiring Teachers to Be Honored for Long Service

On Sunday, June 6, from 2 to 5 p.m. in the Roger McCormick Fellowship Hall at the church of the Straits in Mackinaw City there will be a reception honoring Mrs. Marie Fry and Mrs. Launa Barrett on the occasion of their retirement from the Mackinaw City school system.

Mrs. Fry has taught in Mackinaw City since 1939, and Mrs. Barrett since 1945.

Mrs. Barrett was born in Charlevoix, and came to Mackinaw City when three years old, and has been at home here since.

Mrs. Barrett has two children Janet and Ervin, both graduates of Mackinaw City High School.

Mrs. Fry came to Mackinaw City from Southern Michigan, but loves the North and plans to remain here.

Concerning her retirement Mrs. Fry said, "We all reach an age when we know it is best to step out of the classroom, but this only means the beginning of a new life, not retirement."

The combined years of teaching service for these ladies is 58 years, and we suspect that this Fall they will have many an urge to get ready for school. Everyone in the community is thankful for the dedicated service of these fine ladies, and wish them much happiness in the years ahead.

It is hoped that as many former students and friends as possible will come to the reception. If there are some mementos of these years, 1939 to 1971, you wish to share, bring them along.

L-R Front Row -
 Doris Pettinger, Helen Duffina, Mildred Hilliker, Lela Howard Gowans, Celia Paquet Krueger, Margaret Sullivan, Marian Walters, Loretta Moore, Sylvia Cassidy Morway, Dorothy Ranville, Harvey Douglas - Supt.

L-R Middle Row -
 Julia A. Inglis - teacher, Carl Williams, Charles St. Germaine, Lloyd Dagwell, Elmer Walters, Ronald Moore, Carl Desy, Jack Griffith, Louis Plaunt, John Howard.

L-R Top Row -
 Ada McLean Olsen, Maude Pettinger, Beatrice Brown Cosens, Addie Pierce Desy, Leona Niles Brown, Edith Roll Coleman, Veda Hunt Bonter, Dorothy Roper, Myrtle Wheeler Williams.

Girls Basketball Team and Coach, 1912
(Right to Left): Allie Wickett, Grace Blackmere, Norva Dagwell, Pearl Zimmerman, Cynthia Deitz, Virginia Smith, Helen McVey, Phyllis Robinson, Beatrice McIsaac, Hazel Zimmerman.

Front Row (left to right)
   Kenneth Fulmer, Wm. Plaunt, ? Thompson, Gibb Burroughs, Bun Sullivan, Merl Henry, Ed Dancer.
Second Row
   Helen Jewell, Melba Schepler, Charlot White, ?, ?, ?, Ida Pierce, Mildred Brown (Cousinaw)
Third Row
   ? McGoon, ?, ?, Charley Roper, Lloyd Desy, William Schepler, Homer Walters
Fourth Row
   Phylis Marrel (Burkholder) teacher, ? McGoon, Dannie Gwilt, ?, Sara Schepler, Vera White, Ruth Delamarter, Lula Meski, Flora Miles

First Row: Alvin Bacon, Pearl Zimmerman, Francis Paquet. Second Row: ?, Dan Lamin, Lyle Wheeler, Russell Irwin, Henry Allen, Clyde Parkis, Tom Lamin, Cynthia Dietz, ?, ?, Bea McIsaac. Third Row: ?, Chester LaQuea, ?, ?, Evert Harris, Rose Zimmerman, Virginia Smith, Grace Blackmere. Fourth Row (right to left): Fern Place, ?, Norva Dagwell, Victoria Plaunt, Zella Glen, rest unknown.

184

1927-28 school year

1st row (left to right)

    Bert Niles, Ernie Wallin, Bill Robinson, Forest Barrett, Ivan Barnum, Harold Nau, Mike Krueger, Jim Desy, Harold Flynn, George Hayes, Robert Schwab, Don Galbraith.

2nd row

    Don Thiel, Dan Gwilt, Harold Wallin, Don Ball, Darl Cassidy, Edgar Desy, E. LaFauncy, Ted Dagwell, Don Magoon, Charles Niles, Reynolds Schneider, Bob Schaub, Louis Ziegler, Louis Peppler

3rd row

    Gladys Chapman, Maureen Plaunt, Catherine Peppler (Caswell), Julia Nau, Alice Forgette, ?, E. Delamarter, Margaret Darling (Krueger), Dorothy Pierce, Maxine Krueger, Carolyn Galbraith, Bernice Sommers, Eugene White.

4th row

    Hazel Phillips, L. Caywood, L. Bauers, ?, M. Murray, L. Delamarter

5th row

    Teacher Mr. Brown, M. Litzner, Lucille Pettinger, Edna Thompson, Ellen Olson (Phillips), Ruth Senn, Mildred Brown, Ida Pierce (McKinnon), Helen Bowman Jewell, Cynthia Duffina, Helen Hutchinson, Sara Shepler, Flora Niles, C. White, Nona Cassidy, D. Delamarter.

6th row

    Teacher Mr. Holbrook, Ruby Wheeler, Melba Shepler, Arla Ewalt, __ Magoon, Dorothy Sharp, Dulcie Robinson (Phillips).

Back rows

    ?, Lisa Sheler, teacher Harry Parks, Lena Pettinger, Freda Sands, Mildred Ranville, Ella Hargrove, Ruth Koler (teacher)

Chapter 25

The Mackinaw City
Woman's Club

From Club History Book (prior to June 1968, when Mackinaw City Woman's Club Library joined the Northland Library System.)

In 1912, six enterprising women of Mackinaw City, formed a club to study Shakespeare. They called it the "Shakespeare Club". They were: Mrs. Julia Inglis (the first President), Mrs. Grace Robertson, Mrs. Hattie Stimpson, Mrs. Tena Barrett, Mrs. Blanche Desy and Mrs. Luella Overton. They met in their homes at first, but by 1914, they had over 30 members and became incorporated as the Mackinaw Woman's Club.

In the first yearly program book printed, we find this purpose: to create an organized center of action among women for cooperation in literary, educational and philanthropic work; for the study thereof, and for general culture, for the promotion of practical interest in science, art, literature and music.

They soon were ambitious to start a Library and it was Mr. John B. Stimpson who made a push cart that the ladies took to their meeting places, with a collection of books soon accumulated. They dickered with the town fathers and were allowed to use the Council Chambers as a Library for a time. However, this was not very satisfactory, as it meant the invasion of women with cleaning equipment into one of the men's most treasured haunts, where ash trays and cuspidors were want to occupy conspicuous and handy prominence.

From the Council Chamber the ladies were allowed to move to a room in the schoolhouse. This was not always the ideal arrangement either. The difficulties however, served to fire the ambition of this dauntless group -- namely, they must earn enough money to build and own a combined Library and Clubhouse of their own. Ten cent teas, parties, musicals and programs were held. Finally the day came when two lots were purchased on Jamet Street from Mr. Charles Stimpson at a cost of $550.00, in cash. Fifty women assembled at 9:00 a.m. on the morning of October 5, 1931, to watch Mrs. Overton lift the first shovel of earth for the foundation for the clubhouse.

It was to be a 28'x48' shingle-covered structure with full basement. The building was completely finished and the first meeting held in it January 18, 1932.

Mrs. Grace Barton was President at the time. On the building committee were: Mrs. Luella Overton, Chairman, Mrs. Sarah Irwin, Mrs. Grace Robertson, Mrs. Blanche Desy, and Mrs. Hattie Stimpson. The first meeting in the new building took the form of a Kitchen Shower, and each woman had to bring her own chair. Many and varied were the gifts brought to the Club House, from businessmen and other citizens of the community.

There remained a mortgage of $1,290.00 to pay off. By September, 1938, at a most festive occasion with Mrs. Grace Trumbull, President, the mortgage was burned. From that day to this the affairs of the club, have been guided by the hands of faithful and capable Presidents and Officers. The Club has long been the center of much enjoyable and worthwhile activity, as well as first contributor to the literary life through its Library. The first Monday of each month, from October through May, are Club nights. Once a year, at the end of May, all Past Presidents are honored at a banquet.

WOMAN'S CLUB

A place where womanly thought is cherished,
Where high ideals are fed and nourished,
Where Charity in all its beauty
Is held to be a Sacred Duty.
Where peace and harmony abound,
And members meet on common ground.

*Mackinaw Woman's
Club Library* ➡

Women Realize Long Ambition

Break Ground For Library Building
In Mackinaw City Monday

MRS. LUELLA OVERTON
TURNS FIRST SHOVEL

Basement Will Be Used For Manual Training Room
For Local Boys

From *The Cheboygan Daily Tribune*
October 5, 1931

Ground was broken in Mackinaw City Monday morning for the library building of the Mackinaw Woman's Club, Inc. The first shovelful was lifted by Mrs. Louella Overton, chairman of the building committee, at nine o'clock, in the presence of fifty club women. This step begins the culmination of many years of industry and thrift on the part of the Mackinaw women to realize their ambition for a public library.

The building is to be placed on two lots on Jamet Street, which have a frontage of 100 feet and a depth of 150 feet. The building is to be 28 ft. x 48 ft. and is to have a full basement. A small kitchen and cloak room will be built at one end of the main room. The library room will be 28 ft. x 36 ft. and will contain the books which will be placed in circulation as soon as the building is completed.

The club members plan to fix the basement for a manual training room for the boys so that they may have a warm place of their own in which to meet during the winter. Many donations have been received to help the women along in their endeavor to build a library.

Club Has New Members

The first meeting of the club year was held at the school auditorium Monday night. Twenty-three new members have joined the club this year and many old ones have been reinstated so that the club membership is well over 60 now.

Members answered to roll call by telling of a happy event during the summer.

Mrs. Grace Barton gave the president's address and asked for the cooperation of the members. "The Woman's Club Ideal" was given by Mrs. Louella Overton who also explained the library building plans.

A solo by Mrs. Leo Paquet "When Summer Is Gone" was much enjoyed. Mrs. W. A. Peppler led the singing with Mrs. James Marshall at the piano.

Light refreshments were served at the close of the meeting.

CLUB HISTORY SEALED IN CORNER STONE

First Club President and Present Club President
Place Records

The names of the Board of Directors, the membership list and the history of the Mackinaw Woman's club were placed in a box which went into the cornerstone of the Library building Monday morning.

There was no formal ceremony since the building is being rushed as rapidly as possible, but the records were placed by Mrs. Julia Inglis, first president of the club, assisted by Mrs. Grace Barton, the present president and Mrs. Louella Overton, chairman of the building committee. Pictures were taken of this act to be used in the club scrap book.

The Mackinaw Woman's club now has a membership of seventy – six of whom were members when the club was organized in 1914. These members are Mrs. Julia Inglis, Mrs. Louella Overton, Mrs. Grace Robertson, Mrs. Hattie R. Stimpson, Mrs. Tena Barrett and Mrs. Blanch Desy. The club was federated in 1915 and has been working for the past seventeen years for the betterment of Mackinaw, for a library building and the mutual improvement of members in art, science and literature.

Woman's Club Presidents

Julia Inglis
1914-15
1927-28

Grace Robertson
1915-1916
1930-1931

Mrs. Tina Barrett
1916-1917

Luella Jackson
1917-1918

Mae Galbraith
1919-1920

Millie Stimpson
1918-19

Mollie Hilliker
1921-22

Flora Solomon
1922-23

Rosalie Coffman
1920-21

Blanche Desy
1923-24
1925-26

Hattie Stimpson
1924-25
1928-29
1929-30

Ione Darling
1926-27

Grace Barton
1931-1932

Genevive Dagwell
1932-33
1933-34

Grace Trumbull
1934-35
1935-36
1937-38
1938-39
1939-40

Martha Wilkes
1936-37

Agnes Johnson
1940-41
1941-42

Ruth Bauers
1942-43
1943-44
1944-45
1946-47
1947-48

Jeannette Ryan
1945-46

Pauline Grebe
1948-49
1949-50

Helen Hingston
1950-51
1951-52

Dorothy Wallin
1955-56

Peg Darrow
1956-57

Ida McKinnon
1952-53

Gwen Smith Wilson
1953-54
1954-55

Delores Silfven
1957-58

Laneta Hendrickson
1958-59

Muriel McRae
1959-60

Betty Teysen
1960-61

Helen McCarthy
1961-62

Jean Vachou
1962-63

Florence Tracy
1963-64
1976-77

Florence Walters
1964-65

Diane Fry
1965-66

Martha Darrow
1966-67

Maribeth Barnett
1967-68

Ann Grondin
1968-69

Mona Hughes
1969-70

Nancy Campbell
1970-71

Mary Desy
1971-72

Terri Bach
1972-73

Judy Ranville
1973-74
1974-75

Sue Fuss
1975-76

194

Chapter 26

Looking 'Em Over

by Jim Doherty

from the *Petoskey News-Review*

Deer hunting across the Straits before the bridge was built was an epic adventure almost as big as going abroad.

And a whole new generation of hunters, who will zip across Big Mac with hardly a passing thought to the engineering that made this possible, doesn't even know how it used to be.

They can't remember bumper to bumper lines of cars crawling to Mackinaw City, backed up as far as Cheboygan and beyond.

They can't remember that cars used to run out of gas in these long lines or that gas stations in Mackinaw City had hoses long enough to reach the highway so a hunter wouldn't lose his place in line.

Nor can they remember folks selling smoked whitefish, sandwiches, hot coffee, newspapers and other such necessities to the occupants of these cars as they crawled through Mackinaw City.

Sometimes when those ferries were running you were lucky to move at the rate of a mile an hour--that was fast--just before deer season or most any summer holiday from Memorial Day through Labor Day.

It was not uncommon for some hunters to wait 12 to 24 hours in line to get across the Straits, and still they came.

Some parties in this area would beat the jam by having one guy drive a car up a couple days ahead, take it across and park it at St. Ignace and then take the ferry back as pedestrians for a quarter.

His partner would have another car at Mackinaw City to take him back home. Then when the big day came, they'd all go up in a car and either leave it at Mackinaw City for the duration or somebody's wife had to do the driving if she wanted to have the car while the fearless hunters were gone.

Remember those camps, fellows? Outside of a few posh ones, most of the "good" camps had outdoor plumbing located in a little building behind the shack. Kerosene or gasoline lamps provided the illumination.

Ten, 20 or 30 years ago most of the UP hunters who didn't have a shack made camp in tents, converted trucks, old school busses, beat up house trailers or whatever Yankee ingenuity of the day could improvise.

It wasn't uncommon for hunters to get snowed in on some of those wild back roads. Man, when they talked about roughing it in camp, they meant rough.

Those hunters could eat anything if they could survive camp cooking without dieing from indigestion. Heart attacks? Not many in those days because most hunters were hardened to such difficulties as walking in heavy clothes. That was the day before machines did all the physical work.

A lost hunter in the wilds of the UP before today's helicopter searching and the buildup of our state police and sheriffs' forces was really a matter of life or death.

Back in 1929, there were 68,011 deer hunting licenses sold and 11 hunters were killed or one for every 6,182 hunters. In 1948 another 11 were killed but the ratio per license was one in every 35,454. So, while hunting pressure was building up, we tried various anterless seasons, hunting is actually safer now than it was. That's hard to believe, but as they say, figures don't lie.

As far as hunting pressure is concerned, the big jump has come since World War II. Back in peaceful 1940 there were 176,314 hunters and that was almost three times the number in 1929.

In 1946, first year after World War II, the hunting army jumped to 341,802. By 1954 the number had grown to over 429,000, by 1960 to 460,915, over half a million by 1963 and by 1965 the number of licenses sold was over 600,000!

In the Depression year of 1932 there were only 44,141 deer licenses sold, so there was a gain of almost 15 hunters for everyone in just a little over 30 years.

So much for the statistics.

Those of you who remember those wild November lines at Mackinaw City and those stormy, roaring crossings of the wave-lashed Straits and the gay blades who made them, have something you'll never forget.

Before the advent of auto transportation, the real old timers used to ship their deer back by railroad car and that was quite a sight (they tell me) at Mackinaw City. Freight cars stacked high with bucks, loaded and unloaded on wagons and shipped all over Michigan.

We can't ever turn back the clock, but hunting today is so little like the "gold rush" days before the bridge it's hard to find comparison. And some of those never-to-be forgotten camp stories will be lost and forgotten as a new breed of hunter takes over.

Mackinaw City

Mrs. E.J. Bauers, Corres.

Landmark To Be Torn Down and Replaced

The "Dustin Garage and Storage" on Huron Avenue in Mackinaw City is to be torn down and plans are underway to replace it with a modern garage and storage.

The garage part of the building was formerly a home and fifty years ago was owned by the late Mr. and Mrs. Aroine Kniffen, the former being Mackinaw City's painter, paperhanger and home decorator.

In the late 20's it was sold to Mr. and Mrs. John Laprarie of Cheboygan, who converted it into a hotel-boarding house. A few years later the property was purchased by A.C. Tiffany, M.D. and Clifford E. Dusten, partners, who moved the building back from the street and converted part of the building into a garage, where they sold Standard Oil products, tires, etc., and did mechanical work, as well as renting rooms and operating a small restaurant for their guests.

About 1930 they built the large storage, next to the garage.

In September 1947, Dr. Tiffany and Mr. Dusten sold the business to Fred Roueche and Keith Darling, who have carried on the business of the service station, repairing and storage business, catering largely to tourists going to Mackinac Island and others.

The new plans call for a larger storage to front on the street back of the present storage, instead of on Huron Avenue and continuing in the usual service station business.

During the years two other Standard Oil Service stations have been built, the one on Central Avenue being operated by Fred Roueche; one on Nicolet by Bernard Marshall and Keith Darling has continued to operate the original business on Huron Avenue. (Photos by Rev. Raymond Provost).

Chapter 27

Mackinaw City

from *Michigan State Gazetteer - 1873*

MACKINAW

An incorporated village of between 800 and 1000 inhabitants, on the island of Mackinac, in the straits of Mackinac. It is the county seat of Mackinac, or Michilimackinac County, and is about 18 miles northwest of Cheboygan and 8 northeast of Mackinaw City. From Detroit it is about 350 miles distant, and from Chicago about 400. The island is rough and rocky, and produces but little beyond oats and potatoes. Its principal business grows out of its being the location of a U.S. military post, and being a place of fashionable summer resort, besides which it has a considerable trade in fish. It has 4 hotels, several stores, and one or more churches. The fort is situated on a rocky eminence 150 feet high, overlooking the village, and commanding the straits.

BUSINESS DIRECTORY.
Bailey, Jno. R., physician and dealer in dry goods.
Bates, John, dealer in dry goods.
Becker, John, proprietor Mackinac House.
Cable, James F., proprietor McLeod House.
Davis, John W., general store.
Fenton & Wendell, dealers in dry goods.
Franks, E. A., proprietor Mission House.
Highstone, S., dealer in dry goods.
Madison, A. B., dealer in dry goods.
Madison, Wm., dealer in dry goods.
Muny, Dominick, dealer in dry goods.
VanAllen, capt. Henry, proprietor Island House.

MACKINAW CITY

An embryo settlement at the most northern point of the lower peninsula of Michigan, on the straits of Mackinac. The site, with a large body of land in the vicinity, was, with great foresight and confidence in the future of northern Michigan, bought some years ago by Edgar Conkling of Cincinnati, by whom it is still held. This gentleman has platted a large city and built

a dock, and now patiently awaits the completion of the two lines of railway which are rapidly pushing their way to the straits, to provide a population for his city. When completed to that point, a ferry will undoubtedly be established, and a line of road be constructed from thence across the upper peninsula to Marquette, where it will meet roads already in operation, or on the point of being built, that will connect directly with the great Northern Pacific R.R., and thus a large share of the traffic of the Northern Pacific will pass directly through Mackinaw City. Its prospective railroad importance, with the fine invigorating air of the straits, and the purity of the water, with a rich country lying back of it, and a large share of the commerce of the lakes passing its doors, combine to make this a very promising place for settlement, and for the establishment of business enterprises. The straits here are about 5 miles in width, and form as beautiful a body of water as can be found anywhere. Cheboygan lies 18 miles southeast, and the island of Mackinac, with the fort and village of the same name, already a popular watering place, is distant about 8 miles in a northeasterly direction. Mackinaw City is in the extreme northwestern corner of Cheboygan County, and is on the same meridian of longitude as Quincy, Charlotte and Pewamo, while its latitude is about the same as that of Montreal, St. Johns, Lyons in the south of France, and Venice in Italy. At present the city is merely an insignificant clearing in a dense forest, with no trade but the supply of a few propellers with wood, and the shipment of some cedar posts. But who can predict what it will be in ten years?

Michigan State Gazetteer 1875

MACKINAW

The county seat of Mackinac County, a village of about 600 inhabitants, situated on the south shore of the island of Mackinac, in the straits of the same name, 40 miles northeast of Petoskey, the northern terminus of the G.R. & I. R.R., 18 northwest of Cheboygan and about 350 from Detroit by water. The island is hilly and rocky, and for the most part covered with second growth timber. The village consists mainly of a single street running along the shore with a steep hill rising abruptly in the rear surmounted by the old fort still garrisoned by a company of United States troops. Considerable fish is shipped here, the chief business of the place, grows out of its popularity as a place of summer resort. There are several good hotels in the village which are, during a part of the year, thronged with guests. The walks and drives about the island are very romantic and the air pure, bracing and healthful. A daily boat connects Mackinaw with Petoskey, and it is supplied with a daily mail. James Lasley, postmaster.

BUSINESS DIRECTORY.

Bailey John R., dry goods and drugs and physician.
Bates John, saloon.
Bazear Gaspard, saloon.
Cable James F., hotel.
Chambers Thomas, groceries.
Chapman Mrs. Reuben, hotel.
Davis John D, Railroad agent.
Davis John W, general store.
Fenton & Wendell, general store.
Franke E A, hotel.
Hoban J & J, express agents.
Highstone S, general store.
Jolli Louis, hotel.
Madison A B, general store.
Madison W, groceries and provisions.
Monaghan John W, saloon.
Murray Dominic, general store.
Overall H W, saloon.
Stonax Rev W G (Episcopalian).
Truscott George & Co, general store.
Van Allen Henry, hotel.

MACKINAW CITY

A settlement of about 100 inhabitants, at old point Mackinaw, the most northern point of the Lower Peninsula of Michigan. It is in Beaugrand Township, Cheboygan County, 18 miles northwest of Cheboygan. A city was laid out here on a large scale some years ago by one Edgar Conkling, of Cincinnati, but the enterprise was premature, and up to this time but little development has taken place. There can be no doubt, however, that sooner or later this will be the focal point for the railroad lines reaching out towards the Upper Peninsula, and where the Straits of Mackinac will one day be bridged, tunneled or ferried. Mackinaw City at present has a small trade in wood and telegraph poles. It has a weekly mail. Lewis I. Willets, postmaster.

BUSINESS DIRECTORY.

Stimpson Geo W, justice of the peace and general store.
Stimpson Geo W & Son, wood, telegraph poles, posts and fish barrels.
Willets Lewis I, general store.

from an 1884 Directory

MACKINAW CITY

The northernmost point of the lower peninsula of Michigan, is located on the G.R. & I. R.R., at the junction of the M. div. of the M.C. R.R., in Beaugrand Township, Cheboygan County, 16 miles northwest of Cheboygan, the county seat and bank location, 30 northeast of Petoskey, and 300 by water northwest of Detroit. Its pleasant situation, beautiful and romantic surroundings and bracing air, have gained for it considerable popularity as a summer resort. Each year the influx of visitors is larger than the preceding one, and the village is rapidly increasing in wealth, population and importance. Fish forms the only export. A Presbyterian church, a good school, and several hotels are sustained. The Western Union Telegraph and the United States Express Companies have offices here, and the population is now 500. Land in the immediate vicinity may be purchased for from 14 to $15 per acre. As soon as the title to a certain valuable property in the village has been settled, a large amount of capital will be invested here, and Mackinaw City will soon rank as one of the most prosperous towns in the southern peninsula.

Ames Henry, master steamer *Algomah*.
Anderson Frank, lab, bds A H Buhler.
Andrews Eva, domestic Palace hotel.
Andrews John H, propr Palace hotel.
Ball James, carpenter.
Barnes Robert, lab, bds A H Buhler.
Barrett Devenus, general store.
Bassett Robert, carpenter.
Beck John, car repairer, bds A H Buhler.
Bigelow Orrin E, brakeman.
Bowman Peter, laborer.
Buhler Albert H, car inspector.
Burdett George, baggagemaster M C R R.
Burnett Kent, yardmaster M C R R.
Burns Alexander, sailor.
Cantile Peter, car repairer.
Carlson Benjamin, car repairer, bds A H Buhler.
Carpenter Wm M, ticket agt G R — I R R.
Cavanagh L E, tel opr M C R R, bds Mercier house.
Chamberlin Bros (Samuel B and Harvey W), hardward and groceries.
Chamberlin Harvey W (Chamberlin Bros), res Plainwell, Mich.
Coffman Bros (John H and Joseph S), drugs and jewelry.
Coffman Joseph S (Coffman Bros), res Petoskey, Mich.
Coffman Warren C, clerk Coffman Bros.
Conkling Henry, real estate, bds Stimpson House.
Converse James, carpenter.

Cressy Sarah, waiter Mercier House.
Cunningham Charles B, butcher.
Dalliarg Augustus, laborer.
Davis John G, Propr Campbell House.
Dixon David W, laborer.
Doney Edgar, lab, bds Mackinaw City hotel
Dougherty Kittie, waiter The Wentworth.
Dunham Marvin H, shoemaker.
Dunn John, teamster, bds Palace hotel.
Fee Lewis, barber, bds Palace hotel.
Fox James, Agt M C R R and Freight Agt M C R R and G R — I R R.
Fry & Scranton (Mathias A Fry, Frank Scranton), Saloon and Billiards.
Galvin Patrick, laborer.
Gane George, Real Estate, Insurance, Collection and Justice of Peace.
Goodell Charles, laborer.
Hall Robert, engine wiper, bds Mackinaw City hotel.
Hamlin Joshua, teamster, bds Palace hotel.
Hanley Lucy, waiter Mercier house.
Hansen Christine, domestic The Wentworth.
Harper West, teamster Mercier house.
Harris Wm, conductor M C R R, bds Palace hotel.
Henderson Archibald, watchman M C R R dock
Hill Annie, domestic Mercier house.
Hobbins John, foreman.
Horvan Edward, engine wiper, bds A H Buhler.
Howland Edwin R, clerk Mackinaw City house.
Jacoby Edward engine wiper.
Jameison Martin, meat market.
Karelsey Jacob C, boarding.
Kelker George W, foreman G R & I R R.
Kilmer George, tel opr, bds Mercier house.
Kniffin Adgate C V, propr Mackinaw City hotel.
Laphin Abraham, engineer M C R R.
McKay E D (Young & McKay).
McLennan Belle, waiter The Wentworth.
Marsh Rev Augustus (Presbyterian).
Maxwell Albert, Propr The Wentworth.
Mercier Mrs. Ursule C, Propr Mercier House.
Miller Isaac, porter Mercier house.
Nichols John, yardman Stimpson house.
Notson Dudley B, US signal service observer.
Notson Miss Kittie, bds Mercier house.
O'Brien Kennedy, Mngr Mercier House.
O'Conner Miss Lizzie, milliner.
O'Dell O W, cook The Wentworth.
Olsen John, laborer.
Paden John, railroad contractor and village president.
Palmer Marion, drugs and grocers.
Park Charles, clerk Palace hotel.
Petersen Israel, lab, bds J C Karelsey.
Power Samuel J, physician.
Pyle Joseph H.
Rafferty George L, newspaper agent.
Rafferty Patrick
Ranville Carl J, bartender W S Taylor.
Richards J J G, grocer.
Robinson Sophie, waiter The Wentworth

Robinson Wilbert D, freight clk M C R R.
Scheip Christian, lab, bds A H Buhler.
Scranton Frank (Fry & Scranton).
Shepherd Charles J, clk Jmes Shepherd.
Shepherd James, general store.
Sizeland James K, carpenter.
Stafford Justus E, carpenter.
Stanton Garry J, glove maker, bds Palace hotel.
Stewart Frederick, bartdr, Mercier house.
Stimpson Forest J, Clerk Stimpson House.
Stimpson George W, Propr Stimpson House and Fish Dealer.
Stimpson House, G W Stimpson Propr.
Sullivan W G & Co (W G Sullivan), meat market.
Sutherland Embly M, boots and shoes.
Taylor Wm S, saloon.
Thompson John, laborer.
Todd Bert, laborer.
Todd George H, deputy sheriff.
Von Walthausen Werner, druggist.
Wagner Norman, farmer, bds Palace hotel.
Waite Wm T, express agent.
Walters Tillie, pastry cook The Wentworth.
Washington Lottie, cook Mercier house.
Welch Laurence E, planing mill.
Wentworth The, Albert Maxwell Propr.
West Albert W, carp, bds Mackinaw City hotel.
White Thomas, watchman Mercier house.
Willets Lewis I, gen store and postmaster.
Willets Wm H, dry goods, boots and shoes.
Young Richard E (Young & McKay).
Young Robert E, clerk.
Young & McKay (Richard E Young, E D McKay), wagonmakers.

The Water Wagon

Ground at Mackinaw is very stony, and water wells had to be hand driven or hand dug. This was a very difficult task and so wells were not too plentiful in the 1880's. Mr. McVey had a water wagon – a horse-drawn vehicle, loaded with large wooden barrels. He would drive the horses into the lake and dip the water, bucket by bucket, from lake to barrel until all were filled. Then up and down the streets he went delivering the water to homes for twenty-five cents per barrelful Business was good during a dry spell--but when it rained and everyone's rain barrel filled up, the horses had a holiday. It is understood that drinking water was carried from the nearest well but the lake water, dipped near the horses heels served well for Monday washdays and Saturday night baths.

****Judy Ranville

MACKINAW CITY

Population 900. The farthest-north village of the lower peninsula looks out over the Straits of Mackinaw to the beautiful Mackinac Island and the shores of the upper peninsula less than 10 miles away. As the north ern terminus of the Mackinaw Division of the M. C. R. R. and the G. R. & I. Ry, it is the gateway through which the rail traffic to the upper peninsula flows. The trains of the D. S. S. & A. Ry. reach Mackinaw City on the powerful car ferries Chief Wawatam and Ste. Marie the year, around. The latter boat was selected by the Russian government as a model for an ice crusher in their own waters. Water communication is maintained daily during the season with Mackinac Island and other popular summer resorts in the immediate vicinity. There are many points of historic interest at Mackinaw City. It was here the first fort and block house was erected and upon that site of the massacre of June 4, 1763, has been located the Michillimackinac state park of 22 acres. In addition the village boasts of over four miles of cement walks; a boulevard of about two miles in length along the shores of the straits; a city hall, fire station and council chamber with the second floor equipped as an opera house with a seating capacity of 500; for fire protection a fire engine, hook and ladder truck and 1,500 feet of hose and a volunteer fire department of 40 members, Methodist Episcopal, Presbyterian and Roman Cath olic churches have suitable edifices and a public school of ten grades with 225 pupils is maintained. It is lighted by electricity and has telephone and telegraph communication with all points. The postoffice name is Mackinaw though the incorporated name of the village is Mackinaw City. C. O. Barrett, postmaster

VILLAGE OFFICERS

President—S. J. Smith.
Clerk—Arthur N. Buhler.
Treasurer—Chas K. Fulmer
Assessor—George F. Stringham.
Marshal—A. Desy
Health Officer—Dr B P Pierce
Fire Warden—A. P. Kniffin.
Trustees—Geo. V. Coffman, J. L. Hilliker, H. Z. Galbraith, O. J. Gowans, C.A.Rouche, D. F. Kniffin

ALPHABETICAL LIST OF NAMES

Allen Henry
Allen Trude Mrs.
American Express Co, John L Hilliker agt
Andrews Delia Mrs, propr Palace Hotel
Austin Isaac, laborer
Ayers Paul
Bacon Stephen A, carpenter
Ball Charles L (Sylvia) chief opr Western Union Telegraph Co
Ball James (Emma)
Ball John, Lake Superior lighthouse keeper
Barnum Wm (Sarah) U S Lighthouse keeper
BARRETT CLYDE O, (Irene) Postmaster
Barrett Herbert T, barber
Barrett Margaret M (wid Devenus), dry goods
Boon John Blacksmith
Bowers Emory, switchman
Buhler Anna E (widow Albert H)
Buhler Arthur N, village clk, frt clk M C & G.R&IRR
Buhler, Elizabeth L
Buhler Jennie (wid Albert F) dressmkr
Burroughs, Chas.

Burroughs Iva, tchr
Casino Theater, E A Wheeler propr
Catholic Church, Rev George Nye pastor
Central Drug Store, J H Coffman & Sons proprs
Chapman Wm (Mary), U S Lighthouse keeper
Cheboygan Light and Power Co, George F. Stringham
   mngr
CITY GARAGE, Oscar R Smith mngr
Coffman George V (Rosalie; J H Coffman & Son)
Coffman John H (Louisa; J H Cffman & Son)
Coffman J H & Son (John H and George V) proprs Cen
   tral Drug Store
Cunningham John, laborer
Dagwell Charles T (Norah) marine reporter
Dagwell Elton C, clerk
Dagwell, Norva, student
Davenport Edith
Davenport Harry Y, hostler
Davenport James, U S lighthouse keeper
Davenport Overton, clk Hunt Grocery
Dawson Edward laborer
Dean Eugene, cashier M C R R Restaurant
Deeds Ura (Alice)
Delmarter Harry (Mabel) car repr
Desy Lawrence, R R clk
Desy Come (Virginia) carpenter
Desy Eugene S (Rachel) carpenter
Desy James S restaurant & billiard parlors
Dietz Christian J (Agnes) car repairer
Dorrance Leslie, fisherman.
Dorrance Ray (Janet) fisherman
Drier Walter (Ethel) laborer
Drier, Barney

Duffina Elizabeth
Duffina Margaret (wid Peter)
Duffina Paul Martin
Duffina Theodore
Durham Alma (wid Wallace)
D S S & A Ry Depot, Herbert Z Galbraith ticket agent
Exchange Hotel (A Stringfellow, Prop)
Farwell John (Myrtle)
Fowley J, grocer
Fuller Bert, car inspector.
Fuller John R R clk
Fulmer Charles (Beatrice) clerk M C R R & G R & I
   also village treasurer.
Galbraith Mowat (Lina)
Galbraith Herbert Z, ticket agent M C R R, D S S &
   R Ry and G R & I
Gillis Thomas laborer
Gowans Howard
Gowans Olive F assistant postmaster
Gowans Oliver J (Sylva)
G R & I Ry Depot, H Z Galbraith ticket agent
Green Moses (Mina) laborer
Griffith Frank (Mabel), boiler maker
Hays John (Maggie)
Hartgrove Clarence S
Harding Vine, propr Wa-Wat-Am-Beach
Hilliker John L, agt American Express Co. and Na-
   tional Express Co
Howard John D (Fannie)
Hunt C E & Co, groceries and meats
Hunt Cecil E (Goldie) grocer and meat market

HUNT C E & Co, proprs progressive Store, Special Up-to-the-Minute Furnishings for Men, Clothing, Shoes, Trunks and Bags, Full Line Groceries, Telephone Connection

Inglis Julia A Mrs, teacher
Irwin Jamsc F (Sarah) machinist
Irwin Raymond
Irwin Roy, laborer
Irwin Russell,
Johnson Joseph R R clk
Kinsell Frederick, hostler M C R R
Kinsell Henry, laborer
Kinsell Matilda
Kniffen Almira (wid Chester)
Kniffen Anna, domestic
Kniffen Arvine P, porter
Kniffen Charles
Kniffen Ellsworth L
Kniffen Henry
Kniffen William
Kniffen Belle
Kniffen David F, restaurant
Kniffen Helen
Kniffen Sampson, laborer
Kniffen Samuel W, laborer
Laquea, William
Laquea Reuben
Laquea Chester,
Laquea Frederick, laborer
Laquea Joseph, laborer
Liebeck Louis (Anna) Meat Market and grocer
Lowery Wm J (Anna) marine engineer
Lowery W Marvin

Lyle Melvin J (Mary) lumberman
McIsaac O F, yard master
McVey A W
McVey Charles, conductor
McVey Abbie (wid George
McVey Grover J, clk R R service
Mackinaw City Public School, G H Barr prin
Marshall James W, U S lighthouse keeper
Marshall Mary
Marshall Chester A, R R clk
Marshal George
Marshall George
Martin Clyde O
Martin Nettie, cook M C R R Restaurant
Martin Wm C (Mary) conductor
Martin William E (Emma) switchman
Meeker Thomas, porter M C R R Restaurant.
Menzie Donald, blacksmith
Methodist Church, Rev Emerald B Dickson pastor
M C R R Depot, Herbert Z Galbraith agt
M C R R Restaurant, H L Whitehead mngr
Mirandette Adolph, watchman
Mirandette Edward, laborer
Miske Fred (Fannie)
Murray Alonzo (Rosie) janitor
National Express Co, John L Hilliker agent
New Mackinaw Hotel, Mrs Grace Kelty propr
Niles Vernon
Nye George Rev pastor Catholic church
Olson Conrad, teamster
Overton Luella (wid John M the Rexall Store)
Palace Hotel, Mrs Delia Andrews propr
Paquette Leo, R R fireman
Paquette Anthony, car repairer

Paquet Frances E, waiter Lakeside Hotel

Patrick George W (Gertrude) hardware and insurance

Patrick Marie, clk M C Ticket office

LIEBECK LOUIS (Anna) Fresh, Smoked and Salt Meats, Good Assortment of Canned Goods, Tel 4

PEOPLE'S BANK OF SMITH & CO, Samuel J Smith Pres, Mitchell J Swontek Cashier, General Banking Business, 3 1-2 per cent Interest paid on Savings Deposits, Telephone Connection.

Pettinger Cornelius (Effie)

Phillips Edgar J (Hettie), confectioneries and novelties

Pierce Benjamin B, physician

Pierce Bert B (Mary) dairy

Pierce Carl, laborer

Pierce Earl R, clk

Pierce Earl (Jennie)

Plaunt Helen (wid August)

Plaunt Charles L Ada) car inspector

Plaunt Christ (Emily) fisherman

Plaunt James, laborer

Plaunt Louis N (Stella) fisherman

POST OFFICE, Clyde O Barrett postmaster

Potter Beatrice

Potter Frank J (Addie) farmer

Potter Joshua (Sarah)

Presbyterian Church, Rev W J Cross pastor

Progressive Store The, C E Hunt & Co propr

Ranville Edward, switchman

Ranville George E time clerk

Ranville John (Emma) fireman

Ranville Joseph (Anna) fisherman

Ranville Margaret (wid Alexander)

Ranville, Leo

Ranville, Wilbur

Ranville George B laborer

Reaume Felix J, tel opr

Rexall Store The, L Overton and L G Stimpson proprs drugs

Risk Lina (wid Amos, dry goods

Robinson Charles R (Mabel) switchman

Robinson Ray (Ethel) laborer

Ryan John (Anna) blacksmith

Ryan Edward clk Wm Ryan.

Ryan Wm J (Mayme) soft drink and cigars

Sailler Harvey

Sailler, John

Sands Charles, laborer

Sailer Grace W, propr New Mackinaw Hotel

Schepler Wm, marine captain

Schlief Augusta (wid John F)

Shoemaker Harry, express messenger

Slenters Roy,

Smith D Wellington, baggage master M C R R

Smith D & Son, Samuel J Smith mngr, proprs Stimpson House

Smith Howard

Smith Otis

Smith Oscar R, mngr City Garage

Smith Samuel J, pres Peoples Bank of Smith & Co mgr D Smith & Son

Sousie Silas

Stillwell John (Nellie)

Stillwell George

Stillwell Neal, farmer

STIMPSON HOUSE THE, D Smith & Son Proprs
Mackinaw City's Only Up-to-Date Hotel, Comfort
ably Furnished Rooms, Heat, Electric Light and
Gas, opposite Union Station

Stimpson Ida E

Stimpson Lloyd G (Millie) Rexall store

Stimpson John B (Hattie) contractor

Stringfellow Andrew J, restaurant

Stringham George F (Eloise), mngr Cheboygan Light
and Power Co Tel 5

Sullivan Margaret (wid John)

Sullivan Marie

Sullivan Edward

Sullivan John

Summers Charles (Marcella) section hand

Summers Robert Ins agt

SWONTEK MITCHELL J (Anna) Fire Insurance
and Cashier Peoples Bank of Smith & Co

Thompson Wm M drayman

Trumbull, Clark (Hazel) grocer

U S Lighthouse, Wm Barnum and James Marshalll
keepers

Van Hellen, James S (Helen) janitor

Van Hellen Russell

Wallace Orville

Wallace Ray (Ona) laborer

Walters Charles, fisherman

Walters Leonard R, laborer

Wa-Wat-Am-Beach, Vine Harding propr

Wa-Wat-Am Hotel, Vine Harding, propr

Western Express Co, John L Hilliker agent

Western Union Telegraph Co, Charles L Ball mngr

Wheeler E A propr Casino Theater

Wheeler Lyle

Wheeler R Delbert, pool and billiards

Wilcox Charles R (Mina) car inspr

Wilcox, Chester

Wilcox Chester, freight office clk

Williams Isaac Mrs

Williams Lena, cook Stimpson House

Williams Richard, machinist

Wolford David A, foreman

Wolford George, switchman

Wolford Guy J, car repairer

Zimmerman Alice L

Zimmerman August A

Zimmerman Charles H (Louisa) furniture and under-
taker

Zimmerman Hazel

Zimmerman Pearl, R R clerk

Zimmerman Orin, car cleaner

Chapter 28

World War I and II

American Legion
Clayton Murry Post #159

CHARTER MEMBERS

Clayton Murry (In Memory)
Otis Franklin Smith
Martin Ambrose McIsaac
Russell Curtis Irwin
Leonard R. Walters
Guy J. Wolford
Darrell S. Shank
Alex W. McVey
Arthur Henry Koltz
Paul V. Ayers
Charles Adam Bolinger
Howard F. Donahue
Joseph D. McIsaac
Marvin Lowery
Carl H. Rapson

William Raymond Irwin
Harvey S. Sailler
Jacob J. Ginther
Don Charles Anderson
Joseph E. Thelen
Sampson Kniffen
Alex R. Currie
Clifford E. Dusten
James Edwin Cole
Gilbert Adelbert Nicewonder
Howard Smith
Howard L. Gowans
William L. Ausum
Lyle M. Wheeler

Charter Members
American Legion
Auxiliary - 1918

Mary McIsaac
Philomine McVey
Ruth Barrett
Rosa Murray
Hazel Murray
Cora Murray
Rose Gowans
Helen St. Germain
Hattie St. Germain
Doris Cole
Dorothy Schafer
Clara Smith
Sarah Irwin
Ella Walters
Grace Kelty
Rose Smith

Virginia Ausum
Helen Smith
Hazel Foote
Abbie McVey
Razella Sommer
Norva Lowery
Edna Sailler
Katherine Sailler
Olive Gowans
Katherine Hartgrove
Anna Wolford
Marie Smith
Hannah Coffin
Lilas Widenor
Marian Walters
Myrtle Finnagan

"Young Help The War Effort"

Back Row (left to right): Marybeth Dagwell, Jessie Poter, Perses Glimpse, Jane Dagwell, Margaret Sullivan, Olive Schepler, Marguerite Desy, Hazel Patrick, Vivian Newland. Front Row (left to right): Don and Carolyn Galbrith.

Honors Planned For Grave Of Mackinaw City Unknown Soldier

Cheboygan Daily Tribune - May 1970

Mrs. Celeste Sheldon places flowers at grave of Mackinaw City's Unknown Soldier as these three Legionnaires met to discuss need for a gravestone there in Lakeview Cemetery. From left to right are Robert Wallin, Mrs. Sheldon, and the village resident Ford Martin.

Mr. Wallin is adjutant and a past commander of the Clayton Murray Post of the American Legion, of which Mrs. Sheldon and President Martin are also members. Mrs. Martin was a Navy Wave in the Korean War. She and Mr. Wallin are on the Mackinaw City Cemetery Board.

The Unknown Soldier is buried in a corner of the Irwin family lot in the Lakeview Cemetery. The burial spot was given by Mrs. Frank Foot, now deceased, who was the former Hazel Irwin. Three of her brothers served in the Army. Her daughter Jane is married to Ford Martin.

Nothing is known of the Unknown Soldier except that he came to Mackinaw City during a blizzard in winter of 1918 and apparently fell off the train ferry dock. Snow covered the body, and it was

not discovered until the snow melted in the Spring. There was no identification on it.

Great interest resulted in the town, but all efforts to identify him failed. A funeral was held from the Presbyterian Church.

Some Mackinaw City people have kept his memory fresh over the 51 year span. Bob Wallin has now proposed that a gravestone be placed so that future generations will always remember. There is possibility that the goverment would furnish the stone. It was suggested also that it could be provided as a Legion project or by or with the City. But regardless of who provides it, President Ford Martin assures that there definitely will be stone put there.

The inscription remains to be decided. Mrs. Sheldon suggested the epitaph might be "A man known only to God," or perhaps just, "An Unknown Soldier."

WORK ON GRAVE OF MACKINAW UNKNOWN SOLDIER

from the
Cheboygan Tribune
May 29, 1970

Women of the American Legion Auxiliary at Mackinaw City built a cement base at the Mackinaw City cemetery for a monument to perpetuate memory of

the Mackinaw City Unknown Soldier. The ladies, left to right, are Mrs. Maxine Whittaker, secretary, Mrs. Edna Ranville, chaplain, Mrs. Darlene Thompson, Mrs. Celeste Jewell, Mrs. Gerald Darrow, president, and Mrs. Douglas Bonter. The children Roberta and Nelson Thompson, Douglas and Laura Bonter, and Jackie Hartson, helped by finding and throwing in stones.

The women volunteered for the work because all of the legionnaires were at their occupations or other duties.

A marble stone, 2 feet wide and six feet long, was given by the McCormick Estate. It will be engraved this summer to read "An Unknown Soldier known but to God." The monument was to be put on the grave today, in readiness for Decoration Day observances Saturday.

The grave marks the burial place of a World War I soldier who was found lying dead on the Straits ice in 1918 alongside the Mackinaw City Railroad ferry dock. It appeared that he got off the *Chief Wawatam* from St. Ignace, walked too near the edge of the

dock, and fell off during a snowstorm, apparently striking his head. Snow accumulated over him, and his presence was not known until snow melted in the spring.

No identification was found on him.

The project was sparked by Mrs. Celeste Jewell, who is chairman of the Cemetery Board, as well as being a member of the Mackinaw City Legion post. - TRIBUNE Photo by Gordon Turner.

Harvey Sailler - 1918

WORLD WAR I

Clayton Murry - Killed
Martin A. McIsaac
Alex W. McVey
Joseph D. McIsaac
Gilbert A. Nicewonder
Carl H. Rapson
Leo Ranville
Wilbur Ranville
John Sailler
Roy Slenters
Darrell S. Shank
Otis Franklin Smith
Harvey S. Sailler
Howard Smith
Joseph E. Thelen
Russell VanHellen
Leonard R. Walters
Lyle M. Wheeler
Garrett Windt
Leonard R. Walters
Guy J. Wolford
August A. Zimmerman
Orin Zimmerman

Don Charles Anderson
Henry Allen - Killed
Paul Ayers
William L. Ausum
Charles Adam Bolinger
James Edwin Cole
Alex R. Currie
Paul Martin Duffina
Clifford E. Dusten
Howard F. Donahue
Jacob J. Ginther
Howard L. Gowans
Roy Irwin
William Raymond Irwin
Arthur Henry Kaltz
Sampson Kniffen
Ellsworth Kniffen
Marvin Lowery
William Laquea
Reuben Laquea
Chester Laquea
George LaWay
Clyde Martin

Allie McVey

Mackinaw Keeps Pace
With Boys Now Over There

Report of Mackinaw
Branch of County Chapter
Shows Real Patriotism

from the *Cheboygan Daily Tribune*
Saturday, Oct. 5, 1918

(By Rev. Fr. G. L. Nye)

The Mackinaw Branch of the Cheboygan County Chapter of the American Red Cross Association, was organized June 7, 1917, by Mrs. A. E. Sangster and Mrs. V. D. Sprague of Cheboygan, with a charter membership of ten. A mass meeting was arranged for the next week, with Rev. F. J. Piuskowski, as the principal speaker, which brought the object of the Red Cross before the people in such a way that over two hundred members were obtained.

Mrs. J. B. Stimpson is chairman of the Mackinaw branch, Mrs. Abbie McVey vice-chairman and Father G. L. Nye, secretary-treasurer. There is a board of directors of 15 members and an executive board of five. In the membership drive of December, 1917, over 350 members were placed on the roll.

The people of Mackinaw City take an active interest in all Red Cross activities, as have also the summer visitors. The funds of the organization have been augmented from time to time by donations of individual members; also proceeds from dances, socials and suppers have been turned over for the same purpose.

The rooms of the Eastern Star have been turned over to the organization as work rooms, and when the monthly quotas arrive they have a goodly number present each day, turning out the work. Mrs. Luella Overton has charge of the knitting and has an able corp of knitters ready to assist in turning out whatever may be needed in the knitted line.

During the past winter the school auxiliary was organized and under the able management of Mrs. Julia Ingals has made great progress in their work. At the beginning of 1918, there was a little over $50 on hand for the branch but up to date about a thousand dollars has been collected, from this amount nearly $250 was spent for yarn and an equal amount for supplies and a small amount of incidentals leaving a working fund of $400 with two credits of $100 each still due the branch.

The success of the Red Cross in Mackinaw is due to the interest shown by the members, their willingness to do whatever they are asked and the perfect harmony existing in the board of directors.

The number "over there" from this community, brings the war nearer home, makes us all realize the great need of doing everything possible for the boys at the front. It is for that reason that Mackinaw is 100 per cent with no slackers.

George J. LaWay
World War I

★★★★★★ OUR MEN IN SERVICE OF U.S. ★★★★★★

Mackinaw's patriotic sons, sketches of whom the Tribune has not been favored with, include Otis Smith, Chester LaQuea, L. M. Wheeler, Paul Ayers, Sampson Kniffin, Clare Pierce, James Hartgrove, Christian Plaunt, Leo Ranville, Wilbur Ranville, Roy Schlanter, William Laquer, Rueben Laquer and Howard Smith. Each of these names in the minds of Mackinaw people, call up memories of lads in school and about town, eager and determined to act their part in furthering public enterprises wherein they might be helpful. Many of these boys made records for themselves as mere lads in school, among their playmates; some of them bore responsibilities heavy in comparison with their youth; all of them are writing home of experiences which reflect credit on their early training and the habits acquired in environment of home.

Thirty-two boys were listed last August and since that time some others have taken their places in the ranks for training for Uncle Sam's service in the Army and Navy.

Dr. A. C. Tiffany—

Mackinaw City's popular young physician, Allen Charles Tiffany, was born in Rockford, Mich, near Mancelona. He attended high school in Sioux City, Iowa and also attended the Ferris Institute at Big Rapi where he studied pharmacy graduating with credit to himself. After three years practical experience he took the state examination at Lansing and became a registered pharmacist. He opened a drug store in Boyne Falls where he was located for three years, when he opened a drug business in Pellston. In 1910, he attended the Detroit College of Medicine from which he graduated in 1914. After practicing medicine one year in DeTour he located in Mackinaw City in 1915, where he at once built up a lucrative practice. When the war broke out Dr. Tiffany felt a desire to enlist in the medical relief corps. He enlisted in June 1917, and received a First Lieutenant Commission. He went to Fort Ben Harrison, the following September and later was sent to San Francisco, where he obtained a captain's commission. He was connected in turn with Camp Cody, New Mexico; Camp Gravis, Texis, and Camp Upton, New York. He reached France, July 10, 1918, where he has since been actively engaged in hospital surgical work.

Orin J. Zimmerman—

Orin J. Zimmerman entered service at Camp Custer, Michigan, May 28, 1918. After six weeks training he was transferred to New York from where he sailed to France with the 85th Division.

John Sailler—

"Believe me I'm going to get ahead as fast as I can', writes John Sailler from the Great Lakes Naval Station where he is training. John is but 21 years of age. He enlisted the 26th of June. His training at the Great Lakes station will be finished soon and then he enters the officers training department at Columbus, Ohio university to take a course in aviation.

Harvey S. Sailler.

John's brother, Harvey S. Sailler is 31 years old and is in the service somewhere in France. He enlisted July 14, '17 and left for France less than a month later with Company A. 19th. Reg. Engineers. Both of the boys were born in Cheboygan Co. and are very proud of the fact that they are descendents of a soldier from France who came over to this country with General Lafayette at the time of the Revolutionary War.

210

Paul Duffina—

Paul Duffina is the 26 year old son of Mrs. Margaret Duffina, of Mackinaw and a lifelong resident of the village. He attended its schools participated in its youthful sports, was a member of the boys' choir at St. Anthony's church and from boyhood was devoted to fishing, especially enjoying trout fishing through the ice on Lakes Michigan and Huron .He boasts of having caught as many as 60 pounds of trout at one time, making the trip to and from his shanty with his sled drawn by his faithful dogs "Kelly and "Reefer". He was stationed at Camp Custer for training, and has just arrived over seas.

Leonard Walters

Leonard Walters though a true home boy, devoted to his mother Mrs. Charles Walters and fond of domestic life, is conquering homesickness and making go odin the aviation corps. He is only 20 years of age; was born in Mack. and graduated from Mock. high school June, 1916. shortly after was made a member the Aviation Corps. He was sent to Camp Kelly Field, Texas and three weeks later to the Aviation Mechanics training school at St. Paul, Minn. where he completed his course as electrician. He did some practical work at Minneola, Long Istand and shortly after was mare a member of the mounted artillery. June 25 he sailed for France.

Clarence A. Stimpson—

Cheboygan's first reported casualty startled Mackinaw and Cheboygan county as a whole. Clarence A. Stimpson was so severely wounded in the left arm in action March 28, 1918, that amputation was neccessary He returned to this country for recuperation Aug. 15 and was in a military hospital in Washington, D. C. for some time. He is the son of Charles Stimpson and enlisted in September 1917 with Company B, 6th Engineers. His one regret according to a letter sent home from a Red Cross hospital in Europe was "that they got me so early in the game." Mr. Stimpson is home on a furlough and will report the 20th of this month at the hospital in Washington, D. C., where he will be assigned to special service.

Angus O. Zimmerman

Angus Zimmerman was mustered into service at Camp Custer, December 7, 1917, after training there for two weeks he was transferred to Camp MacArthur, at Waco, and then went to Camp Merritt, N. Texas, where he spent three weeks J., sailing from there to France, with the 126th Inf., A. E. F.

Howard L. Gowans.—

Howard L. Gowans, son of Mrs. Rose Gowans, was born at Gladwin, Feb. 28, 1887. He graduated from the Gladwin High School and then took a course of study at a Bay City Business College. He was employed as bill clerk by the M. C. R. R. company up to the time of his enlistment, December 10, 1917. He is a member of the 281st. Aero Squadron was for a time stationed at Hempstead, Long Island, and is now in France.

Christian Plaunt

Christian Plaunt is one of the last of the Mackinaw City boys to enter the service and he is now in training at Camp Custer with Brigade No. 143. Having been very successful as a fisherman, he will doubtless become of "fisher of Germans".

Fern L. Johnson

Fern L. Johnson, U.S.N., went into training at the Great Lakes Naval Training Station April 7, 1918 and is now in France. Previous to sailing he spent some time at Norfolk. He writes he likes the life in the navy and is wild for a "crack at the Huns".

Clyde Martin

Clyde Martin wears a medal. He has not only shown bravery and loyalty to duty, but is said to be the youngest boy in the American army services. Clyde is about sixteen years of age. He is the son of Mr. and Mrs. W.E. Martin of Mackinaw and while on a visit to his mother who is in Traverse City, enlisted there at the age of fifteen years. He was sent to Grayling for training and later was assigned to the headquarters Co.

McIsaac Boys

Dan McIsaac is very proud of his two sons and their records.

JOSEPH I. McISAAC

Jos. I. McIsaac is a member of a motor truck company now in France and is having a most thrilling experience.

MARTIN A. McISAAC

Martin is spending time as an instructor at Camp Perry, Ohio, and is now a lieutenant in active service.

Pvt. W. Marvin Lowery—

Private W. Marvin Lowery, 13th Co., 160th Brigade, Camp Custer, is the son of William J. Lowery, chief eng. on car Ferry Chief Wawatam He is 21 years of age. Marvin was born in Webbwood, Ont., He came with his parents to Cheboygan, where they resided seven years before locating in Mackinaw in his 14th year. At the time he offered his services to his country he was employed as switchman on the M. C. R. R.

A. W. McVey—

Among Mackinaw boys in the Aviation service is A. W. McVey, who is serving in the capacity of cadet attached to the 87th Aero squadron, at Park Field, Memphis, Tenn.

Clayton Leslie Murray—

Private Clayton Leslie Murray, son of Mrs. Rose Murray, was one of Mackinaw's brave fighters in the big drive the latter part of July. He was reported wounded severely July 31. He is but 22 years of age and is a member of Co. H, 125th Inf.

Ellsworth L. Kniffen.

Ellsworth L. Kniffen, 21 years old has had a varied experience in the U. S. service. At the age of 17 years he enlisted in the Minnesota National Guards and six months later was transferred to the regular army. He served six months in Mexico and was discharged, through disability. He wouldn't stay discharged. He enlisted in the Navy as second class seaman July of this year and is now serving as an expert rifleman at Camp Logan Ill., with the U. S. N. Sharp Shooters.

Irwin Brothers—

Raymond W. Irwin and Russel C. Irwin, are the pride of their family,

"Russel is a soldier and Raymond is a sailor", boasts their sister. Raymond enlisted in the navy at Detroit December 12, 1917 and took his train

RAYMOND IRWIN

ing at the Great Lakes Naval station, later being transferred to Syracuse, N. Y. He is now in limited service at a recruiting camp which he entered early in September. Russell enlisted in the army service at Bay City, and is now in aviation corps training, at St. Paul Minn.

213

Charter Members
1946
World War II

Georgia Yager
Helen Smith
Mary E. Desy
Mildred Martin
Louise Sailler
Rachel Wehner
Helen Carty
Maxine Smith
Harriet Evans
Margaret Sommer
Nancy Kage
Grace Marie Cosens
Alice Collins
Marguerite D. Marsh
Ethel L. Carlton
Blanche M. Davis
Amy Babcock
Ruth S. Barrett
Eleanor Marshall
Kathryn Barnes
Margaret Smith
Dorothy Hayes
Helene Stephany
Grace B. Wheeler
Madanna Marshall
Marcella Sommers
Alvira Cunningham
Mary Ranville
Ann Grondin
Lillian Pope
Loradelle Pope
Irma Moore
Edna Campbell
Betty Bauers
Edna S. Ranville
Catherine F. Backie

Gold Star Members
World War II

Georgia Yager
Flossie Amick
Mertle Smith
Genevieve Kronberg
Ellen Sands

Life Member

Edna S. Ranville

Jack Brown
Killed WWII

PFC Marie Patrick Riggs, USAF, WWII

Honor Roll – World War II

Gerald Amick*
Martin Alger
George Aylesworth
Charles Adams
R. Dale Barnett
Ernest Bauers
Ivien Barnum
Dale Barton
Ervin Barrett
Forrest Barrett
Jack Barrett
Floyd Brown
Jack Brown*
James Burroughs
Robert Babcock
Sidney Babcock
Dan Boone
Clinton Bowman*
Thomas Bricker
Stephen Cosens
Archie Cosens
Rueben Cain
Carl Cassidy
William Chisley
James Colovan
Raymond Desy
Donald Darrow
Everett Desy
James Desy
Keith Darling
Clyde Darling
Edwin Dusten
Thomas Dewitt
Stephen Dombroski
Louis Durand
Wayne Ewalt
George Ewalt

Ralph Flood
Charles Forgette
Harold Flynn
Donald Flynn
Merle Gwilt
Edward Gwilt
Ernest Gwilt
Pat Griffith
Sam Hartgrove*
George Hayes
Harry Heath
Ray Ingels*
Russel Irwin
Cleve Knight
Edward Krueger
Burr Krueger
Jean Krueger
Harry Kniffen
Robert Linklater
William Linklater
Charles LaCombe
Lawrence LaCombe
Raymond LaCombe
Fred Larocque
Ernest Lockhart
Donald Lett
Leonard Lasley
Bernard LaRocque
Aulden LaRocque
Hector LaPrarrie
Allan LaRocque
Alvan LaRocque
Joseph Meagher
Ford Martin
Stuart McVey
Charles McVey
Charles Moore

Robert Moore
George Marshall
Bernard Marshall
Cecil Magoon
Mervil Magoon
Donald Magoon
Ted Morris
Howard Nelligan
William Newsome
Ralph Niles
William Nau
Ray Olsen
Ray Odum
Gerald Ostrander
Walter Peppler
William Peppler
Walter Pope
William Plaunt
Grover Plaunt*
Virgil Plaunt*
Elmer Plaunt
Marcus Plaunt
Leo Paquet
Anthony Paquet
Robert Preston
John Preston
Charles Phillips
Robert Parker
Ronald Parker
Cornelius Reinhout
Friday Robinson
Tracy Ranville
Glen Ritter
Robert Schepler
Reynolds Schneider
Gordon Sattler
Bernard Sullivan
Bernard Sailer
Leslie Sands*
Helios Swontek
Ray Sommers

Joy Sommers
Allen Sommers
Earl Smith
Otis Smith
Marne Smith
Leonard Smith*
Edward Thompson
John Thompson
Ralph Thompson
Kenneth Teysen
Robert Taylor
James Taylor
Ernest Terrian
Clarence Terrian
Albert Thilhorn
Norman Thilhorn
Henry Vieau
Harry Williams
Lyle Williams
Robert Wallin
Ernest Wallin
Lyle Wheeler
Chester Wilcox
John Wilcox
George Wilson
Clare Wilson
Barton Wolford
James Wehner
William Wiedner
Harvey Yeager*
Jack Yeager
Louis Ziegler

*Lost

LADIES

Marie Riggs - Air Force

3 More of County's Soldiers Reported Missing In Action

May 26, 1942

Three more of Cheboygan county's soldiers of the Battle of Battan and Manila Bay have been officially reported by the government as "missing".

Following notice recently received here that Assistant Cook Euclid Vieau, U. S. Marines, was missing, notices have been received by parents stating that Ernest Scott and Harvey and Jack Yeager of Mackinaw City have been listed in status of "missing."

In case of all four men, it was pointed out, that the young men may be Japanese prisoners of war.

Still remaining to be reported is Harvey Pelletier of Cheboygan. Relatives said this afternoon that they still have not been notified by the government concerning him.

Scott was in an anti-aircraft unit on Corregidor(Manila Bay fort. Pelletier and the Mackinaw brothers were also in the Philippines when the war broke out, although it is not known whether they were on Corregidor, some of the other islands, or in the long siege of the Bataan peninsula. Last important American resistance ceased when Corregidor surrendered on May 7. Troops that had survived Japanese attacks were captured.

In letters of notification from the Adjutant General of the Army, parents were told that there was no report of their son being killed, but that casualty reports were incomplete. In lack of definite information, the general said, the men will be listed as "missing."

Chapter 29

Frances Margaret Fox

by Pat Barnett

"One of Mackinaw's prominent citizens, of whom she is justly proud, is Frances Margaret Fox, noted author of children's stories. She was the daughter of the late Mr. and Mrs. James Fox, and was born in Farmington, Mass., in 1870. Educated in the Michigan Seminary in Kalamazoo, she was Mackinaw's first primary teacher. Her stories were published regularly between the years 1900-1939 and she has been listed in the *Who's Who Among North American Authors* since 1929. For many years she spent her summers at her cottage in Mackinaw City and her winters in Washington, D.C., when she was one of the privileged few, having access to the Congressional Library. Because of the infirmities of age, she is now cared for in the Arnold Home in Detroit, but her interest in Mackinaw and her friends of many years standing, still remains."—by Ruth Bauers, published July 2, 1955, in the Cheboygan County centennial edition of *The Cheboygan Daily Tribune.*

Frances Margaret Fox died March 1, 1959, and her ashes were deposited in the Straits of Mackinac by her long-time friend Alan Joslyn, a Detroit attorney. Miss Fox was highly thought of by all who were privileged to know her in our area and she especially loved the children. While she was a teacher here in Mackinaw City she formed a club called the Sunshine Club, and some of the children who belonged were Nina McGregor, Leona Niles, the Barringer girls, the Pettinger girls and the Newland, Griffith, McGinnis, Delmarter and Shepler children.

When Madge Fox and her family first moved to Mackinaw from the east, they resided at 307 Jamet Street, and later she built the cottage at 109 Depeyster Street which she named "Sunny Day". Later she sold the cottage and built "Happy Landing" at 512 Huron Street, where she resided until her death.

Madge Fox used the Straits area as the setting for several of her books, *Nannette, Nancy Davenport, Betty of Old Mackinaw* and *The Magic Canoe,* to name a few. She often referred to local people and places by name. Over the years she dedicated several of her books to the following area friends: Virginia Crane, Bethany Ann Lane, Laura Alice Joslyn, Mary Anna Joslyn, Helen Margaret Parsons, Alan Wilson Joslyn, Lee Everett Joslyn, Jr., Virginia Desy, Lizzie, Edith and Louise Davenport, Frances, Hazen and Elizabeth Rosemary Dodd, Vera, Charlotte, Eugenie and Ruth White and Iva, Leona, Flora, Charlie, Burton, Beatrice, Bernice, Ralph and Katie Niles.

One of her books, *Little Mossback Amelia*, the story of a pioneer family in the Petoskey area, was reprinted by the Little Traverse Regional Historical Society in 1967.

As well as books, she wrote many short stories over the years. They appeared in the Elson-Gray school primers and the following magazines: *Sunday School Times, The Christian Register, Youths Companion, American Childhood, The Woman's Home Companion,The Continent* and *Little Folks.*

Following is a list of the books Frances Margaret Fox wrote between 1900-1940 and two unpublished stories which were found after her death:

Farmer Brown and the Birds
The Little Giant's Neighbors
Mother Nature's Little Ones
Betty of Old Mackinaw
Brother Billy
How Christmas Came to the Mulvaneys
The Country Christmas
Seven Christmas Candles
Seven Little Wise Men
Carlota
Little Lady Marjorie
The Magic Canoe
Little Mossback Amelia
Angeline Goes Traveling
Nancy Davenport
The Kinderkins
Ellen Jane
Janey
Sister Sally
Flowers and Their Travels
Washington D.C., The Nation's Capitol
Nannette
The Rainbow Bridge
What Gladys Saw
Little Toad

Frances Margaret Fox

The First Kerosene Lamp At Mackinac Island

TRUE STORY

There was a time about eighty years ago when Mackinac Island, in the Straits of Mackinac, seemed like a faraway corner of the United States. For long months every year it was separated from the rest of the world by mountains of snow and ice. Even so, those who lived there through the short gay summers and the long winters, had heard of a new invention that would, so it was said, soon be in common use.

This invention was the kerosene lamp. Until that time the islanders had lighted their homes with candles and fish-oil lamps. But the officers and soldiers at Fort Mackinac often talked of the time coming when the fort and village would be lighted by the new lamps. Even the lighthouses at that time were using lard-oil lamps to warn all sailors to beware of rocks and dangers.

One summer day there was great excitement in the village on the island. A ship had arrived with a troop of soldiers and their officers to exchange places with the garrison at the fort. The streets were thronged with friendly islanders who wished to see the departure of soldiers who were leaving the fort and to welcome the new arrivals.

That night, when the candles were lighted in all the homes of the island, a bit of pleasing news was carried from house to house. It was said that one of the officers who had come on the ship that day had brought with him a kerosene lamp. He was a courteous gentleman and had offered to show his wonderful lamp to all who were interested and wished to see it. It was explained that the officer would allow the lamp to burn for about three hours every evening, but no longer. He would show all interested how the lamp was lighted, but he was unwilling to light it more than once a day. This was because he feared that the lamp might get worn out.

The next evening it seemed as if all the fathers and mothers, aunts and uncles, on the Island of Mackinac had climbed the steep path to the fort on the bluff to visit the kind gentleman who lived in one of the apartments in the building known as "The Officers' Stone Quarters."

The Islanders saw the wonderful new invention, and they listened with great interest when the officer explained to them how the lamp worked.

Naturally all the children in the village longed to see the lamp too. And the more stories they heard about it, the more interested they became. They wished to see the officer turn a little knob in the side of the lamp and thus move the wick up or down in the oil, to make the light grow brighter and brighter, or dimmer and dimmer.

At last the officer heard that the children of the island wished to see his treasure. And as he was really a delightful gentleman, he invited all the children in the tiny village to come on a certain evening to see the new light shining in the old historic fort on the bluff.

Now it happens that all the fathers and mothers of that time are gone from earth. But there is yet living one dear old lady of the Mackinaw Country, who was one of the children who climbed the path to the fort that starry evening in the long ago. She is lovingly known as "Grandma Ranville". And only last winter "Grandpa Marshal" was still living. He was a fine old gentleman who was another one of the children who saw that first lamp.

Mrs. Ranville never forgets, and Grandpa Marshal never forgot that wonderful evening. She, like all the

218

little girls of the village, was dressed in her Sunday best for her visit to the fort. He, like all the other little boys, was scrubbed until he was red behind the ears, and then dressed in his Sunday best, copper-toed boots and all, for his visit to the Officers' Stone Quarters to see the new lamp.

The solemn procession of little children marched up the hill, through the gates of the fort, across the tiny parade ground, and were welcomed at the Officers' Stone Quarters by the gentleman who owned the lamp.

It stood on a table in the middle of the room, and the children stood back in far circles to gaze upon the wonder. They had been warned before they left their homes that they must not venture too near the kerosene lamp because it might explode.

So they stood far back in the brightly lighted room and in awestruct silence they looked at that lamp. The bottom of the lamp, which held the oil, so the officer explained, was brass and shaped like a bowl. This brass bottom had a handle like the handle of a candlestick. The light shone through a clear glass chimney.

The officer turned the wick up to make more light in the room, and then turned it down, down, until the light grew dim. The children fairly held their breath, fearing that the lamp might explode, but it didn't. They listened in wonder when the officer told them that every house in the United States would soon be lighted by kerosene lamps. He said that the lightkeepers at the lighthouses would soon be filling big lamps in their high towers with the oil from coal. Everywhere kerosene lamps would take the place of fish-oil lamps and candles.

When at last the children thanked the officer and said good-night most politely, as they had promised to do before ever they left their homes, they walked quietly down the long hill, back to their village. The very moon and stars in the Mackinaw sky looked dim to those darling children of that long ago after they had seen the radiance of the light of the first kerosene lamp ever at Mackinac Island.

And what the Fort Mackinac officer said was true. The time soon came when all the country was lighted by kerosene lamps. But while sweet Grandma Ranville still lives, kerosene lamps have followed the candlesticks to the high shelves, for now the wide world has found a light to rival the stars and put out the moon.

A True Toad Story From Old Mackinaw

by Margaret Francis Fox

Hithertofore Unpublished Manuscripts used by permission of Mr. Joslyn Executor of Fox Estate

The toad lived in Mr. McVey's garden at Old Mackinaw in the long ago. At first Mr. McVey and the toad were polite strangers, but in time they became friends. The toad discovered that Mr. McVey was a kindly gentleman who did him no harm, and Mr. McVey quickly found out that the toad was a great help to him because it ate grubs and all sorts of insects that spoil gardens.

After those two thus learned to respect and like each other, the toad became the family pet. After awhile Mrs. McVey became interested in the toad. Indeed she fed him bread crumbs every day and laughed to see him eat them.

The McVey children used to invite the neighbors to see the toad hopping along the rows of plants, close beside their father while he worked. Sometimes when their father was using the hoe he had to poke the toad out of the way for fear he might, by accident, give him a whack with the hoe.

When Mr. McVey used to get down on his knees to weed the carrots, there was fun for everyone in the garden and for the neighbor's children hanging over the fence, because the toad was funny. He used to put his head on one side and wink and blink and act as if he would like to say to Mr. McVey, "Oh, dig out a good fat grub this time, why don't you!"

For two summers the toad lived and worked in the garden, and at last he became so friendly that he came when he was called. If he heard the voices of his family by day or in the evening he came hopping out to see and be seen.

One day a friend of the family said to Mr. and Mrs. McVey, "How do you know that it is the same toad in the garden this year that was in your garden last year? Perhaps it is not the same one."

Well, perhaps not. The family owned up that toads do look alike and while they believed that their pet year after year was the same old toad, no one could be sure about it. So, one autumn day, about the time when toads back into the earth to sleep under the ground all winter, Mrs. McVey went into the garden and tied four strands of red silk around one of the hind legs of her toad. She tied the silk in a hard knot.

The toad winked and blinked at her in the most friendly fashion and then away he hopped with a band of bright red silk around one hind leg. After that he was seen no more in the garden that season. He didn't even get out of bed to have a look at the Jack O'Lanterns on Hallowe'en.

All winter long the McVey boys and girls wondered if they ever would see their own toad again.

Well, they did. One day in the springtime, when the garden was plowed, Mr. McVey called the family to come out and see their toad. There he was with a red silk band around one leg, winking and blinking in the sunshine and waiting for breakfast.

Everyone was pleased to see him, and the old toad looked happy himself to be with his friends. And to this day boys and girls who live at Old Mackinaw like to hear about the doings of the toad that lived in the McVey garden in the long ago.

Frances Margaret Fox takes a last look across the Straits before the groundbreaking for the Mackinac Bridge.

"Madge" Fox entertaining the children in front of the school.

Mackinaw City Author's Ashes Deposited In Straits

Miss Margaret Francis Fox, noted author, who formerly lived at Mackinaw City, before her death requested that her body be cremated and her ashes deposited in the Straits of Mackinac.

Yesterday Alan Joslyn of Detroit, an attorney, who was a lifelong friend of Miss Fox, fulfilled her wish and deposited the remains on the waves at 512 N. Huron, the former home of Miss Fox.

She was one of Mackinaw City's first school teachers and was noted for a long list of Children's books which won her international recognition.

Mr. Joslyn also presented to the Mackinaw City Women's Club library a group of books written by Miss Fox, and which she had autographed. The Women's Club has undertaken project of assembling a complete set of all books which Miss Fox has written.

Chapter 30

Artists of Mackinaw

By Thelma Shaw

The history, myths and magic of Mackinaw make for a tantalizing beauty which attracts people who work creatively. This includes superb homemakers, skilled craftsmen, those who work in special ways with people, and--as well--men and women in the "fine arts".

Perhaps there are too many such persons for a complete roster of those here on a year-round basis and of those whose creative roots are here but who live in Mackinaw in summers only...Celia Renkenberger, now 95, inspired many with her painting; John Moore, poet; Douglas V. Steere, religious philosopher and writer; Thelma Shaw, whose published work is chiefly for young people; Ralph Shaw, painter in oils; Marie Melms, whose lively verse has brightened and blessed much that is Mackinaw in essence....

There are many others, but special mention is reserved for Mackinaw City's own native son, Lloyd Desy. His paintings are chiefly seascapes, landscapes and portraits of native Americans. They are treasured by many residents, and several local businesses proudly display his work. With eyesight difficulties, Lloyd Desy has persisted and achieved a high degree of excellence. He has lived his life as a true friend of Mackinaw and as an artist of the highest order.

Lloyd Desy, Artist

Northland

How lucky I thought--
How lucky am I--!
As I looked at the stars
And the moon in the sky.

There's our beautiful lake
So much like the sea
That thunders and roars
Yet as calm as can be.

I heard a bird call
In the tree top at dawn.
I sat by a brook
And watched a young fawn.

A silvery rain fell
With a soft soothing sigh
And a golden sun rose
As the seagulls flew by.

I roamed through the woods
And breathed the pure air--
Unpolluted by smoke
Not a worry nor care.

I saw a young mother
In her arms, a wee babe
Untouched by the horrors
That make some so afraid.

I picked a fair lily
As white as the snow.
God's in his heaven--
He caused it to grow.

I looked up at our church
With its high-rising steeple--
Free from all fear
Were its worshipping people.

To sing loud their praises
Of pathways untrod
All Hail and all Glory
And all thanks to our God.

Marie C. Melms

222

Chapter 31

"Recollections"

by Beatrice McIsaac Ackley

The Dan McIsaac family can be justly referred to as the Railroad family, as his four sons made railroading their life work. The Michigan Central Railroad transferred Mr. McIsaac to Mackinaw from Bay City in 1893 to have charge of the maintenance of the Railroad property, including the dock, etc. It included all property between Bay City and Mackinaw, but as the business increased the boundaries were lessened to Grayling to Mackinaw.

As housing was scarce, the railroad built a house for Mr. McIsaac and his family. It had an upstairs that was to serve as living quarters for the Brakeman and Baggagemen who would have to stay overnight and some weekends. (A similar house was built for the roundhouse foreman and the crews who had layovers in Mackinaw.)

These crews would bring their food from their homes and do their own cooking while on their layovers. The McIsaac house was built just south of the tracks on Huron Street. It was razed several years ago. The depot was built when Mr. McIsaac came here, and one of his first projects was to install a steam heating plant and plumbing system. He also installed plumbing in his home, which was a novelty in those early years. The coal stoves were also used during the severe winters. The work was so heavy that a work train was maintained that employed 8 to 10 men during the summer months, and the train would be taken to wherever it was needed. The men lived on the train, and one car was used as a kitchen and dining area.

When moving to Mackinaw, the McIsaac family consisted of one daughter and four sons. The two younger boys started to school in Mackinaw in the same location the elementary school now stands. The youngest of the family was the only one born in Mackinaw. The oldest son, Joe, worked with his Father until slack times came, when he worked at plumbing in Detroit until his death there in 1934. The second son, Arthur, was killed in a railroad accident in Gaylord. Next son, Martin, worked in the freight office until he entered the armed services and attended Officer Training School, graduating as

Lieutenant in the Infantry. He later was employed as a Pullman Company Conductor until his retirement. He now lives in Mackinaw with his wife Catherine. The youngest son, Floyd, or Babe as he was known in R.R. service, was yardmaster in Mackinaw, Battle Creek and Kalamazoo, then was promoted to Assistant Superintendent of the N.Y.C. lines with headquarters in Bay City until his retirement. He always maintained a home in Mackinaw, and his widow, Delvia, now spends her summers here. Floyd died in 1970.

Dan McIsaac retired in 1930. He built a home on the corner of Jamet and Langlade Streets. He died in 1937.

There were few homes "across the tracks", but the McVey and McIsaac families had a group of their own, with the families so close knit they were considered relatives. The mother of the McIsaac family died when they were all very young, and the oldest girl, Margaret, cared for the family, but with the kindness of Mrs. McVey and Grandma Ranville, we were well cared for. They were nurse and doctor whenever anyone was ill. Grandma Ranville was truly a doctor, mother and nurse all rolled into one good soul. They lived in what in recent years was called the "Anchor Inn" and they operated a hotel there.

Other families living down in that area were the Kinsels, LaQueys and Plaunts. About two miles down on the shore was a settlement referred to as "Fly Point". Their main occupation was fishing. They could be seen in the late afternoons bringing in their catch on a sled drawn by a dog team. A priest told one time of getting a telegram reading "Come to the Point at once." He had been serving Mackinaw as a missionary, so readily understood the message. Many of the local homes were used for Catholic services as members of the present parish can remember. Suppers were served up in the town hall to raise money to build a church.

There is something about this small town that draws people back from wherever they lived.

The two surviving members of the McIsaac family, Martin and Beatrice Ackley, have many recollections of the town when it did not have the beautiful motels, gift shops etc.

Martin recalls the factory that was located down in the area of the now state dock. It manufactured railroad ties and telegraph poles. A clothespin factory was also in the area. The logs to be used were floated down from the Upper Peninsula. Martin recalls seeing the first *Algomah* that carried passenger cars on a scow that was equipped with tracks. He recalls an uncle, John Hayes, moving to Mackinaw from the Upper Peninsula, and soon after settling here he organized a band that would play on the sidewalks on Saturday nights. Later the bandstand was built and concerts were given. It was located in the area of the City Hall and Legion Club. Martin prizes a picture of the cast of a Home Talent Show put on by the young people of the town. He recalls their Father sending them to Cheboygan on Saturdays to receive their religion instructions from the nuns in St. Marys School. Beatrice remembers her school days with basketball games between nearby towns, but without a gym it was played in the upstairs of the town hall. One time a game was scheduled with St. Ignace girls, and we were to come home on the 10:00 trip of the carferry, but unfortunately the boat became stuck in the ice and we were there about 4 days. We had a teacher along as chaperone, so her classes were dismissed during that time. We had to be entertained by the St. Ignace team in their homes as no one could afford to stay in the hotel. We all enjoyed the trips, as

we had to stay in hotels and that was a treat. Graduating trips were less glamorous than today. My class went up to St. Helene Island in Roxy Wolford's boat. We picked lilacs to decorate for the graduation. Almost every girl had a turn at clerking in Overton's Drug Store. I worked in my brother-in-law's grocery store one summer. H. Z. Galbraith was agent for the R.R. at that time, and he was one of the first to see the need of women replacing men who were called into armed service. He hired Marie Patrick Riggs to work in the ticket office, and Lucille Robinson Lane and I were offered work in the freight office. A few times we had to check the cars as they came off the carferry. I later transferred to Lansing to work in the freight office there, but by that time many girls were hired for that work. During the war period, Mr. Galbraith was instrumental in setting up a canteen in the depot for the traveling servicemen. Many times he would have us leave our work to handle the canteen.

It is interesting to note the many families who grew up in Mackinaw leave to pursue their careers then return to live out their lives with the memories of their childhood. The McIsaac family follows that pattern. The oldest member lived in Lansing but spent many return visits to Mackinaw, and now her family spends their vacation time here.

Play Group - Upstairs at old City Hall (Shepherd's Hall)
First Row (left to right): Guy Pringle, Helen McVey, Floyd McIsaac.
Second Row: Mitchell Swantek, Anna Dietz, Louie Gahl, Nick Buehler.
Third Row: M. A. McIsaac, Ethel Lawlery, Cynthia Dietz, Grover McVey.

John Hayes, George Hayes, Dan McIsaac

McIsaac Home, R.R. house, stood between Traverse Bay Woolen Co. and R.R. tracks.

Chapter 32

Mackinaw City
In the Old Days
About 1908

I guess I'll have to begin with myself. I was born in the house now occupied by Mr. and Mrs. Lester Stokes. I don't remember much of the first two years, but I remember being very ill at age three. So, my first memory is of when I was pretty well recouperated, the doctor's visits, and he used to bring his boy with him. His name was Max Brown. Anyway, the doctor brought me to a state of good health. My father had been building us a house in the country, about two miles from town, so we moved out there and planted gardens and had chickens and a couple of cows and a pig or two. I recall that my sister, seventeen months older than I, was hand feeding cucumbers to a cow when her dress became hooked over the cow's horn and the cow, in trying to throw her off as she raised her head, was bashing her into the dirt. So I screamed for Mother, who came and lifted her off, glad that she was only scared and dirty and had not been gored. But it was a close call and ever after that she was kind of a fraidy cat. Across the road lived an Irish family by the name of Griffith. They had two boys about my age and a girl a little younger, so we played together, making wigwams, stilts, and ran races and pole vaulted and picked berries. Mrs. Griffith had a sister, Jennie Sousa, who tried to teach us to turn handsprings and told us scarey stories. I remember that she walked on her hands a lot, once she went down our row of little cabbages and chewed off each one. My dad wondered what had chewed the cabbages, but we never told. We had a lot of company from town and had a lot of fun on the farm, but we worked, too, weeding rows of vegetables and riding a horse to cultivate the corn, etc. We also had to keep the woodbox by the kitchen stove filled. My sister helped mostly in the house and I helped outside. I remember getting yelled at, "Clean your feet", "Wash your hands" as I came in the door. My father and I made a root house where we put two barrels of apples that my aunt and uncle sent every fall and the pumpkins, squash, carrots, potatoes, all the vegetables, to keep for winter. We also grew a few sugar beets for the deer so when the deer season arrived he didn't have far to go to get one, and as we harvested the potatoes, the deer walked behind the wagon and ate their fill. In winter we moved back into town sometimes, as I remember living in the little Dr. Pierce house when

Irwins lived where Dick Kage lives now (next door). There was a big barn behind Irwin's, and we played there a lot in winter. Irwins had two girls and a boy, all older than us, but we played with Dorothy. I remember admiring the candy boxes she had stapled to her bedroom wall, and a spanking I got when she sent me for food for a party and I brought out something my mother had planned for supper. At that time there was Sunderland's Good Bakery, where now stands the Masonic Temple. Judge Richards' store was next, then Barret's Clothing, Coffman's Drug Store, doctor's office upstairs (the doctor also pulled teeth), then Zimmerman's Mortuary, then the Mercer house.

Then, turning west on Main Street where the Glass Managerie is, was a saloon, then a feed store, another saloon, Bert Barret's Barber Shop, Peck's Meat Market. Between the saloon and the barber shop was old Doc Kniffin's Soup House, where you got a big fried cake, milk and a good bowl of homemade soup for about fifteen cents.

Then the hardware store, in the back of which was the Post Office, Risk's Big Busy Store, which sold clothing, blankets, etc., then the Liebeck-Trainor Grocery Store, The Overton (later Stimpson, then Linton and Stevenson, now B&C) Drug Store, and the Stimpson House Hotel. Across Henry Street was Hobb's Grocery Store, Rosa Smith's Restaurant, the Macabee's Building, the Mackinaw Hotel operated by people named Blake, then Con Olsen's and another house, then where the Dairy Queen is now, was the Old Casino Movie House and Dance Hall where we held our commencement exercises, home talent plays, which we had more of those days. Then across Ducharme Street was the Smith and Trumbull Garage and Blacksmith Shop. Back to Huron Street, where the cobblestone Village Hall is now, was a two-story wooden City Hall. We played basketball upstairs. Southward was a bandstand and the Windmill Waffle Shop where Kenville's Restaurant now stands.

Down at the waterfront by the railroad tracks was Sheppler's Fish House, and the lake was always full of logs that had been floated there to load on flat cars on the train. A Mr. Mudget had charge of the logs and the loading.

Along Main Street were several hitching posts to

tie horses to and two wells with tin cups hanging on the pumps for people and wooden lard tubs under the spouts for water for the horses. At first there were only four or five cars in town owned by Chris Dietz, Dell Wheeler, Lloyd Stimpson, and a Ford taxi run by Archie St. Germain. I had my first car ride when Mr. and Mrs. Lloyd Stimpson gave us a ride home from Sunday school. The railroad tracks came closer to Main Street then. Once as my sister and I were walking home from school, we saw one man chasing another around a boxcar on a sidetrack with a big knife, but I never heard that anything bad happened.

Three railroads had trains coming in here. The New York Central (which was then the Michigan Central R.R.) came from Detroit, and on the north side of the depot the Grand Rapids and Indiana (later the Pennsylvania) R.R. train came in from Grand Rapids and Chicago. Then on the south side, the Duluth, South Shore and Atlantic from the north came in at night and left in the morning. The depot was also a hotel called The Wentworth Hotel. The dining hall, located in the depot hotel, was a busy place, sometimes with over eight hundred checks for breakfast. Trains came in sections in summer and hunting season, and holidays with about three hundred on each section, two or three sections. I worked at the dining hall and got passes on the trains, so we did our shopping in Detroit. We could get into a berth in Detroit and get off right at home absolutely free because we worked for the railroad. It was hard work, but interesting. We saw all the prisoners going to Marquette Prison – some bad ones: Steve Majac, Killer Burke, Hotelling, Gipsy Bob, and others. Also, we saw the latest fashions going to the Island, as most still came by train. Celebrities: The Gish Girls, Clara Kimball Young, Edgar and Bud Guest, Detroit Symphony Conductor Ossippee Gabrilovich, who married Mark Twain's daughter. In the wintertime when the carferry was stuck in the ice or trains were snowbound, we had a lot of interesting people around for days at a time.

Besides the railroad carferry, we had speedboat service to the Island, and often they took us for a speedboat ride all the way around Mackinac Island free, too.

Our road to school was also used by the Indians, who came to town from Cecil Bay to get drunk. There was a sandy place in the road where the sun made the sand warm, and we would see them lying in the sand on our way home from school. They did break in the door to our neighbor's house and ate the food they found in the cupboard and spilled it around, but they never bothered at our house. They knew my dad to be a strong blacksmith who took no nonsense.

There weren't any houses at Trail's End then, but there was a house at French Farm and on the Wheeler farm across from Bonter's farm. There was a log cabin on the corner across from the Miller farm and two houses near the railroad tracks near where the city dump is now and one a little farther south, Butts' and Stratner's.

They used to have dances at Cecil Bay. There were about thirty houses there and a hotel boardinghouse. The man who played the fiddle at the dance always stopped at our house to visit. His name was Joe Frachette, a Frenchman. My folks always fed the people who stopped by. There were always land lookers, some, who were bachelors, made it a habit to come to eat. They often brought candy for us kids.

In those days, nearly everyone, even in town, had a garden and raised chickens, and the kids had to work more than now. They had to weed the garden, fill the woodbox, feed the chickens, etc. Our school was a big square white wooden building with four big rooms and four teachers, and you learned how the government was run, reading, writing and arithmetic. We also had two years of geometry, two years of algebra and Latin, and the teachers could instill patriotism and right values. During the First World War, they would take us down to the railroad station to watch the Marines drill on the station platform. It was a thrill, also, to be standing there when the big iron horse (train steam engine) came roaring in with the train -- made your hair bristle up! At school we knitted sweaters and washcloths for soldiers at recess. On Monday mornings we all gathered in Mrs. Inglis' room upstairs (called the grammer room) to sing, hear speeches, the latest news, etc. We had to know the Star Spangled Banner and America by heart. We had a Pats Pick songbook. We had some colorful teachers. One professor had a wooden arm (Mr. Chamberlin), another had seizures once or twice, another went insane when his bride-to-be changed her mind. A lot of wonderfully good teachers. Mrs. Inglis was the principal (two of her daughters also taught), and whoever came or went, she was the guiding influence – and a good one. We took a lot of field trips. People walked a lot more then and a lot farther. We thought nothing of a field trip to the old light house and back. Once when it was vacant, Chet Marshall locked three of the girls in it, so we had to backtrack and let them out. The town had a lot more small wooded areas, where there would be hazelnut bushes and apple trees. One stop was at Mrs. Rugg's house. On our way home from school she filled our empty dinner pail with gingersnaps. Those are things you remember. The ripe berries and pretty flowers along the way, especially the last rose of summer and the cherry blossoms in the spring and the picnics in the park on the last day of school. There were animals in the pens, and campers started to come there to spend the summer about the time of the First World War.

People didn't dash around so fast in the old days. They worked harder, lived slower and better. We had better food, took time to prepare it right. There was lots of entertainment. Medicine shows, travelling shows, chautauquas, the organ grinder, our Atwater Kent radios. My father made ours. He also made our first electric lamp. At the medicine show the old Italian would wrestle with a live bear to get a crowd around, then tell how good his herb medicine was, and people bought it for rheumatism, ague, etc. The organ grinder, with his colorfully dressed monkey, always played his grind organ in front of the Stimpson Hotel, and the monkey passed the tin cup for money. There were many tramps, too. They liked to travel – they rode the engine, coal car, or on the rods under the train. Automobiles put a stop to that. I don't see many hitchhikers any more, either. Just imagine Mackinaw with no cement sidewalks, no gas stations, gift shops, motels, even no electricity, no cars. People were more self sufficient then. Kids nowadays wouldn't know what to do to survive without the conveniences we now have.

My father had a blacksmith shop on the now Church of the Straits property. He cut his own nails to put shoes on horses with. My job was to smooth the horses' hoofs with a big rasp so the shoes went on evenly.

Most men worked for the railroads, fishing or lumbering. Everybody was busy.

In the grocery stores, most everything came in barrels: sugar, flour, pickles, pork, vinegar, syrup, molasses, crackers, and all had to be measured out for customers. Tea came in a pretty little teakwood chest with an oriental rug on the top under the cover. Coffee in big bags, dried prunes and apricots, raisins in a big wooden box. The general stores carried about everything you'd need: rubber boots, horse harnesses, saddles, yard goods. Most mothers sewed for their families. The same store sold pianos, dishes, milk cans, etc. Homemakers also made their own butter and bread.

Neighbors had picnics together, especially on the Fourth of July. We used to row boats a lot more then, too.

Mackinaw also had a clothespin factory and a broom factory south of the depot which employed a few people. Young boys worked there, sweeping up the shavings. A lot of good things have vanished, like the settlement where my parents were married between Levering and Pellston, called "Lakewood". Also, the town where my mother was born, Juneita, in Tuscola County, has vanished from the map. My father-in-law came from Ireland, first to Buffalo, then to Cheboygan, where he worked for a dollar a day from sunup to sundown, walked four miles to work, and saved up enough money to open a grocery store. Then he saved up enough to bring all his brothers and sisters over to this country and set them up in business, except one brother who got a job running a streetcar in Detroit.

One memorable day for Mackinaw was when the stores on Huron Avenue burned. I was at school, about in the fourth grade. A Mr. Chamberlain had bought the Sunderland Bakery and turned it into a grocery store. It burned, Judge Richard's store burned, and the dry goods store. The drug store, the little cement mortuary stopped the fire from getting to the Hotel, now the Dixie Tavern. Mr. Chamberlain had a habit of throwing his money bag up to the high top shelf in the store. During the fire and running to carry out all the merchandise they could, Mr. Chamberlain fell dead in the arms of John Hiliker. His last words were, "The money", but the fire was too hot to get it.

the fire was too hot to get it.

Another vivid memory is the forest fire when my dad loaded all our best furniture and the family on a big lumber wagon and brought us to town in the middle of the night, before our escape route was cut off by the fire. He and his friend Joe Barlowe put bed quilts on the roof of our house and climbed a ladder with pails of water to keep them wet so the flying burning twigs could not burn the house down. We stayed at my cousin's house, which is now Martha Wilke's. When we moved back home, it was a dismal countryside, stubs of trees black with soot, but the grass greened up and new trees grew after a rain or two. A lot of wild animals had to find new living space: deer, rabbits, foxes, etc.

The fuel for heating the homes was mostly wood. They all had outside toilets and took their baths in a big wooden tub by the kitchen stove, with bed sheets on wires for a screen. People had to pump their water, the kitchen stoves had a tank on one end called a reservoir, kept filled with warm water which was dipped to a large washbowl to keep our hands washed. Then there was the towel on a roller, about two yards sewed in a circle, to dry your hands on. We didn't have a dime store then, but the pack peddlers came often selling notions and sundries. One, I remember, talked with an accent. He'd say, "Ladies, umbrellas, silek undervare, needles and pins and liddle tings for ladies." I still have some tapestries that I bought from him. I also got a white serge skirt from him that never wore out. If only we could get that quality merchandise these days.

Mackinaw had a lot of colorful people that I would like to write about, but I assume that others are writing about them. One of the early school teachers was Frances Margaret Fox, the children's story writer. Her father was the station agent at one time. She had a step-mother and a very unhappy childhood, so she loved children. She organized a children's club called "The Sunshine Club". She would read her stories to us before she sent them to be published and serve refreshments, and we would play games.

We also had a garden club, eventually called 4-H Club. Our leader was Ruth Wheaton from Cheboygan. I won a medal at the fair for growing the biggest, best potatoes.

In days gone by, Mackinaw had good bakeries and ice cream parlors where you could get a good mixed fruit sundae (no fruit cocktail, just real pineapple, sliced bananas, cherries, strawberries, real whipped cream, with a couple Nabiscoes) for about fifteen cents.

The Gypsies used to come to town every summer. I worked in the hardware store, so my job was to put away all the displays from the top of the counters. One Gypsie woman came begging for food to the dining hall kitchen. Ed said, "I'll give you this pan of baked beans if you have something to put them in." She held up her apron! The women always wore four or five skirts of different colors. The children were sometimes naked.

The police would not let them stay in town overnight.

At the hardware I learned to assemble bicycles, tricycles, little wagons, cut threads on water pipe, make stove pipe and a lot of other things that aren't done any more.

On Labor Day we really had a celebration: bag races, foot races for all ages, the kids scrambled in a tub of flour for pennies, the boys chased a greased pig with a prize for the one who caught it, nail-driving contest for the women, pie-eating contest for the men, climbing the greased pole, etc. Today we wouldn't waste the flour or the grease at today's prices.

"My generation is nearly past -- most everything is different today!"

by Mrs. Leona Brown

Jim Cole, Leona Niles, Charles Ball at the depot.

John Renehan, Leona Niles Brown, Marian Walters Lenke.

The Gypsy Visitors

Roving gypsies used to come into town every year in colorful horse-drawn wagons and would glean whatever they could for their benefit, while here. One day Mrs. Sunderland, who ran a boarding house, around 1907, was busy in her kitchen when she looked up and there stood a gypsy woman eyeing the bread she had just removed from the oven.

Most people were afraid of the gypsies and were careful not to cross them, but this day when the gypsy said, "I'll take that bread," Grandma Sunderland had had enough and she grabbed the meat cleaver and took after the gypsy and chased her out of the kitchen and down the street. The Sunderland's boarders (not the gypsy camp) had fresh bread for dinner that day.

****Judy Ranville

*Windmill Waffle Shop, Mackinaw City
Now Kenville's Cafe*

Fishing on the Straits of Mackinaw at Mackinaw City, Mich.

Hunting season,
Mackinaw City Depot.
Deer to be shipped home.

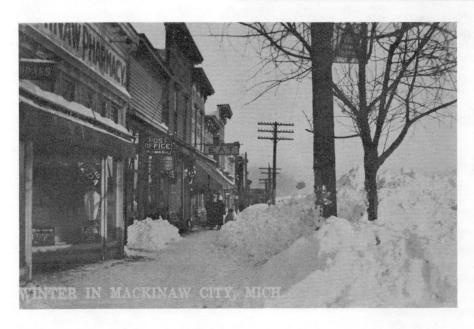

Chapter 33

Memories of Yesteryear

by Marie Patrick (Riggs)

Early in the year of 1897 a young couple by the name of George and Anna Patrick came to live in Mackinaw from Cadillac, Michigan. He was employed in a grocery store located on the southwest corner of what is now Central and Henry Streets. In the very early days the streets of the village running north to south were numbered and those east to west were lettered. When the Patricks arrived they stayed for a short time at the Stimpson House, a hotel built in 1870 and operated by Charles Stimpson, and is now known as the Down Town Motor Hotel. They were escorted to their room by lantern light since the Village at that time had neither electricity or inside plumbing. Water for laundry purposes came from the Straits and was charged for by the barrel. Water for drinking and cooking came from wells which were excavated with pick and shovel and were referred to as open wells.

Two daughters were born to the Patricks, one soon after their arrival and the second a few years later. Since the mother was ill for a time, the older daughter was given to the care of her grandparents, Mr. and Mrs. Byron Sunderland, who lived on a farm at the north end of French Lake. Byron was engaged in carrying freight to and from Cecil Bay with horses and wagons in summer and sleighs in winter. Cecil Bay was then a small settlement operating a shingle mill and employed possibly sixty men who lived there with their families. The small granddaughter often accompanied her grandfather with his loads of freight. The freight would be loaded at Mackinaw and their noon meal would be at the farm after which they continued on to Cecil Bay, spending the night at the mill boarding house there. Next day the return trip would bring whatever freight was available to be shipped out from Mackinaw. Sailing ships could dock at Cecil Bay and load the cedar shingles to be carried to other ports on the Great Lakes. Some of the old dock pilings can still be seen at the waters edge in the Bay.

At the turn of the century, from then on through the 1940's and 50's Mackinaw was a lively place. At one time it had several hotels and four saloons. It also was a terminal for three rail lines. The Duluth, South Shore & Atlantic, operating two passenger trains each way per day; the Michigan Central with two passenger trains each way between Detroit and Mackinaw City; the Grand Rapids & Indiana with the same service between Ft. Wayne, Indiana, and Mackinaw City; and all three with numerous freight trains also. The connecting link between the two Michigan peninsulas were car ferries operated by the Mackinaw Transportation Company. The two older car ferries were the Ste. Maire and St. Ignace which were succeeded by the Chief Wa-Wa-Tam, which is still in operation. The car ferry Wa-Wa-Tam employed about one hundred twenty men and in 1920 went on strike and were out about six weeks. During that time the railroads issued an embargo on selling passenger tickets past the Straits in either direction but in spite of that many people traveling on a limited budget arrived without sufficient funds to pay for crossing the Straits. Meantime a livery stable in St. Ignace established a road on the ice which was frozen solid and charged each passenger two dollars per person for the trip either way to cross the Straits. Many times it was necessary for the people employed in the area to take up a collection to assist whole families in continuing on their way.

In the year 1910 the Patricks purchased a hardware store which he operated for about twenty years. It was located on the site now occupied by the "House of Flavors". In those days the property on the south side of Central Avenue was owned by the G.R. & I. R.R. It was a network of siding tracks and was used for storing old broken down freight cars. In those years both railroads had their own ice houses, which had to be filled with ice cut from the Straits each winter. The ice was used for the dining cars and also for cooling sleeping cars on trains going south to Detroit and some going as far as Chicago, St. Louis, Mo., and Louisville, Ky., since air conditioning had not yet been invented.

In those early days all village children attended a four-room school having but ten grades. It was a two-story frame building and was heated by pot-bellied stoves which burned wood, located where the elementary school now stands.

About the year 1918 the state of Michigan

inaugurated the first of the state ferry boats to accommodate automobiles crossing the Straits. The first one was called the *Ariel* with only a very small capacity for cars. To supplement the steadily increasing demand from motorists, the *Wa-Wa-Tam* had wood planks installed between the tracks on the lower deck and carried as many cars per trip as could be handled in addition to the usual load of freight cars. The charge for such service was three and four dollars per car, depending on the wheel base of vehicles. A bit later on the state ferry dock was built south of the railroad dock, and at the beginning it was just a big rock pile, but as boats were added to the fleet the dock was enlarged to its present size. The *Straits*, *City of St. Ignace*, *City of Cheboygan*, *Mackinaw City*, *City of Munising*, *City of Petoskey* and the deisel powered *Vacationland* comprised the fleet until the advent of the Big Mac bridge which was dedicated in 1957. The discontinuance of the state ferry fleet was a severe blow to the economy in the general area, since a great many families derived their livlihood from employment on both the dock and ferries.

Back in June of 1884 a weekly newspaper called *The Straits Journal* was published by George A. Mosher. In his introductory remarks, Mr. Mosher had the following to say: "In selecting our place of operations it is only a question of time when this beautiful little village will become one of the most important cities in the Lake region. Its natural advantages being located on the Straits of Mackinaw as it is and with the advent of other railroads coming in together with the ones already established will make one of the finest shipping points in the country."

The first edition of the *Mackinaw Witness* was published as a weekly newspaper on April 8, 1893, by George H. Wood. At that time there was local steamboat service between St. Ignace and Manistique by the steamboat *Hunter* on Tuesday, Thursday and Saturday mornings (no time given). The Steamer *St. Ignace* operated daily between Mackinaw City and St. Ignace at 8:25 a.m. and 2:00 p.m.; the *Minnie M.* for Cheboygan on Monday, Wednesday and Friday, also for the Soo on Tuesday, Thursday and Saturday. Two rail lines operated daily between Mackinaw City and Detroit on the Michigan Central, called the "Niagara Falls Route". Even then Niagara Falls was the honeymoon mecca for those newlyweds who could afford to travel. The G. R. & I. also operated three trains each way, two daily and one daily except Sunday from Mackinaw City to Fort Wayne, Indiana. The D.S.S. & A. operated one train each way per day, making connections at Marquette for Ishpeming and Houghton, also Duluth, St. Paul and Ashland, Wisconsin. Hotels advertised in the above-named paper were "Stimpson House", operated by D. Smith and son at $1.50 per day; "Union House", operated by John Olson at $1.00 per day; the "Bay View House" operated by Mrs. C. Walter at $1.00 per day, $3.50 per week; "Mercer House" at the east end of Central

Avenue, which was apparently a boarding house with board at $4.00 per week and transients at $.25 per meal. There was also a good bakery selling all kinds of cake, biscuits, bread and confectionary at reasonable prices. The "Mackinaw City House", located south of the depot by Mrs. A. Ranville, with board at $4.00 per week, transients at $1.00 per day. Two churches, Presbyterian and Methodist, with a resident minister holding services twice each Sunday. Also Episcopal service held in the Methodist Church on Friday evening. A resident doctor, J. J. Reycraft, M.D., had regular office hours each day, 8:00 to 9:00 a.m. and 1:00 to 3:00 p.m. He was a graduate of Detroit College of Medicine and lately House Surgeon of Harper Hospital in Detroit.

The following are some news items from the above mentioned paper:

The young ladies of the Presbyterian Church will give a "Sugar Social" in the church parlors on Monday evening and a "Sweet time" is expected. We have been told that Thomas Welsh and Henry Glaser are running against each other for Constable. Mr. Welsh would certainly make a fine looking officer.

Andy Lamond has got tired of office work and has gone to work switching. He commenced last Wednesday morning, but after this week will have charge of the yard engine at night. Charlie Outhouse is also working in the yard with Sam Middleton and Crackle has gone to Bay City.

The Presbyterian church parlor is now graced with a nice new set of chairs purchased from Hosack and Company.

Cecil Bay contributed items as follows:

A. Flannigan will run the store and hotel this summer. Everything is lively now preparing to begin work in the mill. Mr. Marco has returned and will be in charge this season. Mr. Gorrow is back and intends to move his family here again. We are all glad to see the smoky face of the engineer again.

An Election Notice: A special election will be held in the Village of Mackinaw City on Monday, April 10, 1893, at which time the following officers will be chosen, vis: a Village President, Clerk Treasurer and three Trustees for full term, one Trustee for one year to fill vacancy of O. C. Cope, removed, one Street Commissioner and one Constable. The polls of said election will be opened at Shepherd's Hall at 8 o'clock a.m. or as soon thereafter as may be and will be continued open until 5 o'clock p.m. unless the Board shall at their discretion, adjourn the polls for one hour at noon for dinner.

A. L. Knowlton, Village Clerk

In the same paper ads appear for "Bakers Cocoa", "Rising Sun Stove Polish", "Hall's Catarrh Cure", "Kemp's Balsam Cough Syrup", "Royal Baking Powder" and "August Flowers" for suffering humanity to cure sick headache and palpitation of the heart.

Following are some local ads in the same edition:

J.J.G. Richards, dealer in Groceries, Provisions, Crockery and Glassware, Flour and Feed, Notions and Gent's furnishing Goods. (Store was located in building now occupied by Coffman Hardware.)

D. Barrett, dealer in Dry Goods, Notions and Boots and Shoes. (Store was located on Huron near Masonic Hall.)

W. H. Willets, keeps the largest stock of Dry Goods in Mackinaw City. Hats, Caps, Neckwear, Fine or heavy Suits and underwear, Overcoats, Boots, Shoes or anything in the line of Dry Goods. (Store was probably on west side of Central Avenue on site now occupied by Desy's Gift Shop.)

J. H. Coffman, dealer in Drugs, Medicines and Jewelry, Cigars and Tobacco. Established in 1883. (Store in same location as Coffman store is now.)

C. Cunningham, Fresh, Salt and Dried Meats. (Located in building now occupied by Lella Cain.)

S. B. Chamberlin, dealer in Heavy and Shelf Hardware, Fancy Groceries, Choice Dairy Butter, Eggs, Produce and Confectionery. (Located on the present site of Masonic Hall.)

After completion of the "Big Mac Bridge", both St. Ignace and Mackinaw City became a mecca for tourists from both home and abroad and continues to be so at the present time.

October is a beautiful month in this area. Golden and brown Oak trees, gold and red Maples, White Birch with their yellow leaves, and all waiting for a small gust of wind to bring them fluttering to the ground. Lawns are covered with wet brown leaves, since it perhaps has rained while they were falling, but soon the wind will dry them out and they will blow hither and yon only to be caught and covered with a blanket of snow which means the coming of winter, but the change of seasons is really what this part of Michigan is all about.

George Patrick

Hobo Jungle

Mackinaw had a "hobo jungle". It was located in a wooded area behing Kniffen's Pond, running to the R.R. tracks. Curious boys used to enjoy sneaking around to see how these "men of the open road" cooked up their "coffee and beans" over an open fire. One old "hobo" used to tell how he bedded down after dark for the night, rolling up in his blanket on the ground. In the morning he turned over to discover he was stretched out beside a large bear. "Old Bruin" was still asleep and our friend said he didn't wait to say "good morning"!

****Judy Ranville

Chapter 34

Mackinaw Families

Mr. and Mrs.
George V. Coffman

by Edna Miller Coffman

George's parents, Mr. and Mrs. J. H. Coffman, moved to Mackinaw City from southern Michigan in the spring of 1883. They built and opened a drug and jewelry store July 1, 1883. George was not five years old until September 3rd. He grew up in Mackinaw, and he went to the old school when there was only one room; later a second story was added. The seats were double and he sat with Madge Fox at school. He grew up and finished school here; then he went to Ferris Institute where he finished in 1901 as a pharmacist.

He went to work in Cheboygan for Sangster and Riggs Drug Store, then later moved to work for Ben Cueny Drug Store. Finally he went to work for Frank Brackett Drug Store.

While employed in Cheboygan, he met and married as his first wife Miss Rosalie De Gray on November 4, 1902, at the home of his parents Mr. and Mrs. J. H. Coffman of Mackinaw City.

A few years later he bought one half interest in the store with his father, and they moved to Mackinaw City.

George continued as a pharmacist and a jeweler; he learned taxidermy and worked at that as a sideline for forty years. He was watch inspector for the New York Central Railroad for twenty-two years. He was a licensed funeral director and embalmer for fifty years.

Soon after the Coffmans moved to Mackinaw City, Mrs. George Coffman (Rosalie De Gray) and Mrs. John Hilliker decided the town needed a place where books could be kept for public lending and reading. Each lady picked books from their own homes and took to the old City Hall (now burned) and started a library. They asked other ladies to donate books. This was the start of the library. Through the efforts of these two ladies much credit is due, for out of this came the organization of the Woman's Club and the present day library grew from that beginning.

Mrs. George Coffman (Rosalie De Gray) wrote the Woman's Club song they use today. She was a talented musician and sang in the choir at the church for many years. She was a past president of the Woman's Club and a member of the Eastern Star Lodge of Mackinaw City.

She was a school teacher and taught for several years in Cheboygan. She was also employed as the recorder in the Register of Deeds office in the old Courthouse in Cheboygan; at that time all the recording was done in longhand.

Dean of Druggists 95 on Labor Day

CHEBOYGAN DAILY TRIBUNE   Page Two
Cheboygan, Michigan·   Saturday, August 25, 1973

George Coffman of Mackinaw City, dean of Michigan pharmacists, will observe his 95th birthday on Labor Day, still in business and still dispensing medicines over the counter at his store every afternoon.

He declares his drug store at 109 Huron Street is the oldest drug store in Michigan. It is 90 years old, and has been continuously operated at the same location since being founded by his father John H. Coffman on July 1, 1883.

At the age of 90, George Coffman has curtailed his activity. He closes for the winter, and he does not open up until noon. But every afternoon now he is in the store, doing business until 5:30. He handles only non-prescription products and patent medicines now.

One reason that he is able to keep so active a program is that he has the devoted and efficient help of his third wife, Edna, who is his junior by a lot of years.

Mr. Coffman, though pushing the 100-park, says he has no plans to retire. "I will be here until they carry me out," he asserted.

The passing years have inflicted some infirmities. His

chief complaint is pain which occurs in his knees, and the fact that he is becoming hard of hearing.

His life has been rich and full. He combined several businesses. Besides being a druggest for 72 years he was for 50 years a funeral director and embalmer. Also for 40 years he was a taxidermist. Hundreds of beautiful deer heads which grace the walls in homes and hunting lodges were the work of his hands. Mr. Coffman was expert at watch and clock repair, and for 22 years he was watch inspector for the New York Central Railroad.

Besides all that, he is arch eologist. He was the man who discovered location of the long gone stockade of Fort Michili mackinaw. He showed the loca tion to the Mackinac Island State Park Commission, urg ing that the wilderness fort that was garrisoned by French and British troops 1715-1781 should be reconstructed.

He sparked interest in re storation, and Fort Michili mackinac has been rebuilt, in closed by a stockade on the original location as discover ed by Mr. Coffman.

For his interest and effort in reconstriction of the fort, Mr. Coffman was made a life honorary member of the Mich igan Historial Society.

His interest began when as a boy of 14, with lots of summer leisure on his hands, he began to dig around on the fort site.

Digging was a popular past time for many people. He says there was nothing to be seen of the fort that had once stood there, but the history of the fort was well known. Peo ple dug there for souvenirs.

One of the incentives was a story that a pot of gold was buried there, left apparently by the paymaster or some affluent traders. Mr. Coff man says he knows no his torical basis for the rumor, but a lot of people believed it and tried digging for it.

"A spiritualist came one time with a spiritualist wo man he related. "She went into a trance, and finally she said, 'Drive a stake right there.' The fellow did, and then he started digging. They dug a hole big enough for an elephant, but there was no gold."

He was satisfied to find arti facts, which he collected as a hobby. Down through the years he collected artefacts, and he has a big display in his drug store. He has an artefact board on the wall. On the

board are many of the things he found: a hatchet head, fish hooks, nails, the sawed off end of a gunbarrel, scissors, rings, knives, keys, a bayonet and many uniform buttons. One button is plainly marked with name of the King's 8th Regiment.

A find of special interest is a musket barrel, such as was given by Trader John Astor. Guns were highly prized by the Indians. Mr. Coffman says Astor would stand the long barrelled gun up and tell the Indians to pile a stack of beav er pelts to top of the gun and then they could have the wea pon.

A look at length of the gun shows how Astor was able to do a profitable business.

There was a story that a tunnel ran from the shore into the fort. Coffman tried to find it, with no success, but in digging he found bits of wood under ground. He was struck with the idea that the frag ments might be off the buried end of a palisade from the fort wall.

He started digging in all directions until he found some more wood fragments. He sighted a line and dug some more. He kept finding more bits of rotted wood or wood fragments, and soon he had the layout of the southeast bastion.

The stockade was built of trees trimmed and shaped. He declared the butt of one tree, and the top end of an other tree would be buried side by side for close align ment.

He visited Mackinac Island and reported to the Mackinac Island State Park Commission what he had found. A Commis sion official came to Mackinaw City, and Coffman pointed out the line.

The village of Mackinaw City profited by Coffman's discovery by putting up a fence along outline of the fort.

When the depression came, the WPA finally built a stock ade on the Coffman line. That was start of the restoration, although nothing was done about rebuilding inside the stockade for many years.

Finally about 1959 the Park Commission began restora tion with a new taller stock ade and an archeology pro gram inside the walls to find sites and rebuild the long ago army post.

"I kept urging to officials that the fort should be re built," Mr. Coffman reminis ced. "One day Dr. Maxwell from the Park Commission

Mr. and Mrs. Coffman are shown in their drugstore, where mounted deer heads and large fish remind that Mr. Coffman has also been a taxidermist and an ardent sportsman.

told me, 'You visit the park Monday and you will see 15 men at work.'"

"I went to the fort the next Monday, and there was a man sitting with a gun across his knees. I looked over to the other side and there another man was holding a gun."

The were guards, and the men doing digging and sifting were convicts.

That was start of the re storation of the present day fort.

George Coffman was born at Pewamo in Clinton county, but has lived at Mackinaw City most of his life.

He studied pharmacy at Ferris Institute, and became a registered pharmacist March 5, 1901. His father opened the Coffman drug store on July 1, 1883, so George had a natural inter est in pharmacy. He worked in Cheboygan for the Sangster & Riggs, Cueny and Bracket drugstores.

In 1907 he bought a half interest in his father's busi ness. He became sole owner at his father's death in 1937.

Along the way, he has hunt ed big game in the west and fished barricuda in Florida. Some of his trophies as a sportsman are on the walls of his store in the form of mount ed deer and fish heads.

His most famous exhibit is his artefact board. A lot of people have taken pictures of it.

"I am informed," said Mr. Coffman, "that a picture of my Board is in the Boston Mus um, and even in some place in England."

At age of 95 he can look back on changing modes of transportation. In his early funeral director days, he drove horses for his hearse, and in winter used a hearse on runners.

Living on the Straits, he just naturally developed a love for the water, and operated his own sailboat.

When the Straits froze over, he sailed an iceboat. One of his special pleasures was sail skating.

This is a sport unknown to most present young persons in the Straits Area, but it was popular in his youth.

"A bunch of us would rig up a spar and sail which he would lay across one shoulder, when he skated" he explained. "The wind would drive us along on our skates. When we wanted to turn back, we would shift the spar to the other shoulder and come about to go the other way.

"I have crossed the Straits on skates. with an ice boat, sailboat, and motorboat. I have crossed on the Bridge, and flown over in an airplane."

If as a young man he didn't have a snowmobile, how many present young folks have zipped along on sail skates?

His many years as a businessman and civic leader, recognition. He was honored las year by being made marshall of the Fort Michilimackinac Pagenat parade.

He has one son, Norris, who operates a hardware store in Mackinaw City.

His wife, Edna, has her own business. She operates a museum in Mackinaw City which is one of the places of special interest in the community. Mrs. Coffman includes among her wares wild fruit jams of her own preparation. she makes them from high bush cranberries, choke cherries, and even a "rose hip jelly" from the rose seed balls. Her wild fruit products are a popular novelry, and buyers pronounce them "delicious."

* * *

IN LOVING MEMORY OF

GEORGE V. COFFMAN

Date of Birth
September 3, 1878

Date of Death
December 10, 1975

Services Held At
Church of the Straits
Mackinaw City, Michigan
Saturday, December 13, 1975, 2:00 p.m.

Services Conducted By
Reverend Raymond Provost
and
Wawatam Lodge F. & A.M. 448
Mackinaw City

Place of Interment
Lakeview Cemetery
Mackinaw City

The Desy Family

by Mary Desy (Mrs. Raymond Desy)

The Desy family, Come and Virginia and their two sons Eugene and James, came to the United States from Canada around the year 1882.

Their home was in Prouxville, Quebec, Canada, and it was here that Eugene and James were born. They were around four and six years of age when they came to the United States with their parents.

Their first home was in Manistee, Michigan, which was at this time a very busy lumbering area. They lived there for many years and three more sons were born at Manistee. They were Henry and William, Alphonse and one daughter, Rose.

About ten years later, about 1892, the lumbering era there started to wane and slowly the mills were closing. Now many of the families started to move northward where new mills were starting.

The Desy family and many other families came to the Cecil Bay area (which is about ten miles from our present city of Mackinaw). This was now the beginning of the building of lumber mills all through this area. It was a fast growing little settlement. Many homes sprung up, and it is hard to picture such a busy settlement here when today there are no homes still standing.

The older Desy children also worked at the lumber mills and were now young men when the mills started to slow up, and again the families moved about to different areas, some to towns nearby, and many to Mackinaw City. This was nearing the 1900's.

The Come Desy family now were five sons and one daughter. Their home was built on Sinclair Street (which is now the home of Erwin Flad).

While the home was being built, Mr. Desy worked as principal at the old white schoolhouse in the daytime and with help of friends, worked on his new home whenever time permitted. The old schoolhouse stood where our present elementary school now stands.

Many other homes and families were springing up all over Mackinaw and the city was growing.

The family were now marrying, and while some moved to other areas, Eugene and James remained in Mackinaw and married local ladies.

Eugene, the oldest of the boys, married Rachel Davenport who lived next door, the Davenport family having moved here about the time most of the families from Cecil Bay and railroad workers moved in with their families and friends.

They had three children, Lloyd who is our local artist, Virginia and Roger. Roger died as a very small boy soon after his mother's death. Virginia, after she married, moved away to the Lansing area.

James, who was known to many as either "Jim" or "Pappy", married Blanche Wheeler. Her home was originally Sherman, Michigan, but she moved to Cecil Bay from there with her folks, as her father also worked at the lumber mills there. They married in the year 1904.

Soon after their marriage, they started to build their home across the street from his father's. This is still occupied by some of the Desy family. Jim and Blanche had a family of five sons and two daughters. Their names were Carl, Everett, Edgar, James, Jr., and Raymond, and Marguerite and Rose. Rose died at the young age of six weeks.

All the children attended our local schools, both grade and high school.

James was in the restaurant business. He first started with a small eating place, and it was located just west of our present drug store. This was called "Daisy's". Many did not know how to pronounce the name "Desy", so Jim decided to just call it plain "Daisy's".

Soon this was too small a building, so Jim moved a few doors down the street and called his new business the "Green Lantern". He operated here for quite a few years.

The town was growing and becoming much busier and so again they needed a larger place. The trains were now carrying many people into Mackinaw, and the bus lines were coming into the area also. Mackinaw was like a getting off place, and from here they traveled across the straits into the Upper Peninsula. The bus would go across on the state ferries, and the trains would be loaded onto either the *Ste. Marie* or the *Chief Wawatam* railroad boats.

This is when Jim opened the "Birchwood Cafe". Now it was a restaurant and the Greyhound bus station. It was located where the present Miller Gifts and Pancake House now stand. The "Birchwood" was a great gathering place for the men, and they had one group that was known as the "Coffee Club". What a bunch, and they would congregate here several times a day. There was also a doctor in the group, and he was a typical country doctor and when anyone needed him he was always there.

Jim and Blanche's family were now old enough to help in the restaurant, and that they did for many years. In time they all married and moved to different parts of Michigan.

Carl and his wife Mabel and family live in Florida. The summers they spend in Mackinaw City.

Everett married Addie Pierce, and they lived here in Mackinaw, later went to the southern part of the state, and now Addie lives back here alone. Everett died in 1966.

Edgar and his wife and family live in Grosse Isle,

Michigan.

Marguerite married Earl Marsh, and they had nine children, but lost one while a very small boy. Marguerite was our post office gal for many years. They lived in Cheboygan for a good many years, then back to Mackinaw, and now Marguerite lives in Cheboygan. Earl passed away about 1956.

James married while in the Navy, and he and his wife have two daughters all living in Sterling Heights, Michigan.

Raymond lived with his father after his mother's death in 1934. He finished his high school in 1935. Then he went away to college and helped his dad in the summers at the Birchwood Cafe. In 1940 Raymond married, and he and his wife lived with his father. In late 1943 Raymond went into service and returned in 1946.

During his time in service the Birchwood was sold, and in 1946 when he returned, they built the Desy Gift Shop on Central Avenue.

This was a vacant lot for many years, and the gift shop and Alexander's Electric were built at the same time. They had to make their own cement blocks, as it was too soon after the war to get the necessary materials needed to build with.

The business grew, and they had the help of a few of the older children. They had eight children, four boys and girls.

Jerilynn married Douglas McKinnon from our home town, and they have three boys and live in Sterling Heights, Michigan.

Raymond Allen and his wife have one daughter and two sons, now living in Florida.

Robert is single, and he works at the gift shop and also with the local police department. He lives out in the valley on Valley Drive.

Michael married Gwen Hyatt from Cheboygan, and they are living in Florida. Mike helped and worked in the gift shop while he was living here.

Paul lives here in Mackinaw and assists here in the gift shops and is now married and lives with his wife Loni in Mackinaw City.

Mary Eileen is at home and college and also works at the gift shops.

Theresa and Carmel are also living at home and soon will both be in college also, and work with us in the business in the summer months.

Their father Raymond died suddenly in July of 1972. The gift shops, which are three, are run by their mother and help of the family.

James S. Desy, Sr., passed away in 1957. He came here as a young boy, from Canada in 1882, settling in Michigan and living all his life (but four years) in one state.

Come and Virginia Desy Family
    (Right to Left): James, William, Come (father), Rose, Urane (Come's brother), Sunday, Henry, Alphonse and William. Virginia (mother) can be seen in upstairs window. This is now the E. Flad home on Sinclair Street.

The Daisy (Desy) Cafe
Far left, Mitchell Swantek. Far right, Otis Smith. Next to Smith, Jennie Souci.

Distinguished Alumnus to Be Commencement Speaker

1965   James S. Desy, Jr.

James S. Desy, Jr., a graduate of Mackinaw City High School, class of 1932, will address the class of 1965 at the Forty - Fourth annual commencement exercises Friday.

According to his former coach Maurice Murray, Mr. Desy was one of the finest athletes that Mackinaw City has ever produced. He was an excellent basketball player, and in track he held the state record in the shot put for a number of years.

He entered the Navy in 1933 as an aparentice seaman. After serving on board the USS Arizona and the USS. Yorktown he was sent to Flight School at Naval Air Station, Pensacola, Florida, where he received his Navy "Wings of Gold" in 1938. As an enlisted pilot Mr. Desy flew with Patrol Squadron Eleven, and was later transferred to Naval Air Station, Coco Solo, Canal Zone.

He was promoted to Warrant Officer in 1942, and three months later was commissioned an ensign. By July of 1944 he was promoted to full lieutenant, and was serving as a test pilot at the Naval Test Center, Patuxent River, Maryland, where he was project pilot for many new aircraft armament developments during World War II. At the end of the war Lt. Desy was flight officer responsible for all flight operations for planes flying typhoon reconnaissance from Guam and Okinawa.

His first post war assignment was a tour of duty as chief test pilot, Naval Air Station, Ford Island, Honolulu. In May 1949 he was promoted to lieutenant commander, and was named assistant representative and test pilot at Curtiss-Wright plant, in Columbus, Ohio.

In January 1950, Lt. Comdr. Desy accepted a new position in the Navy, at sea, aboard the USS. Heintzelman, which at the outbreak of the Korean conflict was used as a troop carrier from Japan to Korea, and participated in the famed evacuation of Hungnam.

In October of 1951 he was appointed to the Aircraft Production Resources Agency at Wright - Patterson Airforce Base, and then inspection officer for the Bureau of Aeronautics Office at North American Aviation Inc., Columbus, Ohio. In 1953 he was ordered to duty as administrative officer in the Naval Transport Service, and in 1955 was assigned to Headquarters of the Military Air Transport Service.

Upon retirement for the U.S. Navy his first civilian postition was with the Missile Division of the Chrysler Corporation, where he served as Administration Assistant to the Chief Inspector in Quality Control. Chrysler was making the Redstone and Jupiter missiles at that time, but went out of the missile competition in 1961.

In June of 1961 he became Service Manager and salesman for the Currency Pre-Packaging Machine Company. Inc., a position he presently holds, and which takes him all over the United States.

Mr. and Mrs. Desy and their family presently make their home in Utica.

James Desy, Sr.

Lloyd Desy, sister Virginia Desy and little brother Roger who died shortly after this picture was taken - house in background is Davenport home.

Jim Desy in front of his first restaurant.

Raymond and his father, Jim Desy. The Birchwood Restaurant, owned by the Desys, located where Pancake House is now.

Jim Desy

Desy's Cigar Store, forerunner of Desy's Gift Shops, Inc. Jim Desy on stool, Otis Smith at table.

Theodore Duffina
1877-1958

by Nancy Campbell

Theodore Duffina was born in Leelanau, Michigan, in 1877. As a youth he lived at Fly Point and Mill Creek, both settlements just south of Mackinaw City. Here he fished with his father, a commercial fisherman. On May 17, 1900, he married Nancy Spencer and in 1910 moved in Mackinaw City where he worked as a car inspector for the New York Central Railroad for 28 years, retiring in 1938. He built his home on Langlade Street (now the site of Dancy's Motel and Dress Shop). He later built a small home, fish sheds and dock on the waterfront on N. Huron Avenue (now the site of Shepler's Island Parking). During all his years working on the railroad and after his retirement he did commercial fishing. He had three daughters: Mrs. A. E. Levi Taylor (Helen), Mrs. Charles H. Warner (Christina), Mrs. Henry Hayes (Cynthia), and two sons, Oliver and Frank, Jr.

Theodore Duffina's love of the lakes and commercial fishing is told best in this poem written by his grandson, Ted Warner, when he was a child.

CAPTAIN DUFFINA of the NANCY ANN

The waves were washing
  'Gainst Lake Huron's shore;
"Look", said the lighthouse keeper,
  "There goes Theodore."

As out on the Lake
  All alone he goes
Yes, out on the lake
  That he loves and knows.

Through an early Spring gale
  Through a mid-Summers squall,
Through storm or calm
  To answer the fisherman's call.

"Come you of heart,
  Come you of nerve,
Come you there, Ted,
  The sea you must serve."

And so it was that
  Day after day,
The keeper would watch
  The "Nancy Ann" wend her way.

To the bouy's bouncing
  So gracefully on the sea,
Bearing the black numerals
  That said license "693".

And as the "Nancy" floated by them
  Captain Duffina would reach out
And pull in his catch
  Of perch, whitefish and trout.

And then he would set them
  Again in their place,
With the care of a surgeon
  And with effortless grace.

Then off to the next gang
  Of nets they would float,
Captain Theodore Duffina
  And the "Nancy Ann", his boat.

And again he would raise them
  And quickly remove his haul;
"Got to hurry back home
  To beat that northeasterly squall."

Into his harbor he'd bring her,
  As only he can,
And sell his catch to the people
  Who were waiting on land.

And thus another day
  In his life was done,
And he'd look in the evening
  Toward the setting sun.

You could hear him say
  As it sank in the west,
"Not much of a catch today,
  But I did my best."

Through hell and high water
  I'll take my stand.
Next to Theodore Duffina, captain,
  Of the "Nancy Ann".

Iva Chapman was a summer visitor to Mackinaw City during the 1940's and 50's. She painted scenes typical of the area. This watercolor of Theodore Duffina's fish shed and dock was done for his daughter Mrs. Charles Warner.

Duffina home and fish sheds.

Duffina dock - sunken hull of Algomah I (upper left) - this area now site of Shepler dock and parking lot.

Theodore Duffina

Bert Kelty Hero
Of This Railway Yarn

Popular Conductor on South Shore
Gets Name In Paper

from the *Soo Evening News*
December 31, 1924

The friends of Bert Kelty--and who is not--appreciate the story printed in the Sunday *Detroit News* about him under a Mackinaw City dateline, telling how that popular conductor on the South Shore ingratiates himself with his passengers. Here is the article, which is headed--When a Nor'easter Blows You'll Meet Bert Kelty:

Mackinaw City, Mich., Dec. 17.—When the wind is in the northeast and the ice is thick in the lakes, travelers going to northern Michigan are likely to get acquainted with Bert Kelty. Chances are good these days that they will spend several hours as his guests and be introduced to the "Jolly and Cheer Club of the Straits of Mackinac."

It's a cold winter in the north (6 below zero today as this is written and getting colder) and Bert Kelty is the only ray of sunshine that can melt through the ice packs in the straits and his "Jolly and Cheer Club" has saved many a traveler from despair.

Kelty is a railroad man, conductor having been his title for ten years, but he is also a sailor, mess attendant, social secretary, nurse and messenger boy when he needs to be. For years he has had charge of trains for several railroad lines which are transported on the car ferry *Chief Wawatam* across the eight miles of water that stretch between this point and St. Ignace.

A Slow Journey.

In summertime travelers tiring of the long railroad trip get much relief out of the 30 or 40-minute ride across the stretch of water. But in winter the ice forms in the lakes and when a northeast wind comes up it is frequently blown into the straits, piling high on all sides of the *Wawatam*, and there the ferry is frozen in until it can either buck its way out or be released by dynamite.

Friday the big steel ferry was fast in the ice nearly all day, but it managed to buck its way out of the ice packs which were twelve to fifteen feet high, and reached St. Ignace at 5 p.m. Saturday it started back and before noon again was frozen in.

These are busy times for Bert Kelty and the Jolly Cheer club.

"How long will we be here, conductor?" someone pulling at his coattail asks.

"Mebbe a day or two. Mebbe a week."

Presently Kelty is back with decks of cards, games for children and other things to amuse the passengers. Then the boat carrying the train pushes forward and the travelers get back to their places near the car windows. They are off again. But before they have moved fifty feet the ice is piled up so high in front of the ferry that she cannot move.

Steak Sandwiches.

Meal time arrives and Kelty goes through the cars with hot coffee and steak sandwiches. Sometimes he does the cooking himself. Sometimes he takes the passengers back into a specially fitted car and lets them fix their own food, for the railroads always keep the *Wawatam's* stock rooms filled. This helps them pass the time, he says. After the first meal nobody asks Kelty how long the boat is going to be tied up. Nobody knows or cares.

Bert Kelty - Sunday, April 8, 1928

Welcome to North

Mackinaw, Mich.— The portal to the upper peninsula of Michigan, from the lower peninsula, is the nine-mile stretch of water that constitutes the Straits of Mackinac. At this portal stands--has stood for 15 years--a genial unofficial host, who welcomes with a grin and a joke the traveler from "down below" and conducts him to the northern regions.

Officially, Bert Kelty is Pullman conductor on the day train of the Duluth, South Shore and Atlantic that is assembled in the railroad yards in Mackinaw, goes aboard the big ice-crusher ferry *Wawatam*, lands at St. Ignace and then goes on to Trout Lake and Soo Junction, winding up its tollsome journey by backing into the station at Sault Ste. Marie, whistling like a peanut roaster.

Kelty has spent more time frozen up in Mackinac strait than some men spend in the bosom of the families. Like the rest of the train crew, who live in Mackinaw, he never knows, in the dead of winter, when the cars go thumping and clanking onto the boat, whether the trip across the strait will take an hour or a week.

Five days and nights, stuck in a floe like a polar whaleship, was the luck of the *Wawatam* on one occasion last winter.

The panorama of life that passes before the vision of a trainman at the straits is probably as varied as that at any concentration point in the country. Not to speak of the residents of the north country who have occasion to make their way up and down the route--businessmen, lumberjacks and local pleasure seekers--there is the ebb and flow of summer tourist traffic, and in the fall and winter months the thousands of sportsmen who penetrate the Upper Michigan wilds for game and fish.

Because he is the greeter at the portal he has come to know and be known by thousands of travelers. But the contact is not always so pleasant. There were wild times with the woodsmen in an earlier day, and often there is the sobering spectacle of shackled bad men sitting close with armed guards, on the way from some one of the jails in the Lower Peninsula to that citadel of grim repute, the Marquette Prison. Ninety-nine per cent of the 800 inmates at Marquette passed through the portal at the straits.

from *The Detroit News*

New Mackinaw Hotel - operated at time of this picture by Bert and Grace Kelty. This building was recently torn down and stood just east of Barnett Insurance Agency.

MRS. BERT KELTY WAS A SUPERIOR WOMAN

(By CHASE S. OSBORN)

Death recently took away Mrs. Grace Kelty, wife of Bert Kelty, a Mackinaw City. She had, and Bert has, many friends among the readers of The Evening News.

During his years of critical illness, she was a faithful nurse and helpmate to Bert. Then suddenly he got well, almost mysteriously. Now she is taken.

In her memory, Mrs. Marie Fry has written the following poem, richly deserved.

It was touching of Bert to send his friends a Christmas card from his wife in Heaven as well as himself and enclose a copy of this poem.

—"ASLEEP"—
In Memory of Mrs. Grace Kelty
By MRS. MARIE FRY

The shades are drawn. She is asleep,
To waken in some fairer land
Where griefs and sorrows all disband,
So calm and peaceful in her sleep,
Rejoice we must instead of weep,
For quickly glides time's slipping sands
And all must join that caravan,
Which moves beyond the endless deep,
Into that land of peaceful sleep.
Slumbering on with all who've gone before,
In life she lived and passed its test,
Deserving rest she's earned beyond the door.
Good night, brave soldier, rest in peace.
Much happier art thou that
Severed is life's lease.

The Sailler Sisters
(Left to Right): Edna Ranville, Grace Kelty, Rachael Wehner. Front row (left to right): Georgianna Yager and Sarah Nau.

Grace Kelty was born Grace Sailler, daughter of Frank and Catherine Sailler, and was married to Bert Kelty, known as the Railway Host of the North. The Keltys operated a tourist home, Jamet Lodge, located where Alexander's Lamplighter Motel is now.

The Marshall Family by Keith Widder

GEORGE WASHINGTON MARSHALL

George W. Marshall was born at Fort Pratt Harbor, New York. His father, William Marshall, served as Ordinance Sergeant at Fort Mackinac from 1848 until the 1880's. George fought in the Civil War at the Battle of Gettysburg under George Custer.

Due to impaired hearing, he was mustered out of the Army in 1868. He then returned to Mackinac Island and married Margaret Garrity in 1870. She had immigrated to the Island from Ireland.

In the 1870's he entered the Lighthouse Service being the keeper at Waugoshance and Spectacle Reef. In 1890 he came to Mackinaw City as keeper of the yet to be constructed Old Mackinac Point Station. He held this position until his retirement in 1919.

In 1908, the Marshall's took in their nephew Chester B. Marshall, age 8, and raised him. Like his uncle, he became a Great Lakes lighthouse keeper, serving at Beaver Island and Manitowoc, Wisconsin.

George died in 1932 at 84.

George W. Marshall
1890-1919 Old Mackinac Point

248

James M. Marshall
1919-1940 Old Mackinac Point

JAMES M. MARSHALL

James M. Marshall was born on Mackinac Island in 1882 and became the adopted son of George and Margaret Marshall. When only 18 years old, he followed his father's footsteps and entered the Lighthouse service. He first served as an assistant at Manistee and Skillagalee and later as keeper at White Shoal.

During the winter months when the lights were inoperative, after November 15, he returned to Mackinaw City and worked at Hunt's Merchandise Store.

During 1919, upon the retirement of his father, he succeeded him as keeper at Old Mackinac Point. On December 31, 1940, he retired from the Lighthouse service due to illness. He died on August 23, 1941.

FRANCES R. MARSHALL

Born in 1894 Frances Cox came to Mackinaw City in 1912 from Vestiburg, Michigan. She made her home with the Cecil Hunts, caring for their child and house while they operated Hunt's Merchandise Store. It was here where she met James M. Marshall. They were married on June 10, 1918, in St. Anthony's Church.

They had three children -- George, born on March 5, 1920; James (Bun), born on June 8, 1921; and Madonna, born on February 2, 1926. Following Jim's death, she worked for many years at the Stevenson and Linton Pharmacy and the Desy Gift Shops.

Since 1941 Frances has lived in the house on Straits Avenue built by Jim while he was still keeper at White Shoal. She has nine grandchildren and fifteen great-grandchildren.

Frances R. Marshall

249

Bun, Madonna and George   James M. Marshall
Efficiency Flag - given for having the best score in district inspection on neatness, etc.

In 1928 Superintendent Charles Hubbard of the Lighthouse Board's Ninth District awarded the efficiency flag to Keeper James M. Marshall. This honor went to the keeper of the cleanest station in the district after the annual inspection. The Ninth District included all lighthouses on Lake Michigan.

Holding the flag is Keeper Marshall with his two sons James, Jr., on the left and George on the right. In the center is his daughter Madonna. A few years later, Superintendent Hubbard added to his tour the inspection of Madonna's playhouse on the lighthouse grounds southeast corner. He applied the same rigid standards that existed for her father's building.

The Old Mackinac Point Light guided ships and sailors through the Straits of Mackinac for sixty-five years. Built in 1892, this buff-colored brick structure was the home of both the keeper and his assistant. Keeper George W. Marshall first lit the light on October 25.

Costing $5,500, the fog signal station was built in 1890 and went into operation on November 5. The light station's two other buildings were an outbuilding or barn and the oil house.

When the Mackinac Bridge was completed, the lights on its towers began directing maritime traffic through the Straits. On November 1, 1957, the Old Mackinac Point Light was dimmed for the final time.

The Murrays
of Mackinaw City

One of Michigan's Leading Families Of 4-H Leaders

Cheboygan Tribune - 1941

Mrs. Murray To Receive Pin For 10 Years Service

Mrs. M. B. Murray of Mackinaw City, wife and mother in a family which has 24 years leadership experience in Cheboygan County 4-H club work, will be presented a jewel pin at the county achievement day program at the Cheboygan City Opera House Tuesday. The pin is the award for leaders who complete a decade of service.

Mackinaw's Murray family is one of the outstanding families in the state in 4-H leadership. The family is headed by Maurice B. Murray, school superintendent, who has been a handicraft and forestry leader for nine years. Their seventeen-year-old son Hugh has a three-year electrical club leadership record, and their fifteen-year-old daughter Martha has been a food preparation leader for two years.

Mr. and Mrs. Murray have one other child, a seven-year-old son Richard, and when he is 10 and old

Shown in picture – (back row) Martha and Hugh Murray, and in front row their parents, Superintendent of Schools, M. B. Murray and Mrs. Murray. All four are 4-H club leaders.

enough to join 4-H, chances are he'll get an early start.

Mrs. Murray has been a club leader in Cheboygan county longer than any other woman. She is chairman of the County 4-H Club Council. In 1939 she was the one Cheboygan County woman selected to be initiated into the Service Club of the Northern Michigan 4-H Club Camp at Gaylord. She is a member of the state 4-H Service Club.

She has been a club leader in the county one year longer than her husband. In fact, she has been a leader ever since she came to Mackinaw City. Her project is sewing and at one time while she was helping with the leadership Mackinaw City had the largest clothing club enrollment in the state.

Superintendent Murray is so well known for so many things, that lots of people who know him for other activities fail to connect him with 4-H. In Cheboygan he is well known among men as a member of the Mackinaw American Legion bowling team, which competes here regularly at the Cheboygan bowling alley, and many of the basketball fans recall that he is a former Mackinaw City high school basketball coach who used to bring his teams here to play Cheboygan.

He has relinquished basketball coaching, but still coaches high school golf, a sport in which Mackinaw has made a fine record. He is a good golfer.

His interests are wide. He has his family, his school, his shop, his sports, his resort. For two years the school has had a manual training shop, and he is the teacher, instructing boys in shop craft for high school credit. He has cottages at Carp Lake which absorb a great deal of his summer interest.

Leo Leonard Paquet

by Nancy Campbell

Leo Paquet was born in Mackinaw City on February 4, 1900. His birthplace was the large home of his parents, Alfred and Jennie Paquet. On this site today is the present Paquet Mobile Station. Leo's father came from South Boardman, Michigan, and rode the first trip of the GR&I (Grand Rapids and Indiana) Railroad into Mackinaw after the line had been completed. His father became the first barber in this city. Leo began working for the Michigan Central Railroad in 1918 and retired in 1949. He also started the second gas station in Mackinaw City at the corner of Central Avenue and Nicolet Street—today the site of the Central Avenue underpass of I-75. In 1923 Mr. Paquet married Marguerite E. Burgess, and to this union was born three sons, Leo L., William E. and John H. and one daughter Miriam Ann. Mr. Paquet died in 1958.

Leo L. Paquet and John with catch of lake trout.

Paquet's gas station and garage - corner of Nicolet and Central - now Central Avenue underpass of I-75.

Carl Pierce

by Judy Ranville

Bert Pierce came to Mackinaw in 1896 to work in the woods—wages were $1.00 per day! He had a wife and was expecting his first born. They settled into a farmhouse called "Old Maggie's" which stood where the State Highway Information Station now is, and here Carl was born on February 17, 1897.

Mr. Pierce had a yen to farm and later moved to the Canby area and started raising cattle. In 1913 Mr. Risk, who had a dairy in Mackinaw, talked Bert into moving back to town and starting a dairy also. They purchased a farm situated on the corner where Darrow's Drive In is now. They planned to move on November 10, 1913, but that was the day of the "November 1913 Storm" when many ships were lost. It wasn't a "fit day" for moving, so the Pierces didn't get to Mackinaw until three days later on the 13th.

Carl was 16, the oldest son, so his days were full. He and brother Bob had 30 cows to milk by hand and---30 cows--that's a lot of shoveling, too!! Anyway, when the barn work was finished, Carl went off to work, driving the team of horses, hauling ice in winter and sand and gravel in other months. Oh, yes--there was always wood to cut and haul.

As the family grew, each member was given a job. In a dairy there are so many tasks--milk to cool and bottle and those bottles to wash and sterilize. And milk sold for 5 cents a quart!

On this farm the barn stood where Howard Beech's motel is now, and the cows were pastured wherever there was enough grass to feed them. The Fort area was the nearest pasture, and when that was eaten down, they would drive the cows down the road to areas between the railroad tracks and the lake and toward Cheboygan as far as where the Chief Motel stands. The hired man and the dog would spend the day with the cows and drive them home before evening milking time.

Around 1927 cars began to be more plentiful, and it was no longer safe to have the cows in an open pasture, so the Pierces decided to move out farther. They purchased a tract of land from the McGulpin estate and started to build a house and repair a large barn that stood on the place. Another storm came and the barn was struck by lightning and destroyed, so it was necessary to spend another year on the downtown farm while they constructed the modern barn shown behind the new home in the accompanying picture.

The Pierces moved onto their new farm on the McGulpin tract in 1929. Shortly after, Dad Pierce became crippled by arthritis and spent his remaining days in a wheelchair. A ramp was built on the side of the house so he could get out in the yard, and he continued to guide the development of the farm. Mr. Pierce was also a Justice of the Peace for many years.

There was much work ahead on the new farm. The land was covered with second growth brush and stumps left from the lumbering days. Clearing of this land was done by men with a team of horses. Under all this lay hundreds of tons of stones–these were all picked up and unloaded on fence rows. When the State Dock was first built, all of the stones for it were hauled from the Pierce property.

After the death of Birt Pierce, Carl and his sister Ida and husband Chuck McKinnon continued to run the dairy. It was always a beautiful place, very impressive with its modern and clean buildings, beautiful flowers and shrubs.

In 1961 Carl decided to retire and sold his herd and business. He still resides in his farm home where he enjoys his hobby, handcrafting objects of beauty, varying from oil painting to exquisite rug making, and he made a beautiful grandfather clock.

He says he always wanted one so he made one. Carl also makes windmill ornaments to sit along his garden path.

When talking with Carl, you know that he lives a very busy and happy retirement.

Bob Pierce with the milk truck.

Bob and Carl Pierce, ready to milk - by the downtown barn.

Carl and his horses.

Cows in the barnyard of the "downtown" farm. Woods in the background is where the Fort now stands.

Carl Pierce hauling ice
cut from the Straits.

"Downtown" farm home,
now site of Darrow's
Drive-In

The new home
and barn.

Mother Mary Pierce

Dad Bert Pierce

Youngest daughter, Dorothy

One of the windmills made by Carl during his retirement.

Ranville - McVey - Smith

Edna S. Ranville

Mrs. Ranville descends from a pioneer Mackinaw area family, the daughter of Frank and Catherine Sailler. The Sailler's had twelve children, a son Joseph and a daughter Charlotte both died in infancy. Her sisters were Grace (Kelty), Sarah (Nau), Georgianne (Yager), and Rachael (Wehner). Her brothers were Benjamin, Harvey, John, Charles and Morris. Of this family, Edna, Harvey and John survive.

Edna was born on a farm in Beaugrand Township on August 13, 1898, moving later to Hebron Township where she was the first student to ever pass the 8th grade exam. She later graduated from Cheboygan High School. She then attended Ferris Institute in Big Rapids where she received a "teaching certificate"

and returned to this area to teach in the Freedom and Hebron schools for four years. Some local folks who were students of "Miss Sailler" are Charles Warner, Stanley, Ray and Charlie Bauers and Clarence Nau. In reminiscing about her classes at Ferris, Edna said she attended a 6:00 a.m. psychology class, and the knowledge she gained there has been most helpful throughout her lifetime.

On June 21, 1921, she married George Ranville, Jr., son of Captain Edward and Martha Krause Ranville. Ed was an owner in the Ranville Brothers Fishery and operated a large tug out of Mackinaw City. George, however, chose not to follow the sailing professions of his father and grandfather and at an early age began working for the railroad as an Inspector in the Mackinaw yards. He spent 37 years in this work and died at age 54, in 1954.

Edna and George raised eight daughters and one son, another son died in infancy. Their living son is Edward, and the daughters are Martha, Eleanor, Celeste, Faith, Kathryn, Aurilie, Rosalie and Georgianna. Edna now has 23 grandchildren.

Mrs. Ranville resides in the family home with her daughter Kathryn, and she still bakes the best pies and cinnamon rolls in the county. Her happy smile radiates such happiness that one leaves her presence with that "warm, good-all-over" feeling.

by Judy LaWay Ranville

Edna Ranville

"Little Grandma" Margaret Ranville, wife of Captain Alexander Ranville. She is the Marguerite Courchaine, friend of Elizabeth in the book "Child of the Sea" by Elizabeth Whitney Williams. Grandma, with her family, operated the "Homestead Hotel", now the home of Crispey's Grocery, across from the Breakers Cabins and the state Docks.

MACKINAW CITY PIONEER DIES

Cheboygan Tribune
1935

Mackinaw City's oldest resident, Mrs. Margaret Ranville, died at her home there Thursday, March 7, at the age of 89 years. A pioneer of this region, Mrs. Ranville was born on Washington Island October 17, 1845, and lived much of her early life on different islands in Lake Michigan. With her parents, she was among those driven from Beaver Island during the Mormon persecution of the Gentiles.

Born Margaret Courchaine, Mrs. Ranville as a child lived for a time on St. Helene Island, where her father was engaged in building ships. When she was ten she lost her parents and went to live with an aunt on Mackinac Island.

In 1868 she was united in marriage to Alexander Ranville, and to them seven children were born, three of whom survive.

In 1880 Mr. and Mrs. Ranville and children moved to Mackinaw and were proprietors of the Mackinaw City Hotel (the present Old Homestead) for many years.

The funeral service was held at the home Saturday afternoon, conducted by Rev. R. V. Chaplin of the Presbyterian church. Burial was made in Lakeside Cemetery.

Surviving are one daughter, Mrs. Abbie McVey, two sons, George F. and Joe Ranville of Mackinaw; 13 grandchildren and 30 great-grandchildren.

Also one sister, Mrs. Emily Dobbins, age 92 of Marinette, Wisconsin, and a number of other more distant relatives and a host of friends to whom she was affectionally known as "Grandma" Ranville.

The deceased was a member of Straits Chapter No. 374, Order of the Eastern Star, also a member of the local Parent-Teacher association and an honorary member of the Guild of the Presbyterian church.

Martha Krause Ranville, wife of Edward.

Captain Edward Ranville

Captain Edward Ranville

from the *Cheboygan Daily Tribune*

The people of Mackinaw City were saddened by the death of Ed. Ranville of the Ranville Brothers Fishery. Mr. Ranville died from a prolonged attack of pneumonia. The family, which is well known here, has the sympathy of the entire community. Funeral services will be held in the First Presbyterian Church Thursday afternoon at 2 o'clock.

Mr. Edward Ranville, born October 9, 1869, died February 1, 1930. Ed. Ranville, the son of Captain Alexander and Margaret Ranville, was born on Mackinac Island. The family moved to Mackinaw City when Edward was 12 years of age, and this has been his home since that time. Mr. Ranville has been a well-known businessman and will be remembered as a kind neighbor, a loving father, a devoted son and brother by all who knew him. He leaves to mourn his loss a beloved wife, Mrs. Ellen Ranville, an aged mother, Mrs. Margaret Ranville, three sons, Leo Ranville of Holloway, Ohio, Wilbur Ranville, of Alpena; George Ranville of Mackinaw City, Mrs. Dorothy Norton, Mrs. Abbie Weaver, both of Saginaw, Mrs. Gladys Cecil of Houston, Texas, Miss Mildred Ranville of this city, one sister, Mrs. Abbie McVey, of Mackinaw, three brothers, Mr. John Ranville, Mr. Joseph Ranville, and Mr. George Ranville, all of Mackinaw City.

The Rev. Verne Butler, officiating clergyman. Burial, Lakeview Cemetery.

Left to right: Marne Smith 7, Otis Sr. 37, Harriet (Evans) 3, Otis Jr. (Snuffy). Picture dated about 1927.

 Mr. and Mrs. Otis Smith

Otis Smith is the son of Oscar Smith, one of the Smiths who purchased the Stimpson House, Mackinaw's first business, from the Stimpson family. He owned and operated the Mackinaw Hardware prior to his death.

Mr. Smith was born Helen McVey, youngest child of George and Abbie McVey. Helen died at 72 in August, 1968.

George Gardner McVey

George Gardner McVey fought in the western Indian Wars as a Trumpeter, Troop K. 8th Regiment United States Cavalry (Kiowa, Comanche and Cheyenne Campaign). He was in the west when the first railroad was built there. Later he served in the Fort on Mackinac Island where he met and married Miss Abbie Ranville, aged 18, in 1883. He is the Mr. McVey in the story by Frances Margaret Fox, "The Toad in Mr. McVey's Garden" printed elsewhere in this book.

Abigail Ranville McVey

Abbie Ranville, daughter of Captain and Mrs. Alex Ranville, was born on Mackinac Island in 1869. She married George Gardner McVey and moved to Mackinaw City to assist in operating the "Homestead Hotel" owned by her parents. The McVey's raised five children, Grover, Ethel, Charles, Allie and Helen.

MARNE SMITH RETIRES

from
Cheboygan Daily Tribune
May 15, 1976

Marne Smith of Mackinaw City retires from the State Highways Department after 30 years. He was employed from 1945 to 1957 on the State Ferries as a dockman. After Ferries were discontinued in 1957 he transferred to Southern Michigan as an equipment operator for Road Maintenance. He will retire from State Garage in St. Ignace on May 14. Mr. and Mrs. Smith plan to live in Mackinaw City.

Charles (Mickey) McVey, USAF, WWII - Son of Charlie McVey, Sr.

In Appreciation of a Career
of

DEDICATED SERVICE

The Michigan
Department Of State Highways
And Transportation

HONORS

Marne F. Smith

FOR 33 YEARS SERVICE

And Recognizes A Valuable Contribution
To Michigan's Total Transportation Program

MAY 15, 1976
DATE

Peter B. Fletcher
PETER B. FLETCHER — Commission Chairman

INDIAN WARS.

No. 10,592

Act of March 4, 1917.

s-701

Original

United States of America

BUREAU OF PENSIONS

It is hereby certified *That in conformity with the laws of the United States* Abbie H. McVey

Widow of George Gardner McVey

who was a Trumpeter, Troop K, 8th Regiment United States Cavalry, (Kiowa , Comanche, and Cheyenne Campaign) *is entitled to a pension at the rate of* Twelve *dollars per month, to commence* April 9, 1917

and to continue during her widowhood.

Given at the Department of the Interior this twenty-sixth *day of* May *one thousand nine hundred and* twenty-three *and of the Independence of the United States of America the one hundred and* forty-seventh

Hubert Work
Secretary of the Interior

Countersigned,

Washington Gardner

6—4107

Commissioner of Pensions.

WEB

Widow's Reward, $12.00 per month.

Ethel Marshall Robinson

In the Extended Care Unit of Community Memorial Hospital, Cheboygan, resides a Mackinaw area early pioneer. She's so tiny and frail that she seems almost transparent, but with a mind and voice as clear as a northern breeze she answers questions about her childhood.

Ethel was born in the Lighthouse on the east tip of St. Helene Island on October 4, 1894. Her father, Charles Marshall, was keeper there.

St. Helene Light began operating September 20, 1873 and has been in continuous operation since. The Light was automated in 1923 and no longer manned.

For Ethel's birth, a doctor came from St. Ignace, and Mother Nature helped out by blowing up such a violent storm that the doctor couldn't leave the Island to return to St. Ignace for ten days. A brother, Chester, joined the family also, and they lived in the lighthouse until Ethel was ten years old. At this time her father became critically ill and retired to live his remaining years hospitalized by a terminal illness. When Ethel was twelve, her mother died, and the children went to live with relatives in Mackinaw City, the Marshalls at Mackinaw Point Light and the Barnums.

In young ladyhood, Ethel Marshall married Bob Robinson, who owned and operated the Fishery now known as "Bells". They raised a daughter Dulcie and a son Bill.

Ethel has vivid memories of St. Helene Island. There was a village on the Island of about 500 persons--it was a fishing community owned and managed by the Newton sisters. They bought fish and shipped them in barrels on boats stopping at their large dock in the natural harbor on the north side of the Island. Sailing vessels were also constructed there.

The store and main village were on the northeast end of the Island, a large farm occupied the west third of the Island, and the south shore was dotted with shacks belonging to Indian fishermen who lived in them spring through fall, returning to the mainland for the winter.

Numerous ships went down in the waters around St. Helene. The best known was the sinking of the *California* which went down in 1887, seven years before Ethel entered this world on that cold and stormy night.

St. Helene Island is presently privately owned and uninhabited.

Judy Ranville

Harvey S. Sailler

Harvey S. Sailler was born in Cheboygan in January, 1887, and now at age 89 is a well preserved, friendly gentleman. Asked how he stays so young he replied, "By not working too hard." In visiting with Mr. Sailler one knows this is an understatement, since his work years began at age 15 and continued until age 84 when he retired from the motel business.

When he first came to Mackinaw he lived with Mr. and Mrs. Bert Kelty at the Mackinaw Hotel. Mrs. Kelty was his sister Grace. He went to work for the Railroad, and when the war broke out he enlisted and served for two years, much of this time spent overseas in France. He has many vivid memories of this era of his life and treasures pictures and artifacts from his service years.

Upon returning from the service he went back to the railroad, working in the roundhouse for six months. He then bought a car and started a taxi business. He later acquired a truck and developed a business hauling general cargo and moving buildings. He built a home for himself in 1922 on the corner of Jamet and Nicolet Streets, and it was there he and his bride, Louise Stokes, established their home on April 4, 1923. The Saillers have three sons, one daughter, twelve grandchildren and twenty-one great grandchildren.

When the banks took their "holiday", Harvey had no money and no work, so he went to visit Doctor Tiffany, whose office was upstairs in the building now occupied by the Key Hole Bar, and asked him if he had any money. His answer was, "Yes, I didn't put all my potatoes in one basket."

"He lent me $500.00 without so much as the scratch of a pen and we went into business selling coal. We loaded and unloaded our truck by hand and sold coal delivered into the customer's basement for $8.50 a ton in the winter. If you ordered your coal delivered during the summer you didn't have to pay until wintertime, and it was also fifty cents a ton cheaper. Most families burned ten tons during the winter.

As the depression progressed and men lost their jobs, they couldn't pay their bills and we lost quite a bit of money. That's how we got out of the coal business."

Mr. Sailler talks on, "I was also Street Commissioner in Mackinaw, built some streets, put down sidewalks and water lines. That was around 1924. Prior to that time everyone had their own wells, the only 'city water' being on 'Main Street' and coming from the Railroad tank. Pipes were buried only three feet and used to freeze every winter, so I lowered them to five feet. I didn't know much about the work when I started at it, but I had a man working for me named Ellsworth Kniffen who had put down water pipes in the Army and he told me about it. I sent him out to do the work and he'd do it and then ask me to come and inspect his work. I didn't know how it should be done, but I could tell he had done a good job. He thought I knew all about this work, and I never told him I didn't know. Anyway it all got done and I had no problems with my work.''

At his home in town he had a barn for his team of horses and pigs. (Their dog had puppies and Mother Pig helped out by nursing some of them.) Mr. Sailler, in partnership with Chris Deitz, raised 80 or 90 pigs each year on his farm off what is now Nakomis Street and gathered garbage around town each day to feed them.

Upon receipt of a Veteran's bonus, Mr. Sailler built four cabins to rent and later enlarged and encorporated them into the Sailler Motel, now the "Big Mac" Motel, operated by his son Bernard Sailler. "The Sailler Motel" was ready for the "Bridge Dedication" in 1958, and his first customer was Governor Williams.

And Mr. Sailler said he stayed young by "not working too hard"!

(Written from a taped interview
by Judy LaWay Ranville)

Harvey Sailler - 1918

Schepler Family

*Schepler's Fish House
next to Railroad dock -
Gertrude Crane
(Mrs. William Schepler, Sr., sister)*

Captain William (Bill) Schepler, Sr., captain of the Algomah.

Mrs. Olive Schepler, wife of Captain Schepler, Sr.

Captain William Schepler, II

Captain William Schepler, III

Dr. Tiffany
Old Trail Tavern

Dr. Allen C. Tiffany, Dec. 22, 1879-Aug. 10, 1943

Major U.S. Army Medical Corps. Shown with faithful pal "Topsy", who is buried beside his master in Lakeview Cemetery. Picture dated September, 1936. Building is "Old Trail Tavern", now Masonic Temple. Dr. Tiffany came to Mackinaw prior to World War I.

The "Old Trail Tavern", owned by Dr. Tiffany, located on Huron Blvd., is now the Masonic Temple. At the time these pictures were taken it was being managed by Mrs. Gwen Smith who is shown with her daughter Elizabeth.

Old Trail Tavern - 1937.

Lena E. Wallin

Mrs. Emil S. Wallin, known as "Aunt Lena" to most of her friends, was born Lena E. Thompson, in Rockwood, Ontario, Canada, on November 19, 1892. She was the youngest of 14 children, 8 of whom lived to adulthood.

Mr. Thompson came to Mackinaw City hoping to regain his health in this pollen-free air, and his family followed him on May 7, 1898, when Lena was six years old.

Mrs. Thompson had lived in a more heavily populated area near Toronto, Canada, and her first view of Mackinaw was rather frightening. The town was then a busy railroad terminal, with many tracks and long trains. When the train upon which they were traveling pulled into the depot and stopped, their car was still a long way out (approximately back of the McRae Lumber Company), and the view from the car window was the GR & I roundhouse, tracks, trains, stumps and brush. Mrs. Thompson asked the Conductor when they would be arriving in Mackinaw. He replied, "Lady, this is it." Mrs. Thompson began to cry, and upon greeting her husband at the Depot

begged him to take her back to Ontario. Mr. Thompson's health had improved so he could again be gainfully employed, so the family settled into their new home with only fond memories of a more modern way of life in Rockwood.

Their first home in Mackinaw City was on Central Avenue about a block west of the I-75 Overpass, and Lena says the street was "more brush than Avenue." Her Father, not liking to pay rent, purchased 80 acres of land about three miles south of town and built a log cabin, moving his family there in 1901. Until a school was constructed in that township, Lena had to pay tuition to attend classes in Mackinaw, and walk three miles back and forth on a wagon trail through the brush. Often times a black bear would be walking in one track and "me in the other, I'd run like a deer, scared to death--and I was never late for school." Asked about discipline in school, Lena replied, "The teacher never failed to give you a thrashing when you needed it, and there was no talking back either." When the township school was built about a mile from their log home, Lena would go to school early, chop the kindling wood and build the fire to have the building warm when the teacher and other students arrived. That school is still standing near Potter Road and Old 31 and is now used as a residence.

In 1908 Lena Thompson became the bride of Emil Sigfried Wallin who was born in Edison, New York, on August 9, 1888. "Fred" as he was called by his wife and friends, came to Kegomik, Michigan, with his father, who was a tanner by trade. He came to Mackinaw, where he worked for the railroad and was active in community affairs, being Supervisor of Wawatam Township for 33 years. The Wallins had six children, one girl and five boys. Two sons died during childhood.

Aunt Lena remembers hardships and sorrows in her pioneer life but also remembers with fondness the happy times; her wonderful husband with whom she lived for 47 years until his death in 1969, her loving children and grandchildren and her many, many friends.

Says Aunt Lena, "Life wasn't easy, but we always tried to do right and to be a friend to everyone, and we never missed Church and Sunday School. We walked to the Presbyterian Church every week from the farm."

(Written from a taped interview
by Judy LaWay Ranville)

Lena Wallin

Vernon D. Barnett was born in East Jordan in 1897. He married Marvel Chorpening in 1919 and in 1929 they moved to Mackinaw City where he was cashier in the bank. When the bank closed in 1933, he devoted full time to his insurance agency. He was Justice of the Peace for 38 years and Village Clerk 24 years. He retired in 1962 and turned the family business over to his two sons, R. Dale Barnett and Lowell D. Barnett.

Chapter 35

Biographies

by Nancy Campbell

BAUERS, AUGUST 1858-1939

Born in Germany. Married Louise Schenk in 1885. In 1913 moved from Missouri to Hebron Township, Michigan, and farmed. Moved into Mackinaw City in 1938. Eleven children were born to this union: Catherine (deceased 1922), Mrs. F. W. Archer, Mrs. L. C. Pettingill, Mrs. Hilda Louis, Mrs. G. C. Powell, Fred, Stanley, Emory, Charles, Roy and Louis.

BAUERS, RUTH 1894-1970

Born on June 8, 1894, in Cheboygan County as Ruth Bigger. Married Emory J. Bauers on May 23, 1917. She lived in Mackinaw City for over 50 years. She was a life member of the Church of The Straits, past president of the Women's Club, served 45 years as board member of Mackinaw Methodist Church, was on the Board of Governors of the Church of the Straits and correspondent for many years for the *Cheboygan Daily Tribune*. She had one son, Ernest.

BURROUGHS, CHARLES 1870-1943

Born June 11, 1870, at New Boston, Michigan, and came to Mackinaw City in 1887. He retired from business in 1920 and then accepted a position as Dock Master on the State Dock. He had two children, Clifford and Iva Kerby (Mrs. J.L.).

BIENIAWSKI, FATHER ANDREW 1874-1963

Born in Warsaw, Poland, he began his religious studies in his homeland then went to the Vatican in Rome. He came to the United States in 1897 and was ordained in the Grand Rapids Diocese by Bishop Richter. He served Michigan parishes at Manistee, Standish, Buena Vista and Isadore before coming to Mackinaw in 1928. He served St. Anthony's, Mackinaw City and St. Francis at Alverno as a mission. He continued at Mackinaw until June 29, 1961, when he retired.

COFFMAN, LOUISA HENRIETTA 1858-1945

Came to Mackinaw City with her husband John H. in 1883. She was a member of the Willing Workers Society of the Presbyterian Church. She had one son, George V.

COFFMAN, ROSALIE 1874-1946

Born in Cheboygan, Michigan, as Rosalie DeGrey. She taught school in Cheboygan and married George V. in 1902. In 1906 they moved to Mackinaw City where he operated a Drug Store and funeral home. She was an active member of the Methodist Church and Eastern Stars. She had two sons, Norris W. and Ferris L.

DAGWELL, GENEVIEVE M. 1898-1959

Born in Washtenaw County, Michigan, the daughter of John and Mary Pauline Weber. She attended St. Joseph Academy, Adrian, Michigan, and married Elton C. Dagwell of Mackinaw City in Detroit on February 14, 1917. She was a member of St. Anthony's Catholic Church and Altar Society, the Daughters of Isabella, a past president and member of the Mackinaw Women's Club for 44 years and for 12 years as public librarian. In 1956 she was chosen Woman of the Year by the Mackinaw Lions Club. She had one son, Robert, and three daughters, Mrs. Clare Ecklund (Betty), Mrs. Peggy Erspamer Tollefson and Mrs. Richard Campbell (Nancy).

DIETZ, C. J. 1865-1946

Born in Stutgart, Germany, in 1865, and came to this country in 1881. He lived in Philadelphia, Pennsylvania, for two years, then came to Mackinaw City where he worked for the Pennsylvania railroad. Later he went into the real estate business. He married Agnes Schenk a few years after moving to Mackinaw. He was a member of the Mackinaw City School Board, City Council and director of the Mackinaw City Bank. He had five children: Mrs. Anna Swontek, Mrs. Cynthia Davis, Mrs. O. F. McIsaac, Mrs. Ed Clark and Emery.

DESY, COME   1853-1928
   Born at St. Pite, Canada. In 1875 married Virginia Barbeau. Moved to Manistee, Michigan, in 1880 and then to the Mackinaw area in 1892. Part of these years were spent at Cecil Bay. Mr. Desy was the trusted janitor of the schools for years. He had eight children: Eugene, William, Alphonse, James, Lawrence and Rose. Two died as infants.

DESY, RAYMOND B.   1916-1972
   Born in Mackinaw City, son of James Desy. He graduated from Mackinaw City High School and attended the University of Michigan. He married Mary E. Schiska in Mansfield, Ohio, in 1940, and served in the Phillippines during World War II. He owned and operated four Desy Gift Shops in Mackinaw City. He was a member of St. Anthony's Catholic Church, was a 3rd and 4th Degree member of the Knights of Columbus, chairman of the Fort Michilimackinac Pageant, a member of the Mackinaw City School Board, Village Council, Chamber of Commerce, Lions Club, American Legion and Veterans of Foreign Wars, board member of the Citizens National Bank. He had four sons: Raymond, Robert, Michael and Paul, and four daughters, Jerrilynn, Mary, Theresa and Carmel.

GREBE, PAULINE E.   1902-1974
   Born in Hanover, Ontario, the daughter of Wilhelm and Wilhelmina Messerschmidt. Married Friedrich Grebe in 1927 and moved to Mackinaw City from St. Clair, Michigan, in 1943. She was active in St. Thomas Lutheran Church, Cheboygan, Farm Bureau, Senior Citizens, past president of the Mackinaw Woman's Club and correspondent for the Cheboygan Daily Tribune. She had one son, Kurt, and three daughters: Mrs. John Myers (Pauline), Mrs. Arthur Schneider (Wilhelmina) and Mrs. Larry Eichinger (Katherine).

INGLIS, JULIA A.   1858-1939
   Born in Groveland Township, Oakland County, as Julia Inglis. Married Thomas Inglis in 1873. She taught school in Standish and Frederick, and served as County School Commissioner of Arenac County before coming to Mackinaw City in 1908, where she taught for 17 years. She was a Past Matron of Straits Chapter of the OES, first president of the Mackinaw Woman's Club, member of the Presbyterian Church and former superintendent of the Sunday School. She had four children: Mrs. Lottie Granger, Mrs. Lucy Smith, Mrs. Mariam Jones and Mrs. Agnes Johnson.

IRWIN, SARAH JANE   1866-1940
   Born Sara Curtis at Simcoe, Ontario, and married James Irwin on November 19, 1890. She was a life member of the Maccabees, a member of the Mackinaw Woman's Club, chairman of the Helping Hand Club, a member of the Willing Workers Society and the Presbyterian Church. She had three sons, Ray, Roy and Russel and two daughters Mrs. Frank Foote and Mrs. Jack Barney.

JOHNSON, AGNES   1880-1958
   Born Agnes Inglis at Waterton, Michigan. Married William Johnson who died in 1950. She was a member of the Presbyterian Church, worthy matron and life member of Mackinaw Chapter of Eastern Star, member of the White Shrine and Mackinaw City Woman's Club.

McCARTHY, HELEN   1908-1971
   Born Helen Parsons in Detroit, Michigan, and moved as a child to Kansas City, Missouri, and returned to Detroit in 1925. Graduated from Liggett School in Detroit and Penn Hall College, Chambersburg, Pennsylvania. She spent her summers in Mackinaw City and became a permanent resident in 1942. She was a member of the Presbyterian Church, Mackinaw Woman's Club and Girl Scout leader for several years. She had three sons, Gary, Forest and David, and one daughter, Judy Feneley.

NAU, MARY MARGARET   1876-1950
   Mrs. Nau was one of five children born to William and Catherine Thiesz in Dusseldorf, Germany. At the age of 16, she and a sister came to America and lived for several years in Detroit, where she married John Nau. They moved to northern Michigan and settled near Freedom, and 20 years later moved to Mackinaw City. Eleven children were born to this union: Mrs. Lawrence Doremire (Agnus), Mrs. John Heath (Virginia), John, Clarence, Leonard, Elmer, Harold, Mrs. Keith Romaine (Helen), Mrs. James Kelly (Julia), Mrs. Elizabeth Furstenberg and Mrs. Amy Bricker. Mrs. Nau was an active member of the Mackinaw City Woman's Cub and the W.S.C.S. of the Methodist Church.

OVERTON, LUELLA   1856-1951
   Born Luella Smith in Lilly Bay near Greenville, Maine, to David and Margaret Smith, the fourth of twelve children. Two years after her birth the family moved to California, where they built a home near the gold fields in the Sierra Nevada Mountains. Six years later the family moved back to Maine and after a few years to Duncan Bay, Cheboygan, Michigan. In 1878 Luella came to Mackinaw City and became the first school teacher, teaching in a little log building. In 1882 she married Forrest Stimpson and had two children, Lloyd and Margaret. Mr. Stimpson drowned in the Straits while engaged in the Marine Reporting business. Six years later she married John Overton, a lighthouse inspector. She

owned and operated the Mackinaw Pharmacy, was a member of the Presbyterian Church, a charter member of the Shakespeare Study Club (1912), which a year later became the Mackinaw Woman's Club.

PARSONS, MARGARET E.   1884-1973
Born in Mackinaw City, daughter of Forrest and Luella Stimpson, granddaughter of George Stimpson, one of the early Mackinaw settlers. Her father was the first Marine Dispatcher and lost his life in the Straits while on duty. During her lifetime she lived in Detroit, Kansas City, Lansing, and her hometown Mackinaw. She studied piano at the Detroit Conservatory of Music; was house mother for Chi Chapter of Gamma Delta Sorority at MSU, executive secretary of the Mackinaw Chamber of Commerce, member of the Church of the Straits and served for many years as organist. She was an Honorary Life Member of the Mackinaw Woman's Club. She had one daughter, Mrs. Helen McCarthy.

PEPLER, ANNE   1884-1951
Anne Dufresne was born in Cheboygan, Michigan, the daughter of Mr. and Mrs. Louis Dufresne. She was one of eleven children, four of whom died in infancy. She attended school in Cheboygan and took special training in vocal and instrumental music. On November 14, 1911, she married Walter Pepler and they made their home in Cheboygan until 1923 when they moved to Mackinaw City, where they operated a dry goods store. In 1843 they moved to Detroit where Mr. Pepler was employed. She was an active member of the Cheboygan Woman's Club and St. Mary's Catholic Church. In Mackinaw City she was a member of St. Anthony's Altar Society and church organist and choir leader for 20 years. She was also a member of the PTA, Woman's Club and leader of Home Economic and Girl Scout groups. She had two daughters, Mrs. Merle Caswell (Catherine), and Mrs. Ray Venturini (Mary Ann) and three sons, Louis, Walter and Bill.

STEVENSON, RUTH   1894-1976
Born Ruth L. Hobler in Whitehall, Mcihigan. She moved to Petoskey and graduated from Petoskey High School. On August 13, 1913, she married Elliott Stevenson in Edgemoor, South Carolina. They made their home in Pellston, Michigan, until 1936 when they moved to Mackinaw City. They were the proprietors of Stevenson and Linton Drug Store and Gift Shop from 1921 to 1962. They also owned and operated the Friendly Gift Shop in Mackinaw. Mr. Stevenson died in 1936. Mrs. Stevenson was also proprietress of Ruth Haven Motel until 1971. She was a member of the Church of the Straits, Order of the Eastern Stars and Woman's Club. She had one son, W. E. Stevenson.

SMITH, OTIS F.   1891-1943
Mr. Smith was born in Mackinaw City in 1891, the son of Mr. and Mrs. Oscar Smith, pioneer residents of Mackinaw. In 1917 he married Helen McVey. During World War I he served as a Sergeant in the United States Army in France for 18 months. Upon his return home he and his brother-in-law, Clark Trumbull entered business together. They operated the Smith and Trumbull Lumber Company and also the Smith and Trumbull Hardware and 5 and 10 Cent Store. He was Commander of the American Legion Post, Past Master of the Masonic Lodge and active in community affairs. He had two sons, Otis, Jr., and Marne, and one daughter, Mrs. James Evans (Harriet).

STIMPSON, IDA ELVIRA   1856-1936
Born in Elmyra, Maine, the daughter of Mr. and Mrs. G. W. Stimpson. The family moved to Mackinaw City in 1870. She and her sister, Lydia, were the first white girls to settle permanently in this city. She was an active member of the Presbyterian Church and community affairs.

WALTERS, CHARLES H.   1868-1942
Born 1868. Married Ella Asselin in 1896 at Cheboygan, Michigan. Mr. Walters' parents ran a hotel on the land behind the Anchor Inn (Totem Pole). Charles was a commercial fisherman and also did lumbering in the winter. He built a home in Mackinaw City on E. Etherington Street that is presently occupied by his son, Homer. He had 3 sons, Elmer, Homer and Leonard, and three daughters.

WALTERS, ELLA ELIZABETH   1876-1939
Born in Ontario, Canada, on February 29, 1876, to Mr. and Mrs. Joseph Asselin. She moved to Freedom, Michigan, in her youth and married Charles Walters in 1896 at Cheboygan, Michigan. They moved to Mackinaw City in 1897. They had three sons, Leonard R., Elmer E. and Homer B., and three daughters, Mrs. Fred Moore, Mrs. George Leineke, and Mrs. Eli Sweet. Mrs. Walters was a member of the Mackinaw Woman's Club and St. Anthony's Church and Altar Society.

WILLIAMS, LENA   1881-1936
Born in Canada. Lived in Mackinaw for many years and ran a restaurant on Main Street (Central Avenue). Survived by brother R. Williams.

Photo
Album

Martin Burroughs, father of Charlie, working on the Charlie Stimpson farm.

TOWN FATHERS - Village Council
Back (left to right): Charlie Burroughs, George Coffman. Front (left to right): Sunday Desy, Skip Barrett, Dell Wheeler, George Ranville, Sr.

Central Avenue - Mackinaw City. (Left to right): ?, ?, Bud Liebeck, Mitchell Swantek, Lloyd Stimpson.

Central Avenue - Mackinaw City. J.M. Overton Building, now Village Pharmacy. Second building was Post Office and was moved one block and is now Copper Lantern Gift Shop.

Patrick's Hardware - Central Avenue, Mackinaw City. Far right - George Patrick (Marie Riggs' father), other man with shovel is Cecil Hunt in front of Hunt's Grocery Store.

Central Avenue - Mackinaw City. Fourth of July Parade - Pre World War I - 1912 or 1913.

4th of July Parade about 1912 or 1913

Central Avenue - Mackinaw City (building on right now Keyhole Bar). Dick Williams (with fish), far right **?** Pettinger, Bill Thompson (white gloves), Rutherford Wheeler (white shirt) - next to Wheeler (right to left) **?** Duffina, Pug Kinsell, Charles McVey, Man third from left with hands in pocket is Bill Plaunt.

Railroad Station at Freedom, Michigan. Station Master Joseph Asselin and family (Homer Walters' grandparents.)

Oscar Smith in the blacksmith shop located where Rouche's Standard Service is. The shop later became the City Garage and was torn down for the more modern gas station. Oscar, sitting far right.

Stern arm of the law, Officer Babcock. Harry Hattinger behind bar in Dixie Tavern, in times past known as the Wawatam Inn, Mrs. Clark's Hotel.

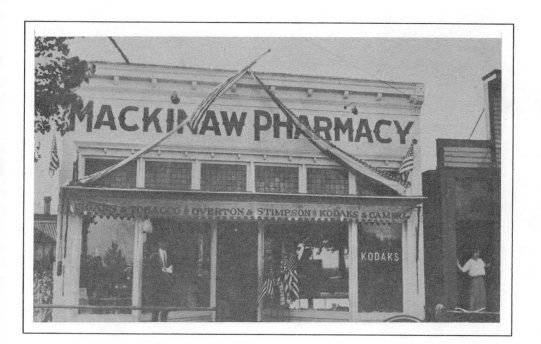

Now the Mackinaw Village Pharmacy

Otis and Sam Smith on porch of Stimpson House. Jim Desy, Helen McVey, Marie Patrick and unknown.

Real Indians visit town.

The 3 little Indians are Fred Rouche and sisters Helen and Esther.

Central Avenue - Tennis Courts are now the site of O'Brien's Miniature Golf.

Mardi Gras Parade
in Mackinaw

Come to the parade.

Saloon owned by Charlie Burroughs in Levering, Michigan. When Emmet County went dry he moved his business to Mackinaw, where Fisher's Pancake House and Gift Shop now stands. Mr. Burroughs is the gent in the doorway with mustache and derby hat. Bartender to the left is Guy Parkas. Identity of other men unknown.

Burroughs Saloon, Mackinaw 1915
(Left to right): Bartender Lee Plat, Guy Wolford, Ed Ryan, Joe McIsaac, Captain Schepler, Bill Thompson, Chester LaQuea, Jack Cunningham, Albert Asselin, Oscar Smith, Unknown.

Booze Special

"How dry I am, how dry I am; nobody knows how dry I am!"

(Old Prohibition Jingle)

When Emmet County was dry and Cheboygan County wasn't, the numerous saloons in Mackinaw City found themselves with increased business. The Anheiser Busch Beer Company sent beer by the carload to Mackinaw, where it was stored in an ice house that stood where the marina area now is. It was hauled from there to replenish the saloons as needed. A special trail, called the "Booze Special", ran between Mackinaw and Petoskey, bringing the thirsty to the bubbling fountains of joy water just over the county line.

Judy Ranville

First car in Mackinaw City - owned by Bill Smith on left. Passengers are Charlie Burroughs and Earl Smith.

Neighboring City Fire Depts. Rush to Cheboygan's Aid

When fire of major proportions consumed the Leonall, Masonic Temple and Clune buildings Friday, Fire Chief Harold Gaynor issued a call for assistance by the Indian River and Mackinaw City Fire Departments. Departments in both cities responded promptly and rushed their fire engine trucks, equipment and crews to help combat the flames. Fire Dept. members from the two Cheboygan county communities are shown in the photos below:

Mackinaw City - Fire Chief Elton Dagwell, Ford Martin, Jack Paquet, George Ranville, Bill Paquet and Henry Vieau - 1953.

Main Street (N. Huron Ave.) before the big fire. Mrs. Callahan, Mrs. Oscar Smith.

*Dock at foot of
Nicolet Street in State Park.*

*Dock where fish tugs unloaded
their daily catch. Behind
Fishery, now "Bell's."*

*Coast Guard
Cutter Mackinaw*

Raising of the Str. Humphrey - sank in Straits of Mackinac 1943 - raised in 1945.

Minneapolis - Sank 1894 in Straits of Mackinac near present site of Mackinac Bridge.

PROGRAMME.

1 Grand March and Waltz............ ....Mackinaw Style.
2 Quadrille............... .... Bon-Ton.
3 Schottische.. Military
4 Gallop............... .... Flyaway
5 Lancers .... Dress Parade
6 Waltz........... ... . Eureka
7 Racquet .... General
8 Quadrille............... .... Caledonia
9 Schottische............... ....:................... Highland
10 Gallop .... Mustang
11 Quadrille............................. As You Like I
12 Polka..Mazurka
13 Waltz........ ....Bankrupt
14 Virginia Reel ....Ye Old Styl
15 Gallop ....Nancy Le
16 Waltz Quadrill............... ....Aesthet
17 Lancers......... .... Acm
18 Waltz................. ....Yum-Yu
19 Schottische... .... ;.........Oscar Wild
20 Quadrille............................. ..... Maple Le
21 Polka.................................Heel and T
22 Grand Medley........... ....“We Won’t Go Home,”

ENGAGEMENTS

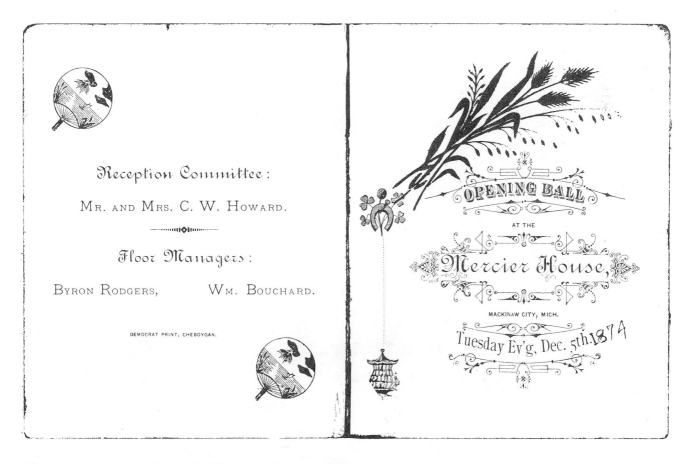

Reception Committee:

MR. AND MRS. C. W. HOWARD.

Floor Managers:

BYRON RODGERS,   WM. BOUCHARD.

DEMOCRAT PRINT, CHEBOYGAN.

OPENING BALL

AT THE

Mercier House,

MACKINAW CITY, MICH.

Tuesday Ev’g, Dec. 5th. 1874

Copy of program of “First Ball” at the Mercer House.

MERCIER HOUSE - Burned in 1890. Corner of Jamet and North Huron.

In the 1920's outside Ryan's Meat Market (in Alexander Electric area.)
(Left to Right): Ed Phillips, Bert Kelty, Charlie McVey, Dell Wheeler, Dr. Pierce,
Bill Ryan in doorway.

Ryan's Saloon, where Key Hole Bar is, around 1905. Bartender is Charlie Burroughs. (Left to
right): Charlie Smith, Mr. LaRocque (barber), Arvine Kniffen, next three unidentified.

Front row (left to right): Earl Martin or John Hayes, ?, Mr. Terrian, ?, ?, Elton Dagwell, Mr. Martin. Middle: Conrad Olson, Charlie Burroughs, Band Master Bill LaQuea, Grover McVey, Sunday Desy, Bill Martin, ?. Back: ?, ?, ?, ?, Harvey Sailler, Emery Bauers, Doc Kniffen, Oscar Smith, Sam Smith.

Play Group - Old City Hall. Only three identified. Left to right, 3rd Row, Nick Buelher (glasses); end of row Kathy Callan, below K. Callan is Hazel Smith.

Mackinaw City Band
In background Stimpson House and Bandstand. Captain William Schepler, Sr. in derby hat, John Hayes front row, third from the right.

Baseball Team - Mackinaw City 1888
L-R Top Row
   W. C. Martin, Unknown, Unknown, Henry
   Todd, Dave Chappel, Charles Dagwell
L-R Front Row
   Unknown, Wilber Robinson, J. Higgins, A.
   Kniffen

"Willie" Taylor - left - last keeper on
Round Island Light. "Farby" George
Ranville. Out on the town at Ty-Jo's
(now Key-Hole). George and Willie
were first cousins.

292

The Suffragettes (1919) - Down with the tyrants, MEN. Shown in front of the Deitz home, now occupied by Mrs. Addie Desy. Left to right those identified are 1 - Rayma Smith, 2 - Tina Barrett, 3 through 7 unidentified, 8 - Millie Stimpson, 9 - unidentified, 10 - Elizabeth Buhler.

Now the R. Phillips home, Corner of Etherington & Henry Streets

Corner of Depeyster and Ducharme Streets before streets and N. Huron Ave. were built.

Krause family --
(Left to right): Cora, Lavina and Dora Krause Grimshaw in back. Lavina and Dora both retired from the Railroad. Dora still lives, an invalid.

"Mackinaw Commons" - now N. Huron Avenue - upper right corner Dagwell Home and Marine Reporting Station - background present home of Lowell Barnett. Left to right in picture, Marybeth Dagwell, Olive Schepler, Jane Dagwell - (front) Ted Dagwell.

LaCombe Children
Top Row (left to right): Raymond, Bill Paquet. Middle Row (left to right): Charles, Richard (Itchy). Bottom Row (left to right): Victor (Bunny) Lawrence (Boots).

R. J. LaCombe - a railroadman - played baseball on the city team. Picture dated 1923.

Ralph and Zelma Preston
in June 1918

William H. Wilkes

Bill and his wife Martha came to Mackinaw City in 1916 from East Jordan. He was yard foreman for the New York Central. He loved to hunt and fish--was a happy, good natured man, well liked by all who knew him. He died in 1951.

Wilbur Ranville 1896-1959. Son of pioneer Captain Edward Ranville.

Gordon, Ann and Joyce Ranville

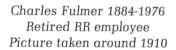

Charles Fulmer 1884-1976
Retired RR employee
Picture taken around 1910

Lillian Beatrice Fulmer 1887-1971
Picture taken around 1910.

Frontier Restaurant
A Teysen Tradition

By Roger Andrews

from the
Mackinac Island News
July 26, 1941

(This voluntary appreciation of the Teysens, written without their knowledge, is as true in 1941 as it was when published in 1934. Since then more than 100,000 copies in pamphlet form have been circulated by Mr. Teysen's friends and patrons.)

The answer is a simple one--just "Teysenize."

Like the old time religion, which was good for Moses and Aaron, "it's good right now."

There is more profit to be made, more health to enjoy, more results to obtain in this wonderful north country today, than there was when lumber barons and mining kings were in their glory.

Believe in your locality, work harder than you ever worked before, shoot square and be an optimist. Sounds like a sermon, but it's the definition of the word "Teysenize," and the living, hustling, successful and famous Harry J. Teysen of Mackinaw City is the proof that it can be done.

Harry Teysen is prosperous, but he has neither enough money to buy this tribute if it were not true, nor to keep it out because he believed the three cheers given for him by the *Mackinac Island News* were too loud or too long.

Fourteen years ago this young man, a victim of hay fever, sought

Below: Ken Teysen at 4 years old and Old Chief Mastow - 1926.

relief in the beautiful Straits country. He had been for years manager of the splendid Saginaw Club. He knew the service people enjoy and will pay for, and he knew the art of friend making. The hay fever might bother him at night, but nothing kept him from working by day. So he opened the now famous Teysen Indian Curio Shop, Museum and Dining Room at Mackinaw City, where he has developed one of the most picturesque resort centers in the

United States or Canada.

Teysen simply "Teysenized". He made his dining room famous for good things at reasonable prices, he developed his patrons into friends, he collected the most interesting Indian handiwork in the northwest, housed in as quaint and unique a building as brains could design, and hard work erect, and a grateful public did the rest.

Indian maidens serve you with genuine coffee and fine food in an atmosphere of the original American frontier. Mr. and Mrs. Teysen give to each guest the attention they would in their own home. There is the Gift Shop with "all season" and not "summer" prices for attractive souvenirs.

In this busy place there is no time for hay fever, hard luck, depression or gloom.

With their son, Kenneth C., the Teysen's have made Mackinaw City famous for hospitality, and have set a marked example of what can be done in developing the tourist industry which is Northern Michigan's pot of gold at the end of the rainbow.

Adventures of Good Eating lists Teysen's as the outstanding place of the North Country.

This book is accepted as a criterion by people who dine out and is America's *Who's Who* of the Catering World.

The plan and its carrying out is not patented. Just roll up your sleeves and "Teysenize" to success. Harry J. Teysen is simply our north country's Exhibit A.

My Personal Memories ...

My Personal Memories ...